FROM POW
TO BLUE ANGEL

Lt. Cdr. Raleigh E. "Dusty" Rhodes, Officer in Charge of the U.S. Navy Flight Demonstration Team, January 1948. Official photograph, U.S. Navy.

FROM POW
TO BLUE ANGEL

The Story of
Commander Dusty Rhodes

JIM ARMSTRONG

Foreword by
CAPTAIN ROY M. "BUTCH" VORIS

University of Oklahoma Press : Norman

Library of Congress Cataloging-in-Publication Data

Armstrong, James L. (James Lowell), 1932–
    From POW to Blue Angel : the story of Commander Dusty Rhodes / Jim
Armsrong ; foreword by Roy M. "Butch" Voris.
        p. cm.
    ISBN 978-0-8061-5342-1 (paper)
    1. Rhodes, Dusty, 1918– 2. World War, 1939–1945—Prisoners and prisons,
Japanese. 3. Prisoners of war—United States—Biography. 4. Prisoners of war—
Japan—Biography. 5. Air pilots, Military—United States—Biography. 6. United
States. Naval Flight Demonstration Squadron—Biography. I. Title: From prisoner
of war to Blue Angel. II. Title.
D805.J3R54 2006
358.40092—dc22
[B]   2005056880

Excerpt from THE RIGHT STUFF by Tom Wolfe. Copyright © 1979 by Tom Wolfe.
Reprinted by permission of Farrar, Straus and Giroux, LLC.

To all the men and women
who have risked their lives or suffered or died
to make life safer and freer for the rest of us

. . . the idea here . . . seemed to be that a man should have the ability to go up in a hurtling piece of machinery and put his hide on the line and then have the moxie, the reflexes, the experience, the coolness, to pull it back in the last yawning moment—and then to go up again *the next day*, and the next day, and every next day, even if the series should prove infinite—and, ultimately, in its best expression, do so in a cause that means something to thousands, to a people, a nation, to humanity, to God.

TOM WOLFE, The Right Stuff

CONTENTS

CONTENTS

ILLUSTRATIONS

FIGURES

ILLUSTRATIONS

MAPS

DIAGRAMS

FOREWORD

To be asked to write the foreword to this inspirational book is a very special honor. *From POW to Blue Angel* is a mind-gripping story about a young U.S. Navy carrier fighter pilot, Raleigh "Dusty" Rhodes, who as a prisoner of war experienced brutal atrocities by his captors as he was shuttled from one prison camp to another in Japan during World War II. At war's end, he returned to duty, refreshing his flying skills and once again pursuing a career in naval aviation.

It was during his refresher training that Dusty had the opportunity to watch three glistening blue and gold F6F Hellcats performing tight formation aerobatics over a naval airfield at Pensacola, Florida. They were the recently formed Navy Flight Exhibition Team, shortly to be named the Blue Angels, now based at Naval Air Station Jacksonville. He was apparently captivated by the precision flying at such low altitudes. After we landed, Dusty approached me and excitedly asked how he might apply for duty with the team. Now a lieutenant commander, he had gained the rank to qualify as a leader.

I have not forgotten those few moments with Dusty. He still had that glint in his eyes, that ever-present tenacity and inner strength that he possessed before being shot down and taken prisoner. When my tour with the Blues was drawing to an end, I arranged to have Dusty ordered as the third leader of the now firmly established demonstration team.

Dusty's naval service, as prisoner of war and later as a leader of the Blue Angels, is a story of strength of character, high initiative, and tenacity, driven by the inner core of a true American hero. When Dusty was a young navy ensign, I saw him as a level-headed, aggressive fighter pilot. With unending purpose, he survived the degrading depths of prison life. It was now his turn to ascend to the heights of leadership of the world's top military flight demonstration team.

FOREWORD

From POW to Blue Angel sets a living example of personal strength and resiliency in a young naval officer, a mantle he proudly and justly wears to this date. Jim Armstrong tells his story with great clarity and feeling.

BUTCH VORIS
Captain, U.S. Navy

PREFACE
THE FIGHTER PILOT

An aging combat veteran, Dusty Rhodes—Commander Raleigh E. Rhodes (USN Retired)—still looks and acts like the fighter pilot he once was. His broad chest and well-muscled arms, toned through a lifetime of swimming and daily workouts, suggest the control he exercised over powerful fighter planes, and his steady gaze signals readiness to meet a challenge.

At five feet, eight inches and a lifetime steady weight of 155 pounds, Dusty always fit comfortably into even a cramped cockpit. He stands more often forward, on the balls of his feet, than on his heels, and hiking behind him once on a rocky trail around Pinecrest Lake, I noticed how lean and muscular his calves still are. Until a couple of years ago, when arterial plaque accumulation in his legs began giving him problems, he took a vigorous walk of several miles at least once a day and played nine or eighteen holes of golf, without a cart, several times a week. Now the pain that sharply limits his walking frustrates him.

Looking at photographs of Dusty from his youth through his aviator years to the present day, you see the same expression of steady alertness and readiness to respond—to a question, an invitation, a joke. His smile comes easily; he loves playful banter or a funny story. You sense his self-confidence and his respectful openness to whatever you have to offer. He seems naturally courteous, even chivalrous, and you can understand why so many men readily trusted him as a leader and granted him their loyalty.

Dusty's blond hair and eyebrows are lighter and thinner than they once were, and the lines of concentration on his tanned face a little deeper. He has always been good-looking, even strikingly handsome, and it's easy to imagine how positively women have responded to him. But he's reticent on the subject, in a gentlemanly way. I mentioned to him once that biographies and autobiographies of fighter pilots usually give the impression that their off-duty activities focused chiefly on women and drinking. Was that true?

He took the question seriously, thoughtfully. "Well, yeah," he said. "I suppose that's true." But he offered no personal examples as confirmation—you might have thought I'd asked him who he liked in the World Series. Maybe he confesses his off-duty exploits more readily when he's among other former fighter pilots. Only long acquaintance might confirm the suspicion that his behavior has ever been less than prudent.

Dusty was seventy-nine, I was sixty-five, when I first got to know him through my wife's uncle and aunt. Over drinks before dinner, I asked him a question about his combat experiences that brought forth a brief version of the events of the first three chapters. I decided on the spot that I wanted to write his story.

Raleigh Ernest Rhodes was born in Madera, California, on June 26, 1918. His father, Welton Capehart Rhodes, progressed through county offices from undersheriff to auditor to sheriff, and eventually became a U.S. marshal. His mother, born Eva Mae Burgess, was a secretary in several county offices. Since his father was known as "Dusty" Rhodes, Raleigh was called "Bud" or "Buddy" until early in his naval career.

Buddy's school years offered him chances to explore his talents for playing the trumpet, swimming, acting in school plays, and scouting. At thirteen he became one of the youngest Eagle Scouts in the country.

Dusty Rhodes as naval air cadet. Courtesy Raleigh E. Rhodes.

James E. "Jimmy" Caldwell as naval air cadet. Courtesy Raleigh E. Rhodes.

PREFACE

Graduating in 1936 from Madera High School after serving as class president every year and student body president as a senior, Bud completed a year of the pre-engineering program at Fresno State University, but he and a classmate dropped out of the fall term the next year to search for a lost mail plane in the snowy Sierra Nevada, hoping to earn a reward. When someone else finally found the crashed plane in the spring, Bud stayed on through the summer as a handyman at a mountain resort where he and his friend had worked while searching. For the next two years he experimented with jobs as an oil field roustabout in Bakersfield and a gas pump jockey at a couple of Shell Oil stations.

Returning to Fresno State in the fall of 1940, he enrolled in the new Civilian Pilot Training program started by the government in colleges around the country to develop a cadre of qualified pilots for military service in case of war. Like many young men his age, Bud had fallen in love with aviation through reading of the exploits of fighter pilots in the Great War, thrilling at Lindbergh's transatlantic flight in 1927, and admiring the acrobatics of barnstorming pilots through the thirties. He excelled in his CPT courses, sharing his enthusiasm and accomplishments with his new friend Jimmy Caldwell, and accumulating several hundred hours of flight experience. The following year, both enlisted as seamen second class in the U.S. Navy.

After Elimination Base in Oakland, where enlistees were required to fly a light airplane solo, Dusty and Jimmy became naval aviation cadets in July 1941 at Jacksonville, Florida, where they were training when Japanese planes attacked Pearl Harbor. In January they moved to Naval Air Station Miami for advanced fighter training. Commissioned as ensigns in March, they were sent to an Advanced Carrier Training Group at NAS San Diego. Shortly after arriving there, Dusty married his college sweetheart, Marian, and Jimmy married his girl, Jean. The two couples shared an apartment off base. Early in July, Dusty and Jimmy joined Fighting Squadron Ten under Lieutenant Commander Jimmy Flatley. Shipping out for Hawaii in early August, the squadron completed its training on Maui and boarded USS *Enterprise* on October 16, en route to the South Pacific. My account of Dusty's war ordeal begins ten days later.

Dusty and Jimmy as newly commissioned ensigns, March 1942. Courtesy Raleigh
E. Rhodes.

AUTHOR'S NOTE

Five years before I began interviewing Dusty in October of 1997, he had retired after thirty years from his second career as a project leader for Lockheed Missiles and Space Company in Sunnyvale, California. His first career of twenty years with the United States Navy had begun when he was twenty-three and led him through adventures as a World War II fighter pilot, a prisoner of war in Japan, a leader of the navy's Blue Angels flight demonstration team, a jet fighter pilot in the Korean War, operations officer at a naval ordnance testing ground, squadron commander on one aircraft carrier and air operations officer on another, and four years as the navy's representative on the Airways Modernization Board, the predecessor of the Federal Aviation Administration.

This book ends with Dusty's return to the United States in 1951 following his Korean tour of duty. It omits the ten years preceding his retirement from the navy in 1961. There is adventure and rare experience in those years, to be sure, but little to match Dusty's years as a POW or as a leader of the Blue Angels.

For the heart of the story, I've relied chiefly on Dusty's memory, prompted by my endless, persistent questions. In over 120 hours of recorded interviews and discussions at his home in Los Altos, California, and at his mountain cabin in Strawberry, on the Sonora Pass road, he's responded willingly and patiently. I've been impressed again and again by the capriciousness of memory—and not just Dusty's. I've also interviewed and recorded eleven of his closest naval aviation colleagues from two to six hours each. Their recollections of events fifty to seventy years ago are sometimes astonishingly detailed and vivid, sometimes uncertain, occasionally blank. Accounts by those who have shared Dusty's experiences are often priceless, but sometimes frustratingly contradictory.

Even historians contradict each other. But out of many sources, a common, convincing story gradually emerges. So I have also drawn on dozens of written sources, including extensive newspaper and magazine clippings, letters, and telegrams collected by Dusty and his family in a very large scrapbook. Rather than employ the usual expository style of biography, I've chosen to embed this detailed and authentic information in a lively, informal narrative for the sake of the drama, vividness, and suspense of a good yarn. The dialogue is a blend of verbatim statements from my taped interviews and imagined extrapolations of the speakers' probable language, based on my ear for their speech and my understanding of the physical and emotional circumstances of the situations.

Dusty Rhodes survived these remarkable experiences, but chose not to write his own story. With his permission, encouragement, and supervision I have written it for him. The sympathetic voice is mine; the adventures, the memories, the judgments are his.

Dusty believes that we have achieved the closest approximation possible of what "really" happened. He has read and approved of everything in the book. The other interviewees have reviewed the parts to which they've contributed. I take full responsibility for whatever huge or trivial errors remain.

Placentia, California
January 21, 2004

FROM POW
TO BLUE ANGEL

TASK FORCE 61

I n late October of 1942, with the Second World War not yet a year old, United States military and naval forces in the South Pacific were trying to recapture territory taken by the Japanese. They were inadequately equipped for the attempt, and often undertrained. Among other causes, America's isolationist policy after the First World War and the economic effects of the Great Depression had left the country unprepared for the aggression of Germany in Europe and the Japanese surprise attack on Pearl Harbor.

The belated mobilization of U.S. armed forces and conversion of industry to war production put many inexperienced and quickly trained servicemen in harm's way with outdated and insufficient equipment. They faced the most experienced, best-trained, and best-equipped armies, navies, and air forces in the world. Before attacking Pearl Harbor on December 7, 1941, the Japanese had been at war in China since 1937.

Guadalcanal, one of the Solomon Islands, was hotly contested, and U.S. intelligence sources anticipated a major Japanese ground offensive, supported by growing Japanese naval forces in the vicinity, including four or five aircraft carriers. Among U.S. forces trying to intercept the Japanese carriers was Task Force 61, consisting of two aircraft carriers, USS *Enterprise* and USS *Hornet*, the battleship *South Dakota*, two or three cruisers, and ten or twelve destroyers. TF-61 was approximately three hundred miles east of Guadalcanal and one hundred miles northeast of the Santa Cruz Islands.

Aboard the *Enterprise* was Ensign Raleigh E. "Dusty" Rhodes, a member of Fighting Squadron Ten, the "Grim Reapers," led by Lieutenant Commander James H. "Jimmy" Flatley. All thirty or so aircraft of this squadron were Grumman F4F-4 Wildcats, single-engine fighter planes. There were also squadrons of dive bombers (SBDs) and torpedo bombers (TBFs) on the *Enterprise*. The *Hornet* was similarly equipped.

In the early afternoon of Sunday, October 25, scout planes spotted a Japanese task force with two carriers heading straight for TF-61. It was still out of range, but if both forces stayed on course at twenty-five knots or more (at least twenty-nine mph), they could threaten each other in a couple of hours. Task force commander Rear Admiral Thomas Kinkaid and *Enterprise* skipper Captain Osborne Hardison ordered out a scout group of twelve SBD Dauntlesses (single-engine dive bombers) in pairs, covering a northwest sector from 280 to 010 degrees. They were followed an hour later by a strike group of thirty-five dive bombers, torpedo bombers, and fighters, including two divisions—totaling eight Wildcats—of Dusty's squadron. Dusty's Division Six stayed put.

The plan was that the strike group would turn back after 150 miles if the scouts didn't locate the Japanese carriers. But there was a spectacular foul-up, with faulty communications and misunderstood orders and wrong assumptions. The result was that the strike group went too far and ran low on fuel. They couldn't possibly find the enemy task force, because it had reversed direction and headed away from TF-61 about the time *Enterprise* planes were launched.

Half an hour after the strike group was launched, there had been a radio report from a group of Army B-17 Flying Fortresses that had accidentally come across the retreating Japanese ships, but Admiral Kinkaid thought that his planes would turn back soon anyway, and he didn't want to give away TF-61's position by breaking radio silence to order them back.

The strike group had flown two hundred miles, more west than north, without any report from the scouts, and then tried another eighty-mile vector to the north before turning back. It was chancy, but it looked like there would be enough fuel to get back safely by sunset. In the meantime, the SBD scout group had given up and gone back, and in order to land them the *Enterprise*, and the rest of the task force with it, had turned and sailed *southeast*, into the wind. In the process, they added about twenty miles to the distance the returning strike group needed to cover to reach Point Option, the predesignated rendezvous point for carrier and planes.

One Wildcat pilot in Reaper Four made it back to the carrier just before dark by following a radio homing signal, but when he'd signaled the others to follow him they'd misunderstood and lost him. Another pilot in Reaper Four ran out of fuel and had to bail out about forty miles short of the task force. He was missing and presumed dead. It was after dark when the rest of the group reached Point Option and found no ships.

The SBD dive bomber pilots decided to lighten their loads by dropping their bombs, and when one of them exploded on hitting the water,

Lieutenant Stanley "Swede" Vejtasa, leading Reaper Seven, could see by the light of the flash that there was an oil slick on the water. He remembered noticing that the *Enterprise* was leaking oil when he'd taken off in the afternoon, and so it seemed logical to follow the oil trail home. By then the full moon was high enough so some of the pilots could see the oil, and they'd finally all caught up with the carrier.

Before all the planes could land in turn, three TBF Avenger torpedo bombers and two SBD dive bombers ran out of fuel and had to ditch near the carrier. Their pilots and crews were rescued, except for one TBF crewman. Two other SBDs were damaged beyond repair in a landing accident on the carrier. Two men and eight planes lost on that mission, and they hadn't even seen the Japanese!

Sunday, October 26, everyone believed, would be different. Lieutenant Commander Bucky Lee, skipper of Scouting Ten, had sent his scout bombers out in ten pairs, he and his wingman heading in what he thought was the most likely direction, and at 0750 hours—7:50 A.M.—they made a sighting: two Japanese carriers, a couple of cruisers, and several destroyers.

"Donald Duck," the intercom, squawked the news through *Enterprise*, ending with "Pilots, man your planes!"

ONE

FIRST BLOOD

From his cockpit, Ensign Raleigh E. "Dusty" Rhodes stared at the plane captain until he signaled "Start your engine." Dusty pressed the ignition button and the engine turned over reluctantly two or three times. It coughed, sputtered, caught, and then as he adjusted the throttle, it roared like a Wildcat.

He glanced at his gauges again and checked the deck crewmen nearby. Two planes ahead of him, Chip Reding's aircraft began to taxi into takeoff position. The flight deck of USS *Enterprise* dipped slowly and rolled gently to starboard. Good weather. Low, light clouds; good visibility.

The only problem at the moment was his rubber Mae West life vest. Climbing into the cockpit, he'd caught one of the toggles on something, and with a whoosh, half the vest had inflated. He struggled to deflate the bulky thing while going through the preflight procedures. It was almost small enough now for him to fasten his seat belt.

The yellow-shirted crewman ahead of Dusty's plane waved him on, so he eased off the brakes and shoved the throttle forward. Clearing the waiting planes on either side of him, he watched for the crewman's signal again and stopped the plane while other crewmen swung his folded wings into place and he locked them. Then, at the crewman's wave, ahead again toward the takeoff position.

Two deck crewmen were holding up white placards. One said "*Proceed* without Hornet." So they wouldn't join up with the *Hornet* planes after all. The other placard listed the speed of the Japanese fleet as twenty-five knots at 0830.

Dusty's watch read 8:55—0855. Ready to launch.

Hornet's Wildcats were already up. A flight of them had swung over ten minutes ago, circling to gain altitude, climbing to rendezvous with their SBDs and TBFs. The sun was well up, too, here in the South Pacific, three hundred miles east of the Solomon Islands. It was October 26, 1942, just four months since Dusty's twenty-fourth birthday on Maui.

USS *Enterprise* (CV-6) at Noumea, New Caledonia, November 1942. Official photograph, U.S. Navy.

A VT-10 TBF Avenger prepares for launch from USS *Enterprise* (CV-6) during the Battle of Santa Cruz, October 26, 1942. The sign visible beyond the plane's landing gear reads PROCEED WITHOUT HORNET, indicating *Enterprise*'s strike is not to wait to join up with a strike being launched by *Hornet* (CV-8). The sign to the left reads JAP "CV" SPEED 25 at 0830." Official photograph, U.S. Navy.

He stopped his plane, set his brakes, lowered his flaps, and waited for the signal to go. High off the port bow, Chip Reding's Wildcat climbed toward the rendezvous quadrant. Dusty would follow Chip up to rendezvous with Jack Leppla's Reaper Six and Jimmy Flatley's Reaper One, then with the SBDs and TBFs. He felt eager, like waiting on the sidelines to go in at quarterback. *Put me in, Coach!*

He watched for the signal, and when it came, shoved the throttle full forward and let go of the brakes. The Wildcat dug out faster than his Ford had ever done, hitting close to twice the Ford's top speed before he reached the end of the deck and pulled back on the stick. With a boost from the carrier's movement into the light morning wind, he took the air once again on a magic carpet of steel.

The Grumman Wildcat wasn't a perfect fighter, but it was the best the U.S. Navy had and the hottest plane he'd ever flown—a real wildcat compared to the pussycat Stearman he'd taken his first aviation cadet lessons in. Still, veteran pilots like Leppla and Flatley and Swede Vejtasa had made him and the rest of the Reapers aware of its shortcomings in combat.

Compared to the Japanese Zero, the F4F-4 was a slow, clumsy turkey. Its predecessor, the F4F-3, had problems enough, but the -4 was carrying extra armor plate and two more wing guns, with the same engine. Zeros could fly circles around it. Nevertheless, this morning his Wildcat was his passport to glory, and there was no place in the world he'd rather be.

Dusty's altimeter read about 1,500 feet when he began to break through the light cloud cover into the clear sky and bright sun. The aircraft of the attack group pulled gradually into formation, the fighters above and ahead of the dive bombers and torpedo bombers, Leppla's division to port and Flatley's to starboard, so that Dusty could see the bombers—the TBFs anyway—behind his right wing and about 1000 feet below.

The four blue and gray F4Fs of Reaper Six moved into a "fingertip" formation, with Lepp in the lead, Al Mead off his left wing, behind and slightly below, Chip off his right wing, also behind and below, and Dusty off Chip's right wing, still lower. A cockeyed-looking formation, but it gave them all great visibility. Well behind the formation came Air Group Commander Richard Gaines in a TBF, without the torpedo.

The two fighter divisions, throttled back so as not to outrun the bombers, still had to weave in a slow serpentine movement to stay in the right position. It was an agreeable motion for Dusty, a little like the swooping zig-zags he used to do on his bike on the streets of Madera, relaxing and almost hypnotic. Except now he couldn't afford the slightest lapse of attention from everything around him—the dark blue sea far below, the other planes of the attack group, especially the sky ahead. A fighter pilot's eyes are as restless as a hunting wolf's, keen for the tiniest unexpected movement in the skyscape.

The altimeter needle gradually moved past 6,000 feet and the formation continued to climb slowly. Dusty knew Flatley wanted a lot of altitude, as much as fifteen or twenty thousand feet, to be in the best position to deal with approaching Zeros, but it didn't look like he was going to get it on this mission. The three SBDs, ahead of the eight TBFs, seemed to be in no hurry to reach their operational altitude. He could see them below each time Lepp led his division in a starboard turn.

The sun over Dusty's right shoulder was warm through the glass canopy, and the radio made only crackles of static. Radio silence was mandatory. They must have been in the air half an hour now . . . yes, his watch showed almost 0930. Probably sixty miles out and at least twice that far to go yet—*if* the Jap carriers turned out to be where they were supposed to be. It was good to have that extra fuel tank slung under the wing—fifty-eight gallons' worth—but he'd drop it in a minute if any Zeros showed up. He'd need all the maneuverability he could get.

Chip passed back the hand signal to charge guns, and Dusty gave him a thumbs up, pulling the right cable first, then the left—like starting an outboard motor, only not quite so brisk. They began a gentle starboard turn, and Dusty looked down toward the TBFs.

What? Smoke! . . . He's hit!

Below the eight TBFs, three Zeros, like mosquitoes, swerved away right as the hit TBF drifted left and began to lose altitude. A second TBF started smoking. The Zeros did matching barrel rolls and climbed toward Flatley's Reaper One. *Swivelneck!*

Bandits nine o'clock high and closing! External fuel tanks were dropping away from the Wildcats ahead of Dusty, and he jettisoned his and switched to his internal tank.

Lepp and Al were climbing, trying to gain altitude they could convert to speed in a dive, but the oncoming Zeros weren't giving them much time. The sky was suddenly filled with the flash of tracers.

Zeros behind us! Chip and Dusty split right, opening space to go into a Thach Weave* with Lepp and Al, but by the time they turned back, Lepp and Al had disappeared.

*Defensive maneuver in which two aircraft or two pairs of aircraft sharply diverge and then turn towards each other so that one unit can fire at enemy aircraft on the other's tail; also "beam defense maneuver." Devised early in World War II by Lt. Cdr. John S. "Jimmy" Thach.

Thach with Chip. Swinging away, then back toward Chip's plane, he could see Chip's prop windmilling and the plane losing speed. *Switch to your main tank, Chip!*

A gray Zero with a black cowl overshot Chip, and Dusty squeezed his trigger as the Jap[†] passed in front of him. Tracers converged on the Zero's right wing and moved toward the fuselage. *Did I get him?*

No time to think. Over his shoulder he could see another Zero moving onto his tail. Hard right, then back down over Chip to keep the next Zero off him until . . . *Squeeze!* The dark shape of another Zero moved between him and Chip. Dusty's tracers raked it from bow to stern, and a puff of smoke erupted from behind the cockpit.

Suddenly the air around his head crackled like cherry bombs exploding, and the gunsight leaped off the cowling and dangled by its electric wires. The instrument panel was full of holes and broken glass, and he had a sudden image of a bullet-blasted panel in a combat-seasoned Wildcat he'd examined on the deck of *Enterprise* back at Pearl after the battle of Midway.

The glass of the cockpit canopy had disappeared. A fire burned on the periphery of his vision. *The tank—it didn't drop.* A flame like a blowtorch spurted from a bullet hole in the fuel tank under his right wing, and Dusty again yanked the toggle that should have released it. It stayed where it was.

Chip was pulling up, gaining altitude. He'd remembered the fuel tank switch. But Dusty needed altitude, too. If you could dive on a Zero you were all right, but climbing you were no match. *Thach again.*

Something streamed past his plane, falling toward the water. An unopened chute? Where were Lepp and Al? Thach Weave with Chip again, back and forth, all the time glancing over his shoulder for Zeros. He saw Chip fire a burst as a Zero crossed their bow. Where were the other Zeros? Above them!

Where was Jimmy's division? Nowhere in sight. Gone on with the bombers?

Altitude 1500. Too low. Do the guns still work? *Lemme find a Zero . . .* Damn it! His guns were jammed. Now what?

Oh, man—no engine. The prop was stuck. Frozen. *Oil line hit. Ditch it.*

He turned into the wind as his Wildcat slowed and began to lose altitude. The fire was out on the wing tank.

[†]*Jap* and *Nip*, now considered derogatory and racist, were commonly used during World War II by English-speaking Allies, both military and civilian.

Hey! His rudder pedals suddenly slammed into the firewall and his goggles flapped against both sides of his head.

I'll be . . . The rudder cables were shot out. He was too low, but he had to bail out. Never bail out under a thousand feet, they said. *Do I have a thousand?*

He reached up with his left hand and threw back what was left of the birdcage overhead. Unfastening his seat belt and grabbing the sides of the cockpit, he pushed himself up awkwardly and kicked the stick hard forward as he grabbed his parachute ring. *Launch 'em!*

As the plane dived, he pulled his ripcord and felt himself catapulted free of the cockpit, flying and waiting tensely for the pop and the jolt of the opening chute. It came in a couple of seconds, snapping his neck and throwing his feet out in front of him, the long pendulum swing downward beginning as the ocean rushed up to hit him—then he splashed feetfirst and plunged into the water until the collapsing chute on the surface jerked him again to an underwater stop.

He had to get free of his gear. He kicked hard toward the surface, pushing away the entangling shrouds, trying to come up alongside the chute, not under it. As he broke the surface, air filled his lungs and relief flooded his brain.

He yanked the left toggle on his Mae West, remembering that the right side had already been inflated and deflated before takeoff. Now he had to use the little tube and blow it up with lung power.

Safely floating, he unhooked the parachute straps and let the chute drift free, but he clung to the seat pack that held the pararaft. He turned gradually in the water as the horizon disappeared and reappeared, scanning the ocean and sky around him. Nothing in the whole 360. No planes, no wreckage. No ships, no other pilots in the water. Just clear blue ocean with swells running four to five feet, lifting him rhythmically and dropping him again. He had to get the raft out.

A growing drone of aircraft engines caught his attention. Four planes were approaching, low over the water. Who? Then he could recognize the shape of an F4F, and the three behind it were Zeros, but not close enough to use their guns. They were passing a quarter of a mile north of him. Dusty was sure it was Chip. He wanted to cheer him on.

One of the Zeros was smoking, and none of them seemed to be gaining. The engine noise gradually faded, and each time he rose to the top of a swell the planes looked smaller, until they disappeared.

He struggled to unsnap the pararaft compartment of the seat pack. The yellow rubber package floated free. But the water around him was colored by blood. What from? The leg. Something had hit him. A bullet or shrapnel.

Then he thought of the sharks. There was no question of using shark repellent, because he'd never gotten around to stocking his emergency kit the way he was supposed to—with sulfa, bandages, shark repellent, flares, all those things.

He turned the flabby raft and found the toggle of the CO_2 cylinder and gave it a sharp yank. A sudden hiss, and there was a yellow rubber doughnut just big enough to sit in, like a kids' toy pool. Dusty wrestled himself across the raft and got his left knee inside, but something was wrong. The raft was collapsing, sinking under his weight. It deflated to a floppy piece of rubber, and Dusty was still in the water, bleeding.

The hand pump. Like blowing up a basketball, or a bike tire. Except that you're not floating in the ocean, worrying about sharks. But the pump came loose in his hand—it wasn't even attached to the raft. He couldn't believe it. There was a threaded brass fitting on the raft around a half-inch hole, but nothing on the pump to screw onto it. He tossed the pump away. Then he took a deep breath and started blowing into the brass-bound hole.

Two . . . three . . . four . . . five . . . six big breaths.

Nothing yet. Seven . . . eight . . . nine.

He watched the yellow rubber intently, waiting for the first sign of life in it. Then he noticed a neat round hole in the rubber, the size of his little finger. Then two more. Several more holes. Bullets. Jap bullets.

There was a patch kit here somewhere. It was a lousy place to have a flat. He remembered a flat he'd had on the old Ford between Madera and Fresno. It was August. No fun working on the hot, dusty roadside with no shade in sight for miles, but he'd fixed it in no time and was on the road again.

In the kit he found two rubber plugs, a small strip of patching material, and a tiny tube of rubber cement. No scissors. There might have been some in his first-aid kit, if he'd had a first-aid kit. But he had his knife.

He worked the two plugs into the holes nearest the pump fitting, and they seemed to fit tight. Then he reached down and pulled the knife from the leather sheath on the right calf of his coveralls. He couldn't see any more blood in the water around him. Maybe it had stopped.

Cutting one patch at a time, peeling off the backing, squeezing some glue on, and sticking it over a hole was tedious, but he worked at it as quickly as he could. And he stabbed himself in the leg with the knife every time he tried to put it back in the sheath.

The strip made about six patches, and that was it. Maybe it was enough. He couldn't see any more holes. Putting his mouth to the brass fitting, he blew a dozen big breaths into the raft and then stopped to check it. Good. It seemed to be holding the air. Now if his lungs held out.

Breath is life, he thought. Blowing, he remembered watching a lifeguard at the beach on Bass Lake blowing life into a boy who'd almost drowned. Now his own breath would save his life, once he got the raft blown up and climbed into it before the sharks came. After each round of blowing, he held his left thumb tightly over the hole.

Again he heard the drone of aircraft engines growing louder. From the crest of a swell, he scanned the sky and spotted three planes flying low over the waves maybe two miles away, one of them trailing black smoke. The Zeros that were chasing Chip. Did they get him?

The next time he crested a wave, he saw the smoking Zero angling toward the water, and then it must have gone in. When he rose again, only two Zeros were flying on to the northwest, and the trail of smoke was fading. Maybe he ran out of fuel. The other two probably wouldn't make it back to their carrier, either. They'd made a mistake chasing Chip. If all three went in, Chip ought to get credit for them. But nobody would ever know.

What if the Jap had a raft? They might run into each other if the wind was right, or if one of them was paddling. There might already be other Japs in the water, even if he couldn't see them. He reached down into the water again, across his body with his right hand, and pulled his .45 from its holster on his left hip. Would it still work?

A thin film of rust coated the barrel. He didn't think it had been rusty yesterday, but maybe he hadn't checked it for a day or two. With both hands above the water, he slid the chamber back, cocking it. Then he straightened his right arm and pulled the trigger. *BLAM!*

It worked. He was ready for Japs or sharks.

Reholstering the .45, he resumed blowing up the raft, watching its contour rise gradually above the water. After five or ten minutes it was still flabby but maybe full enough. In any case, he wanted to get into it right now. Reaching across it and grabbing a handful of rubber on the other side, he pulled and wiggled himself aboard, feeling as he did so that the raft was not much more than half inflated. Still, it would keep him afloat and provide some protection.

When he was settled into a sitting position, his knees drawn up, he bent over awkwardly and blew again into the brass-edged hole. It was a tough angle and hard work. Thumb back over the hole. Maybe a few more breaths after he rested a little. There were three or four inches of water in the bottom of the raft, but that was no problem. He could splash some out, or rig up some kind of bailer. Maybe he'd just leave it alone. Water underfoot would keep him cooler if the sun got too hot.

He looked around, taking stock. What a fix! If he'd been only a hundred yards off Waikiki Beach, he'd be sitting pretty. He'd think about the wage slaves back on the mainland and figure being a naval aviator was the best job in the world.

Here—well, he could be patient. They'd pick him up sooner or later. He could last a few days anyway, and there would be PBY amphibians and other reconnaissance aircraft out scouting for him and others who'd gone in the drink that morning and the night before.

Both calves were sore, the left from the bullet or shrapnel, the right where he'd stabbed it with his knife a few times. There were rips in his coveralls and the sore spots were tender to touch, but they didn't seem to be bleeding anymore. Both feet were bare. The brown loafers he and some of the other Reapers had bought after Jimmy Flatley showed up one day in a snappy-looking pair must have been shaken off when he bailed out. The socks, too, or maybe he'd kicked or pulled them off in the water without thinking about it, because they were heavy and clumsy.

His helmet was gone, and the split goggles. Had a bullet parted his hair like that? The radio cord, still anchored in the cockpit, would have yanked the helmet off when he bailed out. The .45 was a comfort. If he could figure out a way to dry it off and keep it dry, maybe the rust wouldn't be a problem. Right now there was no dry place to put it. He pulled the pistol from its holster and laid it in his lap. Then he unbuckled the belt and pushed it and the holster away from him. Excess baggage.

A little shade would help. The sun would cook his bare head after a while, even with the tan he had. There was supposed to be a little tarp in the emergency kit, but like the sulfa and bandages and shark repellent, it had got left out. His feet, too—in fact, any bare skin was going to take a beating from the sun if he was out here very long. A little sunburn was a cheap price to pay if he got picked up soon, but after a couple of days . . .

He felt of the rubber gunwales and decided to blow a few more breaths into the raft. It was a pain in the neck, about as easy as blowing into his own navel. But it was keeping him afloat.

Well, he'd had bad luck and good luck.

Bad luck to get splashed in his first combat. After a lot of other little pieces of bad luck—half the Mae West accidentally inflating just before takeoff, getting jumped out of the sun by hotshot Nips who'd already had combat experience, Chip's fuel transfer problem, the guns jamming. Then the leg wound, the raft shot full of holes, no first-aid kit or survival rations, no shark repellent or yellow dye, no shade, a rusty gun . . .

But good luck to be alive. Thank Grumman or the navy or somebody for that armor plate behind the seat. If the Japs' bullets split his goggles and hit his leg and shredded his raft, they hadn't missed his head and his body by much. That armor plate must have been full of little craters, like the moon.

And he was able to bail out, and still had enough altitude—barely—for the parachute to break his fall. Just half a pendulum swing and his feet had gone in! No sharks while he was working on the raft. He still had a knife and a gun in case something showed up. The water was warm, not freezing like the north Atlantic. He was in pretty good shape, considering what had happened. He was ready for whatever was next.

He heard more planes. Then he saw them—a whole flight of them.

The attack group! Or what was left of it. Four F4Fs—the skipper's division. One, two, three—all the SB Deuces. But only four Torpeckers. Eight had gone out. He'd seen two of them go down, or at least they were smoking badly.

Hey, guys! Hey! It's me!

The planes passed directly overhead; it was hard for them to see him at that angle. But he waved wildly with his free arm and shouted into the roar of engines. *Hey! Skipper! Hey, you guys! Look down!*

They passed slowly, throttled back to conserve fuel and get back to the *Enterprise*. Dusty dropped his arm and watched the planes grow smaller, headed for the far horizon. The sun was still almost directly overhead.

It had been a busy morning. It looked like it was going to be a quiet afternoon.

TWO

PREDICAMENT

Suddenly he woke up. His arm was dragging in the water and his face was pressed against the gunwale of the rubber raft. He opened his eyes, squinting in the glare, and tried to sit up straighter. His neck was sore, and his lower back too. The water he sat in, floated in, was warm, almost body temperature. But he was deeper than he wanted to be. His left thumb was still pressed over the blow-hole of the raft, but air had been leaking out, and he hadn't blown into it for a while. How long had he been asleep?

He leaned over and moved his thumb aside to blow into the hole again. After a few big breaths he thought he could feel the air in the raft pushing out a little more, lifting more yellow rubber to the surface. He kept blowing for eight or ten minutes, until he was winded. It would have to do for now.

From the sun he guessed it was two or three in the afternoon. He'd have been back on the carrier if everything had gone right. Things hardly ever go right in wartime. He was lucky to be alive. The skipper's division was back okay, probably talking about the mission. And about the odds of finding him and whoever else hadn't come back. Chip might have, but Lepp and Al probably hadn't—he'd seen only four Wildcats in the returning flight.

It would be great to be there, stretching his legs and sipping hot coffee and talking about the battle. There must have been some kind of battle—the Jap task force was close enough, and there were a lot of planes from both sides in the air. If only they hadn't been asleep at the wheel when the Zeros hit. Nobody expected them to be that close, and the attack group was much too low. The skipper would be really ticked off about that.

Images of the dogfight flashed in his memory, and he wondered if he was remembering it right, whether he'd even seen it right in the first

Page of Dusty's flight log, October 1942. Courtesy Raleigh E. Rhodes.

place. Too much going on. But he'd done the right thing covering Chip, and when Chip's engine took hold again they'd done the Thach Weave right. The Zeros kept veering off, bluffed out, even though neither he nor Chip could fire after the first burst or two. *Darn guns.*

He was surprised he wasn't hungry. No food for—what? eight or nine hours. Well, he could afford to lose a couple of pounds. By this time tomorrow he'd be shoveling it down. Maybe. If things went okay.

There were four or five more hours of daylight. A patrol could see him in this light if it was low and close enough. In the morning, at any rate, there'd be scouts and patrols out and somebody would spot him. The task force could even show up, or a destroyer at least, out prowling the perimeter, watching for subs.

His wrists and ankles and feet were bright red. He could imagine what his face looked like. It felt tight and dry, even with the sweat and the water he splashed on it.

Ten more big breaths into the raft, then rest.

Some of his mates were still working, and here he was floating around in the ocean. He felt guilty. *I let 'em down . . . gotta get back. I'll make up for it.*

Marian, too. And Mom and Dad. *They'll worry themselves sick. They'll think I'm dead.* He closed his eyes and tried to imagine what they were doing now. It was five hours later in Fresno—after dinner. Maybe they were listening to Fibber McGee and Molly . . . No, it wasn't Sunday there, only Saturday. They might be seeing a movie. Marian liked movies, and so did her mother . . .

He needed to do something. He thought of the ping-pong paddles, the two little wooden paddles you could strap to your wrists and use to paddle your own canoe. They were still hooked to the raft, the only extra survival equipment he had, because it wasn't up to him to add them—they were already in the raft compartment.

He only needed one, though. His left hand was busy keeping the raft's blow hole plugged. He pulled a paddle loose and tried a few strokes in the water. Not much purchase. Small surface. Better than bare hands, though. Better than nothing. He wondered how long it would take to paddle to the Santa Cruz Islands.

That was a joke. He had some idea of the vastness of the Pacific Ocean. Even of the portion he was in. You could fly for hours and see nothing but more water. He tried to visualize the last chart he'd seen, showing the little dots of the islands a hundred miles or more to the south. He wouldn't even be a dot. A molecule, maybe. An atom.

From where he was to anywhere was . . . endless. He couldn't imagine it. Well, so what. You never know. Paddling was better than just drifting.

You couldn't go in a straight line if you paddled only on one side. He knew that from canoeing on Bass Lake. Maybe a little j-stroke would keep it going. But he discovered it was easier to reach across and paddle a few strokes on the left side every now and then. Besides, it was hard to tell whether you were going straight or not. Not like on a lake where you can keep your eye fixed on some point on the shore. After a while it did feel as if he was making some progress. Impossible to tell how much.

After thirty or forty minutes of alternate paddling and resting, his shoulder was sore. He'd have to take it easier or forget about paddling. He tried holding his right thumb over the blow hole and paddling with his left hand, but that didn't work very well. He didn't have good coordination on that side.

Just paddle and rest. And blow.

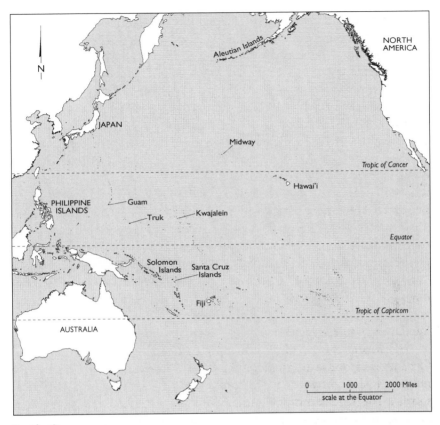

Pacific Ocean

Late in the afternoon—maybe it was the angle of the sun—he thought about sitting in the Officers' Club or at Victor's Bar and having a drink with a few of the guys. He remembered a story one of them told once about a dry martini. Seems that at one time carrier pilots were handed a special small survival kit with the words stenciled on it: "Open Only in Extreme Emergency." The storyteller claimed he'd heard this from an F4F pilot just back from the Battle of the Coral Sea who had to ditch his aircraft when it ran out of fuel.

After leaving the sinking plane and settling into his pararaft, he'd decided the circumstances entitled him to open the miniature emergency kit. Inside he found a thimbleful of gin, an eyedropper of vermouth, a tiny shaker and glass, and a stirring rod. He carefully mixed himself a martini and was just about to take a sip when he heard engines from all sides and found himself surrounded by several small surface craft, a taxiing PBY, and two destroyers.

The skipper of a nearby PT boat hailed him through a megaphone: "Ahoy the raft! That's not the right way to make a dry martini!"

Dusty smiled. Sometimes the mere memory of a drink or a good time with a friend was strangely satisfying. He thought about all the great guys he knew in the Reapers. Knew and felt really close to, even when he didn't know a lot about them. What mattered was that you could depend on them in the air and have a good time with them when you were off duty.

It looked like Chip Reding might have got away, but what about Lepp and Al Mead? He hoped they'd survive too. Jack Leppla was a good division leader, a veteran. He'd flown an SBD off *Lexington* in the Coral Sea. He looked ominous sometimes, with dark bushy eyebrows and a rangy, rugged build like a linebacker. But he knew everybody in the squadron and everybody liked him. Al, his wingman, was tall, too, but more boyish-looking. Al had a keen mind and a sly sense of humor. He and Dusty were both California boys; Lepp was from Ohio.

Dusty was impressed with Swede Vejtasa. He was a tall blond from Montana, friendly and funny. He'd been an SBD pilot in the Coral Sea, too, like Lepp, only he was on the *Yorktown*. He was a crack pilot and a real leader, like Reaper skipper Jimmy Flatley. Flatley had led a Wildcat squadron in *Yorktown*, and after he and Swede came to the Reapers, they spent a lot of time together talking tactics. Swede had already shot down three enemy planes—in a dive bomber!

Jimmy Flatley was even shorter than Dusty, and that led to a funny scene every time he took off. If you were flying near him just after he got airborne, you'd see his head disappear and then pop up again, bobbing like a jack-in-the-box for the twenty-some turns of the crank handle it took to retract the Wildcat's landing gear. You couldn't help smiling.

But he was a crack pilot and a great leader. You knew he wanted to make you into the best fighter pilot he could, by constantly offering advice and tips that might save your life. He'd worked with Jimmy Thach to perfect what started out as the "beam defense maneuver" and came to be known as the Thach Weave. They wanted every naval aviator to learn it. But Flatley was an inspirational leader, too. He really cared about his men's morale. He liked to give them little encouraging talks, either in the ready room or in written copies he'd had duplicated. You knew he was always thinking about how you were feeling, what you might be wondering or worrying about.

It would be good to be back with the skipper and the rest of the guys. The Grim Reapers were a team you were proud to be on.

At last the sun was so low it was about to go under. In the troughs between waves he was briefly in shadow. He'd appreciated tropical sunsets more in other circumstances.

After the sun went down, the light began to go quickly. From the crests of the swells he tried to survey the whole horizon, in case anything at all was within view. But there was nothing.

> *Alone, alone, all, all alone . . .*
> *Alone on the wide, wide sea . . .*

To the east he could see a dark cloud stretching along the horizon. It was probably coming his way. After fifteen or twenty minutes, he was sure of it. Even in the luminous darkness growing around him, the blackness of the cloud was impressive. It seemed to grow faster as it neared the zenith, like a genie from the *Arabian Nights* looming over him.

The rain began with a sudden little shower of drops, like a flicker of spray from a garden hose, and then it came down hard, with quick gusts of wind, but not enough to drive it sideways. As the waves kicked up, the raft shipped more water, but it didn't make much difference. Just a little more rocking and rolling, like riding an inner tube down the San Joaquin River through the foothills, before it leveled out in the Great Valley.

Dusty wondered what it would be like in a real tropical storm. Probably huge waves would capsize you or just smash you with their weight. This was just a squall. He hoped.

Gusts of wind and rain would pelt him for a few minutes and then let up. A few minutes of riding the waves and then another burst. He wondered how long it would last. It was still pitch black and he couldn't see a thing, but it didn't matter. He'd have stories to tell when he got back.

He wondered if sharks hunted in the rain. No reason why they shouldn't. They didn't sleep, either—no eyelids. But they probably depended on surface light to spot their prey. Maybe he didn't have to worry about that.

After half an hour or so, the rain eased up and continued lightly for a long time. Dusty dozed a few minutes, woke up and blew, dozed again, blew again, until it became an automatic rhythm, like breathing. Eventually, it would get light again and he'd get reoriented, when the dawn came up. Like thunder?

It was a long night. At last he noticed he could see the sky above the swells—a lighter shade of gloom at first, then still lighter. He could almost see it changing. He'd watched a few tropical dawns by now and knew how fast it happened. The sky was clear overhead; the clouds had passed. The choppy waves had quieted down, and big easy swells were rolling under him.

He was stiff—legs, back, neck, arms. Stretching helped. When he could see more clearly, he checked out the raft. Still soft and floppy, but enough air to keep him afloat. No changes he could notice, except that his left thumb was numb and paralyzed from stopping the air hole.

The squall hadn't blown anything away. There was nothing to blow. He was cooler than he'd been before, but not chilly. It would be a blessing if there were clouds to cover the sun for a few hours. But not this morning.

On the eastern horizon rays of light stabbed the sky against thin, distant clouds. Then a sharp beam came right at him, switching off again as a swell intervened. And then another, and another, each one seeming a little brighter and stronger, until the whole ball of fire emerged, too bright to look at. Search planes were already up. And Combat Air Patrol. They'd see him if they came close enough.

He wondered what Marian was doing. Maybe going to church. Mom and Dad would go. They hardly ever missed. He thought of Sunday breakfast at home. Poached eggs, bacon, toast and jam. Fresh fruit of some kind. Sometimes pancakes and maple syrup. Hot coffee, fresh orange juice. It had been a while.

Hunger he could live with for a few more hours, even days, if he had to. Thirst was something else. So far he wasn't really thirsty. He didn't feel dehydrated. He'd probably absorbed some water through his skin. But it would get worse with a full day of sun ahead. Maybe he could grab some kind of fish to suck on.

The water was still clear, and he could see down into it twenty or thirty feet. Far enough to see fish coming. Or sharks. If he was facing the right direction. But there was nothing down there right now.

Two or three hours after the sun came up, he heard a distant hum. Aircraft engines. It was hard to tell which direction. He waited for the hum to grow louder, hoping it would be a PBY, flying low. It sounded more like SBDs, though.

Then he could see them, two of them, just specks above the southeastern horizon. SBDs, all right, but it didn't look like they were heading toward him. Probably scouts from the *Enterprise* or the *Hornet*.

After a few more ups and downs, he couldn't see them anymore. Then the sound was gone, too.

He jerked at the noise—a scratchy, squeaky noise just behind him.

He swiveled his neck and saw fins, two of them, only six or eight feet away! Big dorsal fins. Just below the surface were two huge, submarine-like shapes. Eight feet long. Or ten. Sharks, floating there watching him.

He reached slowly for his .45, watching them over his shoulder, out of the corner of his eye. He cocked the gun carefully, hoping the noise wouldn't make them react. Pointing it over his left shoulder, he leveled the .45 at the middle of the right-hand shark's head and kept it there as well as he could while the swells rolled under them. The sharks didn't move, but every few seconds they repeated that weird scratchy, squeaking sound he'd never heard before. It was sort of like a frog croaking.

If they attacked, he wouldn't stand a chance. Maybe he'd get one of them, but the other would have him before he could get off another shot. The knife in his lap would be useless. Should he shoot first? How long would they wait?

Maybe they wouldn't attack if he wasn't bleeding any longer. They probably couldn't figure out what the raft was.

He realized his grip on the pistol was tightening, and he tried to relax it, afraid it might go off before he wanted it to.

Then something else caught his attention as he crested a swell. Off to his right, east or southeast, there was a mast on the horizon, a ship's mast.

Two masts!

Then he was down again in a trough, with a six- or eight-second wait till he was back up. The masts were still there. And then another . . . two more . . . a forest of masts!

As he sank between the swells again, his pulse was racing and for a minute he completely forgot about the sharks. *The sharks!* Where were they?

He couldn't see them anywhere. Were they gone? Or attacking!

Lifted again so he could see the eastern horizon, Dusty scanned the water around him and under him, seeing at the same time that the masts were still there, and moving. There was no sign of the sharks.

Maybe the ships' engines scared them off.

On the next rise he could see that the ships were moving northward, but they were too far away to see him. He couldn't even see the hulls, just the masts and parts of superstructures. It looked like the task force.

The intermittent glimpses continued steadily. He could see that the ships were moving on a course at a right angle to him, and they would never come close, just churning away there toward the north.

He put the .45 back in his lap and started waving his arm over his head, back and forth, back and forth, then in desperate circles.

Hey, look at me! Wake up, you guys! Get those binoculars over here! Look this way! It's me! Dusty!

He stopped waving and blew three big breaths into the air hole. Then he started waving again. He waved until his arm began to ache. The masts were still in sight. But they wouldn't be for much longer.

Then he noticed it. One mast had fallen behind the others. It was getting bigger.

Was it? Was it coming this way?

He watched and hoped. Then he prayed.

Please, God, let them see me. Let them see me.

He waved his tired arm a few more times, and then he was sure the ship was heading directly toward him. More of the superstructure was gradually appearing, and then the hull. Soon he could see the bow wave, and he knew it was coming fast—a small vessel, a destroyer or a destroyer escort. A tin can had never looked so good!

For a minute he couldn't think what to do. It was over. Only a day, and they'd found him! He knew they would. But he felt incredibly lucky. It was a huge ocean, and he was just a speck.

The gray prow of the ship grew higher and sharper. Dusty could just see the forward gun turret, but no ID numbers or marks of any kind. Small as it was compared to the carriers, it began to look huge as it came straight at him, and he wondered if the helmsman had lost sight of him.

Don't run over me now, for cryin' out loud! Starboard two points! Back off the engines! You'll drown me with the bow wave!

But he crested the bow wave easily enough, and as the ship slid by him five or six yards away he heard the huge engines shut down noisily and then go into reverse. The destroyer coasted to a stop twenty or thirty yards past him and slowly began to back up.

The skipper could use a little practice, he thought. *Maybe he's new at the job.*

Keeping his thumb over the air hole, Dusty paddled hard with one hand toward the hull of the ship as it came closer. The water was churning around him. He could flop overboard and swim to the ship, if he could see a ladder anywhere.

Then a heavy line, a hawser, hit the water just in front of him. He paddled another two or three strokes and reached up and grabbed it with both hands. He kicked the raft away and felt his .45 slide off his lap into the water.

Oops! Forgot about that.

Reaching for a new grip on the line, he was surprised to discover he didn't have the strength to pull himself up. It was all he could do to hang on.

Haul away, boys!

He looked up to holler for another line, and the whole rail above him was lined with faces, peering down at him. Not American faces. Japanese faces.

Oh boy.

THREE

RESCUE

He felt the hawser being pulled up, and for a second he thought of letting go. He remembered all he'd heard about how the Japanese tortured prisoners. Not that! But not sharks, either. Or drowning.

He clung to the line, and it jerked him quickly upward, bumping his hands and shoulders against the steel hull somewhere near the bow.

Maybe they wouldn't kill him. Maybe they'd want to question him, and he'd have a little time to figure out what his chances were. But he knew he'd never forget those foreign faces looking down at him. It was the scariest thing he'd ever seen in his life, worse than the sharks.

Hands grabbed his sunburned wrists and arms and pulled him onto the deck. He wanted to say "Easy, boys!" but that would be useless, and besides, he didn't want to show any sign of weakness.

They lifted him to his feet, and he could feel the steel deck burning his soles. He shifted from one foot to the other, and looked around him. They were pushing him and holding him to keep him where he was—crewcut Japanese sailors in khaki uniforms. To his surprise, they didn't look mad at him. They looked more curious, as if they'd just hauled some weird-looking fish out of the water.

They weren't saying much, just jabbering a few words. A couple of them gestured at him to take his life jacket and coveralls off. He peeled off the Mae West and his coveralls as well as he could, trying to keep from stumbling and falling down. When he was stripped to his undershorts, a couple of sailors grabbed his arms, and another snapped handcuffs on him. Someone grabbed the neck chain with his dogtags on it and yanked it over his head. As they pulled him aft along the deck, his feet still burned and his wrists smarted under the tight handcuffs.

They took him to a small portside hatch in the superstructure and shoved him through it. Before they closed the hatch behind him, he could see a steel laundry tub fixed to the bulkhead and nothing else. It was a closet, maybe three feet wide and not much deeper. Then the hatch cover clanged, and he could hear them tightening the screws. Four screws! No need for that. In his condition, he couldn't fight his way out of a soggy paper bag.

It was totally dark in the closet, and there was no ventilation. He stood for a minute holding onto the edge of the laundry tub with his handcuffed hands and leaning against the bulkhead behind him. It was solitary confinement. How long would it last? How long would *he* last?

The thrumming of the ship's engines, which he could feel more than hear, reminded him that they were under way again. He had no idea for where. It was even more humid in the room than outside, and there was no sense in standing on this cruise. He eased himself carefully to the deck and tried to lie down. It was impossible. The closet wasn't even five feet deep.

So he sat, and leaned against the bulkhead. He thought about what could happen next. They might just kill him and dump him overboard. Unless they could think of something better. He decided not to think about torture.

He'd read about prisoners studying every inch of their cells, but there wasn't much to learn about this one. Nothing but the laundry tub. If they used it to rinse out mops, there would be mops in the closet. Maybe the crew washed out their clothes in it. But they probably wouldn't come in while he was there. Maybe it was to throw up in if he got seasick. Maybe this was just the simplest kind of brig they could think of.

He wondered why they took his coveralls. His name and rank were stenciled on them, and USS *Enterprise* was on the Mae West. That would give them clues. They would probably try some sort of interrogation. It wouldn't get very far, though, unless somebody on board could speak English. That wasn't likely, but possible—like in the movies.

"Ha! You surprise I speak your rangridge! Before war I go to UCRA!"

He had to give them credit. There were probably more Japanese who spoke English than Americans who spoke Japanese. The only Japanese word he knew was *sayonara*, and he had thought he would say it to the first Jap he shot down. Maybe the Zero pilots had said it to him.

It was suffocating in the laundry room. He was covered with sweat. His skivvies stuck to him. The handcuffs hurt. The skin on his face and neck and forehead felt tight and dry. It was probably burned red. Nothing was bleeding or broken, though. His left thumb could be a problem. There was no feeling in it, and it still stuck straight out. He could feel it with the fingers of his right hand. His eyes had been closed for a while. There was nothing to see.

He had a mental image of the faces at the ship's rail again, and then he fell asleep.

He woke up when he heard someone unscrewing the hatch. The light blinded him and he could hear somebody speaking to him. He shielded his eyes as well as he could with his handcuffed wrists until he could make out a Japanese sailor looking in at him.

"Dubyaseeka?"

What did that mean?

He raised his eyebrows and shrugged his shoulders. The question came again.

"Dubyaseeka?"

Dusty cocked his head and looked quizzical. He couldn't think of any sign language to try with handcuffs on.

The sailor looked at him expectantly and then said, "Benjo." He stepped forward, took Dusty's arm, and pulled him to his feet. He helped him through the hatch and led him along the deck toward the stern. Dusty's legs felt stiff and tired, and he had trouble at first keeping his balance.

The daylight kept him squinting, but across the water, two or three hundred yards away, he could see a huge ship flanking the destroyer. He knew it right away as a Mogami-class cruiser, and it looked bigger than a battleship. Half a mile or so behind the cruiser, there *was* a battleship. It looked like a task force at least, if not a fleet. He was sure it was the fleet that Task Force 61 had engaged.

Just then he stubbed his toe on a cable running across the deck and let out a yelp as he stumbled. The sailor tightened his grip on Dusty's arm and mumbled something gruffly, pulling him along. Amidships they stepped through a hatchway into a narrow room that smelled like a head. In the deck along one bulkhead was a trough about six inches wide and fifteen feet long.

"Benjo," the sailor announced, and pointed to Dusty's crotch.

"Oh, benjo," said Dusty, nodding his head. The sailor stepped back to the hatchway and stood there looking out, leaving Dusty to his own devices. He was glad his hands weren't handcuffed behind him.

Benjo, thought Dusty. *My second word in Japanese.*

Back in the laundry room, he reviewed his situation. The Japanese ships looked impressive, very businesslike. They were making good speed, maybe twenty, twenty-five knots. He wondered if there were carriers on the other side of them. Maybe next time he'd see something different.

The benjo was peculiar. Was that all there was to it? What if he had to take a crap? Maybe he had missed something, or maybe there was another place for that. He didn't feel the need, though.

The handcuffs were tighter. He could feel that his wrists were swelling, and they were hurting. With his burned and peeling face, he probably looked pretty bad, too. But with no light and no mirror, he didn't have to look at himself. The only thing he could do was listen, and that didn't tell him much. Japanese voices once in a while, the throbbing of engines, an assortment of metal-on-metal bumps and scrapes—normal sounds of a ship running. As heard from a black hole.

But it was all new experience, and he was curious about it. Maybe some of it would be useful some day. In any case, he wanted to remember it all if he survived. Besides, keeping alert would help him survive. He was determined not to let himself go, not give up or get lazy. He should be ready for any chance that came along.

All the same, he couldn't help thinking about what had happened, reviewing the memorable things again and again. There was no point in regrets. He might have done some things different—they all might have. He'd done the best he could. He'd saved his life by getting out of the plane the way he did. He probably saved Chip's life by covering him when he'd lost power. The leaky raft was a disaster, but he'd fixed it and survived. He intended to go on surviving.

An hour or so after he had gone to the benjo, the hatch opened again. This time the light wasn't as bright. A Japanese sailor handed him a metal bowl with some kind of dark liquid in it. It was lukewarm and it had a funny smell. He looked at the sailor and the sailor made a drinking gesture. Just tip the bowl up.

Maybe. Maybe not. He didn't know what the stuff was. He wasn't in any hurry to drink it. He set the bowl down carefully in front of him and nodded at the sailor. The sailor considered for a few seconds, then closed the hatch, leaving the bowl where it was.

It was probably some kind of soup, or broth, but on the other hand, maybe they were trying to poison him. Once he drank it and started flopping around in agony, the sailor would call all his buddies and they'd come running to watch the Yankee fly-boy die. They'd done worse than that in Manchuria, and Nanking.

He realized it must be almost night. That's why it wasn't so bright outside. He lifted the bowl again and sniffed it. It didn't smell too bad, just strange. Maybe a vegetable of some kind. But he didn't need it. He raised the bowl carefully and tipped it over the side of the laundry tub, listening to it gurgle down the drain. They'd wonder if he'd drunk it or not. If it was poisoned, they'd know he hadn't. He'd watch the next Jap's face.

He could lie down on the deck if he bent his knees. Either on his back or on his side. The fetal position. Maybe he'd end up sucking his thumb, or chewing on it, if he started to get hungry.

Good night, Marian, he thought. *Good night, Mother. Good night, Dad*. Then he added, *Please keep them safe, God*.

The night seemed endless, but Dusty fell asleep several times, he had no idea for how long. Waking, he felt stifled in the tiny closet, and all the discomforts in various parts plagued him—his wrists, his thumb, his leg where a piece of steel had ripped it. Not being able to see anything made him more aware of what he was *feeling*. His skin was itching around the waistband of his undershorts, too, probably from the combination of heat, moisture, pressure, and dried saltwater.

In the morning he was taken to the benjo again, and the fresh air and movement were a tremendous relief. He stood at the trough longer than he needed to, until the guard got impatient and threatened to drag him away. Oddly, he saw no other ships on this trip. The cruiser and battleship were gone, but the destroyer's speed didn't seem to have changed, and from the sun's position he judged they were still heading north.

After an hour or two back in the black hole, the hatch opened to show a white-uniformed Japanese officer, complete with white cap and shoulder boards. He carried two small paperback books in one hand, and a long sword in its scabbard hung from his belt. He stayed just outside the hatch while a sailor held the hatch cover open.

Dusty pulled himself up beside the laundry tub and faced the officer. The officer said something and made some gestures that Dusty interpreted to mean he was expected to answer questions. Then he opened one of the books and read something out loud. It didn't sound like Japanese, but it didn't sound like English, either.

Nuts, Dusty thought. *What do I say now?*

The officer glared at Dusty and said what sounded like the same thing over again. Dusty looked him in the eye and shook his head slightly.

The officer's eyebrows twitched and he looked back at the book, holding his finger on a page while he read another statement or question. He looked up at Dusty expectantly.

Dusty couldn't make out a familiar syllable. He shook his head again and tried to look puzzled. He noticed two and a half stripes on the officer's epaulets and decided he was looking at a lieutenant commander, no doubt the skipper himself. He remembered learning somewhere that Japanese naval ranks and insignia were practically the same as the American.

The officer banged his fist on the book and barked a sharp exclamation. Then he tried another question. Everything he said ended with a sound like "ka." Just like "dubyaseeka," except he hadn't said that.

Dusty tried a formula, just to show that he could respond. "Ensign Raleigh E. Rhodes, United States Naval Reserve."

The officer looked astonished, or exasperated, and suddenly grabbed his sword and drew it. He pointed the tip of it threateningly at Dusty's chest, and shouted angry words, not one of which made any sense to Dusty's ears.

Here it comes, he thought, *unless I think of something.*

For an instant he thought of saying "Dubyaseeka," but the context was all wrong. "*Sayonara*" wasn't a good idea, either. What other Japanese words did he know?

"*Benjo?*"

The sword slammed against the side of his head and he stumbled against the laundry tub. Tensing for another blow, he saw the officer turn and stalk away, sheathing his sword. The hatch cover slammed shut, and as he heard the screws tightened, Dusty slowly sank to the deck, holding his head.

It was a close call.

Later in the day a sailor brought him a stub of a pencil and a clipboard with a single sheet of paper on it. Dusty took the clipboard and looked at the paper.

"You must answer all questions correctly. Or else you will not live to see dawn of another day." That was printed across the top. Then there were six or eight questions about the ships in his task force, the types and numbers of planes on the carriers, and so forth. At the bottom he was to sign his name, guaranteeing that all his answers were truthful.

How would they know whether he was truthful or not? They probably had some information from scout planes, or from combat aircraft that might have got close to the task force, but it would be scrappy and approximate. He could shade the numbers a little without attracting too much attention. How would they know? If they already had the scoop, they wouldn't be asking him just to test him.

How could he cause them the most trouble? If he told them less than the real number, they might be more likely to attack. If he told them more than they expected, they might hold back a little. It would be better for our guys to be on the offensive. You always wanted to be ready to put up a good defense, but you only scored points when you were on offense. The attacker had a lot of advantages. So maybe he could scare them a little, or make them think twice.

How about four carriers? Maybe three was more believable. A couple of battleships, four or five cruisers, ten or twelve destroyers. That was a pretty healthy task force. He carefully wrote out his answers.

He didn't know exactly how many planes *Hornet* carried, but it was pretty much like *Enterprise*, and Carrier X was another. He could increase the totals by 10 percent without sounding crazy. After Midway they should be easier to impress, anyway. But what he said wouldn't be taken at face value. They'd want to check his figures against other intelligence they had. He could only hope to tip the scales a little.

His head ached from the whack with the sword, and there was a good-sized lump he could feel with his fingers. He realized he might earn a little more time with the hatch open if he didn't write too fast, so he maneuvered the pencil stub carefully and slowly, making it look like he was really working at it. The sailor on guard wasn't watching him very closely. He was more interested in something on the forward deck.

Dusty sneaked a couple of quick looks past the guard, but he could see no other vessels. He couldn't help noticing his wrists, which were getting really swollen and red around the handcuffs. They were pretty sore. The thumb was still stiff and red. His waistline was itchy under the skivvies. But the slight air movement from the open hatch felt good.

Finally the guard reached in and demanded the clipboard. Dusty nodded and signaled "just a minute" with his hand. He slowly signed his name to the sheet. He hoped the officer wouldn't try to grill him about his answers.

A few hours later another bowl of broth was delivered. It had a white disk of some kind floating in it. It looked like turnip, maybe, or overgrown radish. Taking the bowl from the guard, Dusty set it down again on the deck and nodded "thank you." When the guard closed the hatch, he waited a minute and then felt for the bowl. He lifted the white disk to his nose and sniffed it. It had a faint smell, but not familiar. He nibbled a very small bite and chewed it cautiously. Not much flavor. Crunchy, though.

He lifted the bowl and took a small sip, then another. The rest he poured into the tub and heard it trickle down the drain. He left the vegetable slice in the empty bowl. The nibble and sip would hold him till morning, and if he wasn't sick or dead then, he'd try a little more when the next bowl came.

Just after that, he heard and felt the ship's engines shut down suddenly. It became strangely quiet. Not even muffled voices or the usual footsteps passing his hatch. The motion of the ship changed. They were no longer plowing ahead, but drifting and rocking.

Were they in port? No, it was too quiet for that. Had they run out of fuel? Not likely. If they were taking more fuel aboard, there would be distinctive noises. Had the whole fleet stopped? That was possible. One thing could do it: a sub in the area, an American sub. The Japanese had sonar, he'd heard. If they'd pinged something, they'd try to hide by shutting off their engines.

What if there *was* a sub? What if this vessel took a torpedo amidships? That would be it. They'd sink like a rock. He'd be locked in. Nobody would think about letting him out. He'd be trapped, no matter what happened. The same thing could happen if they were attacked by air. Except that a few .50 caliber slugs might come right through the walls of his compartment. These tin cans had no armor to speak of. They had to be light and fast. They might be able to dodge a torpedo from a TBF or even a two-hundred-pounder from an SBD, but a fighter could rake them from stem to stern.

He felt exposed, vulnerable. A sitting duck for an F4F. He wouldn't see it coming, wouldn't even hear it. Just blam-blam-blam! Curtains.

But right now it might be submarine time, torpedo time. Any minute now there could be a huge blast, and that would be it. He listened to the silence, hoping for some kind of reassuring noises. Nothing.

Minutes ticked by. Then fractions of hours. How long had it been? How much longer would it be? He could go crazy just waiting for the end. Whatever kind of end it was going to be.

It was a long time before the engines started up again, maybe two hours. It was hard to guess. But once or twice he had to work hard at relaxing, because his teeth started to chatter. And once a muscle in his right thigh twitched more than every second for several minutes.

He wasn't sure whether he was better off now than in the raft, or worse. Not that he'd had much choice. If it went on just like this it was better. Two or three days of the same thing in the raft would be worse. And there were always the sharks.

He just hoped the skipper didn't have to shut down the engines again.

When they took him to the benjo that night, they blindfolded him. Likewise the next morning. Why? He'd only seen a couple of ships, but maybe that was too much. Or was something new going on?

His sleep had been fitful and miserably uncomfortable. The steel deck was getting harder by the hour. The laundry room was hotter and stuffier, and it stank. He noticed it coming back from the benjo. The heat rash around his waist was spreading and getting redder. The itching was terrible, and there was no way to relieve it. His wrists looked infected under the handcuffs. There was a line of white skin between the red skin and the metal. His thumb was still stiff, but maybe it felt a little more alive.

Then in the middle of the day he heard airplanes approaching, coming on fast. There was a roar as one buzzed the ship, and he tensed, waiting for an explosion. Nothing—a miss. Maybe next time it would be machine guns. But there was no reaction from the ship's anti-aircraft guns, even when two more planes came close. What were they doing? He was as scared as he was when the engines stopped. The worst thing was being trapped in the dark. If the ship went down, there was no way he could pull a Houdini.

When he went to the benjo the second time that day, he noticed there was pus oozing from under the handcuff on his right wrist. Both wrists looked redder than ever, and they ached. The handcuffs were starting to look rusty. With open sores, he could get blood poisoning—something new to worry about.

His third morning on the destroyer brought a bigger change. During his trip to the benjo, he noticed a new, fresh odor, like wet grass or new-mown hay. It puzzled him for a minute, then he understood. They were near land.

An hour or so later he could hear and feel the engines changing speed, and after that they seemed to go slower for a while. In the laundry room, he could, by then, smell the vegetation.

He was dozing and sweating when they came for him, three sailors this time. They brought his flight coveralls and took off his handcuffs so he could put the coveralls on. His wrists still hurt and looked infected. Pus was oozing from several blisters. But it felt good to have his arms free again. Before they let him out of the hatch onto the deck, one of the sailors tied a rag around his head as a blindfold. They left the handcuffs off.

Dusty figured the destroyer had anchored, because the deck was steadier than usual. The ship's engines had stopped. There were more voices than he was used to hearing, not only nearby, but somewhere off the deck. Even with his eyes covered, it was brighter on deck and hotter than usual. His feet were toughening up, but the steel grating of the steps was painful to walk on when the two sailors holding him by the arms steered him onto a narrow gangway down the side of the ship. There was a handrail, and with one sailor steadying him from in front and the other behind, he didn't worry about losing his balance, just about stubbing his toes. He discovered he could see his feet through a gap under the blindfold.

At the bottom of the gangway, he was maneuvered aboard a small boat bobbing alongside. The sailors sat him down on a narrow bench running along the gunwale, and it was dry underfoot. He'd hoped for some bilgewater sloshing around to soothe his feet.

Then he had a shock. A few inches from his left foot there was another pair of sunburned bare feet. Somebody was sitting across from him. Tipping his head back slowly, he panned up an ankle to a sewn cuff of khaki cloth. Flight coveralls! Just like his! He was stunned and excited.

Who was it? He was sure the body in those coveralls belonged to another naval aviator—maybe from his own task force!

As the motor revved and the boat pulled away from the ship, Dusty thought about what to do. He wanted to hear the voice that went with the feet. He knew it was risky to say anything, but he decided to take a chance. He turned his head toward the guard he could feel sitting next to him.

"Is there another American with us?"

An angry exclamation and a sharp slap on the side of his head.

"Hi, Dusty. It's Al."

Another grunt and slap from the other side of the boat.

Al Mead! Who'd have believed it! It was incredible! How had they ended up in the same place at the same time?

Dusty couldn't believe his luck. His pulse was racing. It was a crazy reunion, but it was better than facing these monkeys alone! He wondered if they'd be able to stay together.

As the boat moved on, he tried to imagine what had happened. He was pretty sure both Al and Lepp had been nailed by the Zeros, just the way he had. Chip was lucky to escape, if he really did. So Al must have been picked out of the water by another Japanese ship—unless he was on the same destroyer as Dusty, but that didn't seem likely. They probably would have been put in the same room.

And both ships had ended up at the same place. They'd probably been in the same fleet. Anyway, they'd come to the same harbor or anchorage. It couldn't be Japan, not in three days. Had to be an island. He thought they'd continued sailing north, but he wasn't sure. He tried to remember names from the maps and charts of the South Pacific he'd studied. Kwajalein? Eniwetok? Guam?

It probably wasn't Shangri-la.

FOUR

TRUK STOP

Blindfolded, they were led ashore on a wooden dock somewhere in the middle of what sounded like a good-sized port or anchorage. There were familiar noises from all sides, some faint and distant. Still blindfolded, they were driven sitting in the bed of a small truck to a small empty building, where their guards removed their blindfolds. Staring sober-faced and wide-eyed at each other, Dusty and Al tried to hide their feelings until the guards left them alone.

Their flight coveralls were taken away again, and they could see a couple of guards with clubs outside the door. The room, or shack, was about fifteen feet square and new, judging from the clean, rough boards of the floor and walls. Overhead there were open rafters under a gabled roof. The door and two small windows had panes of glass with white paper covering them on the outside, so light came in, but they couldn't see out.

There were no obvious air vents, but after the closet on the destroyer the room seemed airy to Dusty. It was going to be hot, though, so skivvies would be okay.

The guards said something to them sharply before leaving, and then they were alone. Al's grin broke through a week-old beard.

"Dusty, you son of a gun! How'd you do it? I thought we were both goners!"

From the looks of Al, he'd been banged around more than Dusty had. There were bruises on his shins and upper arms, and a really ugly one just below his left breast. There was a bloody wound in his foot, too, worse than Dusty's, and it was clearly painful to walk on.

Dusty knew he probably didn't look much better himself. They were both covered with sweaty grime. But that didn't matter. They threw their arms around each other and hugged. Half a dozen times Dusty told Al how excited and happy he'd been to see his feet and hear his voice on the trip ashore.

They spent the rest of the day, from midafternoon until dark, trading stories of their experiences. After dark, they discovered a use for the two thin fiber "blankets" they'd been given. Huge mosquitoes buzzed around them, and they sat cross-legged, huddled under the blankets with only their faces exposed. Waving a hand kept most of the mosquitoes from settling long enough to do any damage. When they finally stretched out and fell asleep on the board floor shortly after dark, the only interruptions had been a delivery of two bowls of watery gruel and an escorted trip to an outdoor benjo, with blindfolds.

Next morning, before the guards entered, they explored the hut and found a few knotholes through which they could see bits of their surroundings. Only one showed anything, and that was a surprise. They were close enough to the harbor—maybe half a mile—to see several ships, including three carriers. At first the view was head on, as the carriers swung parallel with each other on their anchor chains. But later in the day the wind shifted and they turned sideways. Dusty and Al were intrigued.

The silhouettes were different from anything they'd seen. The superstructures sloped backwards instead of rising vertically like the carrier silhouettes they were familiar with. They must be brand new!

"Boy, if we could only get back and tell them about *these* things!" Dusty croaked, his throat dry from lack of water. He imagined the skipper's excitement. Wouldn't our subs and TBFs have fun hunting for these babies!

But escape was a pipe dream right now.

Coming back from the benjo that morning, Al exchanged a few words with one of their guards.

"What did you say to him?" Dusty asked when they were back in the shack.

"I tried to tell him we wanted to wash up. Either he didn't get it or he said 'No chance.' Maybe I didn't say it right."

"Well, when room service shows up with our cup of water, you could dump it over your head," Dusty suggested.

"No, thanks. I need it to keep my radiator from boiling dry."

In the late afternoon, after waking from a hot nap on the floorboards, Dusty urged Al to try his request again. The guards were probably different.

Al looked thoughtful for a few minutes. Then he stood up and hobbled to the door. When he rapped lightly, a guard opened it, holding his club in a defensive position. It looked about two inches thick and a foot and a half long.

Al said something in Japanese—it sounded like a question—and mimed lighting a cigarette and blowing smoke. The guard glanced back at his companion, who looked blank. Then after a slight hesitation he tucked his club under his arm and reached into a pocket of his tunic. Pulling out a small packet of cigarettes, he extracted one and cut it in half with a pocket knife. He stuck one part between his lips and handed the other to Al. Then he produced a match and lit them both. Al took a puff, then stepped back and bowed slightly.

"Arigato," he said.

The guard nodded. They stood smoking together and looking out toward the anchorage.

Al asked another short question, and the guard responded with a few words, at the same time making a circling gesture around the horizon with his finger.

Al pointed down, as if indicating "here, where I'm standing," and raised his eyebrows quizzically.

"Natsu Shima," said the guard, mimicking Al's gesture.

"Natsu Shima?"

"Mmm," said the guard.

Al seemed satisfied with the exchange. When he'd smoked the butt as far as he could, he stubbed it out quickly on the heel of his hand and field-stripped the remaining half-inch or so, scattering the tobacco on the ground and rolling the paper into a tight ball. The guard nodded approvingly and followed suit, collecting Al's paper wad and dropping both into his pocket. Then he motioned Al back inside and shut the door.

Al smiled slyly at Dusty and said, "This is Natsu Shima."

Dusty looked at him doubtfully. "Whatever that is. I never heard of it."

"Me neither," said Al. "But it's a start. How about that cigarette? Next time I'll get one for you."

Dusty had noticed the sky darkening while Al was standing at the open door, so he wasn't surprised a little later when they heard raindrops begin to spatter on the roof. In a few minutes it sounded like a good shower, and the air felt muggier, if that was possible.

"Maybe we could get another drink of water," Al mused.

"Give it a try," said Dusty. "You're the language expert. Better yet, see if they'd let us stand out in the rain and rinse off."

"Good idea," said Al, and he limped back to the door.

A few minutes later they were standing on a grassy patch ten feet from the door of the shack, showering in the warm rain while the two guards stood under the eaves, watching. No blindfolds!

It was great to sluice some of the grime off, even without the soap. Unsure about the guards' expectations, Al grabbed a leg of his skivvies and used sign language to ask if he could take them off. A guard nodded. Dusty and Al scrubbed vigorously, wringing out their underwear a couple of times while they were at it. In too short a time, one of the guards spoke sharply and waved them back inside the shack. They saw him glancing at a white-uniformed figure with an umbrella walking at a distance.

Back inside, Dusty and Al took stock of wounds, bruises, and abrasions. The shrapnel wound in Dusty's left calf was beginning to heal, and the places where he'd accidentally pricked his leg with his sheath knife didn't amount to much. His sunburnt skin had partly peeled off in uneven patches, and his wrists, swollen and infected, were still hurting. His left thumb wasn't as rigid as it had been.

Al had bigger problems, though, with several wicked-looking bruises, the bullet or shrapnel wound in his right foot, and a nasty-looking mess in the middle of his scalp where blood had coagulated over three or four square inches of hair. He had managed to loosen up the tangle a little bit in the rain, but he hadn't had time to work on it. If they didn't get any soap, they'd have to find a way to cut it out.

What had given Al the most relief was rinsing off patches of dried vomit from his neck and shoulders, vomit that turned out not to be his. He told Dusty that when the ship he'd been on had anchored in the harbor the night before he'd been brought ashore, his guards had put him in a small, deep hold. Then they and most of the crew had gone ashore and gotten drunk. Al knew this because they'd returned hours later, leaned over the hold, and yelled something at him. Then, Al said, "They giggled and puked on me."

When found by a Japanese destroyer the morning after he'd ditched his Wildcat, he was picked up in a lowered boat. He remembered thinking, "Now I'm in for it." When the boat pulled alongside his pararaft, he'd been "knocked out cold," he said. He'd seen a rifle and some oars in the hands of the Japanese sailors in the boat, but he wasn't sure what hit him.

"They knocked me out and knocked a tooth out," he said. He discovered the missing tooth and his head wound when he came to later in a stifling "bathhouse" under the aft torpedo tubes. There was a big wooden tub used by the crew for communal baths. Al wasn't handcuffed, but a guard with a rifle and bayonet stood outside the door. To his surprise, one of the ship's officers gave him a packet of ten cigarettes, which he tried to ration and smoke out of sight of the crew, but they were soon found and taken away. The brief grillings the Japs gave him were as useless to them as the ones they gave Dusty. He soon learned to say "Good morning,"

"Yes," and "Thank you" in Japanese. He figured it was better to say "No" as seldom as possible.

Al's Wildcat had been shot up by the Zeros as badly as Dusty's, and when his engine quit after he lost track of Leppla, he managed to make a "good landing, tail down," in the water. As he struggled out of the cockpit, water was already rushing in, and the plane was sinking as he kicked clear of it, pushing his pararaft packet ahead of him.

He'd inflated the raft with no problems, and it didn't leak, but as he sat in it checking out his emergency kit, he found a bullet hole through the small can that had held fresh water. His signaling mirror was also pierced and twisted, and a small tarp that could supposedly be used to catch rain water turned out to be full of holes. He was still able to use it as a sunshade, though.

His foot wound was bleeding and painful, but he didn't have any broken bones as far as he could tell. He thought about trying to bail out some of the water that was sloshing inside the raft, but then he thought the raft might be more stable riding low in the water. And he remembered reading somewhere that keeping his rear end submerged would allow water to be absorbed through his rectum and help prevent his becoming dehydrated.

"I wasn't really worried about anything," he told Dusty. "I could see some small water spouts in the distance, and I knew there would be rain squalls. Besides, it was only about a thousand miles to Australia." He grinned.

Late that afternoon he'd heard a PBY coming, and it had flown within a quarter mile of him. He'd been able to see the forward observer in the nose bubble.

"But he was looking the other way."

Al pulled the tab on his "beer can" emergency flare, but it only gurgled. Then he noticed it had been shot up like his water can. So much for being prepared.

But rummaging in his emergency kit, he'd found a packet of sulfa powder and managed to sprinkle a little on his head and his foot, after propping his ankle across his knee and letting it dry in the sun.

Dusty was impressed by Al's story.

"Did you see Lepp go down?"

"No," said Al, "but he must have. He wasn't even maneuvering, just flying straight on, like his controls were shot or he was dead already. When we checked the guns earlier, Lepp only had one working."

An image flashed for Dusty. "I thought I saw something go streaming past me, like an unopened chute. I wondered later if it might have been Lepp."

Al remembered something. He went over to his beat-up parachute pack, which he'd been allowed to keep with him. Rummaging inside, he pulled out a small plastic packet. He offered it to Dusty.

"Sulfa powder. Might help your ankle."

"Hey, Al, thanks! How come they didn't take that away?"

"I dunno. I tried to tell 'em I needed it. I went through a hell of a sign-language routine. Maybe that convinced 'em. Maybe they felt guilty about beating me up so much."

"You mean they clobbered you again after cold-cocking you?"

"Yeah, three or four times. There were a couple of mean bastards in that crew."

"But you're gonna need more of this."

"It's okay, there's plenty. You only need a little."

"Al, I wish I was as prepared as you. You're a good scout."

"Takes one to know one."

On the third morning, a guard brought Dusty and Al their flight coveralls and ordered them to put them on. Then he blindfolded Dusty and led him on a zigzag route of a quarter mile or so. The guard exchanged words with someone and a door opened. They entered, and the routine was repeated. They stood and waited for five or ten minutes. Dusty heard another door open, and they passed through it and halted again. More words were exchanged in Japanese, and the blindfold was removed.

Dusty was facing a seated middle-aged officer who had turned his chair away from a desk against the wall to face Dusty. He looked Dusty up and down for a minute or two without speaking. His expression was alert but impassive. The collar insignia on his white uniform was three or four gold stars on a red background. An admiral! Dusty was surprised.

To one side and slightly behind the admiral stood a younger officer of lower rank. The admiral said something to Dusty in Japanese. The younger officer translated.

"Rhodes, you are a fighter pilot from the aircraft carrier *Enterprise*." He paused.

"That's right," said Dusty. There was no point in denying it. "USS *Enterprise*" had been stenciled on his Mae West.

"How many aircraft were in your flight group at the time you were shot down?"

"Let's see . . ." He thought a minute. "There were eight torpedo bombers, three dive bombers, and eight fighter planes." They probably knew that, too. Lots of Japs had seen the attack group.

The translator reported to the admiral. The admiral asked another question.

The translator conveyed it: "Is that the usual composition of a flight group from an aircraft carrier?"

"I don't know. I think it varies, depending on the mission, the number of aircraft available, and so on. That was my first combat mission, so I don't have a lot of experience with this sort of thing. I can't give you averages."

He could have guessed the next question: "How many aircraft of each type was *Enterprise* carrying?"

He could fudge a little on that one, but not enough to damage his credibility or risk punishment. He answered carefully, looking upwards and pretending to count each type. But he exaggerated the number of dive bombers, remembering his strategy with the question sheet on the destroyer.

The admiral seemed satisfied with his answers. Neither he nor the interpreter showed any sign of emotion. Their manner was attentive but matter-of-fact. They were just collecting information.

Dusty saw no point in playing the hero, refusing to tell anything but his name, rank, and serial number. He knew he was entitled by the Geneva Conventions not to be abused, but on the other hand, he expected no decent treatment from the Japanese. He'd heard about some of the things they'd done to prisoners on Bataan and other places, and they could do the same to him. It would be stupid to ask for it. He could at least pretend to be cooperative.

The questions continued. What were the names of other ships in the task force? How many aircraft carriers were there? Battleships? Cruisers? Was there another task force nearby?

Dusty remembered a few names of ships. The admiral might not know they weren't all in Task Force 61. He tried to remember the numbers he'd written on the questionnaire. The trouble with lying was you always had to remember what you said before. It would be risky to take chances with these particular Japanese. Both of them were obviously intelligent and probably pretty well educated. They were used to using their minds, not their muscles.

The translator worried him more than the admiral did. There was something nasty in the tone of his voice, the way he insinuated that he thought Dusty was lying. The admiral was impressive. He was methodical and calm, and he always seemed to be thinking two or three questions ahead. He also seemed to know what the translator was going to say even before he'd translated all of Dusty's answer; he would start the next question before the translator finished speaking. But it didn't seem like impatience. More like mind reading.

Ten or fifteen minutes into the interrogation, Dusty realized who he was talking to. He'd seen a picture of Admiral Yamamoto somewhere and read an article about him. He was the commander of the whole Pacific Fleet! He spoke English and he'd gone to college in America.* Of course he understood what Dusty was saying!

Well, he'd spoken to admirals before, and not always under the best of circumstances. He had the greatest respect for Chester Nimitz and "Bull" Halsey, and they'd shown him they were regular guys, not chickenshit like some of the career officers he'd run into. One night when he and Jimmy and Millard Axelrod had had too much at the officers' club near their field on Maui and were staggering along the road toward the BOQ (Bachelor Officers' Quarters), a long black car had pulled up and stopped alongside them. The back door opened and a voice said, "Need a ride?"

They'd climbed in and squeezed onto a couple of jump seats in the back of the limousine, facing Admiral Nimitz and Admiral Halsey. He'd been scared to death, but the admirals acted as if everything was perfectly normal. Dusty couldn't remember a word of what they'd talked about, but he'd never forget the glorious exit the three of them made. They'd backed out of the car saluting and saying, "Thank you, Sir! Thank you, Sir!" and then one of them tripped and they fell on top of each other on the pavement. The car door closed and the admirals drove off.

Dusty knew he might not remember much of the interview with Yamamoto, either. He was apprehensive and thinking of three or four things at once, and he thought he was doing a good job of acting respectful but not too happy at being a prisoner. The questioning continued for maybe an hour, with Dusty often answering "Sorry, I don't know that," or "I'm not sure, but I'd guess . . ."

Trudging blindfolded back to the shack, Dusty was eager to tell Al. Yamamoto himself! It was hard to believe. But the more he thought about it, the more it made sense. Yamamoto had once been an aviator himself, and he had a great appreciation of air power. He'd underestimated the U.S. Navy at Midway, and he'd lost four carriers and a lot of seasoned pilots. He'd be interested in everything that was happening on American carriers, and American pilots could help him out with that.

---

*Isoroku Yamamoto (1884–1943) was commander-in-chief of the Japanese fleet and had been in charge of the Pearl Harbor attack. He attended Harvard University from 1919 to 1921. From 1926 to 1928 he was naval attaché at the Japanese embassy in Washington, and he directed Japanese naval aviation from 1933 to 1936.

There was no chance for conversation with Al, though. Taking the blindfold off Dusty, the guard put it on Al and led him out the door.

Dusty decided to check out the view from the knothole while Al was gone. The first thing he noticed was that the three carriers had moved. In their place was the biggest ship he'd ever seen. It looked half again as long as the *Enterprise*, but it wasn't a carrier. It was a battleship. More than that, it was a battleship he knew. It rode low in the water, as if it was nearly submerged by the weight of its armor. The superstructure towered high above the deck. The single stack sloped aft, and just behind it two long spars made a V in the air. Or a Y. And there, just forward of the superstructure, was an elevated gun turret, clearing the two bigger turrets forward of it.

Yamato! No doubt about it. There was only one ship that big. Yamamoto's flagship! He remembered that silhouette better than any others, even though it had only been a black shape on a plastic-coated card. Maybe every naval aviator imagined himself having a shot at *Yamato* some day, even if the machine guns of an F4F would be peashooters against all that armor. Just to be there when a couple of TBFs planted torpedoes in its hull would be the kick of a lifetime!

Dusty sat with his back against the wall of the shack and began to sort things out. It had dawned on him gradually that this was one of the Truk islands—the headquarters of all Japanese naval operations in the Pacific. Remembering a diagram he'd seen, he turned and looked through the knothole again, consciously readjusting his perspective. He wasn't looking down a long, narrow channel toward the open sea. He was looking across a huge lagoon, with room for heavy cruisers, battleships, and even carriers to maneuver.

But if this was Truk, what was "Natsu Shima"? Another name for the same place? Maybe Al could figure that out.[†]

But when he got back, Al had his own agenda, and Dusty had to wait to spring his news.

"Why do you think they took you first instead of me?" Al asked. "They know I speak a little Japanese."

"I thought about that," said Dusty. "They'd take the senior officer, because they're pretty class-conscious, or rank-conscious, and it wouldn't be the right protocol to let the senior officer cool his heels while they talked to a lower-ranking one."

"Yeah, but we're both ensigns."

[†]After the war, Dusty and Al learned that Natsu Shima was the largest of several islands in the group collectively called Truk.

'Sure, but my serial number is lower than yours, so they figure I'm senior. And I am, strictly speaking. But don't worry. I won't pull rank on you. Unless some really dirty job comes up and they only need one of us."

Al listened patiently to Dusty's discoveries about Truk and *Yamato* and Admiral Yamamoto, but his expression was completely skeptical. When Dusty was finished, he said, "Okay, lemme see."

Dusty watched him squint through the knothole for several minutes. Finally, he agreed that it looked like *Yamato*, all right, but he wasn't buying the admiral story.

"I tell you, that was Admiral Yamamoto!" Dusty insisted.

"I don't think so," said Al. "What would the admiral of the Japanese navy be doing questioning prisoners of war?"

Dusty tried to be patient. "Look, he needs the information, and he needs it now. We're here, and he's here. He knows we came from *Enterprise* and he thinks we know a lot more technical stuff than we do. Besides, I've seen pictures of him. I know that's him. He went to college in the States, and he speaks English."

"Then why does he need an interpreter?"

"I don't know. Maybe it's beneath his dignity to speak to prisoners in their own language."

Al reflected on this. You couldn't be sure of anything in such a chancy situation, but survival could depend on keeping a clear head. The noon sun made the shack like an oven, and he and Dusty had both stripped to their skivvies again.

"Do you think they'll kill us?" Al asked Dusty.

"Naw, they can't. We're prisoners of war."

"That didn't help the poor bastards on Bataan. Or Guam."

"What do you think they make of our stories?"

"I don't know. What did you tell them?"

Dusty explained how he'd exaggerated the strength of TF-61. Al looked concerned.

"Well, I gave 'em a little different story," he said.

It turned out that Al had been given the same kind of question sheet as Dusty had on the destroyer, with the same threat of consequences for lying. But they'd given different answers about the task force strength. Dusty had stretched the numbers, but Al had decided to make them smaller than they actually were. He figured that if the Japs underestimated the size of the task force, they might attack with inadequate forces and get pulverized.

It wasn't hard to imagine how the Japanese might react when they discovered these contradictions. Al and Dusty decided they'd better coordinate their stories from now on. They made plans to review numbers and rehearse their answers, grilling each other in turn. With some things they had to be accurate. The Japanese already knew these things, or they could easily check. But they agreed they could probably get away with misleading the enemy sometimes, without giving away any really vital information. They'd be expected to have detailed knowledge of their planes' equipment and armament, like the differences between the F4F-3 and the F4F-4. But things they were not likely to be asked about, they could "forget"—like the new self-sealing fuel tanks on the F4F-4s. And some of the differences in armament, like the rounds of ammunition each plane carried, they could be a little "confused" about, because they'd done a lot of flying in both planes.

Besides, they didn't know any highly classified material, and the sensitive things they knew a little about, like the radar mounted on one of the TBFs, they could pretend to be ignorant of, or give wild "guesses" with phony sincerity. The Nips obviously wanted every scrap of information they could get, but Dusty and Al eventually decided they could take comfort in the fact that they were pretty small fish and didn't know much that would give aid and comfort to the enemy, even if it was tortured out of them.

Still, they'd already given contradictory information on two different occasions.

"I guess they know we're not stupid," said Al. "They figure one of us is lying. Or both of us."

Dusty stretched out on the rough boards of the floor and stared at the rafters.

"I'm only worried about one thing," he said.

"What's that? Torture?"

"No. I keep thinking about that picture in my wallet I left on the ship. Marian and my parents are gonna see that when my stuff gets sent home."

"What's in the picture?" asked Al.

"You remember when Jimmy Caldwell and I went off base a couple of nights before we left Maui?"

"Yeah. You came back pretty happy."

"Well, we were at this classy bar where they had dancers in grass skirts, and nothing on top except a flower necklace. Between numbers Jimmy saw one of them at the bar, and he talked her into coming over to our table. He'd brought his camera along, and he wanted her to pose with us. He was waving a five-dollar bill at her."

"So you and Jimmy put her between you?"

"No, he wanted us each to pose with her separately. And he didn't want us to look like we were posing for the camera. So he had her stand up on the bench next to me, and I was supposed to hug her knees and smile up at her."

"So did you?"

"Well, sure! She was good-looking, and I was half sloshed and having a hell of a good time, and I figured it was a perfect time to ask her what she was doing after work."

"Was she playing along?"

"Sure, she was there to have a good time, too, and I'm not such a bad-looking guy, you know. So she was smiling down at me and I was smiling up at her, and Jimmy snapped the picture. Then I took one of her with him. My picture turned out best. Jimmy agreed. So I thought I'd keep it as a souvenir. Show my grandkids."

"But not your wife."

"No, not my wife. She's pretty liberal, but nobody's wife would be happy with that."

Al grinned. "So now she'll see it."

"Yeah, and my mom too. She who raised me to be a good Christian young man. An officer and a gentleman."

"Well," sighed Al. "If the war doesn't end too soon, and you stay away long enough, maybe they'll forget about it."

"Sure," said Dusty. "You're always a comfort, Al."

Several days passed without another interrogation, but there was a visit from a doctor who gave Dusty a quick once-over and then settled down with Al to examine his scalp wound. They sat cross-legged on the floor, facing each other, and Al bowed his head for the doctor's scrutiny. While the doctor worked, Al would occasionally try a question in Japanese, and the doctor replied as if he understood. Dusty was astonished at Al's talent for language.

Al winced a couple of times, but before long the doctor triumphantly removed a small black piece of metal—probably a fragment from Al's cockpit canopy blasted loose by bullets from a Zero. They all examined it curiously, but there wasn't much to say about it. Al thanked the doctor profusely, and he left smiling.

Al told Dusty that the doctor said he'd gone to a medical school in Germany. He seemed proud of that, and evidently spoke some German. No English, though.

Dusty told Al he thought they were being treated pretty decently. The shack wasn't exactly comfortable, but it wasn't miserable, either. And none of the Japs had abused them or been hostile. Al thought it probably had something to do with this being the Jap fleet headquarters. There would be a lot of navy brass here, and things were likely to be well run. But even though he'd been getting along well with the guards, his treatment on the destroyer had made him less optimistic than Dusty about the likelihood of their good luck continuing.

A couple of days later, they both had another interrogation by the admiral. Dusty was convinced he'd heard the translator refer to him as Yamamoto, but Al was still doubtful. The questions again focused on the makeup of the task force, and a few of them had to do with the sizes, speeds, and armaments of the ships and aircraft. Al and Dusty were satisfied they'd both been able to stick to the facts and stories they'd agreed on.

Early that afternoon they were standing in the open doorway of the shack smoking half-cigarettes that Al had bummed from a guard. The interpreter suddenly appeared on the path in his white uniform and officer's cap and stopped ten feet from them with his hands on his hips.

"Where do you guys think you are?" he snapped. "The Royal Hawaiian?"

He strode forward, his eyes narrowed. The guards backed away and Dusty and Al stood up straighter, holding their cigarettes at their sides.

"Put those things out and get inside!" he ordered. He spoke sharply to the guards in Japanese.

Inside, he stood with his back to the open door while Al and Dusty stood in the middle of the room, attentive but not at attention.

The interpreter warned them that their present comfort was only temporary. They hadn't seen anything yet. The interrogations were completely unsatisfactory, "a joke." He continued: "But we don't think it's funny. We're sending you to Tokyo, where they know how to get the information they want."

When he left, Dusty and Al agreed they needed to watch out for the interpreter and keep rehearsing their stories. He could be real trouble.

After a third interrogation a week or so later, the interpreter appeared in the shack again. This time they'd been inside, and there was no evidence they'd been smoking, but he seemed to be in a bad temper. He told them he could see through their phony answers. He'd known other Americans in Hawaii, where he'd graduated from the university. Americans thought the world was their oyster. They thought people of other races were meant to be their servants.

Fortunately, he'd been in Japan when the American fleet was destroyed at Pearl Harbor, and he was happy to be of service to the emperor. With his ability to interview American prisoners, he could also help them understand who the real rulers of the world were.

He confirmed his previous threat that Al and Dusty would be sent to Japan for further interrogation. When everything they knew had been squeezed out of them, they'd be "disposed of, like junk."

Dusty was struck by the contrast between the interpreter's behavior and the admiral's. The admiral gave the impression of being a reasonable man, neither hostile nor friendly, but businesslike and competent. He didn't need to bluster or threaten. You couldn't tell what he was thinking, but he didn't make you feel that he was planning a dirty trick on you. The interpreter was nasty, the way Dusty had thought most Japanese military men were.

"He was pretty snotty, wasn't he?" he said to Al.

"Yeah," Al replied. "He's got that race superiority thing. When you see that, you know somebody's made him feel inferior, and he's got to prove he's not."

"Well," said Dusty, "we know who the really superior guys are here, don't we?"

"No question about it," said Al.

Late one morning Al and Dusty were standing in the doorway carefully smoking their cigarette stubs, making them last. Two stocky men wearing dark breechcloths came along the path. One was shirtless and had a white headband. The other had a brown short-sleeved shirt. Both were barefoot.

The bare-chested man carried a machete in one hand and something round in the other. For a minute Dusty thought it was a head. He was about to turn away and go inside when he realized it was something that looked like a huge grapefruit.

The men seemed to be natives of Truk. Certainly they were nonmilitary. The one with the grapefruit held it up, smiling, to show to the two guards, and then he set it down on a low bench near the door and went to work on it with the machete. In a few seconds there were eight or ten neat slices, like pieces of melon, and he gave two to each of the guards. Then he looked at Al and Dusty and said something to one of the guards. The guard nodded and stepped out of the way so he could hand Al and Dusty each a slice. He and the other native took slices.

To Dusty, it tasted like bread. He said so to Al. Al said he was sure it was breadfruit. He'd read about it somewhere. But Al thought it tasted more like some kind of cake—it was too sweet for bread. In any case, it was delicious, a treat after weeks of nothing but starvation rations.

Finishing his piece, Dusty bowed to the natives and said, "Arigato," which he'd picked up by watching Al with the guards. Al followed suit.

Dusty hoped the natives would come back again, and he wondered if there was anything else he could do to express his gratitude.

Not long after their morning "meal" the next day, three guards, all carrying clubs, entered the shack and ordered Dusty and Al to follow them. One of them looked around the room and indicated to Al that he should take his pack with him. Evidently, they weren't coming back. Maybe they were in for the Tokyo trip the interpreter had promised them.

They were blindfolded again and marched to what seemed to be a wooden wharf or pier, where they were helped into a small boat like the one they'd come ashore in. After a short ride, they were pushed up a ship's gangway and led across the deck and then helped down a ladder into a large hold, where their blindfolds were taken off. The hold was crowded with Japanese soldiers in a variety of postures and all stages of dress and undress.

It looked like a troopship, but the soldiers weren't on their way to battle. They were relaxed and casual, and their uniforms looked rumpled and sometimes stained. A few were standing, but most of them were squatting on their haunches in small groups, talking and often laughing. They showed no interest in the new arrivals. Here and there a few were playing some kind of board game. Dusty guessed there might be as many as two hundred in the hold, which was large, but still crowded. The air was warm and stuffy, but not as foul smelling as such a crowd might be expected to make it. There were no weapons that Dusty could see.

Al and Dusty were told to sit together along one side, just out of talking range from a couple of other small groups of prisoners. Two of the prisoners wore flight coveralls like Dusty's and Al's. After exchanging several glances with them as his eyes got used to the dim light, Dusty recognized one of them as a TBF crewman from the *Enterprise*. He supposed the other one was from the *Enterprise*, too, or maybe the *Hornet*. He wondered how many planes had been shot down and how many airmen had been picked up by the Japanese. It must have been a real disaster.

The two guards who stayed near Dusty and Al made it clear that talking wasn't allowed. They seemed to have left their clubs behind, but one of them carried what looked like a riding crop. They watched the soldiers but kept to themselves. There were guards with the other prisoners, too.

Al and Dusty discovered there were thick straw mats they could sit or lie on. It was certainly better than the bare steel decks they'd had on the destroyers. Not long after they'd settled in, a sailor came around to the prisoners with a printed sheet of paper for each of them. The message was in English. It was headed "Regulations for Prisoners." It began:

1. The prisoners disobeying the following orders will be punished with immediate death:
   a. Those disobeying orders and instructions.
   b. Those showing a motion of antagonism and raising a sign of opposition.
   c. Those disordering the regulations by individualism, egoism, thinking about only yourself, rushing for your own goods.
   d. Those talking without permission and raising loud voices.
   e. Those walking and moving without order.
   f. Those carrying unnecessary baggage in embarking . . .

Here Al moved his paper slightly toward Dusty and held his thumb-nail under the regulation. Dusty thought of Al's pack.

   g. Those resisting mutually.
   h. Those touching the boat's materials, wires, electric lights, tools, switches, etc.
   i. Those climbing ladder without order.
   j. Those showing action of running away from the room or boat.
   k. Those trying to take more meal than given to them.
   l. Those using more than two blankets. . . .

That ended the "punishable by death" list. Then there were instructions for using the toilets—buckets in the corners of the room—and explanations of how food would be served twice a day. The list of regulations ended with an encouragement:

6. Navy of the Great Japanese Empire will not try to punish you all with death. Those obeying all the rules and regulations, and believing the action and purpose of the Japanese Navy, cooperating with Japan in constructing the 'New Order of the Great Asia' which lead to the world's peace will be well treated.

Dusty decided it would be a good idea to reread the first group of rules several times. He noticed that Al seemed to be doing the same. Everything seemed understandable and even reasonable enough, except for "Those resisting mutually." Dusty decided he needed Al's opinion on that one. "Resisting" wasn't a problem, but what did "mutually" mean? Al shrugged.

Regulation number 2 said, "Since the boat is not well equipped and inside being narrow, food being scarce and poor you'll feel uncomfortable during the short time on the boat. Those losing patients and disobeying the regulation will be heavily punished."

"Short time on the boat" sounded good. Even "you'll feel uncomfortable" made Dusty think the writer of the regulations was aware of the stresses the situation could create. If the writer was also the enforcer, maybe he'd be a little lenient, despite the death threats. Dusty didn't want to test the limits, though.

"Short time" turned out to be misleading. The days dragged by, and the ship—Al said the Japs called it "something Maru"—churned along the way Dusty imagined an old tramp steamer would. It felt a lot heavier and slower than the destroyer, slower even than the *Enterprise*, although it was nowhere near that big. Well, it wasn't a warship. He hoped that would be obvious to U.S. subs or planes that might come across it. He began to worry again about being torpedoed, the way he had on the destroyer. But he'd cheated a watery grave once, he thought, and maybe he was lucky. If you could call being a prisoner of war lucky.

FIVE

THE QUIZ KIDS

Dusty was having trouble taking it in—the gray-brown clay under his wooden clogs, the dozen or so other bedraggled prisoners lined up behind him, the gray, single-story barracks behind them. Al stood beside him. Several Japanese guards carrying three-foot wooden clubs surrounded them, and a Japanese warrant officer was barking mumbo jumbo.

There were times in the past two or three weeks when he'd felt incredibly alert, as if he'd just downed three or four cups of coffee, but as the days went by, he'd more often felt groggy and confused. Sometimes he couldn't quite focus on what was going on. He put it down to the lack of anything decent to eat—nothing but rice and lousy-tasting cold tea and a few vegetable scraps. Sleeping on steel decks and board floors didn't help, either. The straw mats weren't much better.

The jolting ride from whatever harbor it was on a rickety train with Al and Nelson and Glasser had been nauseating with the blindfold on, and the march through a tunnel before they reached the camp had really disoriented him. There'd been so much strangeness here in this camp for the past few days that sometimes he seemed to be dreaming or sleepwalking, because he could hardly talk with the other prisoners. Late in the morning he'd had his first session with the interrogators the prisoners called the Quiz Kids. It was tiring, but it helped remind him that this was Saturday.

The only things he understood now about this ragtag formation were that he was a "captive," not a prisoner of war, and that for some reason he and Al were the center of attention. Maybe he should be anxious about that. The late hour of the formation and the clubs in the hands of the guards worried him a little.

Wake up, Dusty! Pay attention!

Then Al Maher, the senior Allied officer in the camp, began translating the Jap's words. It was a familiar rigmarole, and Dusty only half listened to it. Something like "You are in Camp Ofuna, and I am Warrant Officer so-and-so, the commandant of the camp, and you are here to answer questions and explain why you have committed aggression against the Japanese people."

Sure, thought Dusty, *and then you're going to give us a nice chicken dinner and a comfortable bed.*

"State your name and branch of military service!"

"Ensign Raleigh E. Rhodes, United States Navy."

"Ensign Albert E. Mead, United States Navy."

"You were aircraft pilots on USS *Enterprise.* You attacked a fleet of ships of the Japanese Imperial Navy, but your aircraft were shot out of the sky by Japanese pilots. You deserved to die. However, you were rescued from the sea by ships of our navy and brought to Japan."

Maher sometimes hesitated in translating, but he managed to turn what the Jap was saying into understandable English.

"Rhodes [it sounded like *Roht-soo* when the Jap said it], you told us that your aircraft carrier was part of a task force consisting of three aircraft carriers, two battleships, four heavy cruisers, and ten or more destroyers and smaller vessels.

"Ensign Mead, you told us that your aircraft carrier—the same one—was part of a task force consisting of one aircraft carrier, two light cruisers, and four destroyers."

But that was a long time ago. We've got our story straight now.

"Ensign Rhodes and Ensign Mead, you lie!"

There was a whoosh of clubs through the air, and Dusty's knees buckled as bolts of pain shot from his legs through the rest of his body. Falling, he took more whacks on his head and shoulders, and then an incredible, unending drumbeat of excruciating blows on his legs and buttocks.

Writhing on the ground, he couldn't catch enough breath to scream, but he could hear himself gasping and moaning as pain and darkness flooded his body and brain.

Terrible pain. Throbbing, incredible pain. It was mostly in the backs of his legs, his thighs—or at least it was the worst there. It was quiet except for his breathing, weak and gasping. The blows had stopped. He was alone in a small dark room. Somewhere outside, a Japanese voice shouted something.

He couldn't have been out very long. Not with this pain. He couldn't just sleep through it. It pulsed and echoed through his thighs and buttocks, and he could hardly think about the rest of his body. His face and head were wet. Did somebody douse him with water? Maybe he was sweating that much. Maybe it was blood.

He thought he was going to pass out again. He tried to hold on, stay awake, even if he couldn't think of anything but the aching in his legs. The worst was in the back of his left thigh, but the rest was almost as bad. He must have felt it even when he was unconscious.

He needed to figure out what was going on. And how he could avoid getting clobbered like that again.

His face was on a straw mat, and he thought it was his own cell he was lying in. Only two or three nights, but that was enough for him to know it.

The Japs had figured out he and Al were lying about the size of the task force. Not too hard if they had notes on both of them, or some kind of dossier. The purpose of the beating was clear. They wanted to scare the shit out of him and Al—a softening-up exercise so they wouldn't get cocky and figure they could outsmart their captors. Maybe the beating was for the benefit of the rest of the guys, too—even though he was pretty sure some of them had already been beaten after the Quiz Kids sessions, or in the compound when they didn't jump fast enough.

He'd figured out that much from looks and gestures and a few things he'd heard some of the prisoners say to the guards. The no-talking rule made it hard to get much information, although a few men had risked trouble by whispering things to him.

He started to move his left arm, but a knifelike stab hit him between the elbow and shoulder. Was it broken? He'd have to take it slow. The legs were out of the question. He didn't have the strength to move them, and if he did, the pain might knock him out again. His right arm was partly under him, and to move it he'd have to move his whole upper body. Maybe later. He was just too tired.

For a while he lay still and listened to some faint sounds from outside. He listened to his own breathing. It was shallower and faster than usual. It was also the least painful thing he could do. He had no desire to try a deep breath. Just wait and hold on and hope for the pain to ease up a little. It was getting darker. Maybe he'd fall asleep.

He woke up sweating and whimpering. Maybe he'd been crying. He was dreaming that he was lying under the big oak dining room table at home and holding his stomach because it was hurting so bad. Then Dr. Ransom was helping to carry him outside to his black Buick roadster with yellow spoke wheels, and he woke up when they were putting the cup over his face. That was the time he had appendicitis. He was three years old.

After thinking about the dream for a few minutes, he decided to try to roll onto his back. Slowly, he worked his right arm far enough under his body so he could push with it against the mat—what did they call it?—and tip himself over. He started sweating again, but he made it. His left upper arm still hurt like hell. It might be broken. There were no words for his thighs. They were swollen like the inner tubes of truck tires, and they stretched the legs of his coveralls tight. They hurt worse than any toothache he'd ever had.

He thought it might help if he could raise his knees a little. Gradually, inch by inch, he maneuvered his feet against a wall of the cell and managed to bend his legs slightly. That felt a little better. He slipped into a light sleep again for a while, the way he'd been doing all night. When he woke up, he remembered hearing the other prisoners coming into the barracks and mumbling as they passed his cell. He couldn't hear what they were saying. He heard the steel doors being latched and locked. Then everything got quiet.

He heard someone snoring before he fell asleep again, and when he woke up during the night there were sounds of men breathing and coughing and moving in their sleep. Or maybe lying awake. Al was supposed to be in the next cell, but Dusty couldn't hear him. He hoped he was alive. Al must be in bad shape, too.

Then there was noise again in the passageway, and the cell doors were unlocked one by one. People got up and moved along the passageway.

"Poor bastards." The voice was soft, almost a whisper.

"They really beat the shit out of them." A different voice. "I never had it that bad."

"They were trying to make a point. Don't lie to them."

"Hell, it don't make no difference. Tell 'em the truth and they still say 'You rie!' And they pound you."

"Yeah, but Blinny says you can entertain them with stories about all kinds of useless shit. He says he puts on an act. He acts like he hates to mention the stuff but kind of gives it up grudgingly. No beating the last two times."

"Let's move it."

He could hear several bodies moving away from him, shuffling clogs on bare earth, a few coughs. The door to the passageway closed and there were fainter sounds from outside in the compound.

He tried moving his left arm again. *Ow!*

But he moved it anyway, a little, just to change position. *Tomorrow it will be better.* That's what his mom used to say.

Maybe he could bend his legs a little more.

Shit, shit, shit, shit, shit!
Maybe he could sleep some more.

Later in the day—maybe it was still morning—he was awake again. He wondered what was going on outside. Prisoners just sitting around, probably. There was nothing to do. You could walk around the compound, but the guards watched you and you didn't want to call attention to yourself.

The first morning he'd watched Dave Hurt talking to one of the guards. Talking English, just a few phrases, like Hurt was passing the time of day, or thinking of something new every once in a while. The guard didn't get any of it. He looked at Hurt, but his expression never changed. He looked like a dog listening for a familiar word.

But Hurt wasn't really talking to him, he was saying things for the benefit of the other prisoners. Especially for Dusty and Al and Nelson and Glasser, the new ones. Hurt more or less reviewed who all was there, who each of the prisoners was and where he came from. Hurt was a sub skipper himself, a lieutenant commander. Same as Blinny—Al Blinn—except Blinny'd skippered a destroyer.

Hurt and Blinn were the next highest ranking under Commander Al Maher, who'd been the chief gunnery officer on the cruiser USS *Houston*. So Maher was the senior officer of the prisoners. That was lucky, because he could speak Japanese. He'd seen a lot of duty in the Orient before the war.

Maher had headed up the morning formation. The prisoners lined up facing west, their backs to the barracks, and after Maher had called them to attention, a guard shouted a command and everybody did a right face. Dusty followed. On the next command they all bowed stiffly, their arms at their sides. That would be for Tokyo and the emperor, Dusty thought. Al had picked that up somewhere and told him about it on the boat. On another command from the guard, Maher dismissed the formation.

For two days Dusty had been out in the compound with the others, mainly sitting on benches alongside the barracks. He'd tried to take in everything, figure out how the system worked. It was pretty cold, maybe forty degrees, and they'd get up and move around every so often, or rub their arms or legs, trying to create a little heat by friction. A few of them had olive drab jackets, probably British, and they'd trade off from time to time with the guys who had less. Dave Hurt, the sub skipper, shared a jacket with Dusty.

Blinny had faked talking to a guard the first afternoon to explain to the new prisoners that nobody here was a prisoner of war, as far as the Japanese were concerned. A real POW was a *horyo*, but in this camp you were a *toriko*—a captive. That meant you didn't have any of the rights of a prisoner of war, like having the Red Cross notified that you were alive. So you were invisible, as if you'd just disappeared off the face of the earth. The Japanese could kill you, torture you, do anything they wanted to with you. Nobody would ever know. Blinny said he'd heard the camp was secret, not even a regular POW camp. The Japanese called it a "questioning camp," and it was run by the Japanese Navy.

The guards wore black and white navy caps, and the rest of their uniforms were brown. They had lightweight black jackets, and they carried short sticks, like a cop's nightstick, that they either twirled by a strap or hung from their belts. In the day and a half Dusty had spent in the compound, he hadn't seen them do much of anything, except break up groups of two or three prisoners so they couldn't talk to each other. There wasn't supposed to be any talking in the compound. The way the prisoners got around it was by pretending to talk to the guards. Sometimes they managed a few whispered or mumbled words when the guards were distracted, talking among themselves.

The whole compound covered maybe an acre. The gray wooden buildings were in an "E" shape, with rows of cells making up the barracks in the three wings, and the main connecting part holding the guards' quarters, the kitchen, and the questioning rooms, where the Quiz Kids grilled them every Saturday. The three wings were called Ikku, Nikku, and Sanku. Dusty's cell was in Ikku. There were some prisoners in Sanku, but he didn't know who they were—maybe civilians. They were kept separate, and didn't show up at the morning assembly. From the buildings to the eight-foot wooden fence around the compound, it was about twenty-five feet or so, on the average. No barbed wire or anything like that. Nobody was likely to go over the fence. Where would you go?

Dusty thought about his first session with the Quiz Kids. It was on Saturday morning, sometime before the noon cigarette break at the barracks door. Knowing it was Saturday—somebody told him that was when the Quiz Kids came—helped him figure out that he and Al and Nelson and Glasser had come on Thursday. By Saturday he was beginning to sort things out, but he was still exhausted and hungry from the long, uncomfortable boat trip. He'd been led into a room about ten feet square in the middle section connecting the barracks wings. Three Japanese men in civilian clothes were sitting behind a narrow wooden table. He was told to sit in a straight chair facing them.

They went through the usual preliminaries—his name and rank, F4F pilot on the *Enterprise*, and so forth—and then they asked about the composition of the task force. He'd answered that one before, both on the destroyer and on Truk, but by now he and Al had worked out their new version. It was too risky to deny either of the carriers, but they left out the battleship *South Dakota* and one of the cruisers, and since they didn't know the exact number of destroyers and smaller vessels, they decided to approximate it at "eight or ten."

Then there were some questions about the size of the *Enterprise*, which Dusty knew pretty well and reported accurately. One odd question, though, threw him for a minute.

What was the headroom between the hangar deck and the flight deck? Each question was formulated by one of two men in dark suits—Dusty thought they looked like typical intelligence service types—and then the third man, also in a dark suit, translated it into English.

"Well . . . I don't know," Dusty answered, trying to visualize the space. "I guess about eighteen feet."

The translator spoke to the others, and they snapped back something the translator rendered as "No guessing, Rhodes. We expect accurate numbers."

"Okay," replied Dusty. "It's eighteen feet and three-quarters of an inch."*

That seemed to satisfy them, and they went on to other questions. Dusty resolved to be clear and certain from then on, even if he had to invent the facts. When he left the questioning session, he thought he'd done okay. That was about an hour before they beat him to a pulp.

It was dim in the cell because there wasn't a window, but light leaked in from some cracks near the ceiling and from the central passageway that had doors at both ends. Dusty had studied the cell pretty thoroughly in the two days he'd spent in Ofuna before the beating. Now he had the time to review it all.

He was lying across two *tatami* mats, each about two feet by seven. That made his cell four by seven. Twenty-eight square feet. The tatamis, woven from straw, were about an inch and a half thick. The walls were plain gray boards, rough sawn, each one about eight inches wide. Old lumber. Tightly fitted, no cracks. The door was made of steel bars about three-quarters of an inch thick and three inches apart. There was a hasp and padlock on the outside.

---

*Actually seventeen feet, three inches. (Source: www.cv6.org)

He could touch the ceiling when he could stand. About seven feet, maybe a little more. Between the ceiling and the tops of the walls between the cells there was a gap of about two inches that permitted a little air circulation and finger contact between prisoners. He and Al touched and whispered a few words the first couple of nights. He didn't know who was on the other side of him.

Al was probably lying in his cell next door now. From time to time Dusty could hear small noises. Twice he'd heard what sounded like a moan. But he didn't feel like trying to communicate. Besides, there might be a guard sitting at the end of the corridor.

Looking up at the ceiling, he remembered his dad's cabin near Bass Lake. It was luxurious compared to this. Certainly roomier—maybe fifteen by twenty. Ten times the size. Bass Lake was a great place. Good memories. His family had started driving up there from Madera for summer vacations when he and his sister Billie Mae were still little kids. He was Buddy then—Dad was Dusty. At the cabin, Buddy and Billie Mae would set up their folding wood and canvas army cots. Sometimes Dad had to help.

He used to lie on his cot when he woke up in the morning, before anyone else was awake, and look at the cabin's beams and rafters and listen to the sounds outside. Mostly birds—sparrows and Stellar's jays and gulls and sometimes a raven.

He wondered why there weren't any birds at Ofuna. Maybe because it was winter. It was chilly in the cell, but he wasn't really cold. He realized that somebody had put a jacket on him. He wasn't wearing that when he passed out. And the two thin blankets helped.

Every once in a while there was a stab of pain in his legs and he winced. Between the stabs there was just a steady ache. He wasn't going to be able to move much until the swelling went down. Certainly not walk. Maybe they'd just leave him alone for a couple of days. Him and Al, assuming that Al was in the same shape.

He didn't remember seeing who hit him, which guards. They all looked pretty much the same anyway. It was just as well he didn't know which ones they were. Thinking about revenge was a waste of time. They were all criminals as far as he was concerned.

The second morning after the beating, Dusty pulled himself up by the steel bars of the cell door when he heard the guard unlocking the doors. His thighs ached and he could hardly bend his knees, but he thought he could walk, maybe with a little help. The guard unlocked his door and he pushed it open, using it to steady himself as he eased his body into the corridor. It was narrow, only four feet or so. Two other prisoners shuffling by stopped and made way for him. One of them took hold of his arm just above the elbow and steadied him as he took his first tottering steps.

"Good show, Yank. You can make it." The mumbled encouragement was barely audible.

The ragged line of prisoners—*fifteen of us*, Dusty remembered—moved slowly outside and turned left around the corner of the barracks. They trudged past the bench to a kind of shack that extended from the main building. Al was several steps ahead of him, limping. Four or five men went into the shack and the rest of the line waited. Dusty remembered it was the benjo.

"Benjo," Dusty's companion whispered in his ear. Dusty nodded.

He glanced at the man and saw that he was watching a couple of guards a little distance away. When they turned to greet a third guard who was approaching, the man looked at Dusty and said softly, "Birch. Leonard Birchall. PBY pilot. RCAF."

"Rhodes," said Dusty quietly. "U.S. Navy. F4F pilot." *Nuts, he knows that.*

Birch nodded, then looked back toward the guards. Dusty liked his friendliness. He'd heard that Canucks and Aussies were good guys. He also liked Birch's amused, sympathetic expression, like he was trying to decide whether to smile or frown.

Dusty's turn at the benjo was easier than he'd expected. There was a long plank six inches wide to sit on, letting your butt hang over, but he didn't need that. He hadn't for a long time. There wasn't even much to piss, but it gave a little relief.

He hobbled slowly back into the compound without help from Birch, but Birch walked next to him just in case. Another prisoner, he guessed an enlisted man, offered him a seat on the bench along the wall of the barracks, but Dusty waved his thanks and shook his head. It would feel good to stand for a little while.

The sky was gray and there was a chilly breeze, but the barracks gave them some shelter from it. Beyond the board fence of the compound, Dusty could see several telephone poles and a hilltop covered with brown grass. Guy wires held by wooden stakes in the ground ran to the corners of the barracks that Dusty could see from where he stood. That seemed funny. Were the barracks that flimsy? Would a stiff breeze blow them down?

He could see two square wooden tubs in the compound, each about four feet square and three feet high and full of water. A couple of wooden buckets hung on each one. Later that morning he learned from Birch that they were reservoirs in case of fire. Sometimes they had to be refilled from a well on the other side of the compound.

The guards stood near the fence in groups of two or three and talked with each other from time to time, but they looked bored with their job. They didn't pay much attention to the prisoners, except when one approached to ask for permission to go to the benjo or for some other question or message, usually a phony one.

Time passed slowly, with not much to look at and nothing to do. Dusty tried to size up the other prisoners without being obvious about it. Most of them either gazed over the fence at the sky or stared at the ground. Once he saw two of them playing "paper, scissors, stone," but not for long. After a while you probably learned to play mental games with yourself to kill time.

Except for the voices of the guards talking with each other, it was quiet in the compound. But in the distance there was the sound of aircraft engines. It was hard to say how far away they were, and Dusty couldn't see them. But they were nearly all to the east. Most of them sounded like they were taking off—single engines and multi-engines. Probably an air base, maybe seaplanes.

Near at hand, but outside the compound, there was a completely unfamiliar noise, a tapping or clicking sound. Sometimes it was quick, like castanets, sometimes slower. Dusty tried to imagine what it could be. A tool of some kind? It was more wooden than metallic. It went on steadily.

Someone had told Dusty on the first day how to request benjo permission, but he'd forgotten. Late in the morning, a slim, studious-looking man reminded him. He stood several feet away from Dusty with his back to the guards, so they couldn't see that he was talking, and introduced himself. Dusty was seated on the bench, leaning against the barracks wall.

"Ensign Larry Coulter," he said, just loud enough for Dusty to hear. "Dopey Clark's copilot, PBY." Sounded like the PBYs were taking a beating from the Nips. No surprise. They were big and slow and had about as much maneuverability as a turkey. Good for long-range reconnaisance, though, and they'd saved a lot of ditched pilots from the drink.

"When you want to go to the benjo"—Coulter spoke the words so carefully Dusty could almost have read his lips—"you have to say 'Ee-ee tee mo benjo yo roshee desKA?'" His intonation and his eyebrows made it clear that it was a question. He repeated it and then waited, looking expectant. When Dusty didn't respond, he looked carefully out of the corner of his eye to check the guards' position. Then he moved slightly to one side, so that his body blocked Dusty's face from the view of the guards. He recited the formula once again and waited.

Dusty tried it. "Ee-ee tee mo benjo yo roshee desKA?"

Coulter smiled and nodded. Dusty said it again, watching for Coulter's approval. Then he rehearsed it three or four times. Coulter was all smiles.

Dusty decided the best way to remember it was to use it. Rising stiffly, he hobbled slowly toward the guards. Each step reminded him that his leg muscles were like raw hamburger. While he walked, he repeated the question to himself, four steps to each repetition.

The guards watched him coming, and he thought he noticed a flicker of a smile on the face of one of them. He stopped in front of them and bowed slightly from the waist, the way he'd seen Al do.

"Ee-ee tee mo benjo yo roshee desKA?"

One of the guards nodded, and Dusty bowed again and tottered on his way. He didn't need to use the benjo, but it was easy to pretend.

I'm learning Japanese, he said to himself.

In the middle of the day—it must have been around noon—the prisoners began to drift slowly toward the door of the barracks. It took Dusty a minute to remember that this was *shigaretto* time. Those first two days in the compound seemed like a long time ago, and he didn't remember much about them.

While they waited at the barracks door, Birch stood near him and introduced his copilot on the PBY, a warrant officer named Bart Onyette. There was also a third member of the crew, an enlisted man, a gunner, who was so badly injured he had to stay in his cell. Birch said he was covered with dirty bandages. Dusty didn't catch his name.

There was another gunner in the group, too, Birch said, a Sergeant Reid, who was the only survivor of Captain Colin Kelly's B-17 that had been shot down in the Philippines.[†] Dusty remembered reading the newspaper story back home in December, not long after the war started. Kelly had ordered his crew to bail out when the plane was damaged, and then he'd crashed it into a Japanese battleship. Colin Kelly was the first big American hero of the war. Reid didn't talk much, Birch said, and he was kind of vague about the details.

[†]The early wartime story was propaganda to inspire Americans. Colin Kelly did not actually crash his B-17 into a Japanese battleship, but he did heroically stay at the controls of his doomed plane to allow his crew to bail out.

The barracks door opened, and a guard began handing out shigarettos to the prisoners, one at a time. Dusty wasn't much of a smoker—he gathered that several of the prisoners weren't—but he took one and waited for a light. It was something to do.

The cigarettes were skinny, loosely packed little things, and the tobacco was strong. No matter how carefully you tried to nurse them along, you couldn't make them last more than five minutes.

After the smokes were gone, there was a chance to scoop a tin cupful of water from a wooden bucket the guard set out, and then the barracks door closed and the prisoners wandered back out into the compound again.

In the afternoon Larry Coulter came over again, and Dopey Clark—Lieutenant Carlton Clark—came with him. They were able to exchange a few quiet words, and Dusty learned that their PBY had been shot down in the north Pacific, flying out of a base in the Aleutians. They were chummy with Birch and Bart Onyette, since they were all PBY men. Dopey had never smoked before he got to Ofuna.

The afternoon was quiet and boring. There was nothing to do but watch the guards or look at the sky. His fellow prisoners didn't look much at each other or make any special effort to communicate. The few exchanges of information that happened were brief and casual. Most of them seemed to know each other as well as they wanted to by now, and there probably wasn't much to learn even from the new prisoners. When there was a lot of time to fill, you rationed out the personal contacts the way they rationed the cigarettes. No hurry for anything.

One thing Dusty noticed was that several of the men reminded him of pictures he'd seen of convicts. It was their haircuts, or rather their shaved heads, a few totally bald, several with only a half-inch growth of fuzz. He remembered having his head shaved the day he'd arrived in the camp. He was stripped and doused with some foul-smelling stuff, too—disinfectant, probably. He ran his fingers over his head. Sure enough. Baldy Rhodes, they could call him.

Dusty was curious about all the men, and he still had a lot to learn about Ofuna, but it would come in good time. He'd learned a lot already. Where was Al, though? He hadn't seen Al since the line at the benjo that morning. He hoped he was okay.

Late in the afternoon it grew dark, and the prisoners gradually moved toward the barracks door. Standing closer together than they'd been doing in the compound, they felt a little warmer. After a twenty- or thirty-minute wait, the door opened and they moved along the dirt floor of the passageway to their cells. Al's was empty, but after a little while he came along the passage and winked at Dusty as he turned into his cell next door. Dusty nodded and smiled. Al seemed to be walking okay, but he moved slowly. He looked exhausted.

Glasser and Nelson were designated to distribute the daily rice bowls up and down the passageway. Rice was called *gohan*. Dusty thought his scoop of rice would just about fill a half-cup measure. Two big bites for a hungry man. But when you were really hungry, and expected to go on being hungry, it was better to make it last. Probably the more you chewed, the more nourishment you could squeeze out of each mouthful. No chopsticks, just fingers. Tonight there was a small piece of dried fish on the rice. Slim pickings for a meat-and-potatoes man.

Oh Lord, for what we are about to receive, please make us truly thankful.

There were two ways to look at everything. The optimist sees the doughnut, the pessimist sees the hole. So far, every meal he'd had as a prisoner had looked more like a hole than a doughnut, but when he thought about it he could see it was slightly more than a hole. He'd keep on trying to be thankful for that.

And then there was the little cup of water—*mizu*—to wash it down with.

Later, stretched out across the tatamis, Dusty realized he hadn't been thinking about the pain in his legs. It was still there, but not as much as it had been the night before or that morning. He touched his legs gently, and decided they were less swollen. He'd been thinking about home and Marian and Mom and Dad, wondering how they'd manage to come to terms with the report that he was missing in action. He wished he could send them a message of some kind. He'd read about mental telepathy, but he didn't believe in it. Still, it was hard to know. Maybe in some kinds of extreme, rare cases something like that happened. Or with people who had special mental gifts. He was pretty sure he didn't have anything like that.

There was a noise overhead, up at the top of the wall between his cell and Al's. Dusty stood up slowly and put his ear against the wall. He stood quietly for a few seconds, and then he heard Al whisper, "Reach up."

Dusty reached up to the little gap at the top of the wall and felt Al's fingers, holding a cigarette. He took it.

"Thanks."

"Treat from the kitchen. I'm working there. Like the food?"

"Delicious."

"More where that came from. The guards don't eat much better. Just more."

"Are you okay?"

"Hurt like hell. I'll live . . . Risky. Let's knock it off."

"Okay. Sleep well."

Dusty slept better than the night before. He woke up once in the middle of the night after dreaming about his mother serving him breakfast in their house on West Yosemite Avenue in Madera. It was poached eggs on toast—three of them—and big slices of honeydew melon. His mother was just watching him eat, and smiling.

After a couple of weeks Dusty could walk without limping, but sometimes he still felt a little pain in his left thigh when he stood up. Somehow he'd escaped more beatings like the one the Nips had given him and Al the first Saturday.

Some of the Quiz Kids still said "You rie!" during the Saturday grillings, usually when he said—honestly—that he just didn't know some things. But he'd only been whacked once with a stick after a frustrated new Quiz Kid had shoved him out the door into one of the guards. Al had been beaten several times, but he didn't want to talk about it.

Still, Dusty was surprised at the detail of the questioning. They even asked him about the pistol he'd had. Evidently, some of the sailors on the destroyer had seen it slide off his lap into the drink. Yes, forty-five caliber, he admitted.

"How big is a forty-five-caliber bullet, Rhodes?"

I'll be darned, he thought. *Don't they know that?*

He held up his hands and indicated the tip of his little finger. "About like that."

"Draw a picture on this paper. Exact size."

Dusty drew the outline of a .45 slug as carefully as he could. One of the Quiz Kids produced a pair of calipers and measured it. The other recorded the number.

Dusty couldn't believe it. He hoped they didn't decide he'd lied.

If Saturday was the most dreaded day of the week, Wednesday was the most welcome. Wednesday night was bath night. The chance to soap off a week's grime, followed by a relaxing five- or ten-minute soak in a hot tub, helped to revive morale and soothe all sorts of irritations.

The bathhouse was in the main part of the building, toward the end farthest from the benjo. Half an hour after the Wednesday rice bowl, four guards conducted the fifteen captives to the bath area, where sometimes they could see wisps of steam leaking out under the eaves or through the crack of a doorway.

With the usual Japanese insistence on rank, Maher and Birch and other senior officers were sent in first. Dusty was in the second group. On the second Wednesday night after his beating, he was anticipating the soothing effect of hot water on his still stiff and tender legs. Standing next to Al Mead in the quiet darkness, he hugged himself against the chill and studied the stars.

Al was telling him about the kitchen work, which was mostly cleaning. He called it "scut work." The cook or the cook's assistant always kept him busy, and there was only a half-hour break or so in midmorning and midafternoon for tea. The guards had a morning meal and came in for snacks in the middle of the day. In the morning they often got a bowl of soup called *suimono*, sometimes with a slice of a large radish called *daikon* in it. That sounded like what Dusty had been given on the destroyer. The guards didn't really bother Al, but some of them insulted him or treated him with impatience.

He'd been called *baka*, which meant "fool," more than once. But he was learning more Japanese every day, and he thought that was worthwhile. He might have been picked for the job because he knew a few Japanese phrases and seemed to pick them up quickly. The cook had told him yesterday that the guards were *kichigai jimita*, which he'd managed to figure out with some questions and sign language meant something like "half crazy." He gathered that the guards weren't considered fit for regular military duty. "Some of them are pretty batty," he said. He'd had more of a chance to observe them than Dusty had.

When it was their turn for a bath, Al and Dusty and the rest of their group were directed first into a small room where they left their clothes and soaped down and rinsed with water from two medium-sized tubs. The water drained away through cracks between the floorboards.

Then they went into the next room where the hot tubs were. There were six small wooden soaking tubs, each heated by a small charcoal burner. Each one was just big enough for one person. Tall guys like Al were a little bit cramped. Dusty couldn't bend his knees enough to sit in the tub comfortably, but after experimenting he managed to slide into the tub butt first and let his feet stick out. The water was really hot, probably well over a hundred degrees, and the red skin where he'd been beaten was as sensitive to it as a sunburn. That was an easy kind of pain to bear, though, and he could feel the heat penetrating deep into his muscles. He was surprised to realize how tense the muscles were between his shoulders and on the back of his neck. It was the biggest luxury he'd had since he left the *Enterprise*.

Any amount of time in the tub would have been too short, but there were still some guys waiting their turn outside, and he was willing to move out when the guard gave the word. Now he had something to count the days for—Wednesday night soaks.

Back in his cell after the bath, Dusty stretched his legs, which had loosened up a little. Lying on his back, he tried pulling them up to his chest. They were still too tight to do that. Then he pushed them up toward the ceiling and did a few bicycling movements. That felt good.

When he tried push-ups, he managed six with a sagging back before his arms gave out. That was something to work on. He was sure he could do better if he practiced whenever he had a chance. If he could avoid another beating for a few weeks, he might see some of his old strength come back.

Be nice with the Quiz Kids, he said to himself. *Pretend you're running for office.*

By the fourth Saturday, Dusty's stretching and exercising were progressing. He could do twelve push-ups with only a little sag. On his back with his arms around his knees, he could pull his bent legs almost tight against his chest. Friday, he'd started sit-ups with his toes tucked under the cell door. He'd done four painful and sloppy ones. Try for six next time.

There was a new Quiz Kid this morning, a young, bright-looking guy with a very short haircut. After a quick review of a couple of items from the previous session, the new kid asked a new question. What radio frequencies did *Enterprise* use in communicating with him and other pilots?

That was a sticky one. He'd have to be a real politician to get them to accept what he'd tell them—unless they already had the answer from another source. He'd have to entertain them the way Blinny did. He leaned forward and looked directly at the new kid, using his hands to show the size and shape and position of the radio dial. Either it was already set when he left the carrier, he explained, or the squadron commander told the pilots during briefing to set their dials at red, yellow, or blue. There weren't any numbers, so you didn't know the actual radio frequencies. Each color setting on the dial tuned the radio to a frequency that had already been set by the technicians. Maybe yellow was 2500 kilocycles. It was easy that way because you couldn't fiddle with fine tuning while you were flying.

He glanced at the translator, then back at the new kid. He couldn't tell how they were reacting. He never could. Evidently, their culture trained them to be expressionless. At least they were paying attention. He might even be telling them something they hadn't heard yet. Or confirming what some other pilot had told them. He hoped he wasn't making trouble for someone else.

But they went on to other questions about homing signals from the carriers and how you picked up the signals. Dusty went on answering quickly and earnestly, like an instructor with a bunch of cadets. He explained more than he needed to, acting as if it was all important stuff, even though none of it was secret or even really interesting. They rarely interrupted him to ask for more explanation or to change the subject. He started to wonder if he might have a talent for this kind of thing. Maybe after the war he'd sell refrigerators to Eskimos.

Maybe they were just letting him hang himself.

But after fifteen or twenty minutes the new kid held up his hand.

"Owari, Roht-su," he said.

The translator said, "You are dismissed."

Three guards with sticks waited outside the interrogation room. But only one looked at him, and he signaled Dusty to return to the compound.

The prisoners in the courtyard watched him as he rejoined them, waiting for reassurance that he was okay. He slowed to a stop a couple of yards from Al Maher and Tommy Payne, a lieutenant who'd flown a VOVS (scouting and gunnery observation) float plane off the *Houston*. Dusty casually folded his arms and gave them a thumbs up. They blinked and shifted their gaze to the rest of the group. Maher winked at Birch.

Nelson and Glasser were standing just beyond Al and Tommy. They tended to stay near each other, and they didn't seem to have much contact with the others. That was probably because they weren't officers. The hierarchy prevailed, even in this situation. Dusty had talked a little with both of them on the voyage from Truk, and he remembered Tom Nelson's anxiety about interrogations. Dusty wondered how he was faring with the Quiz Kids.

Nelson had been the radioman on the TBF piloted by Jack Collett, the skipper of *Enterprise's* torpedo bomber squadron. Collett was leading the first division of TBFs on October 26, and his and Nelson's plane was the first one to be shot down by the Zeros. Nelson made it into the water okay, even though a Zero just missed him with a burst of tracers. His Mae West leaked, and he had to keep blowing it up. When a Japanese destroyer picked him up the next morning, he was glad to be out of the water, even though the Japs bullied and threatened him during the interrogation. What really worried Nelson was that his TBF was the only plane on the *Enterprise* to be fitted with a new airborne radar system, and he was afraid that if they tortured him he might spill the details about it just to save his bacon. He didn't think the Japanese had a clue that any of the planes had radar.

Nelson said that on the destroyer and on Truk they'd asked him about radio terms they'd heard, like "bogey at ten thousand," and he'd given them half truth and half lies. He'd discovered that he could often get them off the track by telling them tall tales about how many U.S. planes and ships they'd destroyed. They liked to hear that, and they seemed to believe it.

Dusty wondered if that tactic was still working at Ofuna. The Japanese asking the questions here were experienced at it, and he knew that some of the guys were beaten up after the sessions. Al Mead had mentioned getting roughed up a couple of times. Maybe the Quiz Kids didn't appreciate his interest in their language as much as the cooks did. Their reactions were unpredictable.

SIX

OFUNA BLUES

One Monday morning the guards in the compound were wearing white uniforms instead of brown. Something special was up. Dusty looked at Birch, standing near him, and Birch mouthed, "Changing of the guard."

Dusty raised his eyebrows.

"Later," said Birch. "Wait."

That afternoon after the cigarette break, more guards began to file into the compound, and after a few minutes the head guard called the prisoners to attention. Those sitting on the bench slowly rose to their feet. They all stayed where they were. It wasn't a formation. They could hear noises from the direction of the front gate. There was a rhythmic thump of footsteps, like a troop of marines double-timing, and then a new group of guards, eight or ten of them, also in white, appeared from around the corner of the barracks.

Jogging briskly, they came to a halt next to the old guards and turned to face them. There was a round of saluting and an exchange of ritual phrases, and then the old troop changed places with the new one, did a right face, and marched away toward the gate.

The new troop broke up and headed for their quarters, except for two who stayed with the prisoners and the head guard, a short, stocky chief petty officer. Holding a riding crop in one hand, he stood staring at the prisoners for several minutes. Dusty thought he seemed annoyed or disgusted. Then he turned and stalked toward the guards' quarters.

When he was out of sight, the two remaining guards relaxed and ordered the prisoners to do likewise. Several of them glanced at each other with quizzical looks or made faces. Any change in the routine was interesting, but not always welcome.

About an hour later the new head guard reappeared and strutted slowly to the front of the compound. He had changed into the usual brown duty uniform. He said something to one of the guards, who called the prisoners into formation and followed the order with "Haraku! Haraku! Speedo!"

When the prisoners were assembled, the head guard spoke sharply to them. It sounded like a scolding. Al Maher, at the right end of the front line, translated. There would be exercises—calisthenics. The foreign captives were getting soft because they had no work to do. That was not permitted! Everyone must follow the commands and not lag behind!

The head guard gave the commands and began counting.

"Ichi, ni! Ichi, ni! Ichi ni! Ichi ni!"

One of the guards demonstrated deep knee bends, then gestured for the prisoners to begin. They responded unevenly. Dusty, in the second row, couldn't get all the way down, the way he used to, but it wasn't bad. He'd expanded his stretching and exercise routine in his cell to include a session at night before sleep.

Ahead of him, Blinny and Dave Hurt squatted pretty well but were slow to rise. Maher was struggling but making it. The count continued, slow at first to allow all the prisoners to get with the rhythm, and then a little faster.

"Ichi, ni! Ichi, ni!"

To Dusty it sounded like "Each . . . knee! Each . . . knee!"

His knees began to hurt after ten or twelve squats, and he wondered how long it would go on. Dave Hurt was way behind the count, and Blinny was having trouble keeping his balance. Al Maher was heaving his lanky frame up with great effort, gasping, and throwing his arms up instead of keeping his hands on his hips the way the guard had demonstrated.

After about twenty repetitions the head guard took several steps forward and stood directly in front of Maher. He was grinning. When Al's arms came up with his next attempt to stand up, the guard cracked one of them sharply at the wrist with his riding crop. He stopped counting and said something to Al, who huffed desperately and made one last effort to stand up with his hands on his hips, then fell over on the dirt.

The guard started beating Al fiercely on his head and face with the riding crop, grinning widely as he directed each blow, some striking Al's hands, which he'd brought up to protect his face, some any exposed part of his head. Dusty was outraged. He could imagine Al's pain with each blow, and he remembered his own beating before he'd lost consciousness.

Most of the prisoners had stopped their knee bends when the counting stopped, but someone at the end of the line was still going, though slowly. Two men were sitting on the ground. Hurt and Blinny seemed to be holding each other up. They were all watching the beating. Dusty thought if they all rushed the guard they could overwhelm him and kill him before any other guards could arrive. But nobody moved.

Dusty was monitoring the rhythm of the blows, and it seemed like one was coming every two seconds, except for brief pauses when the guard moved around Al's head for a different angle. Al was gasping and moaning, reaching out feebly with one hand toward the stick, which he never succeeded in intercepting. The beating went on for about two minutes, maybe three, and the guard was grinning the whole time.

When he finally stopped, he straightened up and stared at the other prisoners, still grinning and not even breathing heavily, in spite of the viciousness of the blows. It wasn't clear whether he was daring them to react or looking for another victim. Then he turned slowly and strode back to the guards' quarters, never looking back.

When he was gone, Birch was the first to reach Maher. With help from Coulter and Dopey Clark, he half carried him to a place near the bench along the barracks. Coulter said, "Mizu," and went to talk to the guards. Two other men followed him, and in a minute, they began bringing double handfuls of water toward Maher from one of the fire reservoir tubs. Others joined them and soon a line of water carriers was moving back and forth.

The water helped to revive Al and wash away some of the blood. He managed to drink a few swallows. After a few minutes, he motioned that he wanted to get up, and Birch helped him to a sitting position.

Then, to everyone's astonishment, Al smiled.

"Thanks," he said. He looked from one to another.

"Anybody got an aspirin?" asked Coulter, and they all laughed.

The atmosphere was different in the compound the rest of the day. Everybody was alert for the reappearance of the head guard. Mick Glasser posted himself near the center of the compound, where he'd be the first to see the petty officer come out of the guards' quarters. Glasser had got their attention with a distinctive two-tone whistle like the first part of the well-known wolf whistle that none of them had had a reason to use for months. With a brief charade he indicated that he would be lookout.

Dusty remembered talking with Mick Glasser on the tramp steamer trip from Truk to Ofuna—actually to the port of Yokosuka, near Ofuna and not far from Yokohama and Tokyo, as Maher had explained to him. Mick had been turret gunner on John Reed's TBF in the second division of TBFs in Dusty's attack group. The Zeros hit them hard on the first dive. Mick saw some tracers and then some planes flash past just as a piece of the TBF's greenhouse sailed past his turret. Over the intercom he heard Reed yell, "Bail out! Bail out!"

Glasser kicked his shoes off before his parachute hit the water, but he still had his helmet and goggles, which helped shade his head from the sun the rest of the day. He didn't know whether there were any other pilots in the water with him. He couldn't see evidence of any. Late in the afternoon a couple of porpoises swam up to him. When he first saw their fins, he thought they were sharks, and he gave himself up for dead, but when they got within a few feet of him they raised their heads out of the water and he recognized the familiar bottle-shaped snouts. They circled him slowly a couple of times and hung around for a little while. Then they swam off. Mick wished they'd stick around and take care of him. He'd read somewhere that porpoises would drive sharks away.

Dusty had been genuinely interested in Glasser's story, as he'd been in Al Mead's. Everybody had a story to tell, and every one of them was as interesting as his own. The scary part about Glasser's story was that the Japanese on the destroyer that picked him up early the next morning pretended they were going to behead him with a sword when they thought he wasn't cooperating with their questioning. They'd even blindfolded him and had him kneel on the deck. Again, he'd thought he was a goner. He'd had just one close shave after another. But here he was at Ofuna, a survivor, like the rest of them.

Several hours after shigarettos, they heard Glasser's whistle, and all eyes went to the spot where the head guard would appear. When Maher saw him, he slowly turned around and faced the other way. Dusty saw the guard glance in Maher's direction. Then Birch and Dave Hurt turned around, not so quickly as to be obvious, but the movement gradually included the rest of the prisoners, and within a minute or two they had all turned their backs toward the head guard.

They waited to hear his voice, but nothing happened. For several minutes it was quieter than usual in the compound. They could hear a low conversation among the guards some distance away. Then there was another period of silence and tension. Finally, Dusty thought he could hear two or three nearby men begin to breathe more deeply, and there were sounds of movement. They looked at each other and turned around slowly. He was gone.

Coulter hissed a word—"Scheisskopf!"

Dusty looked at him quizzically.

"That's German," said Coulter, "for Shithead."

Dusty grinned, and the word was passed carefully from one prisoner to another. Like all appropriate nicknames, it stuck. Shithead was on their shit list.

The next day Dusty had a chance to talk briefly with Coulter while the guards were changing shifts. He asked Larry where he'd learned German. It turned out that he knew only a few German expressions, as well as some French ones. He'd picked them up when he was touring Europe with the Fred Waring orchestra before the war started. He'd played piano for the orchestra, and had enjoyed the life of performing and traveling. He knew he might have been able to get a draft deferment and keep playing, or maybe even play in some military band, but after Pearl Harbor he decided to volunteer for the navy, and an uncle helped steer him toward the flight program. He'd always been interested in flying, and he thought that if the music business ever dried up for him, he might like to become a pilot for one of the airlines, especially one with overseas connections.

Dusty liked Coulter's boyish expressions and his friendliness. He was good at passing on things he'd learned, like Japanese expressions he had a knack for, the way Al Mead did. He seemed to have read a lot as well as traveled, and various things he said made Dusty think he was one of those naturally curious guys who just enjoyed picking up new things.

Four days later Shithead appeared again. It was Friday. Nobody had seen him since Monday, except Al Mead, who had to serve meals to Shithead, along with the other guards. Al thought he had a really evil face, and he told Dusty the other guards pretty much avoided him.

It was the middle of the morning when Shithead entered the compound. Just as he'd done before, he had one of the other guards order the prisoners into formation, and then he repeated his scolding about getting soft. This time they were going to run. He made a counterclockwise sweeping motion with his arm around the compound, and then another guard started pushing Birch and saying "Ee-tay! Speedo!" Birch gave him a dirty look as he started jogging. The guard took a swing at Birch with his stick but missed. He waved the stick threateningly at the others as they passed him, but he didn't try to hit anyone.

By the time the line of prisoners made two circuits of the compound, the guard with the stick had stopped threatening and was just waving them on with one hand. Then Shithead shouted "Hayai!" and Birch, running ahead of Dusty, said back over his shoulder, "Faster." The prisoners picked up the pace slightly.

Running in the wooden clogs wasn't easy. Dusty hadn't run any-where for a long time, but the pain had pretty much gone out of his legs and he was surprised that he could keep up the pace. Not that they were running fast. The real problem was going to be wind, depending on how long Shithead made them keep it up. Dusty had been counting laps, but he lost track around seven or eight.

"Hayai!" Shithead shouted again, and he moved closer to the line of runners and raised his riding crop.

"Speedo!" hollered the guard.

Most of the prisoners were panting hard, and a couple of them were beginning to stumble every few steps. Maher wasn't doing badly, but Dave Hurt was slowing down and limping on his right foot. Blinny was pale and gritting his teeth, and Birch was gasping. Then Hurt stepped outside the line to get out of the way of the others and slowed down to a painful walk, with a conspicuous limp.

Shithead was on him in a minute, cracking him across his thighs with the riding crop. Hurt resumed running, or trying to run, still limping, and Shithead turned to look for other prey. Blinny and Birch were down. Dusty saw them stagger and fall.

Shithead yelled, "Tomari nasai!" and rushed to Blinny, who saw him coming and wrapped his arms around his head. The guard attacked Blinny's ribcage with his riding crop, slashing hard. Blinny kept his arms around his head. Bloodstains began to appear on his khaki shirt. Mean-while, the guard who had been threatening them with his stick lit into Birch, beating him savagely on the buttocks. Birch had also covered his head and pulled his knees almost up to his chin, but there was no way he could protect his butt. The rest of the men had stopped running at Shit-head's command, and the third guard brandished his stick to warn them to stay back.

To their surprise, the head guard stopped the beating sooner than he had with Maher. Straddling Blinny, he waved his arm at the whole group and shouted something in Japanese, which Maher later translated for them as "Your turn is coming!" or "You'll get yours!" Then he spat on Blinny's quivering form and marched back to his quarters. There were traces of his former grin, but this time he looked more angry.

The other guard had let up on Birch when Shithead stopped, but after taking a step or two away, he'd look back, swing around, and return for another whack. He did this two or three times and then finally gave it up and went to talk with the third guard.

Fellow prisoners helped Blinny and Birch to their feet and back to the bench by the barracks wall. They stripped Blinny's shirt off and rinsed it in a fire reservoir tub. Two or three other prisoners, including Maher, took their shirts off, dunked them, and helped to sponge the blood from Blinny's torso. Birch didn't want to sit on the bench and stood leaning against the barracks wall, with Dusty and Onyette helping him. It was almost like a silent movie. Weeks in the compound had conditioned them to near silence, and besides, there was nothing to say.

Dusty was having murderous fantasies about Shithead, especially at night in his cell when there was nothing to do but think. He knew that that ugly face and evil grin were imprinted in his memory forever. When would *he* be the victim? He needed to step up his morning and evening exercises. The best defense was to stay as fit as he could. He was doing twenty-five pushups now and thirty deep knee bends, although his energy seemed to disappear suddenly on the last few repetitions. His baggy coveralls showed he was continuing to lose weight, but toning his muscles was the best way he could think of to burn up the few calories he took in each day.

He knew he could be tough. He'd been through a lot already, including the worst beating he could imagine. Staying mentally tough might be harder. He was sure there was a lot of value in positive thinking, the way Reverend Axworthy had explained. Negative thoughts had to be squelched. He wasn't pessimistic about his situation, but he had regrets that he hadn't been a better son and husband. Too often, he'd put his own interests ahead of everything else.

Well, he'd make up for that when he got home. He'd tell Mom and Dad and Marian how much he loved and appreciated them. No taking them for granted anymore. He'd go home a better man, a stronger one. He'd be more religious, living by the Golden Rule.

Each day was a test. And each day was a preparation for a better future.

Days would pass without sight of Shithead, and then suddenly he'd appear and demand a new round of knee bends or running. There was always a victim, sometimes two. He kept them going until somebody couldn't take it and collapsed. They were all weak from hunger and sometimes dysentery. The older officers—Maher, Birch, Hurt, and Blinny—were the hardest hit. Maher had some ribs broken or cracked when Shithead kicked him. Somebody tore up a shirt and helped him wrap strips of it around his chest. You could tell he was still hurting after a couple of weeks.

Kicking had begun to replace beating with the riding crop. Usually Shithead would unleash four or five hard kicks aimed at whatever part of the prisoner's body was nearest, and then he'd turn and walk away. Dusty wondered what triggered his outbursts. The unpredictability kept them all on edge.

Then one Monday afternoon late in January there was a surprise. A new troop of guards arrived and Shithead and his crew left. Somebody mumbled, "Good riddance to bad rubbish." Dusty hoped he'd be gone from Ofuna by Shithead's next tour of duty. There didn't seem to be a reason for any of them to be kept there longer. The Quiz Kids rarely came up with a new question.

The days dragged by, but maybe they'd be a little less brutal now.

It wasn't hard to keep track of the days of the week, with Wednesday night baths and Saturday morning quiz sessions as markers. A few of the men had made secret calendars of one kind or another and could tell you the day of the month as well, but that didn't interest Dusty much. It was enough to know that it was January or February, 1943, and that the freezing weather would eventually give way to warmer days in the compound. He wondered what summer would be like. And he wondered how much longer he'd be kept at Ofuna, and what would be next.

Christmas had come and gone with little attention. The irony of wishing each other "Merry Christmas" or "Happy New Year" was too painful. Quite a few of the prisoners seemed quieter and sadder than usual that last week of December, and Dusty thought a lot about past Christmases with his family. Those simple activities of the season seemed so rare and precious now. He hadn't realized how lucky he'd been. When he got home again, he'd live such days with new appreciation.

Meanwhile, the daily boredom of the compound was at least better than another rampage by Shithead. Sometimes he felt relieved that nothing was going to happen that day. Other times he felt anxious that something might. There were a lot of gray, cloudy days and a few bright, sunny ones. During occasional rainstorms, they were permitted to stay in their cells.

A couple of times there was a light snowfall, enough to cover the ground and the roofs of the barracks. But the snow didn't last, it melted by midday, and there were puddles around the courtyard. Dusty watched a guard walk into one of the larger puddles and push his stick into the ground several times before moving on to another puddle and repeating the operation. There were bubbles where the stick had punched into the ground, and Dusty thought the puddle had begun to shrink. Within a few minutes he was sure of it. The water was draining into the holes the guard had poked! How could that happen? He had no idea.

On extremely cold days or very rainy ones it was a relief to be confined to the barracks, and the prisoners spent their time napping or exercising their memories or imaginations. But once in a while there was other entertainment. The new head guard was also kichigai jimita, but in a harmless way.

He earned the nickname "Co-hee," because he'd seen some American movies before the war and picked up a few English words he liked to show off. Unlike Shithead, he took turns with the other guards patrolling the barracks. He'd sometimes walk up and down between the locked cells and put on a performance. He'd pantomime pouring himself a cup of coffee, slurp it loudly, and then announce, "Co-hee!" He'd grin widely and follow up the coffee with "Donatsu!" Then he'd nod his head vigorously and look around for appreciation. The prisoners would nod and smile wanly. Thank God for small favors.

One cold and rainy afternoon, for some reason, Co-hee left their cells unlocked when they returned from smoking their shigarettos at the entrance to the barracks. They stood at the doorways of their cubicles, leaning against the bars and waiting for the lockdown. Co-hee started parading up and down the dirt-floored corridor, doing his coffee and doughnuts routine, his kendo stick under one arm. Suddenly, he stopped at one end and leaned his stick against the wall. Raising his right arm straight above his head, he shouted something nobody could understand. Then he brought his arm down sharply and looked expectantly at the prisoners. They gave each other puzzled looks.

Co-hee raised his arm and shouted the phrase again.

"Arya maru, gasayo, go!"

Was it Japanese or English? They looked at him and shrugged.

Finally Co-hee pointed at Dopey Clark, standing at a doorway next to him. "You say!" he commanded. Then he crouched down with his hands spread on the dirt in front of him, like a runner taking a starting position.

Dopey finally understood. He smiled and stepped forward, standing just behind Co-hee.

"On your mark, get set, go!" he yelled, and shoved Co-hee's butt with his foot, just hard enought to upset his balance. Co-hee lurched forward and sprawled in the dirt. Laughter exploded in the passageway.

Dusty laughed, too. He couldn't help it. But his gut tightened when he thought about the consequences. He watched Co-hee push himself up from the floor and look with surprise at his grinning audience.

Then Co-hee grinned, too. He was pleased. It was the best response he'd ever got from anything he'd said or done to show off for the prisoners.

He pointed to Al Mead. "You say!" he ordered, and took his starting position again. Al looked at Dopey doubtfully. Dopey smiled and nodded.

Al shrugged and stepped behind Co-hee. He raised his arm. "On your mark, get set, go!" Putting his foot firmly on Co-hee's rear, he shoved hard.

Co-hee hit the dirt again, then quickly got up, brushing himself off and grinning broadly. This time there was applause along with the laughter. Co-hee smiled and bowed, like a proud entertainer. Then he detached the key from his belt and waved the men into their cells, shaking his head and smiling to himself.

It was one of the memorable days. One of the better ones.

One morning early in February, Dusty was sitting on the bench in the compound when he felt an earthquake. He grabbed the edge of the bench and spread his legs for support. The prisoners who were standing were staggering like people on the shaking floor of a carnival funhouse. A couple of them lost their balance and went down. There was a rumbling sound like an avalanche. Over the fence top, Dusty could see telephone poles swaying and the lines swinging.

Water was sloshing out of the fire emergency tubs. Dusty could see the guy wire vibrating at the corner of the barracks. He hoped the barracks were strong enough to stay up. The shaking and rumbling let up after a few seconds, and then there was another sharper shock. The water sloshed farther from the tubs.

When it was quiet again, more guards appeared from their quarters. Some of them ordered prisoners to follow them to the other side of the compound, past the Sanku wing. Others grabbed the wooden buckets hanging on the fire reservoir tubs and began pointing to the prisoners nearest them. Dusty stepped between Al Maher and a guard and grabbed a bucket. Al had been moving slowly the past few days and obviously wasn't feeling well. Dusty hoped there would be enough bucket carriers without him. They'd have to make quite a few trips between the reservoirs and the well on the far side of the compound.

The bucket brigade lasted a couple of hours, until all the big tubs were filled to their previous level. Dusty was surprised to see that the earthquake had shaken out all but a few inches of water in all of them. After the cigarette break, he saw a couple of the guards walking around the compound and poking their sticks into the ground in the middle of several puddles of water. Again, as he watched, the water slowly disappeared, as if someone had pulled the plug in a bathtub.

On the day after the earthquake, there was a midmorning formation. Extra formations always made him anxious. More often than not, they were bad news. But whatever it was, it wouldn't involve Shithead this time. He and his crew had been gone for more than a week.

Co-hee said a few words in Japanese, and then in English he announced, "We taking a walk." He sounded like Edward G. Robinson or maybe Jimmy Cagney in a gangster movie. They were all marched around the barracks and out the main gate. Al Maher asked the guards where they were going, but all they would say was "We're going for a walk."

Were they finally moving to another camp? Not likely, since there was no preparation, no formal announcement, no reading of names. Maybe it was a work detail—something nearby that had to be moved or cleaned up. Possibly something worse, but nobody wanted to think about that. At least, it was another break in the routine, like yesterday's earthquake.

Dusty half expected the guards to put blindfolds or handcuffs on them, but they were just herded along a dirt road toward low, rolling hills covered with brown grass and scattered trees bare of leaves. Fifty or sixty yards outside the gate, three small houses huddled alongside the road. As they passed, Dusty could hear the familiar tapping noises coming from inside. Not pounding, not as if work of some kind was going on, or something was being made. What it was he couldn't guess.

Farther on, they met a man driving an oxcart, with several big clay pots or jars in it. There was no sound or smell to offer a clue to the contents. Maybe they were empty. For all that Dusty had heard about how crowded Japan was, this part was evidently an exception. Maybe in summer it would be busier. The fields surrounded by dirt berms or dikes were probably for rice. He supposed crops of some kind must be grown on the hillsides.

There were eight guards for the fourteen prisoners, who walked two by two. Behind the group came two women who worked in the kitchen, according to Al. One of them was old and bent, the other around thirty. Al had told Dusty about taking a leak in the benjo outside the kitchen one morning when the old woman came out of a nearby stall and stood next to him, talking to him. He was flustered, but she seemed very matter-of-fact about it.

The younger woman wore a colorful kimono around the kitchen, as a geisha would. At first Al thought she was a servant bringing special food to the guards, but then one day the cook asked Al if he'd like to screw her. He said no thanks. He decided she must be there as a whore for the guards. But Al said "concubine" instead of "whore."

There was no clue why the women were along on this trip. It was unusual that Al had been excused from his kitchen duty, too.

The guards carried their sticks, and two of them had rifles slung over their shoulders, but they didn't seem worried that the prisoners would try to escape or cause any trouble. Dusty walked with Lou Farran, the only civilian in their barracks. He was with them because he'd been taken prisoner along with the naval contingent at Wake Island, where he'd been a construction superintendent in charge of various building projects on the base. He was an older man, over forty.

Dusty hadn't had a chance to get to know Lou yet, but he seemed like a friendly and helpful guy. Dusty had noticed him a couple of times working on somebody's getas, or wooden clogs, making some sort of repairs or adjustments. He seemed to be good with his hands.

There was no chance to talk on the road, though. The guards were too near and nobody wanted to risk punishment. The day was turning out to be warm for February. Patches of blue began to appear through the gray-white clouds, and after half an hour or so the sky had opened from broken to scattered clouds. On one stretch of road going up a hill, Dusty thought he could see the ocean in the distance. Several times he heard and saw aircraft—bombers and seaplanes—landing at the airbase or taking off.

A guard near the rear of the column called out something, and the other guards signaled the prisoners to stop. They came to a halt and stood looking around. Dusty saw the younger woman walk off the road a few yards into the grass and squat, hoisting up her kimono. Dusty was surprised and looked away. He couldn't imagine an American woman doing that. The Japanese were much more matter-of-fact about toilet matters. In a minute the guards waved the prisoners on again.

A heavy grove of trees appeared ahead, mostly pines, and in the middle of it there was some kind of large building. As they turned off the main road onto a footpath leading toward the building, Dusty could see curved sections of roof through the trees and a couple of supporting columns looking like good-sized trees themselves.

The guards nearest them were talking with each other, and Lou said quietly, "Temple. Shinto or Buddhist."

Dusty hadn't expected a sightseeing tour, but it still seemed likely they would end up doing some sort of physical labor. The earthquake had probably damaged something.

It was shady and dim in the temple. Half a dozen short candles here and there didn't add any light, but they made the atmosphere cheerier. A dark wooden statue of Buddha sitting cross-legged on a low platform filled about half the small room. Dusty guessed it was eight or nine feet high.

The priest—Dusty had remembered the word—stood on the other side of the statue with his hands clasped and spoke to the prisoners, aided by a translator. He talked about the life story of Buddha and his discovery that all life was suffering but at the same time all suffering was an illusion. That was the word the translator used—"illusion." Dusty wondered if the Buddha had ever been pounded with two-inch wooden clubs until he passed out from the pain.

Dusty gradually lost interest in what the priests were saying. His mind wandered to the younger woman, kneeling in front, who had been offered to Al. Even after months of abstinence, he would have rejected her, too. Too risky—and he wouldn't want that on his conscience when he got together with Marian again.

The priest and translator had stopped talking. They were staring at the prisoners. Then the translator said, "If you would like to come back another day and learn more about the teachings of the Buddha, please raise your hand."

There was a short silence. The eyes of Co-hee and the two priests moved slowly over the faces of the *gaijin*. Somebody cleared his throat, and Dusty heard a couple of men breathing. Nobody moved. After bows and sayonaras, Co-hee motioned the prisoners out of the temple, and the waiting guards escorted them back to the compound.

Dusty wondered if anyone else was asking himself whether it would have been smart to raise a hand in order to get some more trips outside the gates. But for him the answer was clear. Definitely no. Too many unknowns. And the worst thing would be to break up the solidarity of the group. Other guys would wonder what you were up to. They wouldn't trust you anymore.

Stick together, guys.

That night in his cell, thinking about the trip to the temple, Dusty wondered why religion wasn't more interesting to him. He believed in God, and he wasn't uncomfortable at a church service, but Bible stories and Jesus and that sort of thing never seemed to have much to do with his day-to-day life. A couple of men in the camp were Catholic, and he'd seen them crossing themselves a time or two, but nobody talked about religion. He guessed most of them felt pretty much the way he did. You went to church at Christmas and Easter, and you got married and buried with a church service, and that was about it.

He remembered the day Reverend Axworthy, pastor of Madera's First Baptist Church, persuaded him and Jaydolph—just Everett then—to get baptized. Some of their friends had been baptized, and they couldn't think of any good reason not to be. They agreed to go to the 9:30 service the following Sunday morning. But they decided not to mention it to their parents.

So they were baptized. But after Everett was immersed, he shook his head vigorously, drenching the Reverend's face and eyeglasses until he couldn't read from the Bible, and Dusty, following him into the water, forgot to bend his knees and hit his head on the side of the tank.

It wasn't a painful bump, but he could hear more giggles from the spectators as he climbed from the tank and joined Everett in the room behind the altar. When the door closed on them, they sputtered and choked, trying not to let the congregation hear their hysterical laughter.

That was the most memorable of Dusty's religious experiences. It was a hard one to top.

With Co-hee in charge, things were easier in the compound. The camp's commandant, a warrant officer, rarely appeared. Co-hee was a chief petty officer, like Shithead, but he had a different attitude toward Westerners, maybe because of the American movies he'd seen. The other guards in his troop were more easygoing than Shithead's troop, too. Dusty hadn't seen or heard of any beatings lately, and the guards on duty in the courtyard were lax about the no-talking rule.

A couple of them who usually distributed cigarettes at the noon break dreamed up a game to amuse themselves and provide a few more cigarettes to the prisoners than the usual one a day. When everyone had smoked his butt to the last puff, one of the guards would light up a new shigaretto and smoke a few puffs. Then he'd toss it four or five yards out into the courtyard. Any prisoner who could walk on his hands until he touched the cigarette could have it.

Dusty thought the guards probably got the idea from seeing him demonstrate his hand-walking ability for Birch and Bart Onyette one morning. He'd been practicing in his cell for about a week, but he couldn't go very far there. He'd learned to do the balancing part in high school, but he'd never had the strength to walk more than a couple of hand-steps. Now he'd discovered that he could stay up on his hands quite a while because he'd lost so much weight. The first time he tried it in the courtyard he covered eight or ten feet.

Birch tried it, too, that day but had trouble keeping his balance. Bart was smaller than Birch and stronger than he looked. He balanced pretty well with a little help from Dusty and even managed to take a couple of hand-steps.

Dusty was easily best at the cigarette-retrieval game, but instead of making it an all-out competition the way the guards wanted, he insisted that each prisoner should have a turn, one at a time. Bart made it halfway to the cigarette the first time he tried, and they gave him a round of applause. Most of the men either lacked the strength in their arms or couldn't keep their balance. Payne, the *Houston's* pontoon plane pilot, and Reid, Colin Kelly's gunner, made great efforts on their early tries, and on the third day Reid went all the way and won a cigarette.

Dusty continued to claim the cigarette most days—in fact, whenever he got a turn. But Birch was practicing seriously, and Dusty coached him. Once Bart got close enough to fall into a somersault on the last few feet and come up with the cigarette in his hand. He pretended to be a winner, but several loud hisses and a few downturned thumbs rejected his claim.

The guards were enthusiastic spectators. Like the prisoners, they applauded success, but they were more entertained by the struggles of the losers—those who never got close to a cigarette and those who made heroic efforts and failed at the last minute. They cheered Birch on until he finally went all the way, and Dusty was proud of his student.

Some of the guards were curious about America, and they would ask prisoners questions, using a combination of Japanese, English, and sign language. These two guards were impressed by Dusty's hand-walking skill. One of them bent his arms to flex his biceps and nodded approvingly. The other asked him something that sounded like "America gin desk-ka?" Dusty nodded and added helpfully, "California wine."

"Ah!" said the guard. "Carifonia!" He smiled and nodded vigorously. "Shree-mahss. Hahrywood!" He squinted and pretended to turn the crank of a movie camera. Co-hee wasn't the only guard who'd seen American movies.

The days of March were cold and blustery, and the prisoners didn't spend much time sitting on the benches. Walking around kept your blood circulating better. You could be shielded against the wind in the lee of a building or a wall or by the bodies of other prisoners. The guards were more tolerant than usual about letting two or three huddle close together.

They welcomed any activity. Maher or Blinny would frequently organize a session of light calisthenics, with mostly jumping jacks or jogging in place. Toe touches or deep knee bends rounded out the exercises, but their execution was sloppy, even with the leader counting cadence. You weren't doing it for anyone but yourself, just enough to stretch your muscles and warm up a bit. Dusty's morning and evening exercises in his cell had reached the point where it didn't make much sense to continue increasing the number of repetitions. He was as fit as he was going to get on a near-starvation diet. He figured he must have lost forty or fifty pounds.

Twice he'd been assigned with Birch to a wood-piling job on the other side of the compound. A pile of split logs cut in foot-and-a-half lengths had been dumped in a corner from an ox cart the previous day, and their orders were to stack the wood in neat rows. It looked like firewood, but Dusty wasn't sure where the Japs used it. Maybe in the kitchen stoves.

It would have been fun to swing an axe and split the wood, too, but that job had already been done. He remembered chopping wood at the Bass Lake resort where he'd worked a couple of summers. The aim was to build a big enough pile—usually several piles—to get the resort comfortably through the winter.

Another job at Ofuna, a less pleasant one, also reminded him of a Bass Lake experience. Once a week, usually on Tuesdays, an ox-drawn wagon arrived to clean out the benjo, and Dusty tried to be as far from the guards as possible and looking the other way when they picked out the two or three prisoners needed for the work.

But he'd had his turn, using a long-handled wooden scoop to transfer a half-gallon or so at a time of stinking slop from under the benjo into a bucket, which was then emptied into the wagon. The wagon was called the "honey wagon," and they filled it with "honey-dew." The Aussies and Canadians had a fancier name for it—"night soil." Dusty figured it was just one of those jobs that had to be done. You couldn't keep digging new holes and moving the benjo, the way people did back home with their outdoor privies. The camp had limited boundaries, and outside the camp, everybody's plot of land was probably pretty small. Japan was a lot more crowded than the States. Besides, they used the honey-dew as fertilizer on their rice and vegetable fields. Back home, cows and pigs furnished the manure. Here there were a lot more people than cows and pigs.

But even at home there were cesspools that sometimes had to be cleaned out. Dusty learned all about them while he was working at The Pines resort at Bass Lake. That was in the spring of his second year at Fresno State, after he'd dropped out with his friend Bill O'Hara to help search for a lost DC-3 mail plane that had gone down in a snowstorm somewhere near Bass Lake. There was a reward offered that was big enough to pay for a lot of college and other things, and Dusty thought he knew the area well enough to have a good chance of finding the plane.

He and Bill talked the owners of the resort into letting them live and do odd jobs there while they searched for the plane, and after it was found by someone else, Dusty—still called Bud then—decided to stay on at the resort through the summer and return to college in the fall.

One day in the late spring, before the season had really started, the owners had decided the cover of the resort's big cesspool needed to be repaired, so they'd asked him to help their regular handyman, Paul Bollinger, do it. To make a long story short but no less dirty, Bud slipped into the pool of stinking sludge and was pulled out by Paul, who laughed uproariously as the befouled Bud ran blindly to the lake, plunged in, and thrashed about like a madman. Upset and humiliated, he refused to help Paul finish the job.

Ladling waste out of the benjo turned out to be a cleaner job than fixing the cesspool cover at The Pines, but it was unpleasant enough, and the stink stayed in Dusty's nostrils even the next day. Still, it was a change from the daily boredom of the compound. Even on easy days when nothing bad happened, the monotony of the place, the food, and the routine made it a kind of group-size solitary confinement.

There were worse things than boredom and monotony. Just when you got to wishing something different would happen, something did. And then you wished you had the monotony back.

On a chilly, gray Monday morning late in March, the guards turned out in their white navy uniforms, signaling another change of the guard troop. Early in the afternoon all the guards assembled in formation, while the prisoners watched with interest and a touch of anxiety. Co-hee's troop had been the easiest bunch of guards so far. The next ones were likely to be tougher.

Then they heard the jogging of the new troop coming through the main gate and along the back side of the barracks. From around the corner they appeared, moving smartly, with a familiar figure in the lead. Shithead! Dusty shut his eyes in disgust, and he heard low groans and mumbled curses around him.

He realized he'd never hated another human being as much as this one. Hated and feared. This time it could be his turn to be one of Shithead's victims. He'd rather dive head first ten times into the cesspool at The Pines than face another month or six weeks of that son of a bitch. He knew he couldn't keep his opinion from showing on his face, and that could get the bastard's attention. His only safeguard was that all the rest of his companions probably had the same expression.

Shithead was grinning his evil grin, as usual, but he looked only at Co-hee and the other guards, not at the prisoners. When the formalities were over and Co-hee's troop had marched away, Shithead marched directly to the guards' quarters without a look in their direction. The prisoners exchanged expressive glances—dismay, contempt, loathing, anger, resignation. There were bad days coming. Shitty days. Today could be the first.

The next day, midmorning, Shithead appeared and called a formation. Maher translated the familiar harangue about their disgusting weakness and laziness, and then they were off and jogging around the compound. Shithead watched them intently, holding his riding crop in front of him with both hands. None of the prisoners could be described as physically fit, but none of them had been beaten for more than a month, either, and the moderate workouts that Blinny and Maher conducted had helped them make the most of the health they had. Nobody stumbled or fell. Dusty could see the stress in some of their faces and hear some labored breathing, but they hung on as the run continued.

Dusty imagined that they were all thinking, "Not this time! I can last! Just one more round. Then one more."

At last Shithead called a halt and waved his hand at them dismissively. Then he said something they couldn't clearly hear and walked back to the guards' quarters.

When he was gone they looked at Al Maher.

"Tomorrow," he said. "Ashita."

Each knee, thought Dusty. *He'll get us with that one.*

The next day brought another surprise, though—a more welcome one. For the first time since Dusty and his three companions from the *Enterprise* had come to Ofuna, some new prisoners arrived. There were three of them, brought in by half a dozen armed Japanese sailors in the morning, about the time they were expecting Shithead to run them through deep knee bends till somebody dropped.

They were British Navy, it turned out, from the submarine HMS *Griffin*: the skipper, the exec, and another officer whose duties Dusty missed hearing. They were a tight-lipped group, unwilling to say much to the Americans or Canadians. Maher and Birch and Hurt all had a shot at finding out what had happened to their vessel, but they didn't come up with much. Word got around that they thought information they shared with other prisoners might be pried loose under torture by the Japs. So far, they claimed, they hadn't told the Japs *anything.*

That Saturday the Quiz Kids apparently didn't have much luck with them, either. The skipper came back from his quiz session with a bleeding gash over his left eye. Dusty could see him just shaking his head when Hurt tried to talk with him in the compound. One of the other Brits seemed to be walking very carefully, trying not to limp.

Not long after the noontime cigarette break, Shithead stalked into the compound and ordered the prisoners to line up along the north wall. Then he called Maher to stand near him and translate. He ordered the three *Griffin* officers into the middle of the compound and told them to run in a small circle. Three guards carrying heavy sticks came out and spaced themselves around the outside of the circle in which the sub officers were jogging. Then they began swinging the sticks at the Brits, hitting them hard on the butts and upper legs. The Brits lurched and staggered, and Maher's voice kept relaying Shithead's commands:

"Keep running! No stopping!"

It was horrible to watch. Dusty had an impression of what the others must have felt when he and Al were beaten.

The executive officer went down first, and one of the guards stood over him with the stick, swinging at him like a golfer hitting a ball out of the rough. The sub's skipper and the third officer had to run around him and duck to avoid the guard's swinging club, all the time being pounded by the other two guards.

The skipper suddenly crumpled to the ground, and Shithead was on him in three strides. He waved away the guard who'd last hit him, and the guard turned to help his buddy with the third officer, who didn't last long.

Shithead cut sharply at the fallen skipper half a dozen times with his riding crop, and then he moved on to the exec, motioning the guard to take the skipper. All three officers were unconscious in a minute or two. Shithead ordered the guards to drag their limp bodies to the other wing of the barracks. That was the last Dusty saw of them.

Heavy, dark clouds hung low over the camp the next morning, hiding the tops of the hills around the camp. The smell of rain was in the air, and not long after the morning formation big drops began to splatter in the dirt of the compound. The guards waved the prisoners toward the barracks, and they were half-soaked by the time they got inside. The pounding of the rain on the roof grew steadily louder. Separated in their cells, the prisoners gave up trying to talk.

There was no cigarette break at midday, and it stayed nearly as dark in the cells as at night. Dusty sat in the roaring gloom with his back against a wall and the two thin blankets wrapped around him. The rice bowl was hours away. Nothing to do but think. That was the only freedom. Think about food, or making love to Marian. Drinking bourbon, or walking on a sandy beach on Maui or in San Diego.

What would he do after the war? Stay in the navy or find a job at home? Hard to guess. Too many unknowns.

Try not to think about Shithead and tomorrow. Better to just let your mind wander. Drift and dream.

It rained steadily for the next two days and nights, and the only breaks in the monotony were trips to the benjo and the evening rice bowl. Dusty did calisthenics twice a day.

Then one night they were herded out to the baths, so it was Wednesday. The heat felt wonderful for those few minutes. He wished he could have stayed longer.

The rain stopped that night, and they were called out for formation the next morning. Shithead appeared, but he wasn't grinning. After the count-off, he read a short announcement off a piece of paper he carried with him, and Al Maher translated.

The following captives would leave Ofuna today: Birchall, Coulter, Rhodes, Onyette, Reid, and Farran. They would report to the gate in fifteen minutes. *Owari!* Dismissed!

Shithead stalked toward his quarters, and as soon as he was safely out of sight, the lucky six were mobbed by the others, smiling uncertainly, questioning each other. What did it mean? Where were they going? Most likely to a real prisoner of war camp. Congratulations were probably in order, but at least good luck wishes.

Dusty was overwhelmed. Why him? The rest of these guys had been here longer. Getting out of Ofuna was great, but he'd hate to see the last of his companions. Maybe they'd find a way to stay in touch. Maybe the rest of them would come later to the same place today's group was going. But he was afraid it wasn't likely.

There was nothing to pack. He was wearing his possessions. The barracks was unlocked for a few minutes, though, and he checked his cell just to make sure. The other five were doing the same thing. Al handed him a scrap of paper with his parents' address written on it. If Dusty had any chance, would he try to notify them that Al was alive? He gave Dusty a pencil stub and another small piece of paper and had him write down his own parents' address.

There was no time for proper good-byes, but that was just as well. Save the tears and regrets. Dusty made sure to say good-bye and thanks to Al Maher, Dave Hurt, and Al Blinn, and in the remaining few minutes on the way to the gate he managed to at least touch the rest of them.

A truck was waiting, and the six of them climbed in. Looking back at the faces of the rest, some smiling, some looking worried, he was sure he would never forget them. They were heroes, all of them. He was glad that

Birch and Lou and Coulter were going with him. Except for Al Mead, they were his closest pals at Ofuna. The truck jerked into gear and ground slowly away as a guard pulled the gate shut. There were people standing ankle-deep in the flooded rice paddies around the camp. They straightened up to watch the truck. The morning clouds were beginning to break up, showing patches of blue.

SEVEN

THE STADIUM

Dusty had only a vague idea where Tipperary was—that Tipperary in the old World War I song that the British prisoners still sang sometimes—but he knew it stood for "home." And he knew it was still a long, long way to his Tipperary, whether you measured it in miles or in days. But he knew he was going to make it.

He was still a prisoner of the enemy. He was emaciated and sometimes weak. He had no idea how much longer he would have to hold out, or what the next day or next week would bring. But he already knew that the Yokohama Stadium prisoner-of-war camp was miles better than Ofuna, that hellhole he'd endured for five months. Some unforeseen thing—typhoid, a bullet, a bayonet, a bomb—could put an end to him, but his chances looked better than even right now.

At first, on his way to the stadium camp, bouncing around in the back of a truck with Birch, Coulter, Lou, Bart Onyette, and Sergeant Reid, he'd felt great relief just to be out of Ofuna—to be away from the threat of Shithead's vicious beatings and the shivering cold and the mind-deadening boredom of the place. The next place might be no better, he'd thought then.

But it was. The guards at the stadium were from the Japanese Army, not the Navy, so Shithead would never show up. The camp, in the middle of the city of Yokohama, was closer to the ocean, or the harbor, and it was warmer. It was May now, the beginning of summer.

The daily physical labor was often tiring, but it beat doing nothing. And one other thing—he was no longer a "captive," a nonperson. He was officially a prisoner of war, and that meant the Japanese would at least pretend to treat him according to the Geneva Conventions. Mom and Dad and Marian would be notified that he was still alive. He might even get some mail, eventually.

Maybe it was crazy to be counting his blessings, but he really was better off. He got fed twice a day. He had some new clothes to replace the coveralls that had been worn to threads. He didn't have to sleep in a steel-barred cell. He could go to the benjo without asking permission. There was no weekly grilling by the Quiz Kids. And there were so many other prisoners here—maybe five or six hundred—that he could disappear into the crowd and not be noticed. The stadium camp helped him see how grim Ofuna really had been.

The daily work detail made the biggest difference. Their first day there, he and the others got their assignments, and after mealtime they met some of the other prisoners and got the scoop on the way things were. At least half the prisoners were Brits, or Canadians, or Aussies. They were friendly and helpful, like Birch. Birch, an RCAF group leader, equivalent to a commander in the U.S. Navy, was now the highest-ranking prisoner in the camp. There were five other officers, and Birch and Dusty and Coulter and Onyette moved in with them in a room partly partitioned off from the enlisted men's barracks under the stadium bleachers, a big structure of concrete and wood.

Captain Caesar Otway had been the ranking officer until Birch arrived, and the rest of the prisoners, especially the Brits, looked up to him. He was a great organizer, and the camp authorities seemed to respect him. Dusty was glad to find that one of the other officers was an American army doctor, Captain Nelson Kaufmann. He was very friendly, even fatherly, like Lou, though he was only a couple of years older than Dusty. It was always good to have a doctor on hand.

Lieutenant Jack Ford was one of a number of Royal Scots among the British contingent taken prisoner in Hong Kong. He was friendly, too, and jaunty in a way that Dusty had begun to think of as typically British. There was a tall, red-haired Royal Air Force pilot officer, Charles Hard, and a warrant officer from the Royal Navy, Neil Waring.

All the camp's indoor facilities were under the bleachers—the kitchen, the benjo, the bath, the guards' quarters, the commandant's office. In front of the bleachers there was a large oval track, probably a quarter mile around, and inside the track there was a baseball diamond. Evidently, nobody used either one now. That was it, except for a ten-foot-high wooden fence surrounding the whole works. The prisoners' quarters were crowded. Both officers and enlisted men had tatamis to sleep on, laid on wooden frames a foot high, strung with rope. By the terms of the Geneva Conventions, the Japanese couldn't require the officers to work. The catch was that if you didn't work you got reduced rations. Every officer worked.

After the weigh-in and superficial medical exam on the day they arrived, Dusty and the others from Ofuna were assigned to work details. It took only a couple of days to catch on to the work routine. Each work detail of a hundred prisoners or more assembled outside the barracks doors in front of the stadium, one group at a time. Birch had taken charge of the prisoners reporting for the lumberyard group. Dusty was glad to be with Birch. He was always great company. As the men bound for the lumberyard slouched and shuffled into two ranks near the truck pick-up point, Birch called them to attention.

It sounded like "Kyutske!" to Dusty.

Al Maher had done the honors at Ofuna, and like all the other prisoners, Dusty had learned to respond to the sounds of the Japanese commands, even though he couldn't have spelled them.

"*Bango!*" sounded like "Bongo!" It meant "Count off!" But you had to count off in Japanese, and that had been tricky at first. At Ofuna, though, there wasn't much else to do besides practice a few useful Japanese words and phrases, and the numbers came quickly. If you got stuck, there was always somebody nearby who'd been there long enough to know all the numbers, and he'd whisper them to you.

After everyone had counted off and Birch knew his group was all present, he hollered, "Quirei!" at which they all turned in the direction of the Emperor's palace in Tokyo and bowed stiffly from the waist, arms at their sides. If there was any news Birch had to communicate, he called parade rest: "Yasami!"

Then he called them to attention again, and on the command of "Owari!" they fell out and headed for their truck. The truck was enclosed, and they sat on benches along the sides or else on the floor. The benches were better, but they couldn't hold everybody. There were several trucks in the convoy. They rode along in a bumpy, swaying daze until they reached the lumberyard. It was hard to tell how far they'd traveled—maybe four or five miles.

The lumberyard was huge, with piles of logs and cut lumber covering several acres. All day long for a couple of days Dusty and Birch stacked and restacked lumber of various sizes, moving pieces from one pile to another on a two-wheeled wooden cart they had to balance between them, one man pulling from the front, the other pushing at the back. That kind of cart turned out to be the standard vehicle at all the work sites. Over the next few weeks Dusty went to two others—a peanut oil factory and a brickyard. He never got to the fourth work site, the Osano dockyard, but he heard about it from other prisoners.

Coulter and Lou went there once, and they and fifty or sixty other prisoners had spent the whole day carrying bales of cotton from a cargo ship to the wharf. The bales must have weighed sixty or seventy pounds, and maneuvering them on a two-wheeled cart down a shaky wooden gangplank was tricky. Other prisoners said that most of the time they had to carry bundles of foodstuffs in slings hung from both ends of a wooden yoke they carried across their neck and shoulders. They called it "coolie labor." The only good thing about the dockyard detail was that there were chances to swipe food now and then, but you had to eat it on the spot. It was too risky to try to smuggle it back to the camp.

Lou was showing the strain of heavy work details. He was older than most of the other prisoners, maybe forty-five or so, Dusty guessed. He usually stayed on his cot in the evening, and Doc Kaufmann had noticed. One morning before the work details left the stadium, a couple of guards came in carrying a sewing machine with a foot treadle. Doc met them at the door and asked a couple of enlisted men to take the sewing machine to a place along one wall, where there was good light from a window. Dusty saw Doc talking with Lou, and Lou didn't go to work that day.

That evening word was circulated that Lou was going to be repairing clothing for anyone who needed it. You could bring him anything in the morning and he'd have it fixed for you by the end of the day. Nothing else was ever said about it, but Dusty was sure Doc had persuaded the camp authorities to provide the sewing machine. It was the first of many times Dusty noticed that Doc Kaufmann took care of his people almost before they knew they needed it.

For a couple of weeks Dusty and Birch traveled by truck with twenty others several miles to the peanut oil factory, where they moved bags of peanuts and copra from a large storage yard into the factory. The bags were then dumped into huge presses to extract the oil. Copra, Dusty learned, was coconut meat that had been cut out of the shells. They lugged the bundles on the two-wheeled carts. It was heavy work, but there were rest breaks while the crews of Japanese civilians at the presses caught up with the accumulating piles of peanuts or copra. The civilians were mostly grown men, some of them over sixty, with a few boys between twelve and fifteen. Most of them were friendly and good-natured, and they seemed to appreciate the help of the prisoners. A couple of supervisors made it clear by gesture and a few words what they wanted done. Often it was just sweeping the floors indoors or raking the dirt yard outside. Unlike the camp guards, the civilians were patient about misunderstandings, and sometimes they and prisoners even shared a laugh.

The guards who went with the prisoners to the factory generally stood on the edge of the activity, usually near the outside walls. They carried rifles with mounted bayonets, but kept them slung over their shoulders. They were as bored and inattentive as the guards at Ofuna, and in the large space of the factory Dusty and the others were able to just sit and rest a fair amount of the time. The civilians would keep an eye out for the guards and tell the prisoners when one was coming.

It was clear to Dusty that the morale of most of the prisoners was better than at Ofuna. For one thing, there wasn't the threat of Shithead's deep knee bends or run-till-you-drop routines and the ruthless beatings. There wasn't much rough stuff at all. In fact, you were as likely to see a senior guard slap a junior one as to see anyone slap a prisoner. The Japanese guards were big on "discipline," which meant that a guard of higher rank could instantly punish one of lower rank for the slightest slip-up—maybe even for wearing the wrong expression. Maybe that was why most of them looked so deadpan all the time.

But prisoners rarely got slapped or beaten at the stadium camp. And there was more food than at Ofuna—two meals a day instead of one. No better tasting, but more of it, and after a couple of weeks Dusty was sure he was starting to gain back some weight. Upon arrival, he'd had to stand on a scale marked in kilograms, and his weight was 42, which in pounds was about 92. By the third or fourth week he was probably pushing 95. He felt better. So did Coulter and Lou and most of the other guys he was getting to know—better than when they'd arrived at the camp.

Instead of the white rice they'd had at Ofuna, the food now was mainly a mixture of boiled millet and barley they called "black gunk." Birch said it was more nutritious than the rice, and Doc Kaufmann agreed. Sometimes there was soy sauce for the black gunk. And the prisoners who worked at the oil factory were sometimes able to smuggle in small quantities of peanut or coconut oil, which helped the flavor. Once in a while there was also salt stolen by prisoners who worked at the dockyard. Every now and then they got some thick soup, called *miso*, made from fermented bean curd, and it usually had a slice or two of daikon in it. Dusty told Birch about his first encounter with daikon on the destroyer, when he thought they might be trying to poison him.

Dusty and Birch soon had their chance to share in the small-scale smuggling operations. One morning a member of the camp "surveillance crew," whose job it was to scrounge for useful trash, brought Birch two empty small-mouthed glass bottles with corks. He and Dusty each carried a bottle to the oil factory hidden in their sleeves, and it wasn't hard to move out of sight of the guards to fill them from some large jugs of peanut oil. The problem then was to get them safely back to the stadium kitchen crew. Birch explained to one of the civilian supervisors that he needed some string to help hold his baggy pants up, and the supervisor obliged. At the end of the day Birch and Dusty retrieved the filled and corked bottles from where they had hidden them and tied them around their waists under their clothes.

Birch's bottle was filled too full, and when he carefully put the cork in, there was no air space left. He was sure he could handle it by moving slowly and being careful. They managed to climb into the truck without spilling any oil, but half-way back to the camp the truck had a flat tire, and the prisoners had to march the rest of the way. It was a very warm late afternoon, and the peanut oil may have expanded or the bottle was jostled against Birch's legs. In any case, when they lined up for inspection by the guards after they got back to the stadium, Dusty noticed a pool of oil around Birch's feet. He nudged Birch and pointed, and Birch said, "Oh, my god! Me for the marble orchard!" Punishment was certain if he was caught. It might go really hard on him as the senior officer in the camp.

Luckily, the guards were in a hurry, and they didn't come close to Birch and Dusty. There were happy grins among the other prisoners that night when they heard about the adventure over their bowls of black gunk flavored with peanut oil.

The prisoners noticed small signs in the stadium camp that their captors were giving at least token recognition to the idea of treating them in a civilized way. Every couple of weeks they all received a small ration of Japanese money, at the rate of twenty-five sen per day for the officers and fifteen sen for the enlisted men. They could use this to buy poor-quality cigarettes, which were delivered to the officers' quarters periodically and distributed from there. The scarcity of both cigarettes and sen meant the prisoners had to ration their cigarettes carefully, even when they got a pack of ten at a time. Since there was very little to take pleasure in, lousy cigarettes seemed like a luxury.

A true morale builder was mail from home—for most of the men. Dusty hadn't gotten any. Nobody at home even knew he was alive, unless the camp authorities had actually notified the U.S. government the way they were supposed to. They'd permitted him to write a postcard home, to his folks and Marian, in May, not long after he'd arrived at the stadium, but who knew how long it would take to get there? If it got there at all. Still, he could share in the other guys' excitement when they got something. Not all of them did. Lou and Coulter hadn't received any yet, and he didn't think Birch had either. What mail there was came every couple of weeks, and it was passed out from a kind of "office" window between the corner room of the barracks where the officers had their beds and the main room. Dusty volunteered to hand it out as often as he could. It felt good to give something valuable to the others. Besides, if he ever did get something, he'd see it first.

He often had dreams about what he thought of as "real food"—milk, eggs, bread and butter, meat of all kinds. The food was always there, looking and smelling wonderful, but for one reason or another he could never get to it. Once a couple of the guys who were working at the brickyard were given some eggs by a civilian woman who was visiting there. They scarfed them down raw. Dusty would have done the same.

Jack Ford, the Royal Scots lieutenant, was keeping a secret journal. He'd started it not long after the British garrison at Hong Kong had surrendered, on Christmas Day, 1941. Dusty noticed him writing, and occasionally he talked to him about it. Jack said it helped to pass the evenings and exercise his mind. He wrote down things that happened, if they were interesting enough. He wrote out rhymes and song lyrics he'd known for years, some of them since school days. Sometimes he composed original things, especially funny poems. Now and then he read aloud what he'd written to Dusty and the other officers. Usually there was laughter, but sometimes there was silence, and once or twice Dusty felt tears in his eyes.

He'd never been much of a writer himself, but he wished he could copy down some of the things he heard. He asked Jack if he could see his journal to look at a couple of poems he'd liked. Jack wasn't sure who the first one was by—it was an American woman named Millay or something like that, he thought. Dusty read it over a few times and soon had it memorized. It went like this:

> My candle burns at both ends;
> It will not last the night;
> But ah, my foes, and oh, my friends,
> It gives a lovely light!

The other—"At Night"—wasn't as good, and he didn't want to memorize it, but it reminded him of summer nights at Bass Lake when he'd stood on the shore and looked at the sky. Jack knew the poem by heart, and he'd written the author's name, Ralph Hodgson. It began:

> I stood and stared; the sky was lit,
> The sky was stars all over it . . .

It went on to tell how the poet stared at the sky without a thought in his head or a feeling in his heart. He was just there, and there was nothing to say. Just witnessing the stars and the sky was enough. Dusty remembered what that was like.

When he told Jack he'd like to copy the poems sometime when he could find something to write them on, Jack smiled and said, "Say no more. You shall have it." Two days later Jack gave him a piece of corrugated cardboard he'd brought back from the dockyard and a sheaf of rice paper, twenty or thirty sheets.

"Fold this over for the covers, you see, and then stitch the pages in. Or have Lou do it for you."

Dusty cut the covers to size with a knife borrowed from the kitchen and stitched the pages in with some heavy thread Lou gave him. On the cover he lettered diagonally "Ensign R. E. 'Dusty' Rhodes USNR." Having such a thing was forbidden by camp rules, but so were a lot of things they did. The guards never searched their belongings, as far as they knew. If it was ever discovered, he'd have to deal with the consequences.

Making a start in the journal was harder than he'd expected. He had one thing he could put in it, though. Coulter had found a tiny photograph of the Grumman F4F-4 that Dusty had flown in a Japanese newspaper given to him by a civilian worker at the brickyard, and he'd torn it out and given it to Dusty. With a touch of the rice glue Lou kept on hand, Dusty stuck it in the middle of the first page. That had been his plane, and now it was at the bottom of the ocean. Under the picture he started to letter the name of the fighter, but then he hesitated. "Bulldog"? Grumman Bulldog? Somehow that didn't seem right. He couldn't think of anything else, though. So much had happened since then.

Finding something to say wouldn't be easy. He wasn't a poet, and he sat down to write only if something really important was on his mind. There *was* one important thing he could keep a record of—mail, what he sent and what he received. It would be easy to start—there was only one entry.

He headed the second page "LETTERS," and then under that he made two columns—"SENT" and "RECEIVED (?)." The sole entry in the first column was for the postcard he'd written soon after he'd arrived at the stadium camp, when the guards gave him and a few others a blank card about three by five inches and told them they could write one piece of mail. "1 POSTCARD—MAY 1943."

There were Jack's poems he could copy. Jack and Doc Kaufmann were probably the most literary guys in the camp. Birch was a reader, too, and he'd enjoyed the journal readings as much as Dusty had. When he saw what Dusty was doing, he decided he was going to start a journal, too.

Some of the funny poems in Jack's journal had been written by a friend of his, another Royal Scot called Mac—Second Lieutenant J. K. R.

MacGregor. Mac had evidently gone to another POW camp in Japan. One of the poems Dusty borrowed to copy into his journal was dated March 1942. The one he and Birch liked best, though, was about everybody's hatred for the rice that kept them alive. They'd repeated the last stanza together and immediately committed it to memory.

> We've no blankets or clothes and we sleep on the floor.
> We have scarcely a window to close and no doors.
> And a problem most weighty for someone to solve
> Is how to maintain some hygienic resolve.
> But who gives a hoot for the menace of lice,
> As long as those b—— keep giving us—rice.

Birch was so inspired he went off and wrote a funny one about a POW who long after the war meets a Nip in a bar and chokes him to death with a daikon radish he's carried with him for years. Dusty was tickled with it, and Jack and the other officers liked it, too. Dusty doubted that he'd ever write anything original, but he was sure he could find other things worth recording.

One of the evening pastimes he'd started to enjoy was reading the small stock of magazines the Brits had managed to bring with them from Hong Kong. They called it their circulating library. The ones he liked best were tattered copies of *Reader's Digest*—probably because Mom and Dad had subscribed to it and there was usually a copy or two in the bathroom at home, where everybody could take turns at it.

Every issue had a "condensed book" in the last thirty or forty pages, usually a new popular novel or a nonfiction book on some current topic. He'd already read three or four condensed books, as well as a lot of articles and excerpts, which were nearly all reprinted from other magazines and newspapers. In one issue he'd found an article on clever sayings, called "maxims," and one evening he filled a whole page of his journal with a dozen or so of the best ones.

He especially liked this: "WHEN WE RESIST TEMPTATION IT IS USUALLY BECAUSE TEMPTATION IS WEAK, NOT BECAUSE WE ARE STRONG." At the bottom of the page, when there was only room for one more, he chose a statement about death, not because it was particularly memorable or because he agreed with it, but because he'd been in the vicinity of death a couple of times, and he'd done some thinking about it. "FEW MEN HAVE AN INTIMATE KNOWLEDGE OF DEATH. WE DIE NOT BECAUSE OF RESIGNATION, BUT FROM STUPIDITY AND CUSTOM, AND MOST OF US DIE BECAUSE WE CANNOT HELP IT."

Close as he'd come to it, Dusty didn't think he had "an intimate knowledge of death." He wasn't sure, either, that he wanted any more knowledge than he already had.

Once the journal was under way, he began to take it seriously. He spent an hour or so with it every three or four evenings. It was satisfying to see it grow, and to collect some of the things the other journal-keepers shared with him. It was nothing like his aviator's log or a ship's log, but it preserved some of his thoughts, when he had time to think about more than the daily routine. Maybe some day he'd be glad he had it.

He decided to start a list of books he'd read, or wanted to read. There were a lot of stories he'd read in pulp magazines about aerial combat in the Great War, but he couldn't remember their titles. In high school, though, he remembered reading *Rebecca*, by Daphne Du Maurier, and being surprised that he liked it. He wrote that at the top of a new page. Then there was the first full-length flying book he'd read, *Squadrons Up*, by Noel Monks. And another good war story, *Three Comrades*, by a German, Erich Maria Remarque. Funny name for a man—Maria.

That reminded him of Marie Carmichael Stopes, who'd written a book called *Contraception* that his friend Jaydolph had shown him in high school. Something everybody ought to know about. But he'd decided not to take it home. He read it a few pages at a time, at Jaydolph's house.

Now that the list was started, he began to think of other books, and by the time his memory ran dry he had twelve titles and authors, including *Gone with the Wind* by Margaret Mitchell, *The Glorious Pool* by Thorne Smith, and *North to the Orient* by Anne Morrow Lindbergh.

A couple of nights later, he shared his list with Jack and Doc Kaufmann and asked them if they had any suggestions of books he ought to read. Doc said that if he'd found the Stopes contraception book interesting, he ought to try one called *Encyclopedia of Sexual Knowledge*. Dusty nodded and wrote it down. Doc listed the multiple authors for him. Jack recommended a book called *From Day to Day* that was translated from German, and quoted a line he remembered from it: "Reality is never so awful or so splendid as we imagine it to be." Dusty wrote that down, too. And then there were several "thrillers" by John Buchan that Jack remembered.

Gradually the list grew, and Jack and Birch recommended other titles. Birch had his own list, as it turned out, and he commented on several books on Dusty's list. Dusty wrote "G" or "VG" in the margin in front of some of them. In a couple of weeks he'd filled the page and started a second one. He included books he read from the well-worn collection the British officers had brought along from Hong Kong.

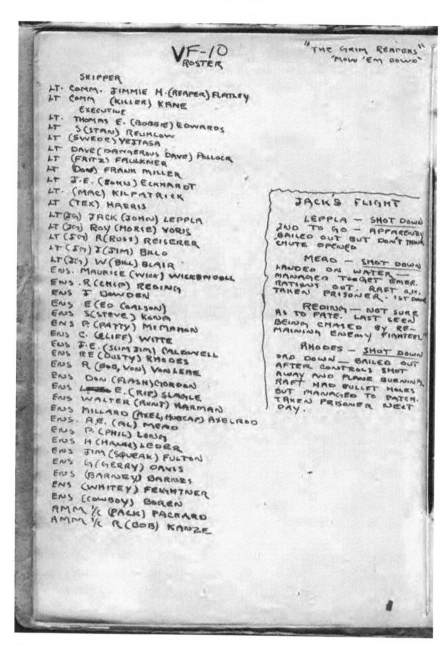

VF-10
ROSTER

"THE GRIM REAPERS"
"MOW 'EM DOWN"

SKIPPER
LT. COMM. JIMMIE H. (REAPER) FLATLEY
LT. COMM (KILLER) KANE

EXECUTIVE
LT. THOMAS E. (BOBBIE) EDWARDS
LT S (STAN) RUEHLOW
LT (SWEDE) VEJTASA
LT DAVE (DANGEROUS DAVE) POLLOCK
LT (FRITZ) FAULKNER
LT (DON) FRANK MILLER
LT J.F. (JOHN) ECKHARDT
LT. (MAC) KILPATRICK
LT (TEX) HARRIS
LT(JG) JACK (JOHN) LEPPLA
LT (JG) ROY (HORSE) VORIS
LT (JG) R (RUSS) REISERER
LT (JG) J (JIM) BILLO
LT (JG) W (BILL) BLAIR
ENS. MAURICE (WICK) WICKENDOLL
ENS .R (CHIP) REDING
ENS J DOWDEN
ENS E (ED CARLSON)
ENS S (STEVE) KONA
ENS P (PATTY) McMAHON
ENS C. (CLIFF) WITTE
ENS J.E. (SLIM JIM) CALDWELL
ENS RE (DUSTY) RHODES
ENS R (BOB, VON) VAN LEHE
ENS DON (FLASH) GORDON
ENS LESTER E. (RIP) SLAGLE
ENS WALTER (RUNT) HARMAN
ENS MILLARD (AXEL, HUBCAP) AXELROD
ENS. A.F. (AL) MEAD
ENS P. (PHIL) LONG
ENS H (HANK) LEDER
ENS JIM (SQUEAK) FULTON
ENS G (GERRY) DAVIS
ENS (BARNEY) BARNES
ENS (WHITEY) FEIGHTNER
ENS (COWBOY) BAKER
AMM ½c (PACK) PACKARD
AMM ½c R (BOB) KANZE

JACK'S FLIGHT

LEPPLA — SHOT DOWN
2ND TO GO — APPARENTLY
BAILED OUT BUT DON'T THINK
CHUTE OPENED

MEAD — SHOT DOWN
LANDED ON WATER —
MANAGED TO GET EMER.
RATIONS OUT, RAFT O.K.
TAKEN PRISONER. 1ST DAY.

REDING — NOT SURE
AS TO FATE, LAST SEEN
BEING CHASED BY RE-
MAINING ENEMY FIGHTERS.

RHODES — SHOT DOWN
3RD DOWN — BAILED OUT
AFTER CONTROLS SHOT
AWAY AND PLANE BURNING.
RAFT HAD BULLET HOLES
BUT MANAGED TO PATCH.
TAKEN PRISONER NEXT
DAY.

Page of Dusty's secret prison camp journal, showing his recollection of VF-10 squadron personnel. Courtesy Raleigh E. Rhodes.

The BOOKS TO BUY list was shorter, and included *Anthology of World Prose*, *Complete Works of Nathaniel Hawthorne*, *Ideal Marriage* by Van der Velde, *Encyclopedia of Sexual Knowledge* by Drs. Costler et al. He bracketed four titles in the list and labeled them TO READ. They were *Moby Dick*, *The Yearling*, *Anthony Adverse*, and *Dodsworth*, all American novels. And he added a short list of MAGAZINES TO SUBSCRIBE TO: *Reader's Digest*, *Life*, *National Geographic*, and *Esquire*. After the war he was going to make up for lost time.

In late June, Dusty's twenty-fifth birthday came and went with no special attention. Only a year ago he'd celebrated his twenty-fourth in Hawaii. Hard to believe. But with a little luck, the war could be over and he'd be back in Fresno for his twenty-sixth. Cards and presents and the birthday dinner would be nice, but they'd be small potatoes compared to being home again with Mom and Dad and Marian. He'd been in the stadium camp nearly two months now, and there was no evidence that anyone outside the camp knew he was alive. The Japs were supposed to notify somebody—the U.S. government, the Red Cross?—of the names of prisoners of war they were holding, but he wouldn't bet his life on that.

Then in mid-July there was a surprise. The camp authorities announced that fifty prisoners would be chosen by lot to record a radio message to their families that would be broadcast on Radio Tokyo. Each of the fifty could list the names and addresses of up to ten other prisoners, so that everybody was accounted for. The prisoners were skeptical, but even grasping at straws was better than nothing. When the lots were drawn later that day, Dusty was lucky. He'd be making a broadcast! Maybe the folks back home would find out at last that he was alive and okay.

It didn't take long to find several other prisoners to mention. Through Sergeant Reid, who'd come from Ofuna with Dusty, he'd gotten to know a couple of other U.S. Army sergeants—Ralph Boyd and Nick Kentis. Larry Coulter was going to be named by another broadcaster, but Dusty would list Lou Farran and Al Mead, who as far as he knew was still alive and maybe still at Ofuna, though chances were he'd been moved to another camp by now. He and Al had promised they'd notify each other's parents the first chance they had. He had the address of Al's parents on a scrap of paper he'd brought with him.

The next day, the lottery winners were excused from the work details in the morning and told to line up outside one of the service rooms under the bleachers. The door opened and a guard led the line inside up to a free-standing microphone. On a nearby table, there was a tape-recording machine. Dusty was third in line, and after the two men ahead of him had been given the signal and read their messages and moved aside, he stepped forward and read from the sheet of rice paper he'd kept folded in his pocket:

> Anyone hearing the following broadcast please notify those concerned and the United States Navy Bureau of Personnel. This is Ensign R. E. Rhodes, U.S. Naval Reserve, calling Mr. and Mrs. W. C. Rhodes, 2939 Lamona Avenue, and Mrs. R. E. Rhodes at 4905 Maroa Avenue, Fresno, California.

Dusty fought down a swelling in his throat and blinked away tears before he could continue.

> Hello Mother, Dad, and Marian. I am speaking to you from Tokyo Prisoner of War Camp Number Two in Yokohama, Japan. I hope you are all well and that everything is okay. Don't worry about me, because my health is excellent and my outlook optimistic. Please write often and ask my friends and relatives to do likewise.
>
> Here are the names and addresses of some of the other men who are in the same predicament. Sergeant R. E. Boyd sends his love to his parents, the William A. Boyds, at 3560 Gaviota Avenue, Swanton, California. Sergeant Nick Kentis sends his love to his wife Winifred at Silver City, New Mexico. Ensign A. E. Mead, U.S. Naval Reserve, also sends his love to his parents at 2545 Monterey Road, San Marino, California. Sergeant S. E. Reid sends his love to William A. Reid at Ligonier, Indiana. L. L. Farran, formerly of Wake Island, sends his regards to friends in Glendale, California.
>
> Well, dear folks, keep your chins up and don't forget to do a lot of writing. I send you all my love. Good luck and goodbye for now. This is Ensign R. E. Rhodes of Fresno, California, signing off.

Leaving the room, he was still excited, but anxious. There was no guarantee the recording would be broadcast, or that it would be heard if it was. It was better than putting a message in a bottle and throwing it in the ocean, but it might be a long time before he knew whether it got through. Still, it was something to hope for.

After a couple of months Dusty and Birch were reassigned to different work details. Dusty and Coulter went with maybe ninety or a hundred others to the brickyard. The work there consisted of pushing and pulling heavy cartloads of sand, gravel, or cement from the yard into the furnace rooms and dumping the loads on the concrete floors. Again, the civilian workers were easygoing and never seemed to lose patience with the prisoners. At all four work sites there was a noon break for green tea shared by the civilians and the prisoners, and occasionally there were brief attempts at conversation between the civilian workers and prisoners who had picked up some Japanese. They called it "pidjin Japanese." But the guards usually objected to this, and communication with the civilians had to be done while working and when there were no guards near.

The brickyard, called Taika-Ringa, was the best of the three work sites Dusty had been assigned to, and he hoped they'd let him stay there. In addition to Coulter, there was Martin Ivey, a broad-shouldered National Guard private from New Mexico, and a number of other enlisted men he was getting to know better. Since Birch was on another detail, Dusty was the senior officer at the brickyard, so he was in charge of the morning assembly in front of the stadium. The routine and commands were familiar to him from watching Birch, and the work went smoothly. Several truckloads of prisoners made the trip six days a week. Sunday, they all stayed in the barracks.

Months of malnutrition, physical and mental stress, overcrowding, and poor sanitary conditions had affected many of the prisoners. During the winter there had been three cases of pneumonia in the camp, and there always seemed to be a few guys suffering from amoebic dysentery. Doc Kaufmann reported that two new prisoners had symptoms of what was probably beriberi, because of the vitamin deficiency from months on a diet of white rice. He thought the millet and barley black gunk would help them. It tasted awful, but it had some vitamins.

Yellow jaundice—a sign of liver problems—appeared in the middle of August. Dusty had been feeling strange lately, and he and Birch had both noticed their skin looking yellowish. They asked the doc about it, and he confirmed their suspicions. He really went to bat for them, and persuaded the camp commandant to let them rest in the barracks for a week. He inveigled medicine of some kind—maybe it was quinine—from the Japanese medical orderly. He had to pay for it out of the pool of sen the officers all contributed to. Doc also advised Dusty and Birch to thin out their black gunk with water. By the second week they were both feeling better, and they didn't mind going back to work.

Jack Ford memorialized the event with an original poem:

YELLOW JAUNDICE STRIKES THE OFFICERS

WE ARE YELLOWER MEN IN THE LAND OF JAPAN
THAN THE NATURAL JAPANESE.
WE ARE MEN WHO WERE WHITE AND HAVE CHANGED
    IN A NIGHT,
AS IF THEY WERE TRYING TO PLEASE;
NOW THE JAPANESE MAN ALTHOUGH PROUD OF HIS
    TAN
IS A LITTLE ASHAMED OF IT TOO.
HE IS JEALOUS OF WHITE AND HE ALWAYS DELIGHTS
IN THE SIGHT OF A WHITE CHANGING HUE.
SO STICK TO YOUR COLOUR AND TAKE MY ADVICE—
IN FUTURE NOTHING FOR YELLOW BUT RICE.
A LITTLE BIT CRAWLING IS NOT OUT OF PLACE,
BUT IT'S GOING TOO FAR IF YOU YELLOW YOUR FACE.
AND REMEMBER MO S'KOSHI, WHEN ATO DE'S HERE.
A WHITE FACE IS PASSPORT, A YELLOW—NO FEAR—

As Dusty copied it into his journal, he admired how Jack had included a couple of Japanese phrases they knew—*mo sukoshi*, even more, and *ato de*, later.

In early October the nights were getting cooler, though the days stayed warm. Lou decided Dusty needed a jacket, and in a couple of days he ran one up on his sewing machine from what was left of Dusty's flight coveralls. Dusty had stopped wearing them soon after his arrival because they had holes in the knees and he'd received a brown wool tunic and a pair of pants from the store of uniforms that had come with the British prisoners from Hong Kong.

Lou had even sewn homemade ensign's bars on the jacket. It felt good on cool mornings and in the evening while sitting around the barracks. Lou was all heart. In the six months he'd been in the camp he must have made or mended something for half the guys there.

As Larry was helping him move a cartload of sand at the brickyard one afternoon, Dusty felt a jolt of pain in his right jaw. It was such a shock that he let go of the cart and stood grimacing and pushing hard on his jaw with his hand. After a minute the pain ebbed, but his jaw still ached. By bedtime the ache wasn't much worse, and he fell asleep quickly, as usual. But an hour or so before dawn—it might have been four o'clock—he woke up with his whole mouth throbbing. It was surely a toothache, but he couldn't tell which tooth it was.

He found Doc Kaufmann before morning assembly, and after assembly the doc persuaded the camp authorities to let him see a dentist. An armed guard led him through the streets for a mile or so, to a doorway opening on steps leading to the second floor. There in a crowded room they found a row of seven or eight occupied dental chairs and eight or ten patients waiting crosslegged on the floor. The dentist, wearing an army uniform, was moving from one chair to another, followed by a young woman assistant in a loose smock and trousers.

A couple of the patients were moaning softly, and each time the dentist bent over one for a minute or two, there was a yelp of pain. But the assistant was right there with a big wad of cotton and sometimes a strip of gauze bandage that she wrapped around the patient's head. Then she helped him out of the chair and pushed him firmly to the door, meanwhile waving another waiting patient into the chair. Somehow she was at the dentist's elbow in time for the next procedure, and found time to carry instruments back and forth from a counter behind the chairs. She was impressively efficient.

Sometimes, though, the dentist needed her while she was attending to another patient, and he called her urgently with a word that sounded like "Musume!" Dusty learned later that it meant "Girl!" Shortly after she motioned Dusty to a just-vacated chair, she rushed back to set a couple of instruments on a chairside tray—a rusty-looking knife or scalpel and an equally rusty pair of pliers. Distracted by all the noise and action, he had partly forgotten about his aching mouth, but now the pain completely disappeared. There was no reason for him to be here!

Before he could mobilize his muscles to leave, the dentist was leaning over him, tipping his head back, and prying his mouth open wide. Dusty squeezed his eyes shut tight and held his breath. There was a short pause while the dentist located the problem tooth. He signaled his decision with a soft grunt, and then one of the steel tools was in Dusty's mouth. He barely had time to hope it was the pliers, when he felt a jolt of pain like the one he'd had at the brickyard. The dentist shook his shoulder and said something. Dusty opened his eyes. The dentist was pointing to the bloody tooth he was holding in the pliers and saying something again. It must have meant "That was it!" Then the dentist was gone and the musume was there stuffing a wad of cotton in his mouth. She motioned that he could leave. Dusty climbed shakily from the chair and stumbled toward the door. The guard who had brought him intercepted him and steadied his arm while they went down the stairs.

Walking back toward the stadium, he tried to decide whether the pain was receding. It had to be. He was sure he wasn't going back to the dentist. Among the civilians they were passing on the street, he saw a tall blond man in a western-style suit and tie walking toward him. As he passed by Dusty he said quietly out of the side of his mouth, "How are these little bastards treating you?" Dusty was too surprised to respond, but he kept himself from turning around and walked on with the guard. When he told Birch about it later, they decided the man was probably either German or Swiss, and he might have been with a Red Cross team visiting the prison camps. Some of the Brits had told them that the Red Cross was supposed to have access to POW camps, but so far as anyone knew, the stadium camp had never been visited.

EIGHT

YOKOHAMA CHRISTMAS

Dusty watched his shaking hands open his journal and grinned. Writing was usually a way to exercise his mind after another long, boring day. Copying Mac's funny poems passed the time and gave him a chuckle. Birch was copying some of them, too, and sometimes they'd read them to each other. There'd been only four more entries on the "LETTERS" page, all under "SENT," but there was a growing list of things he'd read in the tattered "circulating library" the Brits had brought with them. He'd even copied out all seventy-five stanzas of Omar Khayyam's *Rubaiyat*.

But now—a letter from home! The first in over a year! The first ever in Japan! That was worth writing about! Of course, it was from Jaydolph—Everett Bondesen—the faithful old pal. Jaydolph's mother had relayed to him by mail the news that Bud was alive, and he'd sat down to write that same day, "somewhere in the North Atlantic," on his destroyer. The same old Jaydolph, jokey and optimistic.

The letter was safe in his shirt pocket. He knew it by heart already, after three or four readings. It was wrinkled and some of the ink was smudged. It was scissored up by the censors, too—either Japanese or U.S. Navy, or both. Written August 27, 1943. Today was December 14. No telling where Jaydolph was now.

So start a new page. "LETTERS RECEIVED." *I before E, except after C.*

He remembered Jaydolph in his officer's uniform in Miami, impressing him and Jimmy with his ensign insignia. Pretty sharp. Good-looking guy. The destroyer he was in, USS *Davis*, was just back from South Africa. They reminisced about Bass Lake. How they'd decided they'd have to bring the girls up there to the cabin for a cookout or something. He and Jaydolph had both had good luck with girls. And they'd made plans. But they'd never written them down.

Now was the time. On a new page he described the business venture he and Jaydolph had planned for after the war (assuming neither of them

Lt. Everett "Jaydolph" Bondesen and Ensign Dusty Rhodes in navy blues at Jacksonville, Florida, March 1942. Courtesy Raleigh E. Rhodes.

stayed in the service). They would operate a summer resort at Bass Lake in the Sierra Nevada mountains. If they could raise the capital. He should have something coming from Uncle Samuel, and Jaydolph would have something set aside.

Owning controlling interest, they would live at the resort, which had about forty housekeeping cabins for rent. Dusty thought of possible improvements: installing a bar, enlarging the store. They could lease the lakeside property, which could be subleased to people wishing to build summer houses. Other income would flow from selling groceries, ice, and beer in the store; the dining room and soda fountain; the gasoline pump; boat and riding-horse rentals.

Dusty stopped and stared at what he'd written. More than a page. More than he'd written in a long time, except for a couple of the long poems he'd copied. Two or three postcards home, the first one in May. Those were no more than telegrams, limited to forty words by the Japanese regulations. Hopeless to try to say much more than "Hi, folks. I'm okay. Just a little thinner. Glad you're not here."

This was different. Reading it over, he could see some real hopefulness. He could believe in it. Believe that some day he and Jaydolph would really make those dreams come true. Even if they didn't, they'd go back to Bass Lake together. It was a great lake, a great place to fish, loaf, fool around. The cabin would still be there, and the old rowboat. They'd put a new outboard on her and really take off!

It was just like Jaydolph. He always made a guy feel better. Maybe the ideas were crazy, but heck. It didn't hurt to dream.

A couple of days before Christmas, when Dusty and Coulter got back from the brickyard, they heard a rumor that a truckload of Red Cross packages had been delivered to the camp. But nobody knew who'd heard it first, or how they knew. A few guys were hopeful enough to make guesses about when they'd get the packages, but most of them took their usual wait-and-see attitude. Whatever was going to happen would happen, and guessing wouldn't make any difference.

After work the next day—it was Christmas Eve—there was big pile of cardboard boxes outside the barracks. As each work detail returned, guards directed each prisoner to take one box from the pile. They all bore Red Cross symbols and the words AMERICAN RED CROSS and "Prisoner of War Food Package." Some men sat down with the packages on benches or on the ground, and some carried them into the barracks. Dusty took his and went into the barracks. Ripping open the boxes took seconds.

Dusty found two packs of Chesterfield cigarettes, a safety razor and packages of double-edged blades, a small bar of Ivory soap, a tube of Colgate toothpaste and a toothbrush, a package of Oreo cookies, packages of raisins, dried prunes and apricots, some Planters peanuts, some oatmeal, two bars of dark, hard chocolate, and small packets of tea, powdered coffee, and sugar. Whoopee!

It wasn't a lot, but it was American! The timing was perfect, whether it was planned or accidental. A Christmas present from home on Christmas Eve! The Red Cross had come through at last. All over the barracks and outside the door, prisoners were tearing open the boxes, loudly itemizing the contents, crunching on cookies, lighting up cigarettes.

Besides that, there was mail! Dusty got seven letters, including one from Mom written in September, and one from Sis written on July 31st. Sis told how a ham radio operator in Fresno had called them the day before to say he'd recorded a shortwave broadcast from Radio Tokyo, and Dusty was on it! They were delirious to learn he was alive. The radio man had invited the family over to his house to hear the recording. Sis said the local paper was writing it up, and everybody in town would be writing Dusty as soon as they could.

It would be an unforgettable Christmas. The best thing was the feeling of reassurance that they hadn't been forgotten.

The next morning they reported for assembly, but Birch had received word from the camp authorities that there would be no work parties since it was Christmas. Dismissed, they wandered back into the barracks and turned their attention to what was left of the loot from the Red Cross packages. A jury-rigged Christmas tree began to take shape in one corner, assembled from a few scraggly pine branches from a tree in the compound and decorated with paper ornaments. Scraps of paper were also twisted and folded and glued into chains and streamers hung from the ceiling.

Just before noon Caesar Otway and Jack Ford distributed to the other officers homemade booklets covered in yellow rice paper, bearing the handwritten words "Menu" and "Christmas 1943." There was a line drawing of an old-fashioned horse-drawn passenger coach with the legend "Horyo Service. Yokohama to Home." At the bottom of the page was the "Passenger List," with the names, ranks, and services of the nine officers. Inside, the menu listed three meals:

> Breakfast: White rice. Soup.
> Lunch: Roast beef. Sweet potatoes. Boiled carrots and cabbage.
> White sauce. Raisin pudding. Scones.
> Dinner: Fish. Bread. Scones.

Everybody grinned and chuckled, and there were a couple of rude comments. Dusty was tickled, and amazed at the endlessly inventive humor of the Brits. If you couldn't feed your belly properly, you could always feed your imagination.

In the middle of the afternoon, four guards came to the barracks carrying armloads of musical instruments. The prisoners were incredulous. Were the guards going to play for them?

But they set the instruments in the middle of the floor—an accordion, a trumpet, a clarinet, a fiddle, two guitars, a mandolin, and a lute.

One of them motioned for the prisoners to help themselves. Then they turned and left. Larry Coulter grabbed the accordion and held it up.

"Anybody else know how to play this thing?"

There were no takers, so he settled down on a bench with a smile and began coaxing happy sounds out of the squeeze box.

Others picked up the rest of the instruments and examined them with interest before passing them on. They appeared to be used but in good condition. There were no volunteers for the trumpet except Dusty. Ivey seemed to know what to do with the fiddle, and several Brits and Aussies were trying out the other stringed instruments. A man Dusty didn't know claimed the clarinet.

Tentative squeaks, toots, and thrums filled the room. Dusty was sure he'd lost his lip, but he puckered and blew. The first few notes sounded like farts, and a couple of guys laughed. Then they started to sound like music. Dusty tried a scale or two.

After a few scales and squeezes on the accordion, Coulter began playing "Deck the Halls with Boughs of Holly." Dusty tentatively picked up the tune, and Ivey and a guitarist followed. The clarinetist was next. Before long the other guitarist, the lutenist, and the mandolin player were picking out notes more or less in tune. The improvised combo ran through three or four choruses of "Deck the Halls" before Dusty led it to a close. There was a flurry of applause, punctuated by cheers and whistles.

Coulter was ready with the next number, "O Little Town of Bethlehem," and the listeners grew quiet. Expressions reflected a respectful mood. After a couple of more carols, Coulter seemed stumped for a minute. He looked thoughtful. Then he broke into "Begin the Beguine," and grinning, two of the men grabbed each other and began dancing. In a minute nearly everyone was dancing. Some of them had put on shiny paper party hats that either came from a Red Cross package or were handmade.

Two of the guards had returned, entering the room quietly, and as the song ended and the dancing paused, they stepped forward. One of them held up his hand. He had a camera with a flash attachment, and he motioned the members of the combo to move closer together on a couple of benches. Other prisoners crowded in behind, and the guard with the camera held it to his eye. He motioned for quiet, and then the flashbulb popped. There were shouts of approval, and the guard turned to focus on another bunch of prisoners. Some of them held up goods from the Red Cross boxes. Dusty and Coulter passed their instruments to others to hold. "Snaky" Kerr, one of the two Royal Scots who worked as cooks, squeezed into the front row, wearing his tartan-trimmed cap. Another flashbulb went off. Ivey managed to get into another picture, still holding his fiddle

Allied prisoners at Yokohama Stadium prison camp,
Christmas 1943. Trumpet, Dusty Rhodes; accordion,
Larry Coulter; violin, Martin Ivey; coffee, Lou Farran.
Courtesy Raleigh E. Rhodes.

and wearing an army hat. The guard shot five or six more before waving
his thanks and heading for the door.

There was a minute of silence as everyone exchanged smiles and
looks of surprise. Then Coulter hit the accordion keys again and launched
into a familiar swing tune. The combo picked it up. Dusty couldn't
remember the name, but he'd played it often with the dance band at Bass
Lake. The pictures would probably be used as propaganda, to show how
well taken care of the prisoners of the Japanese Empire were, but who
cared? Everyone who knew or hoped he was in the pictures had the same
thought—maybe they would be published and circulated and someone
out there would recognize him. The music and dancing went on for a couple of hours.

The Christmas camaraderie had a bittersweet quality about it—sharing memories and regrets of the season with fellow prisoners instead of loved ones. The mail delivery, the Red Cross packages, and the musical instruments and carols brought a certain amount of solace and cheer, but the reminders of their isolation and powerlessness were depressing. The new year arrived without fanfare, noted only as another marker of passing time, like the months and the seasons.

Dusty was glad to have something to do, instead of sitting listlessly on a bench at Ofuna, even if it was only going daily to Taika-Ringa to push and pull cartloads of sand and gravel. The winter cold was much less punishing than last year's because he had wool trousers and a jacket, instead of his flimsy flight coveralls. Except for the jaundice and the infected tooth, he'd been in decent health and continued to gain weight slowly. His morning exercise routine, on top of the labor at the brickyard, kept him fit. The mental challenge—staying optimistic—was harder than the physical one.

Any change in the routine was usually a good thing. It gave him something new to think about. So the rumor that the Taika-Ringa work party would soon be moving to barracks being built in a small compound adjoining the brickyard was tantalizing. The word was that other work sites—at least the peanut oil factory and the lumberyard—would have their own barracks, too. No word about the dockyards. The source was one of the civilian workers at the brickyard.

It seemed plausible. Cutting out the travel time would mean more work time, more productivity for the Japanese. Dusty didn't know what the firebricks they were making were used for, but they probably went into boilers, either in factories or in the engine rooms of battleships or aircraft carriers. It didn't matter. Working meant eating, and staying warm, and keeping fit, and avoiding boredom.

Early in February there was another mail delivery. In addition to the mid-December letter from Jaydolph and the Christmas eve batch of seven letters, there had been the biggest bundle so far—nine letters!—on December 29th. Those included three from Mom and a couple from Mr. Martin, Neil's dad—real encouraging stuff, with news of friends and neighbors and relatives, and hopes for the end of the war. Some of them were dated as recently as September, but all the letters he'd gotten had been triggered by the July 30th broadcast of his recorded radio message.

February's bounty was even better—thirteen letters! He sorted through them quickly, looking at the return addresses. Three more from Mom, two from Sis, a couple from Mr. Martin again, Aunt Lil, his cousin

Pym, Aunt Ruby, Aunt Betty—it was old home week! When he recorded them in his journal, he'd arrange them by date, in the order they'd been written, but most of the postmarks were smudged or too faint to read, so he read Mom's and Sis's first. Still nothing from Marian. That was a disappointment.

One of Mom's letters was dated August first, just two days after the broadcast, when she'd received in the mail a written transcription from another ham radio operator who'd recorded the broadcast. She told about going to the Fresno radio operator's house to hear the recording, and how thrilled they all were when they heard Bud's voice. Until then they'd thought he was dead, because the navy had told them that way back in December 1942.

He'd heard from Aunt Marjorie and Aunt Gladys in the last batch, and now here were Betty and Ruby and Lil. He opened the letter from Betty first, and the first line of the second paragraph stood out like a neon sign.

"Your father died last January from a massive heart attack," Betty wrote. "I hate to be the one to have to tell you, but . . ." He couldn't read any more. The ink was already running from tears dropping on the letter. His throat ached and it felt like something was squeezing his chest, hard. He dropped the letters on his tatami and headed for the door. Thoughts were whirling in his head. January. Last year. His dad had been dead a year already. He was only—what? In his mid-forties.

Why hadn't his mom said anything? He'd had six or seven letters from her, including the one today she'd written right after the broadcast, the first one after she knew he was still alive. Nobody else had mentioned it, either. They'd all sounded like everything was perfectly all right at home, nothing changed. Were they afraid to tell him? Had they forgotten he didn't know?

Now he'd never be able to tell Dad what he'd meant to him. Dad would never get to see the new Dusty, the grown-up veteran, the ex–prisoner of war, the "Gob of Gobs," as he'd called Dusty in one of his letters before he'd left the States.

Those letters—there'd been several of them while he was going through training, after he'd been commissioned, while he was flying with Fighting Ten at North Island. Dad had called him "dear boy" in one letter, and ended it by saying "Take care of yourself, dear lad, with so much love, Fondly, Dad." He'd never forget those words. Dad had never said things like that to him face to face. It wasn't his way. Or Dusty's. They'd both had that feeling of closeness and love and respect for years, even though they'd never talked about it. It was just sort of understood between them. Dusty knew he'd made his dad proud by joining the navy and becoming a fighter pilot and going off to defend his country. But he'd never see his dad's face when he got home after the war. Never. Never again.

He felt an arm across his shoulders and looked to see who it was. Lou Farran was walking alongside him, along the track around the empty baseball field. There was nobody he'd rather have seen then than Lou. Lou understood. Even though he hadn't seen the letter or talked to Dusty, he knew that something bad had happened, and it didn't matter what. He just knew it would be good for him to be there.

They walked a long time around the track without saying anything. Finally, Dusty was able to get a few words out, and after a few snuffling false starts and a couple of deep breaths he was able to explain to Lou what it was all about. Lou didn't say much until Dusty ran out of words. Then he just said a couple of very wise, very sensible, very comforting things. He gave Dusty something good, something encouraging, to think about. Dusty nodded. He knew he'd be all right. Lou would be there to back him up, and the other guys would, too. They'd all understand.

When they walked back to the barracks at last it was dark and chilly. There wasn't anything for Dusty to say except "Thanks, Lou."

He discovered that he had a lot to think about over the next few weeks. He knew he was quieter and less talkative than usual, but the other guys didn't bother him about it. He kept remembering all the years he and his dad—and Mom and Sis—had had together, all the good times and some of the hard times. And he knew over and over again he could have been a better son, could have behaved a lot better, if only he'd thought about it. If only he'd stopped to think that Dad wouldn't be there forever.

On the 27th of March—the days were getting warmer and things were greener around the stadium compound—he wrote a letter and then copied it into his journal.

My dear mother, wife and sister—I hardly know how to start. Since I last wrote to you have received mail with news of dad. It was a terrific shock but I have had a fear of such a calamity since the time I was captured. I had made so many plans for us all when I get back. Am very thankful to hear otherwise OK. Received 30 letters from you so far mother, sis, aunts, Neil, Bill McNally, Pym, Lil, Aunt Glare, Aunt Ruby, Al Martin, Vada Lewis, Herb, Steve. Please give them my best and sincere thanks. Would like to write all, but impossible (1 quarterly). Surprised you all writing. Please send snapshot of family. Food Parcel would be greatly appreciated. Take care of selves and don't worry. Give love 2 Bertha, Ada, Ray, Don & all relatives. Tell Everett still 100% future plans. All my love to you, Bud.

In the margin he added a notation: 600 LETTERS
30/LINE
20 LINES.

It was a reminder to himself of the six-hundred-character limit his captors set for outgoing letters, along with the one time quarterly he'd mentioned in the letter. It was good that there didn't seem to be any limits on incoming mail, except that of course every letter had been opened and most of them had words and lines clipped out by the censors, either U.S. or Japanese. He wondered if for some reason they'd clipped out other mentions of his dad's death. He'd probably never know.

NINE

THE BRICKYARD

The announcement came the first week in April: next week the Taika-Ringa work group would be moving to new barracks on site, at the brickyard. Since the move had been rumored for a couple of months, the news was no surprise. Another announcement, though, *was* a surprise—on Sunday there would be an Easter service conducted by the Reverend Mr. Watanabe. He would visit the camp on Saturday to discuss the service with the officers.

Mr. Watanabe, it turned out, was an English-speaking Japanese Christian minister. He invited the officers to participate in the service by reading Bible passages of their choice or offering personal statements. Warrant Officer Waring and Pilot Officer Hard volunteered to read, and Doc Kaufmann said he would represent the American contingent. Birch and Jack Ford wrote out a program, and Mr. Watanabe had a couple of hundred copies made.

On Easter morning Dusty estimated that about half the prisoners were choosing to enjoy the fine weather instead of attending the service, but he was happy to be there. Coulter played a couple of hymns on a small piano brought in for the day, and for Dusty the service's theme of Resurrection and renewal was reassuring. Since the news of his dad's death, he'd been thinking a lot about the ways he could be a better man when he got home. Being a more sincere Christian was one of them.

They all liked the new two-story wooden barracks in the compound next to the brickyard. Coulter, Lou, and Ivey went, as well as Dusty, and the rest of the company was about half Americans and half Brits—Englishmen, Scots, and Canadians. The two Scots who'd been working in the stadium kitchen would be the cooks at the brickyard, aided by rotating shifts of volunteers or appointees. For Coulter and Dusty, the officers' quarters were a small room near the main door on the ground floor. They were joined by a prisoner sent there from another camp, U.S. Army Lieutenant Alex Kelly, a medical doctor. Again, Dusty was thankful to have a doctor aboard.

The American enlisted men filled the rest of that floor, and the troops of the British Empire took the "first floor," as they called it. That provoked playful arguments about which group really had the *first* floor and which first floor was the better lodging. Lou was on good terms with the enlisted men and was contented to be among them, as long as he had a table for his sewing machine. He was used to repairing clothing and footwear for the Brits as well.

As the senior officer, Dusty was in charge of the morning assembly, filling Birch's former role. He was also the moderator of communications between the prisoners and the commandant of this POW outpost, as well as between the Americans and the Brits. The need for moderation appeared before the end of the first week. Dusty was aware that there were some arguments between the troops of the first floor and those of the ground floor about whose daily food portions were larger. Then a couple of British enlisted men arrived in the officers' quarters one evening to present their complaint. It seemed that an undetermined number of the Brits had concluded that the buckets of soup or gunk delivered to the first floor contained smaller quantities, per man, than those going to the ground floor. The evidence for this complaint was vague, but it apparently derived from both "reconnaissance"—spying—and scuttlebutt.

Dusty was skeptical, but he promised the British envoys he would look into the matter immediately. They seemed satisfied with that. When they'd gone, he turned to Coulter and Kelly.

"Is there anything to that? Are they right?"

"I don't know," said Coulter. "Sounds like another limey prank to me. They like to stir things up just for the hell of it."

Kelly agreed. "That's probably it. Still, you can't just ignore the complaint. You've got to play along. Make it look like you're taking it seriously and solving the problem."

"No point in involving the commandant, is there?" asked Dusty.

"No, of course not," said Kelly. "It's not his problem, it's ours. And we don't even know if it's a real problem."

The solution was simple. The next morning Dusty announced at assembly that starting that evening, each floor would choose a representative—preferably a noncommissioned officer—to go to the kitchen just before meal times and cooperate with his counterpart in weighing the wooden food buckets. Each representative would make sure his floor's portion was adequate and the other's was not excessive. New representatives could be chosen at any time.

"Any questions?" asked Dusty.

There weren't any.

"Owari!" he said, and they broke up to go to their work stations. Later in the day one of the British envoys told him they were satisfied with his solution. Even impressed.

"Somebody said you was a bleedin' King Solomon."

Dusty nodded. He hoped all his administrative problems would be solved as easily.

There were other problems and disagreements as the days passed. In any group there were bound to be different opinions, and in a hierarchy like military service it was a tradition to gripe about the way things were being run. With nearly a hundred possible sources of discontentment—more, when you thought of all the possible combinations—you'd expect complaints. But as the weeks went by, there were no major conflicts, and the morale overall even improved.

There were several reasons for that. The weather was better—warmer, with more sunny days. The prisoners had long since adjusted to their diet and the work schedule. The work at the brickyard wasn't unreasonably hard, and the prisoners weren't mistreated. They'd learned to take care of themselves, and they were determined to survive. Alex Kelly was a good doc, like Kaufmann, and he kept close tabs on the men.

But the biggest reason for the good morale was Sergeant Ito, the commandant of the camp. Dusty had met Ito-Socho the day the brickyard group moved from the stadium to the new barracks. He had apparently just arrived, and he was getting things organized in his office, which was in the front section of a wooden building about twenty feet from the barracks. His living quarters and the guards' quarters were in the rear. Ito-Socho was about Dusty's height and obviously muscular, even in his loose-fitting brown army uniform. He was probably two or three years older than Dusty. He had short-cropped brown hair and a calm, interested expression.

That first day the prisoners had filed through the commandant's office, where they were asked to sign a statement pledging they would make no attempt to escape and acknowledging that they would be severely punished if they did. That was no problem. Nobody took it seriously. Dusty had already promised himself and the U.S. Navy he'd do everything in his power to escape, and that promise had priority.

Ito-Socho stood silently observing the procedure, while a couple of guards directed the signing and moved the line along. Having led the line and been the first to sign, Dusty stepped forward and introduced himself to the commandant with his name and a slight bow. Ito acknowledged him with a nod and a few words in Japanese, spoken in a way that sounded genuinely hospitable, though Dusty wasn't sure of their exact meaning. In the days that followed, their encounters continued to be polite. Dusty thought they were understanding each other as much through good will as through words and gestures.

A few days later Dusty saw Ito supervising some Japanese workers who were putting up a wood and steel frame between the commandant's office and the barracks. It turned out to be a gymnastic high bar. When it was completed, Ito-Socho called the prisoners together in the free period before the evening meal to demonstrate its use. The steel bar, about seven feet off the ground and five feet long, was set between two wooden posts six inches thick. Ito stripped off his tunic and stepped smartly under the bar. He stretched up to grasp it with both hands and did a few quick chin-ups. Then he swung his legs up through his arms and let his weight carry his body as far as it would go without releasing his hand grip. It was the classic skin-the-cat movement every school child tries on the playground.

As Sergeant Ito did it, though, he kept his legs straight and his heels together, and he made it look graceful and effortless. Reversing the movement and dropping to the ground, he faced the watching prisoners and stepped back, sweeping his arm to indicate that the bar was theirs to use. Then he picked up his tunic and walked back to his office.

The prisoners looked at each other, but no one moved. Then someone said, "Go ahead, Dusty!" Dusty shrugged and stepped forward. Pretending to spit on his hands, he rubbed them together and jumped for the bar, swinging his legs between his arms to skin the cat and letting his feet lower as far toward the ground as he could without dislocating his shoulders. His knees were not as straight as Sergeant Ito's, and he knew he didn't look as graceful, but he came out of it easily. Then, before letting loose of the bar, he did ten one-arm chin-ups with each arm. Amid scattered hoots and whistles and applause, he grinned and bowed and walked toward the barracks, waving the rest of the men toward the bar.

It was clear that Ito-Socho wanted to do what he could to keep the prisoners healthy and reasonably comfortable. There was probably nothing he could do about their diet, which after all wasn't a lot different from that of the guards, as far as they knew. But he responded promptly to Doc

Kelly's requests for medical supplies and was attentive to every issue that Dusty raised with him. When their pidgin Japanese and pidgin English were inadequate, Dusty called in Coulter, whose Japanese was improving daily, or one of several British noncoms who had picked up some Japanese on tours of duty in the Far East.

Though Dusty usually worked with the rest of the men in the brickyard next door, he sometimes stayed in the barracks compound to attend to small administrative duties or discuss a problem with Sergeant Ito. Now and then he would notice Ito exercising on the high bar in his shirt sleeves, having taken off his tunic. The brown army breeches and leggings always stayed on. Once Dusty saw him pull his upper body smoothly above the bar and then press easily into a handstand. When he mentioned this to Coulter and Kelly, Coulter said some of the civilian workers had told him that Ito had once been a gymnast in the Olympics. They also said he'd been wounded in the war in China by bamboo splinters from a grenade, which had seriously damaged his legs. That was why he was here with the POWs instead of fighting in the war.

Dusty never detected a limp in Ito-Socho's movements around the compound. Neither did he see him performing any unusually difficult movements on the high bar. But from his gracefulness and ease, it was believable that he could have been an Olympic athlete. In any case, he carried out his duties as commandant in a way that commanded respect without being harsh or even threatening. He observed every morning assembly, but he rarely had anything to say. The relaxed behavior of the guards seemed to reflect the commandant's expectation that the prisoners would do their work and not cause trouble.

Once in a while, though, somebody misinterpreted Sergeant Ito's seeming lenience. A new prisoner, an Australian bomber pilot named Noel Quinn, arrived at the compound during the evening black gunk serving. Dusty sent him to the first floor, where he was given a tatami and brought up to speed by his new mates. The next morning Dusty took him to Sergeant Ito's quarters, and the commandant asked him to sign the pledge that he wouldn't attempt an escape.

Quinn's response surprised Dusty. "No, I'm not going to sign it," he said.

Sergeant Ito was unruffled. Through an interpreter he said, "I will give you one hour to reconsider. When you are ready, you will come back and sign."

Quinn and Dusty left, and Quinn began walking around the compound with his hands clasped behind his back, looking thoughtful. Dusty kept an eye on him, and after twenty or thirty minutes Quinn said he was ready to return to the commandant's quarters.

Sergeant Ito rose from his desk and Quinn stood directly in front of him.

Shaking his head, he said, "Nah, I'm not going to sign it."

Dusty heard a sharp *crack!* and Quinn crumpled to the floor. Ito had slapped him, hard.

Quinn scrambled awkwardly to his feet, holding his jaw and shaking his head. His face was red and blood trickled from his mouth.

"Okay, I'll sign," he said. And he did.

Dusty told Coulter about Quinn's sudden change of heart, and the story spread among the American prisoners. By the next day the Brits knew about it, too, maybe because Quinn had been obliged to explain his damaged looks and pride. The prisoners' consensus was temperate—Quinn got off easy. It could have been worse. They'd all seen or heard of prisoners being treated far more brutally.

Ito's reputation rose another notch when Dusty reported his reaction to the arrival of several Japanese army officers just when a truckload of Red Cross packages arrived. The officers immediately began opening the packages and rifling through them—not looking for contraband but just helping themselves to cigarettes, candy, and even food. Ito was furious, as he later told Dusty with angry expressions and violent gestures, but he could say nothing because of his rank. The officers knew they were wrong, and they also knew Ito wouldn't attempt to stop them. Dusty knew Ito's frustration was sincere. He was a good soldier but also a good man.

He was especially friendly to Dusty, and he often invited him to work out on the bar with him. He nodded his approval of the one-arm chin-ups, but as they took turns it seemed to Dusty that Ito wanted to communicate that the usefulness of the bar was simply to keep fit, not to compete or show off. Dusty had the feeling he was holding back so as not to diminish his guest's prowess.

Every couple of weeks Dusty and Coulter and Ivey and an Aussie guitar player, who'd all brought their instruments with them from the stadium, got together to practice a few tunes. After working up half a dozen new numbers, they'd organize an evening performance for the rest of the prisoners, and Ito-Socho was always invited. He always came, bringing a folding metal chair from his office, and sat close to the combo near the officers' end of the barracks. He seemed to enjoy himself, smiling at the players and nodding and smiling at other nearby prisoners as they applauded. Ito always applauded, too.

With good will between commandant and prisoners, and with the comparatively easy circumstances of their daily lives, signs of rebelliousness or even restlessness were few. Still, some of them had been prisoners for two and a half years, and early hopes for a quick end to the war had died. They often speculated about the future, and they fed on clues from the Japanese brickyard workers as well as from news reports that Coulter translated from newspapers smuggled to him by one of the workers. With practice, and his knack for language, Coulter had steadily been getting better at reading Japanese. He would stick the paper under his tunic and read it on visits to the benjo, looking for news of the war. There wasn't much, he told Dusty, but from what he could make out, glorious victories of the Imperial Japanese Army and Navy were so common that you'd think the war would be over by now.

One report of a "glorious victory," though, ended with a mention of considerable Japanese casualties, which surprised Coulter. He thought it might have been a slip-up, and that casualties all along just weren't being reported to the Japanese people. Another clue that the war might not be going so well for Japan was that, although locations of the battles were rarely named, there had recently been a mention or two of islands only 1,500 miles from the Japanese mainland.

The most interesting news so far was a report of a bombing attack on a harbor city to the south, on the island of Kyushu. American bombers of a new type, called *bi-nijuku*, or B-29, had flown very high, at 30,000 feet or more, beyond the range of anti-aircraft fire. But several squadrons of fighter planes had intercepted them. There were twelve bombers and half of them had been shot down. Most bombs had missed their mark. Over the next few weeks, Coulter looked hard for more news of bombings on the Japanese mainland. But there was nothing for some time.

Then in early July he found an item mentioning another bombing raid in the same area. The bombers had come at night, however, and there was no mention of the type or number of planes or damage from bombs. A night attack might have helped the bombers to avoid fighter defense, but they would have had to fly much lower to find their target. It was hard to know what to make of the report. Coulter promised to keep watching. Maybe the *bi-nijuku* would fly again.

Though Sergeant Ito had made it plain that the horizontal bar was intended for use by all the prisoners, as well as by himself, the only one besides Dusty who used it regularly was Ivey, who often took turns with Dusty and Ito-Socho. Despite this underuse Dusty was convinced, and he urged the others to believe, that Ito was genuinely concerned for their physical welfare.

Another sign of this was the frequent availability of the large wooden hot tub, where they could soak and relax. Three or four evenings a week they heard the wood-fired water heaters going and saw steam coming from the small bathhouse across from the barracks. The tub, filled with piping hot water, was about twelve feet long by six feet wide and four feet deep, with an underwater bench you could sit on while you soaked. As usual in Japanese baths, it was a communal experience, and after soaping and rinsing in an adjoining room you joined whoever else was already there. Sometimes a couple of the guards were bathing at the same time as the prisoners. They avoided eye contact and clearly didn't want to talk, but they seemed comfortable with sharing the bath.

The summer days of 1944 were long and hot and humid. Frequent rainshowers alternated with blazing sun. The work in the brickyard was by now simply a habit. There was nothing to complain about, since it wasn't difficult and there was no trouble with the guards. One day passed into the next with little change except in the weather. The meals of black gunk with occasional small fish or vegetables were so uninteresting they didn't warrant comment. The hot baths were not as valuable as they'd been in cooler weather, but a relaxing soak after washing off the day's sweat and dust was still satisfying.

Mail deliveries were about the only thing that brought a break in the routine. They had been coming about once a month. Dusty had been lucky, he thought, with at least one letter every time, and sometimes two. His mother and Mr. Martin, a neighbor to the family, were the most faithful writers, and in September and October there were newsy letters from his sister. Most of them had words or lines snipped out by a censor's scissors, and sometimes what was left was puzzling.

October brought cooling breezes and lower temperatures. With the first day of November came the first remarkable event in months. In the middle of the day one of the prisoners working in the yard noticed two parallel white lines crossing the sky high overhead. He called attention to them, and soon nearly everyone could see the airplane—a silver four-engine bomber—just ahead of the condensation trails caused by the cooling of the engine exhausts in the stratosphere. But there were no sounds or other signs of bombs falling. What was going on?

"Reconnaissance," said one of the British prisoners, and Coulter and Dusty agreed. But it was three weeks before their conclusion was confirmed.

Shortly after work had started on the morning of November 24, air-raid sirens began blasting the steady squawks that supposedly meant enemy aircraft had been reported in the general area. The alert might mean only that planes had crossed the coast somewhere south of them. But an hour or so later the sirens changed to the more rapid bleating indicating bombers were very near. Then in the midmorning light the sky was suddenly filled with contrails. It looked as if two or three dozen B-29s were heading for Tokyo! You couldn't count them among the contrails and the puffs of flak from anti-aircraft batteries. Every man in the yard stood frozen in place, staring at the miracle.

"That's them!"

"Go get 'em, boys!"

"Hot dog!"

Not shouts or cheers, just scattered eruptions of uncontrollable excitement. Dusty couldn't have spoken a word, nor could most of the prisoners. The feeling was too much for words. Even the guards looked paralyzed.

The sharp-eyed among them could see tiny fighters—probably Zeros—attacking the high-flying B-29s. They were over Tokyo now, but the fence around the brickyard made it hard to see whether bombs were hitting the city. One contrail began to curve, and the plane veered slowly away from the formation. Then the contrail disappeared, and they could see the B-29 was losing altitude. In a few minutes they lost sight of it.

They listened for the sound of explosions and watched for traces of smoke above the brickyard fence, but there was nothing to confirm the effects of the raid. Maybe the target was too far away. They talked about the B-29s the rest of the day, when they could, and that night the barracks were full of speculations, predictions, and bets. They didn't know much, except that the B-29s had come. But they were sure they'd hear more.

They did. News trickled in during the next couple of days. The newspaper reported that the target had been an aircraft engine factory, but that little damage had been done. Most of the bombs had missed the target and killed innocent civilians. At least eight or ten bombers had been destroyed. The civilian workers said they had heard about a lot of damage from the bombs, but none of them had gone to see it.

The day after the bombing, Ito-Socho directed the digging of a bomb shelter in the barracks compound. There were prime targets nearby, in Yokohama. The prisoners were more than willing to dig, and to dig fast. With a limited number of shovels, they worked in teams, trading off for rests.

The shelter was a hole five or six feet deep, about eight feet wide, and thirty feet long. The next day a truckload of railroad ties arrived, and these were laid across the hole and covered with the dirt that had been removed. The shelter would be useless against a direct hit, but it would provide protection against shrapnel and flying debris from bombs that lit outside the fence. You couldn't stand straight up in it, and there probably wasn't enough room to hold all the POWs and Japanese workers and guards, but it was better than nothing.

Three days after the bombing, the shelter was finished. Dusty was checking the condition of the pipes and buckets in the part of the compound where they got their water, beyond Ito-Socho's office. If there were fires, they'd need water quickly. Suddenly, he heard a roaring noise that grew quickly louder. It sounded like two or three trains bearing down on him. He started to run toward the shelter behind the barracks, then he saw he might not have time to get there. So he headed for the bathhouse—there would be at least some protection there. He threw open the door and dived headfirst into the big empty tub just as a thunderous explosion rocked the building and shattered a couple of small windows.

Startled grunts and cries came from the two guards he landed on, who'd just taken shelter in the tub themselves. Rolling off them, Dusty saw their usually composed expressions replaced by frightened scowls. "Gomen nasai!" he blurted. "I'm sorry!" They shook their heads angrily and muttered something he couldn't make out, just as they all became aware that the explosions were moving away from the compound. Dusty couldn't help thinking, *Any port in a storm.*

The formation of B-29s had again appeared about midday, but the bombing in Yokohama seemed to have been light. Maybe they'd gone back to do a better job in Tokyo.

Smoke showed where several fires were burning near the brickyard, and there were sirens. Only a few of the prisoners had made it to the shelter because the bombs came so suddenly. That evening several of the noncoms began working out a system to get people into the shelter as quickly as possible. They made plans for practice drills. Things were heating up. The war was coming to Japan.

For a couple of weeks it was quiet. Then in mid-December they heard reports through the civilian workers that B-29s had bombed the Mitsubishi works at Nagoya, on the coast two hundred miles southwest of Tokyo. A few days later Coulter said a newspaper report had confirmed this news. Then they heard there had been another raid on Nagoya five days after the first. The attacks seemed to be coming in pairs.

Christmas came and passed at Taika-Ringa, then New Year's. The musical Christmas party at the stadium seemed as long ago as Christmases at home. The year at the brickyard had been fairly easy, but over the past two months Dusty had seen most of the prisoners getting more tense and

Korea and Japan

anxious. The B-29 raids had caused excitement and hope at first, but out of the discussions and arguments about the effects of the raids came new fears about their probable fate as prisoners. They could be either accidental victims of the bombings or intentional victims of vengeful Japanese. A feeling of gloominess, gray as the weather, permeated the brickyard and the barracks.

The days were chilly, often cloudy, with blustery rainstorms. Some nights were bitterly cold, and the little iron stove in the middle of the barracks didn't put out enough heat to be felt more than ten feet away. They let it go out after everybody sacked in, anyway, to save fuel. Only their body heat made the barracks warmer than outside. Maybe if he and Larry and Alex could put a curtain of some kind in their doorway, they'd keep their body heat in. Or maybe that would only shut out the body heat of the forty-some others in the main room.

The wooden shelf kept you off the floor, but the tatami wasn't much insulation. Thank God—or thank the Brits—for the wool tunic and pants that came from Hong Kong. Either they were extras or the men they'd belonged to had been killed. The woolen army blankets, too, were precious. Even the jacket Lou had sewed for him out of the top half of his flight coveralls after the bottom fell apart—that was a little extra help.

Still, it was cold and uncomfortable, and the nights were long. He thought again and again about the evening discussions they'd been having. In the hours of darkness before sleep came, Dusty found his mood changing, too. Sometimes shivering, he began to think seriously about something he hadn't considered for months.

Escape.

He could do it. It was possible. Nobody had tried it here, or he would have heard. Scuttlebutt traveled fast, even if a lot of it turned out to be fairy tales. You'd better know the true dope because your life could depend on it.

There were good reasons why nobody had tried to escape from the brickyard. Even though there was little security, everybody said it would be stupid to try. Any *gaijin* would stand out like a sore thumb in the streets of the city. There was no place to hide. Even at night you'd look suspicious if anybody saw you skulking along like a murderer or thief.

But the idea had been nagging at him ever since he realized how close the brickyard was to the seaplane base, where he could hear the planes taking off on reconnaissance flights at dawn and in the late afternoon. Probably no more than two or three miles, to judge from the sound and from what he'd seen of the city's layout when they'd been trucked here from the stadium camp every day. During those rides, they could see the water of the harbor at a distance between the buildings at certain corners.

It wouldn't take him long to cover the distance. At night he could move through the streets so fast he'd be out of sight before anybody who heard his footsteps could open a door to look.

To be warm! Even the activity, the excitement, would make him forget the cold for a while, but to really get out of here, and back to a carrier again—he'd walk across ice floes for that.

Just the usual night sounds in the barracks now. A chorus of soft breathing, with a few snores and a lot of hacking coughs. A creak of a bedframe and a rustle of cloth every time somebody turned over. Almost time to go to the benjo.

He hadn't told anybody about his plan. Not Coulter, not Alex, nobody. He didn't have the right to risk anybody else's life. Besides, the whole operation depended on quickness and stealth. More bodies, most of them in worse shape than his, would increase the risk.

The benjo was the key to the gates of freedom. Just get up as usual, like you were going out to take a leak, and then go around the benjo instead of into it, and there was the wood fence, eight feet high, hammered together out of one-by-twelve boards. No trick to get up and over it—easier than swinging up on the horizontal bar—and not even any barbed wire to worry about. The lone guard that patrolled the perimeter would be around on the other side of the brickyard, near the entrance gate. Dusty knew the routine, and it was obvious they didn't expect anybody to try an escape.

Then he'd drop down from the fence and be on his way. At the seaplane base there'd be some Kawanishi flying boats anchored in the harbor. He'd never seen the planes, only heard them, but he knew the sound of multi-engine planes, and the Kawanishis were the only four-engine seaplanes the Japanese had. He knew them from the recognition drills they'd done on Maui and on the *Enterprise*. A crew of nine or ten. He'd have to surprise them to have any chance at all.

First he'd locate the guard or guards and wait till the coast was clear. That might be the tricky part. But then he'd quietly paddle a little boat out to the nearest anchored plane, which would be empty. Once he got aboard, he'd have the rest of the night to figure out the best hiding place, somewhere in the back. Then just settle down and wait. Halfway home.

The riskiest part would be when the pilot and crew came aboard in the morning. But since they took off at dawn, it would probably still be dark in the plane, and the crew would be sleepy and just going through their familiar routine—all to his advantage. Nobody'd expect any trouble.

Once the engines were running and the plane was airborne and the crew were busy with their work, he'd crawl out carefully and coldcock 'em, one at a time. There'd be some kind of steel tool or piece of equipment he could use. Even his bare hands if he had to. He'd be keyed up enough to strangle them without a sound. It'd be better to find something heavy or hard to use, though. Just one vicious blow.

If he was lucky, the Jap would have a sidearm, and he'd be in business. Maybe he could knock out a few more, or maybe he'd have to shoot. But he'd still have the advantage of surprise.

Clobber the pilot, or shoot him, and grab the yoke and push the body out of the way. Stay low to keep under the radar, and head northwest, toward Vladivostok, about three hundred miles. The Russians weren't exactly U.S. allies in the Pacific—they'd never declared war on the Japanese as far as he knew. But they wouldn't welcome a Kawanishi flying in their direction. He'd have to set her down in the water before they decided to take a shot at him. Or maybe he could work the radio and establish some kind of contact and explain what he was doing. He'd figure it out. Man, if he got that far he could do anything!

G'bye, you guys, he thought. Wish me luck. He pushed back the blanket and swung his boots to the floor. Just act natural. Don't skulk around. Somebody might be awake. Guys go to the benjo all the time in the middle of the night. He casually opened the door, stepped out, shut it. Two steps down, a dozen steps on the frozen dirt around the corner to the door of the benjo.

It was clear and cold. Millions of stars, no moon. Over the fence behind the benjo he could see the glow of a few small lights from the sleeping town. Mostly blacked out because of the air raids.

Dusty walked past the benjo door, quieter now and faster. Between the fence and the benjo he was out of sight to anybody in the compound. One foot against the fence, a jump, and his hands gripped the tops of the boards, his arms easily lifting his hundred-and-twenty-pound frame up and over, his head swinging down and his feet up as he pivoted and let himself down quietly on the other side. Crouching, he sized up the scene while he felt for a big splinter in his left hand and pulled it out.

Dark houses twenty feet in front of him. To the left, fifty or sixty yards away, a small streetlight at the corner and two figures standing under it. Police. Nuts! To the right, eighty or a hundred yards, another light and a lone human silhouette. It was moving towards him. Across the street he could see no open spaces between the houses, only fences and gates. Climb over a gate into a dark yard, and then what? Stumble around in the dark, knock things over, wake up people. Uproar! The police come running and you can't see where to go.

Hurrying now, Dusty jumped and hoisted himself back over the fence. *Hope they didn't see me.* He listened. No one in the benjo. He stepped inside and stood listening to his heart beat. Not breathing hard, but his heart was thumping fast. *Shoot!* Why couldn't it have been better?

He waited for several minutes, until his heart quieted down. Then he walked carefully back to the barracks and got into bed. He stared into the darkness. If one of the street corners had been empty, he'd have gone for it.

But what about the next corner, and the next? Sure to be patrols at some of them. How many corners to the harbor? It was hopeless. He never would have made it. What would they have done to him? Nothing good. He'd heard stories. And even if he'd made it, what would they have done to the rest of the prisoners? They'd figure everybody knew about it. Everybody would suffer. Even Ito-Socho.

What had he been thinking of? Himself. Home. Food, warmth. Getting back into a Wildcat and splashing a few Zeros. But it would have been ugly for Coulter and Kelly and probably all the rest of them. The Japs would never believe that the POWs' senior officer could go AWOL without everybody knowing about it. And Ito-Socho would get it in the neck, too, no matter what he did to the prisoners. The higher-ups would think it was his fault. After everything Ito had done for them, he didn't deserve that.

Dusty didn't sleep for the rest of the night. Over and over, he replayed all the scenarios he could think of, and the answer always came out the same. He was lucky he'd stopped when he did and got back safely.

At first light he heard a Kawanishi taking off from the seaplane base. He imagined himself aboard. *Nope. Impossible.* He couldn't believe in that dream anymore. Just face another day in the brickyard.

Late in January the prisoners heard about another bombing raid on Kobe, a hundred miles west of Nagoya. The target there was the Kawasaki aircraft factory. They waited for news of a second raid on Kobe, but none came. A week later, though, air-raid sirens sounded late in the morning, and in less than an hour a flight of B-29s appeared over Yokohama and Tokyo Bay, but much lower than in the previous attacks—maybe only 10,000 or 12,000 feet, under a high overcast. Anti-aircraft fire was fierce, and it looked like the bombers were being peppered with buckshot. Dusty saw at least three planes hit. It was hard to tell with so many black puffs of flak up there and so many planes. But the ones he was sure of spewed smoke from one or two of their engine nacelles. Two of them seemed to be losing altitude as they disappeared in the north beyond Tokyo.

He counted twenty or more three-plane divisions, arriving at irregular intervals for half an hour or so. Heavy clouds of smoke rose over a part of Tokyo maybe fifteen or twenty miles away. It was hard to tell.

Then Coulter found news of a second attack on the Kawasaki factory in Kobe. It had come two weeks after the first one. The article claimed that twenty B-29s had been shot down. There was no way to tell whether it was true, but if that many planes were claimed, there must have been a lot more in the raid.

On the second Saturday in February, another big flight of B-29s came over Yokohama under high clouds as they had exactly two weeks before. It was a carbon copy of that earlier raid, even to several bombers being hit by ack-ack fire and the smoke clouds rising in the same area of Tokyo. Somebody who'd been keeping track of raids said that they almost always came on a Saturday or Sunday. Was that an accident, or was there a strategy behind it? Discussions in the barracks at night heated up, and Coulter was called on to share his supposed knowledge or expert opinion.

Then, in the middle of February, the U.S. Navy arrived! The appearance was spectacular. First, just after dawn, there were sirens from the direction of the air base at Yokosuka to the south, and some that sounded nearer. Soon they could hear distant aircraft engines—big planes, bombers or flying boats, and then from another direction the higher-pitched drone of smaller planes, fighters, coming nearer. By now the prisoners were in the compound, standing in line for the benjo. When they searched for the source of the sound, they saw flocks of Zeros diving sharply in the eastern sky and disappearing below the line of the fence. Some fighters were diving and others were chasing them. Dogfights over Tokyo Bay!

Suddenly, a drone grew into a roar and a plane flashed over the compound, pulling into a fast, climbing turn. Gull wings? An F4U! A Corsair!

Incredible! Dusty knew Corsairs had been in the pipeline. He'd seen pictures and silhouettes, but they hadn't been delivered to the Pacific by the time he'd gone down. Now there was a carrier full of them off the coast of Japan! Doolittle's B-25s had taken off from the *Hornet*, but that was three years ago! Carrier planes had never hit Japan since then, as far as Dusty knew.

Some prisoners stood frozen in place, others waved and shouted. Nobody moved toward the bomb shelter. This show was too good to miss!

Then two other fighters rose above the fence line to the east, half a mile or so away. Wildcats? Hellcats! F6Fs! Dusty knew them, too, from photos he'd seen. This was fantastic! Two new carrier fighters hitting an air base in Japan! And there were no doubt dive bombers and torpeckers hitting the shipping in the harbor, as well as the air base.

How long the melee continued Dusty had no idea, but before it ended he saw more Corsairs and Hellcats, as well as some new Japanese fighters. What a blast! Maybe this was the beginning of the end.

Only a week later—it was about eleven o'clock on a Sunday night—those prisoners still awake heard the air-raid sirens begin the rapid squawking indicating an imminent raid. Then they heard a distant deep drone that quickly grew louder. Multi-engine aircraft, a lot of them! Slipping getas on and grabbing jackets or blankets, prisoners began pouring out the barracks doors into the freezing air. B-29s—no telling how many—were over Tokyo Bay, much lower than they'd been in daylight—maybe under 10,000 feet. Searchlights were picking them out, and it looked like they were flying single file!

Bomb bay doors were open or opening, and when the bombers reached a certain point over Tokyo bombs began tumbling earthward, clusters of them lit by searchlights probing for planes. But they were small bombs, or clusters that broke apart into even smaller ones. Incendiaries, for sure! The racket from Japanese anti-aircraft batteries near the harbor was audible over the noise of the planes, and they could sometimes see the flak bursts up there among the line of planes, which were arriving at the bomb release point twenty or thirty seconds apart. More dramatic than the little black puffs of flak were the lines of tracer bullets converging on the bombers like fiery hose jets.

It was crazy! The B-29s had to be taking hits. Each one came over on exactly the same path as the one before, and the searchlights had them perfectly framed. They must be flying through a regular curtain of ack-ack fire. And still they kept coming! Some of the prisoners had started to count them, and they numbered well into the forties or fifties. They didn't think they'd counted the first ones in the line. But how many of them were being hit?

Distant flashes of light from the ground and billowing clouds of black smoke lit from below by fires confirmed that the bombs were incendiaries, not the high explosives that the daylight raiders had dropped. If civilian neighborhoods were being hit, there'd be no stopping the fires among the wooden houses. But even steel and concrete buildings would burn, with all the combustible stuff inside them.

It was some part of Tokyo, not Yokohama, that was taking the brunt of it. Despite the chilly night air and their thin clothes, the prisoners stayed outside in the compound, transfixed by the show. They watched and talked, trading opinions about the implications of what they were seeing. After at least an hour since the first ones made their runs, the B-29s were still coming.

Suddenly, an explosive flash silhouetted a bomber, and it slowed, faltered, and lurched into a dive toward the east. It was a goner. But it was incredible that they'd seen no others hit. There must have been others. Maybe they were heavily armored. More likely, they were out of sight by the time they went down. The Japanese anti-aircraft batteries couldn't have missed so many.

After a while there were no more B-29s, though the searchlights continued to rove the sky. Sounds of distant voices and sirens came intermittently, but otherwise it seemed nearly as quiet as usual. The counters said there had been at least 150 bombers! That seemed believable from what they had all seen, but still it was hard to comprehend. To the north, over Tokyo, massive clouds of smoke rose thousands of feet, tinged near the ground with wavering orange light.

When they retreated to the comparative warmth of the barracks, they talked long into the night. The low-altitude bombing would score more hits than the high-altitude, and the incendiaries would probably cause more destruction than high-explosive bombs. But coming in one after the other on the same flight path was suicidal! Once they got over their surprise, the anti-aircraft crews would be deadly. The next day a civilian brickyard worker reported that his younger brother, an anti-aircraft gunner, said that at least three B-29s had been shot down. None of the crews had survived. If they had, they would have been killed by whoever got to them first. The gunner called the bombers "birds from hell."

Exactly a week later, there was another raid on Tokyo—this one in daylight. But the planes were high, and the prisoners could see nothing because of an overcast sky. In fact, there were more cloudy or rainy days than clear ones in these winter months. With better weather, the raids might come more often. On this Sunday there were only the muffled sounds of distant explosions and anti-aircraft fire, as well as a couple of columns of black smoke, to show that a raid was under way.

It was less than a week, however, until the next raid, and it was at night again. It was more than exciting. More than frightening. It was awesome. The high winds that had been whipping through the brickyard all day, and probably through the whole area, made everything more dramatic. Nearly all the prisoners watched at first, but the chilling winds were hard to take. Some of them went and sat in the bomb shelter. Others returned to the barracks. A few stayed for the whole show, and it lasted over three hours.

The first B-29s arrived around 11 P.M. They could hear the guards shouting "Bikko!" as they had taken to calling the B-29s. There seemed to be only five or six of them, but they appeared to come from more than one direction. A few distant explosions started fires, and the wind-driven billows of smoke traveled more eastward than upward. There was a lull, then, of half an hour or more, and nearly all the prisoners had returned to the barracks. But a few minutes after midnight the main force arrived.

They sounded much louder than the night raiders two weeks ago. Prisoners spilled from the barracks again to stare at the wonder. Maybe there were more planes or maybe the high winds made a difference. Some of the prisoners thought the bombers weren't flying in a single line, as they'd seemed to do before, but were in two or three parallel lines, not very far apart, so that sometimes they seemed to be coming in two or three abreast over Tokyo Bay to the east.

But the biggest difference must have been their altitude. Everybody agreed they were lower, maybe by three or four thousand feet. Some of the men swore they couldn't be more than 5,000 feet above the bay. Others said no more than 6,000 or 7,000. In any case, the armada must have been twice the size of the previous one. From that altitude, those thousands of incendiary bombs falling like rain would absolutely obliterate their targets!

The bombers were more silvery in the searchlight beams than before. Sometimes they looked golden or even blue. Their wings were like long, sharp blades. The shower of incendiaries did indeed look like rain, or like a blizzard of tinsel from thousands of Christmas trees. They seemed to be trailing thin silver filaments, which may have stabilized their flight, like feathers on arrows. What would it have felt like to be directly under that deadly rain?

There were fighter planes up there, too, and they saw one of them crash head-on into a B-29 with a tremendous explosion. Two or three times there was a sudden glow just ahead of a bomber's tail—a hit on oxygen stored there? Twice an engine nacelle fell away from a plane. Streams of tracers crossed the sky, following the pointing fingers of the searchlights. The noise was not deafening, but it continued as a great, throbbing roar punctuated by the combined rattle of hundreds or thousands of distant automatic anti-aircraft guns.

Two hours after midnight, the B-29s were still coming, and a great incandescent column of smoke and gasses leaned eastward from over Tokyo, brighter than any of the firelit clouds from the previous firebomb raid. Most of the prisoners were too overwhelmed by the spectacle of it all, or too overcome by their thoughts of what it must be like in the hellish fire of Tokyo, to try to say anything above the noise. They watched in silence, shivering in the freezing winds even when huddled in the lee of a building. It was nearly 2:30 in the morning when the sounds of the last departing bombers disappeared. Ten minutes after that, the all-clear signals sounded.

The next day there was no newspaper for Coulter. The brickyard worker who supplied him said none had been printed. He didn't know why, but he thought the printing office might have been burned down by the fire. Much of the area where there were many factories had been destroyed. Many people had been killed, too, not by the bombs but by the fire. Whole sections of Tokyo had been burned to the ground, and people had been unable to escape the flames moving fast on the wind. Those who were alive but homeless were leaving the city, by foot or on bicycles or in oxcarts.

The wind was still blowing, and clouds of smoke continued to climb skyward and seaward from Tokyo. Some of the smoke had spread south over Yokohama. By midday it was still darker than usual in the brickyard and the barracks compound. The prisoners went on with their daily work. Inside the buildings, the civilian workers seemed subdued or distracted. They worked steadily without talking to each other.

The following day was Sunday, so there was no work in the brickyard and no news of the city or world. The sky was still smoky, but a brisk breeze from the southwest was clearing it. Many of the prisoners stayed in the barracks, napping or reading or writing letters. Four prisoners were picked by a couple of guards to do some digging beside the guards' quarters. They reported later that it was going to be a vegetable garden, not another bomb shelter. Ito-Socho told Dusty to take a few men and find out whether an old fire pump in the brickyard was working. The pump was mounted on a four-wheeled cart and consisted of a large wooden tub into which water had to be poured, and then a two-handled pump, like those on railroad handcars, pushed the water through a two-inch fabric hose. Dusty and Ivy and two other enlisted men finally got the pump working after an hour or so, but it didn't look like it would be much help if there was a lot of fire.

Conversation in the barracks had turned optimistic again. The increasing tempo and intensity of the air raids had convinced everyone that Japan couldn't hold out much longer. The distant hope of last year's slogan, "Golden Gate in '48," had been accelerated to "Home alive in '45!" Wagers and betting pools were concentrating on the most probable date for the end of the war. Noel Quinn offered to bet Dusty, and after an agreeable discussion of worthwhile stakes, they settled on this: if Noel won, Dusty would give or send him a Japanese-made telephoto lens for a Leica camera—worth at least fifty dollars. If Dusty won, Noel would send him fifty dollars' worth of the best Australian beer.

There were blustery spring rains for several days, then a couple of clear days. The newspaper began coming again, and Coulter said there were brief reports of bombings on Nagoya and Kobe. Then on Saturday, just a week after the last Tokyo firebombing, the paper reported another large and very destructive night bombing raid on Kobe.

The prisoners waited expectantly on Sunday night, but no bombers came. The next weekend was stormy, so they didn't expect any raids. The Sunday after that was the first day of April, and it dawned clear and warm after a rain shower in the early morning hours. Prisoners strolled around the compound in the sunshine. Some took their shirts off. There were no bombers overhead at midday, and none came at night, though everyone was expecting them. The quiet night came as a relief.

On Monday there was a rumor that a couple of excited prisoners picked up from worried brickyard workers. American forces had tried to invade the island of Okinawa, which was only a few hundred miles from Japan. But the Japanese army was driving the Americans back into the sea. It seemed unbelievable to the Japanese workers that enemy forces could be so close to the Japanese mainland. But they had been reassured that the enemy could go no farther. Japanese defenses would hold.

Clear skies through the week kept hopeful eyes glancing skyward. The B-29s wouldn't miss such an opportunity, and the next attack could be even bigger than the previous ones. But no bombers appeared until Saturday noon, and then they came in low, at 10,000 or 12,000 feet, under high clouds. The surprise was that when they were attacked by a swarm of Japanese fighters, a bigger swarm of American fighters suddenly appeared and started knocking the Japanese planes out of the sky. But what were they? Nobody recognized them. They had a clear bubble cockpit cover amidships and what looked like an air scoop on the belly directly below. They were silver and fast and highly maneuverable. The Japanese fighters were no match for them, and they soon fled or went down.

The B-29 target was Tokyo again, and some of the prisoners had begun wondering aloud when Yokohama would be hit. Surely there were targets in Yokohama! Why was it being spared? How much could be left of Tokyo?

The answers to both questions came the following weekend. Around eleven o'clock on Friday night the low-flying B-29s came in, heading for

Tokyo. Searchlights fanned the sky and picked them out. Anti-aircraft fire looked heavier and more deadly than ever. There were Japanese fighters up there, too, and the American bombers kept coming and coming. Dusty saw three of them get hit; one just exploded in the air, and the other two trailed flames. There was a brief lull after midnight, and then another wave of B-29s arrived. The plane counters reported about a hundred bombers in the first wave. The third wave finished its run and departed about three o'clock in the morning. Three hundred B-29s!

The huge illuminated smoke clouds over Tokyo indicated that there was still a lot to burn in the city. One area was much brighter than the rest, and the clouds of flame and smoke billowed upward at an amazing rate, climbing to heights impossible to estimate.

But Sunday night it was the turn of Yokohama, along with an area just to the north that Ito-Socho had told Dusty was called Kawasaki. The familiar scenario was repeated—the bombers arriving half an hour before midnight and meeting searchlights, heavy anti-aircraft fire, and many fighter planes. Dusty thought he saw five or six B-29s get hit. Four of them fell apart in the air. But the incendiary bombs were hitting close this time. The noise was like strings of huge firecrackers half a mile away. The whole area immediately east and northeast of the compound was in flames—for how many miles it was impossible to tell. No bombs came within half a mile, as far as they could see, but winds from the north were blowing smoke and flames in their direction.

There was no sleeping that night. Between five and six o'clock, morning light began to penetrate the clouds of smoke, and guards reported that a fire was getting close to the north fence. Dusty directed his pumping crew to haul the pump wagon closer to the fence, and a line of other prisoners formed a bucket brigade to refill the pumper's tub if it began to run dry. Sergeant Ito moved about the compound and into the brickyard, receiving reports from guards and directing them off again on missions. About an hour after first light, Ito-Socho told Dusty that flames were within fifty meters of the fence but advancing slowly. Fortunately, there was not much wind.

Dusty decided to test his crew. Two men began pumping, their heads and shoulders bobbing steadily up and down with the pump handles. Two other men held the hose, directing the nozzle toward the board fence, no more than ten feet away. The pumpers kept working for two or three minutes, but nothing happened. They paused and looked to Dusty for direction. He urged them on again, just as the hose carriers looked back over their shoulders. Beyond them, Dusty saw the head of a guard named Hyashi appear over the fence, looking into the compound. Just then, as the pumpers increased their tempo, a jet of water surged from the hose nozzle and struck Hyashi full in the face. He disappeared, and the hose carriers, who'd felt the water coming through and turned back to see where it was going, half collapsed in sputtering convulsions. They barely managed to keep the hose aimed toward the fence.

Dusty ordered a halt and, smothering a grin, glanced back at Ito-Socho. The sergeant had turned away, both hands cupped over his mouth, and was walking slowly toward his quarters. Dusty congratulated his crew on a successful test. They were ready for the fire.

The fire arrived from several directions and at several points along the fence. The pump crews labored heroically, and volunteers replaced them every five minutes or so. When one portion of the fence was thoroughly soaked and the fire seemed momentarily stopped, they moved to another section. The bucket brigade followed them, conveying water from outlets on the other side of the compound. But the fire quickly burned through the wooden boards and flames licked out toward the barracks. The hose was turned on the barracks, and several prisoners moved in on the burning fence boards with rakes and shovels, knocking them to the ground. A corner and part of one side of the bathhouse was singed and blackened, but the flames didn't take hold.

Working their way through the broken fence, the rake and shovel crew beat at the flames on the edges of the burned grass and shrubs outside. Before long, the immediate danger was over, but here and there through clouds of smoke they caught glimpses of a crumbled and blackened wasteland where there had once been a city.

No one had thought about breakfast—the usual black gunk and hot water—or about the morning assembly. Too much was going on. Then a guard told Dusty that Ito-Socho wanted him. Sergeant Ito startled Dusty by telling him that all the prisoners were going to be moved immediately. Why and where to were not explained. Dusty was to call an assembly so the announcement could be made.

Dusty called the ragged formation to attention and the ritual bow was made in the direction of the emperor's palace. Then Sergeant Ito spoke to the prisoners in Japanese, and a guard translated. All prisoners were to be ready to leave the compound in one hour. They would march to the train station and make a long journey. Each prisoner would take with him only what he could easily carry. Everything unnecessary would be left behind.

As they assembled their belongings in the barracks, the apprehension was something new. Some prisoners were optimistic—almost any change was welcome, and maybe it meant the end of the war was near. Besides, they didn't want to be around when the next firebombing came. Others were worried. Maybe they were being taken somewhere to be killed. Maybe they'd be put in work gangs to clean up the bombed areas or carry away bodies or build more air-raid shelters. In any case, Sergeant Ito wouldn't be looking after them. Life at the brickyard might look like a picnic in retrospect.

A guard notified Dusty that it was time to assemble the prisoners. When they were formed up in the compound, Ito-Socho appeared, and after an exchange of salutes with Dusty, he indicated that he would march with them to the train station. That was good news. Dusty wondered whether he was concerned about people taking out their anger on the prisoners for the bombings they'd suffered. There had been rumors that surviving crew members of downed B-29s had been beaten and even killed. Or maybe Sergeant Ito was as sorry as Dusty was to see a fairly trouble-free period come to an end.

Two guards led the way, and others brought up the rear. There were still about ninety prisoners in the formation as they walked, two by two, out the gate and through the blackened, battered streets of Yokohama. The sky was gray.

Hardly anything functional was still standing. Here and there stood charred and broken parts of buildings. In two or three completely demolished buildings stood steel safes, the only things left unburned. In nearly every direction you could see for hundreds of yards with few obstructions except these fragments and a few poles carrying broken telephone or power lines. Smoke rose from smoldering debris, but flames were visible in only a couple of places, at a distance. Maybe most of the fires had burned out because there was nothing left for them to feed on.

They saw no bodies, which was surprising. People must have been killed, unless somehow the whole area had been previously evacuated or everyone had made it safely to air raid shelters. At a distance they saw small groups of people moving slowly among the ruins. Strangely, a streetcar moved smoothly along unobstructed tracks, and later, half a mile away, a train was heading north.

Ito-Socho walked silently beside the column, showing no emotion that Dusty could detect. He was wearing his cap and full army uniform. There was no talking in the line of prisoners. They just looked, taking it all in, wondering what was coming next.

After an hour or so, they turned at an angle to follow two train tracks leading toward a large building that looked half collapsed. It turned out to be the station. Coming closer, they could see a couple of lines of train cars, with a locomotive at the far end of the closest one. When the guards brought them to a halt between the remains of the station and the standing trains, Ito-Socho indicated to Dusty that he wanted the prisoners to face him. Dusty gave the command, and they stood waiting. Ito looked up and down the double line of men, slowly making eye contact with them. Then he saluted smartly. Dusty returned the salute for them. Ito took two steps forward and extended his hand to Dusty. As Dusty took it, Ito said only, "Sayonara," then turned and walked away, back toward the brickyard.

After a wait of half an hour, they were loaded on a train, where they sat quietly for a long time, talking very little. There was nothing new to say. They had shared the same experiences for a year or more. They knew nothing about their future. Many of them napped, or tried to. No one had slept last night. Late in the afternoon intermittent rays of sunlight began to flicker through the windows. Then the car lurched, and after a pause, they began to move slowly toward the night and—maybe—the next day.

TEN

WAR'S END

The train traveled slowly through the night, lurching and swaying, sometimes stopping for a while. The prisoners tried to sleep, leaning against each other or stretched out on the wooden floor with an arm or a folded piece of clothing for a pillow. A few dim lights were just enough to see by. At each end of the car a guard sat braced against the door, cradling a rifle and dozing. The brickyard prisoners were spread among two or three cars. Whether there were other passengers Dusty couldn't tell, but the train seemed short, maybe four or five cars behind the engine.

For an hour or more in the middle of the night the engine strained on a series of upgrades. Then there was easier, smoother movement, as though they'd crossed a mountain pass and were heading downhill. Morning light came slowly, but those who were awake could gradually make out mountains to the right, where the sky was lightest. They were heading north.

After a while buildings began to appear along the track, and the train slowed as they moved through a good-sized town. At what was apparently the center, there were several five- or six-story buildings among many smaller ones, spread out over a few square miles. There was no sign of bomb damage, and people seemed to be going about their business normally.

Then there were more tracks and a station, where they stopped. Dusty heard one of the guards say something like "Nagaoka." Maybe that was the name of the town. After they had sat for a few minutes, the door at one end of the car opened and a couple of guards brought in some buckets from which they served tea and rice. Paper bowls were passed among the prisoners the length of the car.

In half an hour the train started up again, and they settled down to stare out the windows or sleep some more. Another couple of hours passed as they moved across flat countryside among fields and rice paddies, a range of mountains still to their right. Then they began to have glimpses of water ahead and to the left—evidently the ocean. They seemed to be traveling on a coastal plain. They entered a large town again, maybe larger than the last. They passed through one station without stopping and came to a halt in another, alongside a long wooden loading platform with a railing. A guard announced, "Niigata!" and they left the train and trekked in a double column three or four miles up a dirt road to a group of single-story and two-story wooden buildings, similar to the barracks at the brickyard. This was their new prison camp.

It was bigger than the stadium camp in Yokohama. Prisoners already there, mostly British from Hong Kong and a few Americans, confirmed that the town was called Niigata, and that it was the only major port on the Japanese mainland that hadn't been bombed. There were between nine hundred and a thousand prisoners. Work details went mainly to the dockyards, but there was also a coal yard from which ships were refueled, and a steel foundry. The camp's commandant was a Lieutenant Kato, and he was tough. You didn't want to tangle with him. The ranking prisoner was an American Army major named Fellows. He was a nice guy, very helpful.

Dusty's group was directed to a single-story barracks with low bed frames and tatamis, like those at the brickyard. But they were advised to use the two blankets they were issued—British woolens, brought from Hong Kong—to rig a hammock of some kind that would keep them off the floor and less vulnerable to bites from the fleas that infested the place. There were no separate quarters for officers. Dusty and Lou and Coulter and Doc Kelly settled in near each other.

In the middle of their first afternoon at Niigata, the new prisoners received a visit from Major Fellows and from a tall Canadian named Arthur Rance, who said he'd been with the Hong Kong Volunteers. Rance was friendly and full of information and advice. He stayed more than an hour, giving them an orientation to the place, while Major Fellows, after a short speech of welcome, went on about his business. Fellows, Rance wanted them to know, was renowned in the camp for his weekly lectures on the U.S. Civil War. He was an expert on the subject. The guards were neither hostile nor friendly, for the most part. They kept to themselves, though they were sometimes willing to talk with Rance, who spoke Japanese "well enough," as he said. The commandant, however, was a by-the-numbers army officer, and if the guards took a prisoner to him for any reason, the punishment was harsh. There was a story that either he or the previous commandant of the camp had personally beaten a prisoner for stealing something, and then had him tied out in the compound for a whole day in freezing weather. The prisoner had developed gangrene in his legs and had died from it.

What Rance knew for sure was that a prisoner named Frank Spears had escaped from the camp by going over the wall at night, but he had been captured the next day and brought back to the commandant. Kato was furious, but he didn't beat Spears. He just told him "I will kill you" if he ever tried to escape again. And Spears believed he meant it.

One of the brickyard prisoners asked Rance if it was true what he'd heard from another Niigata inmate—that there was a big pit outside the compound that would be a mass grave for the prisoners if the Allies invaded Japan.

Rance smiled. "Oh, the air-raid shelter?" he said. "That's what the guards call it. Nobody believes them. It wouldn't shelter anyone from a snowfall. I don't know. We hope for the best."

That wasn't reassuring. It dovetailed with other old rumors about the fate of POWs in case of an invasion, and with more recent stories they'd heard about the treatment of downed B-29 crews. But Dusty couldn't imagine Ito-Socho ordering his prisoners executed. He'd been upset and angry when their Red Cross parcels had been rifled. And the civilian workers at the brickyard had never shown any hostility to the prisoners, not even after the firebombings. Still, it all depended on unpredictable circumstances and who happened to be giving the orders. Hoping for the best was all they could do.

Well after lights out the first night, Dusty woke up to the sound of excited voices. Then he heard the familiar distant drone of aircraft engines.

"B-29s!" several voices exclaimed.

Most of the prisoners must have hit the deck simultaneously, climbing or falling out of their hammocks and stumbling in the dark toward the barracks doors. As they poured into the courtyard between their barracks and the one opposite, some planes were passing directly over the camp. Their bomb bay doors were open and they were heading for the harbor. They couldn't be higher than two thousand feet, but they were invisible until the searchlights found them. They were PB4Y Liberators, not B-29s! It was impossible to guess how many. A few anti-aircraft guns opened up, without any apparent effect. Parachutes were visible in the searchlight beams, at a distance of three or four miles, but they seemed to be attached to bombs, not people. They waited for the aerial bursts.

But there were no explosions. It was strange. The bombs couldn't all be duds. Maybe they had some kind of delayed action fuses. The Liberators disappeared into the night, and the prisoners waited for the explosions to come—in vain. It didn't make sense. Disappointed, they trooped slowly back into the barracks and crawled into their hammocks. There were a few quiet conversations, and then they tried to go back to sleep.

The explanation came late the next morning. The sound of a terrific explosion came from the harbor. They rushed to the fence and could see brilliant pulses of light flashing one after another and fiery streamers flying in all directions from a ship in the middle of the harbor. It must have been carrying munitions! Multiple thunderclaps continued for several minutes, and billows of smoke rose above the harbor. Then they could see the bow rise, and the ship slid quickly beneath the water. Cheers rang out. It was a mine! The bombers had dropped mines in the harbor and the ship had run into one. With any luck a few more would blow up. But there were no more explosions that day.

There was another the next day, though, and at intervals through the week. A number of ships hit mines, and several were apparently sunk, though it was hard to tell how many because of all the smoke over the harbor.

The consensus after the raid was that Niigata was no longer protected by its distance from the bomber bases, wherever they were. The new prisoners were instant experts among the older ones, confidently predicting that there would be another raid in a day or two. That's the way they'd seen it happen over Tokyo and Yokohama. In fact, it was three days—or nights—before the next raid, and this time it was B-29s, coming in a little higher than the Liberators, but dropping incendiaries and getting two direct hits on ships in the harbor and leaving much of the port in flames.

Since the long gradual slope down to the harbor wasn't heavily built up, scuttlebutt agreed that the camp was probably safe from bombings, except for an accident or fluke. And they had grandstand seats. They looked forward to repeat performances.

The fleas were a constant nuisance, and nobody escaped their bites. Out in the compound or in the barracks you were constantly swatting or scratching your feet and ankles and wondering if you'd eventually develop an immunity. The makeshift blanket hammocks helped at night. But then with warmer weather came the mosquitoes, and they were worse here than at the stadium or the brickyard. You brushed and swatted them automatically all day long, and at night you covered up.

There were frequent outbreaks of amoebic dysentery, and the benjos stunk worse than usual. When it was your turn to suffer, you hoped it would be a mild case and ate a watered-down version of the cooked barley until it went away. One building served as a kind of sick bay. If you were really miserable or too weak to get out of bed, you could go there for a few days. Alex Kelly spent most of his time there, helping a couple of other doctors. He said there were hardly any medical supplies available. A certain number of prisoners died from one thing or another, and the doctors felt frustrated and helpless.

In late June another contingent of prisoners arrived. They turned out to be from a camp in Kawasaki, apparently not far from the brickyard. Most of them had worked at a rail freight yard, and they said the daily workload had been increasing steadily for months, except for some interruptions after the biggest incendiary raids. They'd been burned out of their camp eventually, just the way the brickyard prisoners had been.

Lou Farran said he felt lost without his sewing machine, and Coulter said he understood. He missed his accordion. They both seemed to find ways to fight off boredom, though, partly by making acquaintances with other prisoners. Dusty saw less of them than he had at the brickyard. There were ten times as many prisoners here.

In July, Art Rance shared some bad news with a few of the officers. Frank Spears, who'd been warned by Lieutenant Kato that he'd be killed if he tried to escape again, had evidently cracked despite warnings from other prisoners, and he'd tried again—and failed. A guard who'd helped bring him back told Art that Kato had ordered Spears to be taken out in a small yard behind the commandant's office, and there he'd borrowed a rifle with a bayonet from a guard. Spears's hands were tied behind him, and with guards holding him from each side, Kato had run him through with the bayonet three or four times. Major Fellows knew about it. Kato had told him to continue carrying Spears on reports as "absent and confined in a military penitentiary."

A few days later Rance reported more bad news. A guard had told him that the commandant had received an official order from a very high-level officer, Field Marshal Terauchi. It said something like "At the moment the enemy lands on Honshu, all prisoners will be killed." The news came as no surprise, but it was depressing anyway. Did they have any chance? As the word spread among the prisoners, there were serious discussions. If they heard that they were going to be killed, couldn't they take the guards by surprise and all break out of the camp together? But some argued that they wouldn't stand a chance against active military units in the area. Even if they were killed, though, it would mean that Japan had been invaded and would soon be defeated. That would be worth dying for.

Barley and rice rations were cut to one a day, and they heard that even the guards were getting less to eat. A prisoner who worked in the camp kitchen said that some guards were shooting rats that prowled the camp at night and bringing them to the kitchen to be cooked.

One evening just before dark Dusty and five other prisoners were taken by three guards in a truck to a sandy beach along the ocean. There they met several civilians, apparently fishermen, who had a small boat with a large fish net coiled in it. Two guards stayed on shore to supervise the prisoners, while one went in the boat with the civilians. While the prisoners held a line attached to one end of the net, the boat headed straight out from the beach. About thirty yards offshore it turned, and the men on board threw out the net as the boat moved parallel to the beach. Then after forty yards or so it turned back toward the beach, trailing a line to the end of the net. There was enough light from the sky to see the shadowy figures in the boat riding the gentle swells.

The second line was handed to another group of three prisoners, and all began to haul on the lines, pulling the net in. The water inside the net began to boil as it got close to the beach, and then they could see swarms of phosphorescent fish thrashing around in it. The fishermen waded out above their knees and began grabbing fish and throwing them into wooden tubs that were floated and then dragged up the beach as the net continued to be hauled in. The fish, mostly eight or ten inches long, looked like bonito, smaller cousins of tuna. The next day, pieces of boiled fish arrived with the prisoners' bowls of barley.

The following week, on another fishing trip, Dusty sensed that something unusual was up, because of excited talk among the guards. He could make out "bi-nijuku" and a few other words, but it didn't make sense until a guard talked to him as they were working together throwing fish into a tub. With an elaborate pantomime and a few words of pidjin English, he told Dusty that a single *bi-nijuku* had dropped a "new invention" over a big city in the south, and the whole city had been destroyed. Thousands of civilians had perished. Looking worried, the guard pointed at Dusty and indicated "Soon I will be your prisoner."

Dusty was unsure how seriously he could take that, but it certainly sounded better than "I will be your executioner." He hoped the guard was right.

For a few days there was more than the usual anxiety and tension in the camp, among the prisoners as well as the guards. Rumors about the "new invention," about an American invasion, about being moved to another camp, continued to feed arguments in the barracks. A breeze from the shore nearly every day gave some relief from the heat, but the fleas and mosquitoes were worse than ever. In the meantime, there was another night fire raid on the harbor, this time with PB4Ys again. As the smoke drifted over the camp all the next day, Dusty wondered what there was left to bomb. The Liberators had a free hand—no fighter planes had gone up to meet them, and the ack-ack looked thin, as if the gunners were firing only occasionally instead of throwing up a barrage of flak.

A week after Dusty's unusual conversation with the guard, the prisoners were confined to the barracks the whole morning. Shortly before midday, all the guards lined up at attention at one end of the compound, near the commandant's quarters and the gate. They were hard to see from the barracks, but they appeared to be bowing. The prisoners could hear a strange, high voice that seemed to be coming from a radio, but those who understood some Japanese looked puzzled and shook their heads. Even Art Rance said he could make out only a few words. Then they could hear some music, like a military band.

For a few minutes after the radio voice stopped, the guards stayed more or less in formation. Some of them seemed to be talking quietly to each other. Then they began drifting away, disappearing one by one around the corners of buildings. No one came to say the prisoners could leave the barracks.

About midafternoon they heard that Major Fellows had been called to the commandant's office. Then they heard that he'd told a dozen or so prisoners to get buckets of white paint from one of the supply rooms and climb up on the roofs of two of the buildings. Lieutenant Kato had said they were to paint on the roofs in large letters *P W*. He had not explained the reason. But many prisoners believed it was intended as protection against bombers—at least bombers that came in the daytime and were flying low enough to see the letters. Why was this being done just now?

While the painting crews were at work, the rest of the prisoners decided to leave the barracks if the guards didn't object. But only a few guards remained. Most of them had disappeared. A prisoner who'd been working in the kitchen that morning said the chief cook and a couple of assistants had been called to the formation but never came back. He guessed that he and a few other prisoners would prepare the day's meal themselves. If the cooks didn't come back by the next day, maybe there would be two meals.

Lieutenant Kato was still in his office or living quarters, but he refused to see Major Fellows again. Some prisoners checked the main gate and found it was unguarded but still locked. They said they were going to break the lock after dark. Some of the remaining guards were carrying rifles. The day's meal—rice and slices of some kind of boiled vegetable—was served late in the afternoon. As daylight faded, the barracks were buzzing with questions and guesses, some plausible, others unbelievable.

Shortly after first light the next day, the news spread. The war was over! Japan had surrendered! The emperor had announced it in his radio broadcast—that was the strange voice they'd heard on the loudspeaker. Art Rance and several others had gone out of the camp and found some civilians who'd explained it to them. But there were still questions.

Were they in danger of being killed by hostile Japanese? Had Allied troops already invaded? How could they get more news? What should they do? With so many prisoners in the camp, and so many rumors, you couldn't be sure what was happening. They heard that some of the prisoners had found the old civilian man who daily emptied the benjos with buckets on an oxcart, and they'd bought the starving, decrepit ox from him with a few yen they'd saved. Then they'd slaughtered and butchered the ox, and it was being roasted over a fire on the other side of the camp.

For a couple of days nothing much happened. The prisoners were unsure what to do. They'd been confined so long that staying put was a habit. If they left the camp, where would they go? Wouldn't American reconnaissance planes find them quicker if they stayed where they were? They continued the daily routine of the camp—meals, cleaning the barracks, lying in their hammocks—assuming that something would happen soon. Dusty noticed that the Japanese flag that had flown from a pole over the commandant's quarters was gone. Some of the prisoners had taken possession of a small store of rifles and ammunition left by the departing guards. What use they would be was hard to imagine. No armed guards remained, only a few who had surrendered to Major Fellows. Lieutenant Kato was gone.

Scavenging parties in nearby neighborhoods brought back some chickens and a couple of pigs. The Japanese civilians gave them up with no resistance, even though it looked as if they had little to eat themselves. Senior officers in the camp insisted that civilians must be treated respectfully, and there must be no looting or violence. Any food that was "liberated" should be in the nature of "excess." But with the news of victory and the anticipation of freedom, appetites were growing.

On the fourth or fifth morning after the Japanese surrender, they could hear a flight of small planes approaching, and then they arrived, wheeling in a great circle at a thousand feet or less—SBD scout bombers and F6F Hellcats. It looked like a good part of an air group. Several planes swooped low and dropped small bundles. They turned out to be tee-shirts wrapped around handwritten notes saying that B-29s would drop food and other supplies soon, and in the meantime these planes would be back as soon as they could pick up a few things from their carrier. On a second pass, five or six pairs of shoes came tumbling down—the high-top black work shoes usually worn by gunners and other air crewmen. The prisoners cheered and waved, and several of the planes rocked their wings in answer.

The next day they were back, with more and bigger bundles to drop, laundry bags holding candy bars, cigarettes, miscellaneous pieces of clothing, and even a few cigars. There were notes saying the goods had been contributed by sailors aboard the carrier and wishing all the POWs good luck in getting home soon. Dusty was happy to get two packs of Lucky Strikes. He gave one of them to Lou.

The day after that, there was manna from heaven. About ten o'clock they heard the distant drone of multi-engine planes, growing steadily louder. Then they could see the B-29s coming over low—about 2,000 feet—and parachutes opening behind them. There were two of the silver beauties, and everybody in the camp was out in the spaces between the buildings, waving and cheering.

The parachutes came down fast. It was obvious their loads were heavy—huge cardboard cartons and metal drums or cannisters. The bombardiers were good! Nearly all the parachuted cargo was headed right for the camp. A few bundles were going to land outside, but they'd be close. Then one of the steel drums hit the roof of a building with a tremendous crash, and they knew it had gone right through the roof. They watched the descending loads carefully, making sure they stayed clear of where they were landing. A couple more drums or boxes landed on roofs, and it sounded like they all went through.

In a few minutes the bundles were all on the ground, and men were swarming over them, prying them open. Some of the cardboard cartons had already broken open, spilling their contents. There were boxes of candy bars—Hershey's and Baby Ruth—and whole chickens that looked frozen. Coffee, sugar, powdered eggs, even tin cans of pressed meat—Spam or something like that. The metal drums and cannisters held cocoa powder and fruit salad—at least some of them did. Dusty didn't scramble to open tins or boxes. There were already more than enough guys doing that.

But he wandered through the compound, watching the openings, watching the men with their hands in the cartons and cannisters passing the loot to those behind them as fast as they could, or even tossing smaller boxes back over their heads. It was another prison camp Christmas, early but much more abundant than the Red Cross parcels they'd gotten at the stadium camp and the brickyard. Some of the big cartons contained

Marine Corps combat boots, leather ones, and they were prizes, as long as they fit you, more or less. There were packages of tee-shirts and skivvies and socks, and toilet articles of all kinds. Dusty heard there were boxes of medical supplies like sulfa powder and bandages and vaseline and rubbing alcohol. He hoped nobody would drink the alcohol. A couple of days ago six men on a scrounging mission outside the camp had found some cans of ethylene glycol—antifreeze—and, desperate for any kind of alcohol, glugged it down. When they started to cramp up, a medic in camp diagnosed the problem. Now they were all in the sick bay, probably dying.

Under the direction of Major Fellows and other officers, most of the parachuted supplies were brought to one of the central barracks, where they were organized and then shared out among the men in a reasonable facsimile of fairness. Dusty collected a few pieces of clothing and a box of Baby Ruths, and another box with toothpaste and a toothbrush, a safety razor and a small jar of shaving cream, as well as a small towel and a washcloth. There was no sense accumulating more than he needed.

Dinner that night was different than it had been for years. Instead of rice or black gunk, there were scrambled eggs, and even salt and pepper. There was a kind of hardtack that wasn't bad if you could find some grape or apple jelly to put on it. Coulter handed Dusty a couple of slices of canned meat to go with his scrambled eggs. That was a welcome addition. For dessert there was a lot of fruit salad, and most men ate a couple of bowls of it. Cocoa, too—delicious even with water instead of milk.

Another prisoner told Dusty that he'd eaten a piece of the roasted ox—or tried to. He'd gnawed on it, anyway. "It was the toughest piece of meat I ever had," he said. "But it tasted pretty good."

The next morning they heard that a steel drum had slipped out of its parachute harness and landed outside the camp, bouncing through a house and killing two Japanese civilians. That was bad news, even if it was nothing compared to casualties from a bombing raid. Everybody would be looking sharp the next time the bikko came over. Watches were posted, and when they came again that afternoon all the prisoners cleared out of the camp and watched from a safe distance. The parachuted boxes and drums were much the same as before. Only one hit a building this time, a benjo, but luckily nobody was in it. The boxes that had crashed through the barracks roofs hadn't done much damage, and it didn't matter, anyway. Nobody was going to live there much longer.

After another B-29 drop, there was a navy sortie, this time two divisions of F4U Corsairs, swooping low and slow so the pilots could throw bags of goodies—candy and cigarettes—and bundles of printed messages into the camp. The messages all said the same thing:

USS Lexington, August 27, 1945

To Former American Prisoners of War:

Hearty success in your approaching liberation, which will occur tomorrow in conjunction with the landing of airborne troops of the United States Army at Tokyo. The Marines and Navy will follow shortly into Tokyo Bay. So it looks like there will be a hot time along the ginza any minute now. . . .

Wonderful news! But it was a week and a half now since the end of the war. What did it mean, their liberation "will occur tomorrow"? If troops were landing only in Tokyo, it could be several days, at least, before they got to Niigata. Anxiety and impatience were growing, but most of the men seemed to be content with filling their bellies and enjoying their freedom.

The next day there was no sign of anything that looked like liberation. In the barracks and around the compound some men were finding things to keep busy with, but many were just loafing, waiting for something to happen. They were confident they'd be taken care of in good time. The great war machine that had defeated Japan might take a few days or weeks to gear down to dealing with postwar problems.

Three days after the messages were dropped, four U.S. Navy planes buzzed the camp. There was wild cheering. When he got to the courtyard, Dusty could see two TBF torpedo bombers and two F6F fighters circling the camp at less than a thousand feet. Some prisoners had pieces of paper the planes had dropped. The F6Fs—Grumman Hellcats—came back over slowly, losing altitude fast. It looked like they were going to land nearby. They disappeared behind a line of trees a quarter of a mile away. In a couple of minutes the torpeckers followed them. Fifteen or twenty prisoners were already out of the camp, trotting toward where they'd landed.

Twenty or thirty minutes later the visitors appeared with their enthusiastic escort. There were four pilots in flight coveralls, two aviation crewmen, and two navy officers in white uniforms. One of the officers introduced himself as Commander Harold Stassen.* He said the navy was well aware of the large number of "former Prisoners of War"—Dusty liked the sound of that—and was doing everything possible to see that relief was delivered immediately. The Tokyo area was overcrowded with Allied

---

*Governor of Minnesota since 1938, Harold Stassen (1907–2001) resigned in 1943 to join the navy and become chief of staff to Admiral William Halsey. After the war, he was president of the University of Pennsylvania from 1948 to 1953 and a "perennial candidate" for many high offices, including president of the United States (nine times).

men and materiel coming ashore, and General Douglas MacArthur, the Supreme Commander of Allied Forces in the Pacific, wanted the former POWs to stay in their camps for a few days until the congestion eased. Then they'd all be moved to the Tokyo harbor area, given a medical checkup, and repatriated just as soon as possible. That was another term Dusty liked—"repatriated."

Commander Stassen said that on Sunday, September 2, the peace treaty would be signed aboard the battleship *Missouri* in Tokyo Bay. That was just three days away. By then everything should be secured in the Tokyo area, and probably convoys of trucks would arrive soon afterward in Niigata to move the men there. Commander Stassen repeated General MacArthur's request that they sit tight for a few days.

But Dusty wondered if it would be only a few days. With thousands of troops and vehicles and supplies coming ashore in a limited area, and having to be dispersed, it could stay crowded for weeks. It was hard to say how long the prisoners—the *former* prisoners—would be willing to wait.

Commander Stassen left shortly, saying he had to ferry to his carrier an injured American POW coming from a camp fifty kilometers south, at Naoetsu. A bale of boots dropped from a B-29 had gone through the roof of a benjo—Commander Stassen said "head"—and clobbered him. Somehow a phone call from another POW at the camp had gotten through to Stassen, and he'd promised to pick up the injured man if he could be trucked to Niigata. This had been accomplished. The Niigata prisoners heard the story with a mixture of amusement and amazement. They swapped ideas about how they could qualify for aerial ambulance service.

The two F6F pilots announced that they were going to stay overnight and fly back to their carrier in the morning. They wanted to see for themselves how their mates had been living, and they had a lot of news to share. They were cheered and led off to the nearest barracks.

In the morning it was raining hard, and Dusty heard that the field or strip of road where the planes had landed was too muddy for the pilots to take off. They'd have to stay until things dried out. The rain gradually diminished during the morning, and then in the early afternoon the weather began to clear. The pilots went to look at the field and evaluate the possibility of taking off. They decided to wait a few hours, and then in late afternoon they took off successfully, with plenty of daylight to get back to their carrier.

The next day was Saturday, the first of September. The war had been over for two weeks. The peace treaty would be signed the next day, and then in a day or two the trucks would show up. Maybe. If not, something would have to be done.

All day Monday, Dusty could sense a growing expectancy through-out the camp. The men were ready to leave, ready to go home. There were no bags to pack, just ragtag little bundles of minimal possessions sitting here and there on the barracks floors, or hanging from nails on the walls. Dusty had his journal, which he hadn't written in since leaving the brick-yard, a toothbrush and razor, two or three extra pieces of clothing, a cou-ple of candy bars. Everything could be tied up inside the jacket Lou had made for him from his old flight coveralls. The heavy wool blanket he'd been using as a hammock could stay behind. So could the overcoat.

No trucks on Monday, no word of any kind. By Tuesday noon, more men were beginning to agree with those who'd been urging action for days. By two days after the peace was signed, five days since Commander Stassen's visit, they should have heard *something*. Arguments became live-lier, and those who'd been advocating patience, like Lou, had grown quiet. Various plans of action were proposed. By the end of the day the senior officers announced their decision: in the morning the prisoners would march to the Niigata train station and get on a train for Tokyo.

ELEVEN

HOMEWARD BOUND

It was Wednesday morning, September 5, 1945, when Dusty began his homeward journey. The war had been over for three weeks, and his patience, like everyone else's, had run out. He didn't need to be at the head of the column of a thousand "former POWs" marching down the road to the railway station in Niigata. It was enough to be moving. He and Lou walked together. Coulter was somewhere up ahead. Two long trains were sitting at the station. Dusty was confident that Major Fellows and Art Rance and some of the other senior officers or Japanese-speaking non-coms were taking charge of things. All he needed to do was get aboard the train. He and Lou followed a couple of other men into one car and found spaces near each other on the benches that were quickly filling up. There were no arguments over seating, no pushing or shoving. They'd lived together too long in close quarters to be pushy.

Either the train would eventually start moving, or somebody would tell them to move to another train. This train was pointed in the right direction. Some men lit up cigarettes they'd brought along, and the car got smoky. Dusty lit one himself, and was glad he was sitting near an open window. From across the car, Lou smiled and puffed away too.

The train shuddered, jerked a couple of times, and slowly began to move. They were on their way, heading south. He remembered little of the trip north from Yokohama, over the mountains at night. He couldn't remember the name of the last town they'd gone through before getting to Niigata. Some of the men in the car talked quietly to each other. Others just sat, looking out a window or at nothing, or dozing, leaning against the side of the car or each other.

Eventually, word was passed through the car that Art Rance and some others had climbed into the train's engine and told the engineer he was taking them all to Tokyo. There was no objection, but half a dozen Japanese passengers already aboard decided to get off when all the ex-POWs started getting on.

The train stayed on the coastal plain and came to a town called Nagaoka. Maybe that was the name he'd forgotten. There was some noise and confusion on the station platform. It looked like other POWs standing there. Sure enough! They waved and smiled and began climbing aboard. It was getting crowded, but nobody seemed to mind. Everybody squeezed closer.

Dusty struck up a conversation with one of the newcomers, a U.S. Navy pilot who'd been in a prisoner-of-war camp called Naoetsu, several miles south. They'd done the same thing as the Niigata group, commandeering a train that morning, but it had turned out to be headed in the wrong direction, and at Nagaoka turning around or switching was too complicated, so they'd decided to change trains. The man's name was Chuck Bransfield; his grandfather was the founder of the Miller Beer Company. He and Dusty swapped information for a while, and then as the train started up again, they grew quiet.

The train turned inland toward the mountains, and as the grade increased, it began losing speed. Everyone was hoping the extra passengers wouldn't turn out to be too heavy a load. Not only was Dusty's car full to bursting, but some men were hanging out the windows. But the engine chugged steadily, and even though in some stretches they weren't moving more than ten miles an hour, they were headed in the right direction. Dusty had a chance to see some of the mountain scenery he'd missed in the darkness on the way north, but his thoughts were racing far ahead of the train and eastward across an ocean.

The train picked up speed on the downward slope, and there were a few cheers and hurrahs. A couple of bottles were being passed through the car, and Dusty was invited to take a couple of swigs from one. "Saki," said his neighbor. Evidently it had been brought aboard at Nagaoka. Food was also being shared, mainly candy bars. The saki was warm, but it tasted good. Anything tasted good after years of black gunk and white rice.

The train was making good speed downhill, and on some of the curves the cars swayed more than Dusty was comfortable with. At one point there were shouts and then laughter from the car behind them, and a while later word was passed forward that an American aviator had gotten blind drunk on saki and fallen out an open door on a curve. It wasn't clear whether anything was done to rescue him. Late in the afternoon the train came out of the mountains and into the Tokyo area. At first things looked normal, but then there were areas that were completely burned out, like the part of Yokohama Dusty had seen leaving the brickyard. Then normal-looking stretches again, and one burned-out area from the tracks as far as they could see. Finally they came to a train station not far from Tokyo Bay, and there the train stopped. There were U.S. Army Military Police with their black and white armbands all around the area, and troops moving through on foot and in four-by-four trucks. MPs waved the former POWs off the train and directed them down a street toward the harbor area. They straggled along, all in a cheerful mood now, joking and kidding each other. They were back among friends at last, and on their way home. Dusty lost track of Chuck Bransfield.

In the dock area the POWs were assembling near a warehouse. A couple of MPs were talking to an army officer who was shaking his head and looking doubtfully at the bedraggled former prisoners. Shortly one of the MPs approached them and announced that they should stay where they were. "We weren't expecting you today," he said. "But that's okay. We'll have things ready in just a few minutes."

While they waited, they watched the activity around them—the jeeps and trucks and skip-loaders, and crews of soldiers, sailors, or Sea Bees moving, stacking, and loading supplies coming in on landing craft from the bay. After thirty or forty minutes, a warehouse door opened and the ex-prisoners were waved in. Inside, they found lines strung across the open space and pieces of canvas being hung from them to make smaller areas. Several young men in white shirts and pants, apparently medical corpsmen, were directing them this way and that. Dusty ended up in a partly draped canvas room where he and six or eight others were told to strip off their clothes and step into the next room, where a corpsman waited with a large metal spray can.

"Delousing!" he announced. "This is DDT. Close your eyes and hold your nose." Dusty could hear the hissing spurts of the DDT can and feel the misty spray on his bare skin, with extra squirts to his head and crotch.

"Okay, that's it! Move on through!" came the order. Dusty stepped back quickly into the previous room and grabbed the jacket Lou had made from where he'd dropped it on the floor. He carried it with him into the next area, where several shower stalls had been improvised and he was handed a small cake of soap and a towel and then waited in a short line until it was his turn to scrub down in a spray of warm water that seemed to be running off toward some unseen drain. He kept his jacket fairly dry by hanging it over the shower head, and then joined the line of naked men furiously toweling off as they moved into the next room. There he was directed to help himself to a new outfit from piles of dungarees, chambray shirts, shoes, socks, and underwear.

Before he could put on more than the skivvies, though, he had to submit to a quick physical. His temperature and blood pressure checked out okay, but the medic didn't like the sound of his breathing. He moved his stethoscope around several times. Finally he said, "Pleurisy. Check in at the hospital ship." He scribbled a quick note on a sheet of three-by-five-inch notepaper and thrust it into Dusty's hand. The note said "Benevolence." Dusty finished dressing in a more open area of the warehouse, wondering how many days a visit to the hospital ship would cost him.

He couldn't see Lou or Coulter anywhere, but he figured he'd connect with them later. He left the warehouse through a door that led to a marked route directly across a broad wharf to a dazzling white ship moored there. "Next stop, hospital ship," an attendant at the door told him after glancing at his note, pointing the way. Dusty had gathered that he would be given a more thorough physical and then possibly held for treatment before being sent home. Walking toward the ship, he looked around at all the activity on the wharf crowded with stacks of crates, skip loaders, and jeeps. Men in navy dungarees and white hats were moving every which way. He wondered where all the other ex-POWs had gone to.

The name stenciled on the bow of the white ship was USS *Benevolence*. A good name, reassuring. He stepped thoughtfully up the gangway, surprised at the apparent lack of people and activity on the deck. *This will really hang me up,* he thought. *I'm not sick. No broken bones, no diseases. Pleurisy's not serious. I'm healthy enough if I've survived this long. I don't need to go through this.*

He folded the note sheet and stuffed it in his pocket. Then he stepped onto the deck and walked straight ahead across the ship to the other side. On the way, he slipped his old jacket on and buttoned it up. The ensign's bars that Lou had put on the shoulders gave him some status.

A gray destroyer was moored alongside the *Benevolence*, and a ramp connected their decks. Dusty hailed the Officer of the Deck.

"Request permission to board," he said.

"Permission granted."

Dusty stepped down the ramp and saluted the U.S. flag flying at the destroyer's stern.

"I need to see the skipper, please," he said.

The OD nodded. "Right this way, mister." He led Dusty toward the stern, where they found the destroyer's captain talking to another officer. Dusty waited respectfully until they finished their conversation. The captain turned expectantly toward him, and he saluted.

"Begging your pardon, sir," he said. And then he explained who he was and what his situation was. The skipper, about Dusty's age and a couple of inches taller, looked interested. Dusty continued, emphasizing his good health and his urgent desire to avoid any unnecessary delays.

"It's been three years!" he concluded.

"I understand, Mr. Rhodes," said the skipper, smiling. "You know, it's about lunch time. Let's go down to the wardroom."

In the wardroom, the skipper called to a mess steward, "Bring this man the two biggest and best steaks you have." To Dusty he said, "Medium well?"

"Great!" said Dusty.

While he was waiting for his steaks, Dusty was introduced to a couple of other young officers sitting at the table, and they invited him to join them. The skipper excused himself to return to the deck, and the mess steward brought to the table a glass and a pitcher of ice water.

The officers at the table, both lieutenants, began asking Dusty about where he'd come from and how he happened to be there. While he answered, they passed him plates of bread and butter, which he began eating as he talked, washing it down with ice water. The lieutenants were finishing up bowls of soup, and politely took a little bread when Dusty pushed the plate their way. Then they pushed it back.

By the time the two T-bone steaks arrived fifteen or twenty minutes later, Dusty had emptied the bread plate and the pitcher of water. He thanked the steward and looked at the steaks doubtfully. They were steaming and sizzling, and they smelled wonderful. Maybe stuffing on the bread had been a mistake.

He cut a bite of steak and chewed it slowly, thinking of all the food dreams and fantasies he'd had in the past three years. He'd truly forgotten that anything could taste that good. There'd been chicken and cold cuts and Spam and other great things in the food drops, but no steaks. He swallowed, realizing that his stomach felt very full.

The two lieutenants were talking to each other, leaving him to enjoy his steaks, but he noticed they were glancing curiously to see how he was reacting. The second and third bites were also delicious, but swallowing them was harder. His stomach was beginning to hurt a little. He cut the fourth bite, took a deep breath, and then common sense kicked in. He laid down the knife and fork, shaking his head and grinning. The lieutenants looked up.

"I can't do it," Dusty said. "My stomach's shrunk. There's no place to put it. I sure hate to waste good meat, but . . ."

The lieutenants nodded sympathetically. One of them suggested he might like a little walk on the deck. They'd give him a quick tour. Dusty agreed.

On deck, they found crew members casting off lines to the *Benevolence*. The destroyer's engines were turning over and she was beginning to drift away from the hospital ship. The skipper approached.

"I just phoned that hotel ship anchored out there," he said, pointing, "and they've got a bunk for you tonight."

"You know," Dusty said, "I'm supposed to report to *Benevolence*."

"I thought you didn't want to."

"No, definitely not! It's the last thing I want to do."

"Okay, then," said the skipper. "You don't have to. We're going to get you to Kisarazu. That's where the stateside air ferries are flying from."

In what looked like the middle of Tokyo Bay, the destroyer approached an LST, a large, shallow-draft landing craft designed to carry armored vehicles close to the beach. Cutting engines and easing alongside, the skipper yelled to the LST skipper through a megaphone, "Get this man over to Kisarazu first thing tomorrow morning. Put him up for the night and get him over there tomorrow."

"Aye, aye, sir!" came the response.

"I don't know how to thank you," Dusty told the skipper. "You've really been generous to me." The skipper extended his hand and they shook. "Good luck, Mister Rhodes," he said.

Quickly crossing to the LST, Dusty was taken to a room with half a dozen bunks, all empty, all with clean sheets and pillowcases. He undressed and climbed into the nearest bunk. It was more luxurious than anything he could remember. He was asleep in a minute.

Dusty woke up before dawn. For a minute he lay soaking up the bliss of real sheets and a mattress after three years of steel decks, board floors, tatamis, and blanket hammocks. Then he found the showers, shaved and dressed, and followed his instincts and nose to an urn of coffee in the mess area. Taking the mug of steaming java with him, he found the OD, who told him a motor launch would arrive at 0600 to carry him to Kisarazu. It was now 5:30. Dusty's luck was holding.

He'd seen hundreds of sunrises over Tokyo Bay from Ofuna, the stadium camp, and the brickyard—though the view had been obstructed—but none had been as beautiful as the one he watched while skimming eastward over the bay toward Kisarazu. Ashore, he asked the nearest Shore Patrol where former POWs were supposed to report and was sent to a navy R5D four-engine transport on the tarmac at the airfield. Other men were already climbing the ramp, and he joined the boarding party, still carrying only his small bundle of essentials. He found a seat along the bulkhead next to a tall, gaunt, red-haired man, who answered Dusty's self-introduction by saying his name was Red Bullard. They swapped recent personal histories while they waited for the plane to take off. It turned out that Red had been the exec of Butch O'Hare's squadron and had taken over as CO after O'Hare was shot down.

That was sad news. In February of 1942, the month before Dusty received his commission, Butch O'Hare had become the first naval ace of the war by shooting down five Betty bombers in one day in the South Pacific. He won the Medal of Honor for that. Then he'd gone back to duty, been promoted two grades to lieutenant commander, and led his own squadron. And, killing the Bettys, he'd flown an F4F, the same plane that Dusty did. The last Dusty had heard, O'Hare was still flying.

Red himself had been shot down and taken prisoner. Like Dusty, he'd been taken to Truk—this was many months later—and he'd been brutally beaten day after day. He refused to give any information but his name, rank, and serial number. Major Pappy Boyington—like O'Hare, a famous ace—was a prisoner there at the same time, in the next filthy little cell, and he advised Red to stop stonewalling and tell the Japs *something*, anything that sounded plausible—close to the truth but not the truth. He'd probably saved Red's life.

As the transport's hatch was secured and it began taxiing for takeoff, someone asked where they were headed.

"Anywhere but here," was the first response, and they all laughed. Then a couple of voices said they were going to Guam. Everyone accepted the news. Then came the accelerating rumble down the runway and the little bump and smooth sailing as the plane left the ground. They banked slightly to port, then more steeply, giving the passengers on Dusty's side a view out the windows opposite them of the ground below. Parts of the city—Tokyo or Yokohama—a mile or two across, maybe more, looked totally flattened. Hardly a building was standing. That must have been where the incendiaries landed. From above, these areas reminded Dusty of the part of Yokohama he'd seen while marching from the brickyard to the train station, as well as some of the neighborhoods the train from Niigata had passed through before coming to the harbor in Tokyo. The images overlapped, and they all told the same story. *When the fires were burning, nothing could have lived there.*

Tokyo Bay was full of ships and boats of all sizes. Dusty thought he caught a glimpse of the impressive bulk of the USS *Missouri*, where the peace treaty had been signed. The plane completed a circle and then leveled out, gaining altitude. Settling back in his seat, Dusty felt again that sense of comfort and satisfaction that had come repeatedly over the past few days. *Everything's going okay. One more step on the road home.*

It was a long, droning, vibrating trip, and most of the passengers—all former POWs, it turned out, the first group to be heading back to the States—didn't feel the need to try to talk over the noise of the engines. After a few hours a couple of stewards brought everybody cold lunch packs and cold bottles of Coca-Cola. There were whistles and playful cheers of appreciation for the Cokes. Dusty had always liked his with a shot of bourbon, but this one was the best he'd ever had.

Noticing that the R5D continued to fly straight south, to judge by the changing sun, Dusty realized his mental map of the Pacific was a little foggy. He thought Guam should be at least a little bit east. Then he wondered why they were going by way of Guam, when Midway—as he remembered—lay on almost a straight line between Tokyo and Pearl Harbor. Maybe Midway was farther than Guam, beyond the range of the R5D. Or maybe it was a safety precaution. There were islands—all of them now under Allied control—between Japan and Guam, in case of mechanical problems or bad weather. And there was nothing much between Japan and Midway.

Oh well, he thought, *ours not to reason why.*

Dusty noticed that the pilot had come back into the cabin and was slowly making his way aft, chatting with some of the men. When he got to Dusty, he glanced at his jacket and ensign's bars. "Navy?" he asked.

Dusty nodded. "*Enterprise,*" he said. "Fighting Ten. Santa Cruz Islands."

"Like to come up front for a while?" the pilot asked. Dusty gratefully accepted, glad for a change of seats. In the cockpit, the pilot slid into his seat and suggested that his co-pilot take a break while Dusty sat down for a little while. The pilot briefed Dusty on their location and bearing, and then asked where he'd been held prisoner. After hearing Dusty's brief summary, he said, "Did you know there's another guy aboard who was in Ofuna? Right back there." He turned in his seat and pointed. "Name's Condit, I think."

After talking with the pilot a few more minutes and thanking him, Dusty went back to the area of the cabin where the pilot had pointed. "Condit?" he asked. One of the seated men looked up and said, "Jim Condit, U.S. Navy."

"Dusty Rhodes. I understand they put you up at Ofuna."

The man sitting next to Condit offered Dusty his place and moved to a vacant seat. Dusty sat down and explained that he'd spent about six months in the questioning camp, from late 1942 to May 1943. Condit said he'd arrived at Ofuna in September of 1943, after his TBF had been shot down in a raid on Marcus Island. After a year at Ofuna, he was sent to a camp called Omori, on an island in Tokyo Bay.

According to Condit, the Marine Corps ace Major Greg "Pappy" Boyington came to Ofuna in March 1944 and got in trouble because of his compulsive smoking. He'd been caught smoking in the benjo and the other prisoners had to witness his punishment of being beaten with clubs on his buttocks and legs, just as Dusty and Al had been. Other prisoners were heavily beaten for looking at a Japanese newspaper in the benjo, or for farting or spitting while they were bowing to the emperor in the morning assembly.

Condit didn't remember meeting Al Mead at Ofuna—Dusty thought Al was probably gone by then—but he remembered somebody by that name at Omori. He thought Al worked in the kitchen. That seemed likely to Dusty because that's what Al did at Ofuna.

After the Japanese surrendered, Condit was sent aboard a destroyer and then somehow selected to represent aviation POWs aboard the *Missouri* at the surrender ceremony. He was impressed by how formal and quiet it all was. He said one of the Japanese held out his hand to MacArthur, and MacArthur just ignored it. When the signing was over, hundreds of planes flew over in formation. It was really something to remember.

Dusty wished he'd been there, but he was happy just to be headed home. Maybe he'd see the surrender signing at the movies, in the newsreel.

The morning coffee and lunchtime Coke required visits to the head at the rear of the plane. Otherwise, Dusty stayed seated, strapped in, and stretched now and then to relieve stiffness in his legs and shoulders. Talking with Jim Condit helped pass the time. It was midafternoon, he figured, when he could feel the plane begin to descend toward the airfield at Guam. It had been about eight hours, somebody said.

Guam was U.S. territory! It had been so before the war, and now it was again. The numbers of uniformed men and the stacks of materiel on the airfield and in adjacent areas seemed even greater than on the docks in Tokyo. Of course he'd seen only small parts of the scene in both cases, but still it was impressive. More of everything than he remembered from the beginning of the war, at North Island, and San Francisco, and even Pearl Harbor.

Shortly after landing, they all had a chance to send a cablegram home, and Dusty lost no time in writing out the good news for his mother—he'd just arrived at Guam from Tokyo, the next day he'd fly to Pearl Harbor, and the day after that he'd be home! She'd probably get the message before he got to Pearl.

For most of the ex-POWs, the great thing about Guam, before, during, and after dinner, was the beer. Real, honest-to-God beer! In black cans, still camouflaged, the way all canned goods were in wartime—except those blessed Cokes on the plane. He drank two cans before dinner, and then slowed down, afraid he'd do a repeat of the bread-versus-steaks routine on the destroyer. He and the others bedded down in a BOQ not far from the airfield. Lights out, deep sleep, no dreams.

Departure time the next morning—same plane, different crew—was 0800 hours. Another eight hours in the air. On the eighth of September. The destination, they heard, was Kwajalein—an island in the Marshalls that had been taken from the Japanese. And then there'd be an even bigger hop to Pearl—twelve hours. The Pacific was one big ocean. And they still wouldn't be home. One more day after that, another twelve hours, to San Francisco.

It was good to see they were heading east now. The day passed much like the previous one, and after landing, more beer and more good food. But no comfortable cot in a BOQ. The plane would leave at ten o'clock that night, and they'd have to catch what sleep they could aboard. That might be a hard night, a long twelve hours. But when they got to Pearl Harbor, maybe ten o'clock in the morning, it was still going to be September 8. Sometime in the early morning they'd cross the International Date Line and lose a day. No, they'd gain one! They'd left Tokyo on the 7th, they'd be in San Francisco on the 9th. Four days in the air, but only three on the ground.

And Pearl Harbor was something special—not only for a navy man. For all Americans, the war had begun there. It was the center of operations for the whole U.S. campaign in the Pacific. For Dusty, it was completing a circle that had started three years earlier, on the 10th of October, 1942, when he'd landed a Wildcat for the first time on USS *Enterprise* off the coast of Hawaii. Six days later the *Enterprise* was steaming toward the South Pacific.

The third leg of the journey was indeed a long one, but they were still heading east—a little north but mostly east, and it was midmorning when they saw the green hills of Oahu, then passed over Pearl Harbor and landed at Hickam Field. Some of the R5D's passengers dropped to their knees on the airfield's parking strip and kissed the ground. Dusty understood their feeling, but he didn't need to perform the ritual. Still, Hawaii was more like home ground than Guam had been. Even though he hadn't been at Hickam Field before, it was next door to Pearl Harbor and Ford Island, and all the naval facilities. And just a few miles away was Honolulu, and Waikiki—evoking memories of good times. But he was in no mood to interrupt his homeward trajectory.

There was shuttle bus service to Pearl, though, and time after an early lunch to travel to the navy exchange there and buy a new uniform of navy gray, with ensign's bars. The dungarees he'd been given in Tokyo were okay for traveling, but he'd need something dressier soon. He paid with some of the cash they'd been issued soon after landing.

The schedule was still being accelerated. At 1800 hours—six o'clock—they'd begin the last leg, and sleep on the plane overnight. Before that, there were a couple of other drills to run through. They were all herded into a hangar where an army major in the Intelligence division told them about the work being done to identify Japanese war criminals, who would be hunted down, as far as possible, and brought to justice in a series of war crimes trials. Every former POW could help by telling the army investigators all that he knew about the Japanese guards and commandants in the camps where he had been held.

Dusty's interview was with a lieutenant who worked from a list of questions. First he wanted to know all the places where Dusty had been held prisoner. Then he asked Dusty to describe in detail any kind of treatment that he thought was criminal or unnecessarily brutal under the circumstances. And to name or describe any guards or camp authorities who were involved or responsible. Dusty wished he'd learned the real name of the chief petty officer at Ofuna they all knew as Shithead. But the lieutenant said that with converging details of physical descriptions, approximate times of encounters, and corroborating accounts by other former POWs, a pretty accurate profile would eventually accumulate for every Japanese guard or camp authority who should be arrested and tried.

Dusty understood the importance of the opportunity—no, the duty, the obligation. They'd talked about it sometimes in the last few weeks at the brickyard, when it seemed pretty clear that the war would soon be over. He knew that a lot of prisoners would be tempted to try to settle old scores, to get some revenge for their suffering. But he felt a responsibility to be accurate, not to exaggerate or to minimize. He wanted justice, for the victims and for their tormentors. People's lives could hinge on what he and other former POWs said. Even though he'd rather have been thinking about good things to come, he tried to remember everything that could matter. He was careful to detail the fair and considerate way that Sergeant Ito had treated the prisoners at the brickyard. He was glad that he knew Ito-Socho's name, and he could certainly describe him in detail. He told the lieutenant that everything he knew about Ito showed he was anything but a war criminal. He hoped his report would be given strong consideration against any accusations another prisoner might make.

At the end of the interview, the lieutenant thanked him and said a transcript of his deposition would be mailed to him in a few weeks at his home. He could sign it then after he'd read it over and made sure it was accurate.

He had one more duty before eating a light supper and boarding the plane—reporting to the base medical unit for a physical exam, which turned out to be more thorough than the quick check he'd had on the docks in Tokyo.

They took off with the sun low in the west behind the plane. Except for the roar of the engines, it was quiet during the flight. Everyone was talked out and tired from the long hours in the air and only intermittent napping the previous night. It would be early Sunday morning, September 9, 1945, when they arrived over San Francisco Bay. Pearl Harbor had been attacked on a Sunday morning nearly four years ago. Tomorrow would be one of the most special days in Dusty's life. The last three years were probably the worst years he would ever have. He was on the verge of a whole new beginning.

TWELVE

HOMECOMING

The first rays of the morning sun shot through the plane several hours before it began the descent over San Francisco Bay. As it grew lighter, there were sounds of stretching and yawning, hushed scraps of conversation. Faces turned expectantly toward the windows, necks craned for the first sight of land. About 7:30, someone said, "There it is!" It was the Golden Gate Bridge. Tired as they were, most of the men were on their feet, peering out the small windows on both sides for glimpses of a country they hadn't seen for months or years. Dusty could hardly believe he was nearly home. In a few minutes he could call Mom in Fresno, and that would make it real.

They landed at Oakland airport on the east side of the bay. A bus took them to Oak Knoll Naval Hospital, where they had a late breakfast in the cafeteria before being shown to their beds in a large, empty ward. There were lines at the pay phones outside the cafeteria and the ward, but after a little wait Dusty got his chance. A cheerful long-distance operator dialed his mother's number, and when she said "Hello?" he said, "Hello, Mom."

"Buddy! I knew it was you!"

Then she started crying, and it was hard for either of them to talk. Another familiar voice came on the line.

"Hi, Buddy! It's Gladys." Aunt Gladys was visiting from Madera. She asked him where he was, when he'd arrived, how he was feeling, and then said, "Here's your mom again."

Mom's voice was still shaky, but she had more questions than Aunt Gladys. He tried to answer a few, and then explained that there were other men waiting to use the phone. He assured her he'd tell her everything when he got home in a couple of days. In the meantime, could he talk to Marian? Sorry, Mom said, but Marian was at her mother's house. Okay, then, would she let everybody know he was at the hospital? She would, and they said good-bye. He decided to wait till the next morning to call Marian. He was anxious about that. He didn't know what to expect. In all the time he'd been a prisoner, he'd received only two letters from her.

On Monday morning, he began his first full day on American soil for over three years. Oak Knoll was big and clean and efficient, and there were male orderlies and pretty nurses bringing the former POWs breakfast and morning newspapers, and anything else they could think of. Compared to their Japanese accommodations, it was like a luxury hotel. They reminded each other they didn't have to gorge—the supply was endless. One man told Dusty he'd got a box of two dozen Milky Way candy bars from one of the air drops over his POW camp after the war ended, and he'd eaten eighteen of them in the space of three or four hours.

Dusty finally called Marian, and she seemed cheerful and glad to hear from him. They agreed they'd have a lot to talk about, but they found it hard to say much on the phone, and the conversation was short.

It was after lunch before he saw a doctor, who checked him over, listened to his chest with a stethoscope, and asked him questions. Yes, there seemed to be some pleurisy, but it wasn't bad. After a couple of days resting in the hospital, he'd be ready to go home. The doctor said he seemed to be remarkably fit, and encouraged him to keep eating well and gaining weight. He was already back to 135 pounds, from the improved diet of the last three weeks.

Later that afternoon, the men were all called to an office on the main floor, where they filled out some papers and were given their accumulated back pay. For Dusty and a few others, there was flight pay as well. Dusty's payoff, in cash, came to just over six thousand dollars. He was a rich man! He was also promoted from ensign to lieutenant junior grade, with a notification that he could expect further promotions soon. A clerk handed him a small envelope, explaining that he'd been awarded two medals, an Air Medal and a Purple Heart.

The next day Dusty received three telegrams, all welcome-home greetings, from Mom and Sis, his Aunt Betty, and Jean Caldwell, Jimmy's wife. "So happy for you. Will be waiting to see you," Jean said. "Will"? Had she meant "We'll"? What about Jimmy? He didn't like the sound of it.

Just before lunch a nurse's aide came to the patients' lounge where he was reading a newspaper to tell him there was a telephone call for him. It was Aunt Betty in San Francisco, and she sounded excited and happy. She and Uncle Clifford were going to take him out for a really nice dinner just as soon as he was available. Betty had always been close to him, and it was in one of her letters he'd received at the stadium camp that he'd learned of his father's death. He thanked her and told her he'd look forward to the dinner, and he'd call her soon.

There was a bus going from Oak Knoll to the navy exchange at Alameda Naval Base, and any patient not restricted to the ward was free to go. Dusty needed new rank insignia as well as a few more uniform pieces, so he took advantage of the opportunity. Anticipating more promotions, he bought the insignia for lieutenant and lieutenant commander as well.

Wednesday morning the doctor listened to Dusty's chest again and told him he was well enough to leave. Completing his paperwork for dismissal, Dusty learned he was beginning a ninety-day rehabilitation leave. He discovered that the chief administrator at Oak Knoll was Ralph Jack, now a navy captain, whom he'd known as a physics professor at Fresno State College six years ago. When Captain Jack learned Dusty was headed for Fresno, he said his wife was driving their car back there that afternoon and wondered if Dusty would like a ride. As a matter of fact, he'd really appreciate it if Dusty would do the driving, since his wife didn't like to drive. Dusty could hardly believe his luck.

Mrs. Jack was a pleasant and chatty passenger, but Dusty had trouble paying attention to her questions. His thoughts were on Marian and Mom and how they and Fresno and the whole country must have changed in the last three years. He knew he'd changed. He wondered whether they'd think he looked different.

It was a three-and-a-half-hour drive. He would have driven faster, he thought, if he'd been alone and in his own car. Coming into Fresno on Highway 99, he couldn't see any obvious changes. At Shaw Avenue on the north side of town, he turned left and drove east five miles to Palm, making sure he stayed under the speed limit. A few blocks past Palm, he turned right onto Maroa Avenue. Two blocks and he was at Marian's mother's house. He stopped and thanked Mrs. Jack for the ride.

"No, thank *you*, Dusty," she said. "I really appreciate your driving. Hope we'll see you later. Good luck with everything!"

He got out, picked up the small bag he'd bought at the navy exchange, and watched as Mrs. Jack drove off. He turned toward the house and took it in at a glance. He was wearing his new gray uniform with lieutenant's insignia. He hoped he looked all right.

Marian was just as pretty as he'd remembered, and her mother, Mrs. Lowe, was gracious and bubbly and happy to be making a fuss over him. She served iced tea and sugar cookies, and then after a few questions about Oak Knoll and his drive to Fresno, she excused herself, saying she had to get things ready for supper.

Dusty had hugged and kissed Marian at the door, but they were both tense and awkward. Since they'd said good-bye at North Island in San Diego, they'd been apart for longer than the period they'd known each other before that. A lot had happened. They'd both changed. Everything had changed. It wasn't going to be like old times. It was like starting over again.

Conversation was more awkward than if they'd just met on a blind date. A question, an answer, a pause. The problem was not just what to ask next, but what not to ask. Some things needed to be talked about later, not now. For the moment the problem was solved when Mrs. Lowe reappeared with an album of newspaper clippings and letters, all the memorabilia accumulated since he and Marian were married. It was strange for Dusty to see the first notices in the *Fresno Bee* and the *Madera Citizen* that he was missing in action. Then the follow-up articles that he was presumed killed in action. Letters of sympathy to Marian from Jimmy Flatley, the skipper of Fighting Ten, and Secretary of the Navy James Forrestal. Some reports of Allied victories in the Pacific, and an article about American Prisoners of War of the Japanese—not very encouraging. Then there was a transcript of the short-wave radio broadcast Dusty had made from Tokyo. It was picked up by several ham radio operators on the West Coast who were monitoring Radio Tokyo. That stirred questions from Mrs. Lowe about the prison camps, and suddenly there was plenty to talk about. Dusty was conscious of censoring certain details, as he'd already had practice doing with Mrs. Jack and some of the people at Oak Knoll. There were years ahead of telling war stories and POW stories, and every story would be tailored to its audience. Some stories would get better with practice, and he'd probably get tired of telling others.

It was already nearly supper time, and Mrs. Lowe understood that he was anxious to see his mother. She'd phoned Mrs. Rhodes to tell her he'd arrived. So he excused himself, and Marian said it would be best if she stayed home and let his mother have him all to herself for the evening. Dusty could take her car.

It was less than ten minutes to Mom's—three miles south on Palm, then east on McKinley, zigzagging south on North Fresno Street, and east again to 2939 Lamona. Mom was sitting on the porch waiting. He parked at the curb and ran up the walk and grabbed her in his arms at the bottom of the steps. He had to fight to hold back the tears. Mom let hers flow. "Oh, Buddy!" she said. "Oh, Bud!"

When they got control of themselves, he helped her back up the steps and into the house, where she led him straight to the dining room. Sis got up smiling from the table to hug him, and Mr. Martin from next door was there, and Bob Wynne, who owned the gas station in Madera where he'd worked part-time when he was in high school. Then Bob had moved to Fresno, and Dusty had worked for him again when he was going to Fresno State. An unfamiliar man at the table turned out to be Sis's new husband, Don Fault, a regional manager for Gerber's baby food.

There were too many people to talk to, too much to take in, to think about Dad for a few minutes. But his absence was almost a presence in the room, and after a few minutes, when they were all seated again and Mom and Sis had brought in several hot dishes and platters from the kitchen, Mom asked Sis to tell Bud about how it happened. Dusty managed to keep eating, but his eyes grew wet as he listened.

Dad and Sis had driven up into the mountains about forty miles east, and Dad had stopped the car just off the road at the mouth of a little deserted canyon, so they could have a few minutes of target practice with his Colt .45. No sooner had they started to shoot than he grabbed at his chest and fell to his knees. For a minute Sis thought he'd been hit by a ricocheting bullet, but then she realized it was his heart. She helped him to his feet and half carried him to the car.

"I can't drive, Sis," he groaned. "You'll have to do it."

As she got him into the passenger seat, he passed out.

She dug the keys out of his pocket and got in behind the steering wheel before she understood her predicament. She had to get him to the hospital in Fresno as soon as possible. But she'd never driven before—not once.

"I was terrified," she said. "I was just paralyzed."

She took two or three deep breaths and tried to remember what to do. She knew the clutch pedal had to be held down while pushing the starter button, and then she had to shift into low gear, but she wasn't sure where that was. She got the engine started, but then killed it because she'd forgotten to take off the parking brake. After a few jerking tries, she finally got the car rolling and started to learn how to coordinate clutch and gearshift, brake and accelerator.

A quarter of a mile up the road there was a wide turnout on both sides, and when she was sure there were no cars coming, she slowed as much as she dared and did a careful u-turn. From then on back to Fresno, she said, "it was a piece of cake." But she worried more and more because Dad was still unconscious and seemed to slump farther against the door.

The attendants who came out to the car at the hospital confirmed her fear. Dad was already dead.

There was a long silence after Sis finished the story. Everyone seemed to be concentrating on chewing quietly. Dusty was nearly as over-whelmed by Sis's heroism as he was by the thought of Dad's dying so sud-denly and so young—he was only forty-four. He'd tell Sis later. Then Mr. Martin helped out by asking Dusty—he and everybody at home still called him Bud—what he'd done and thought about to keep his courage up, all those years in the Japanese prison camps.

Dusty tried to tell them. The fitness routine, the secret journal, the belief that America was strong enough to win. Determination not to give up, desire to come home for his family's sake, and the hope of making up—. He stopped there. It was getting emotional again.

Mr. Martin asked him if he'd prayed. Somebody during the war had said that there were no atheists in foxholes. Was that true?

Dusty said he didn't know about that. But he'd certainly done a lot of praying, especially when he was locked up in a tiny dark cell alone, and hurting, and didn't know whether he was going to be allowed to live or not. He'd made resolutions, he said, to try to be a better son and a better man and a better Christian when he got back.

"But I guess that's easier said than done," he added. "We'll see about that."

The supper was roast beef and gravy and baked potatoes and onions, with green beans and freshly baked biscuits. For dessert there was peach pie with a big scoop of homemade ice cream. Dusty had a second helping of dessert. It was hard to believe that just a week ago he couldn't eat two beautiful steaks. He told them about that, and they all laughed.

After supper it was time to highlight all the other news—family, friends, city, state, country, and world. Dusty could see it was going to take a while to catch up on all the happenings and changes. Bob Wynne observed that everyone was saying it was going to be a very different world after the war, because all the energy and materials and new technology that had gone into the war effort could be turned to improving everyday life. They all nodded. It seemed reasonable. A long, hard chapter had closed in their lives. A new one full of promise was just opening.

He stayed at Mom's that night, and breakfast the next morning was another dream fulfilled. He'd often fantasized about Mom's breakfasts while he was a prisoner, living on half a cup of rice a day or a couple of dol-lops of black gunk.

First there was a small glass of freshly squeezed orange juice, sweet and pulpy. Then a bowl of hot Cream of Wheat, which he covered with milk and sugar. Next, the main course: three poached eggs on toast and several slices of cool orange muskmelon alongside. And more toast to hold the strawberry jam, and a big mug of steaming coffee. It was heaven, and he thought he could have died happily right there.

Meanwhile, Mom sat across the table from him with a mug of coffee and smiled in a sad, wistful way. It looked as if she couldn't decide whether to laugh or cry. Sis had gone to work already, and Dusty had forgotten what day it was. It didn't matter. There was nothing he absolutely had to do. He was on vacation. If breakfasts at Oak Knoll were like a luxury hotel, this was better yet—like coming home for a few days back when he was working on the oil wells near Bakersfield. No, better still. With ninety days stretching ahead of him and an endless supply of ready cash, he could be king of the castle for a long, long time. All he needed to do was sort things out with Marian, and there was no rush about that. Neither of them was going anywhere for a while, and they could take it nice and easy.

Mom chatted about the neighbors and the relatives and her flowers and vegetable garden, keeping him anchored in the present. That was luxurious, too. There was no place he'd rather be, no need to imagine himself enjoying better times, as he'd done daily and nightly for the past three years.

At last she said, "Dad took it so hard about your being missing. That was in November. He listened to the news every night, and he read the newspaper from front to back. Then in December we heard from the Navy Department that they'd decided you were killed in action. That just broke his heart. He didn't know what to do with himself."

"It was in January he had the heart attack?"

"Yes—although you know he'd had high blood pressure for years, and he'd had some chest pains two or three months before that."

Dusty shook his head. "He was too young."

"I know," she said. "I miss him."

She grabbed a dishtowel and got up and turned toward the sink. Dusty got up and cleared the breakfast things off the table.

That evening he drove to Marian's for supper. Mrs. Lowe served roast chicken, with mashed potatoes and giblet gravy. Dessert was apple pie, and he gratefully accepted Mrs. Lowe's offer to make it à la mode. After dinner Marian suggested they go for a walk.

Dusty asked about her work at the doctor's office. His name was Dr. Standiford and he was a cardiologist. Marian was his receptionist, answering the phone, making appointments, and keeping patients' records. She said she liked the job—it felt like she was helping people, and she enjoyed meeting them. She asked him if his mom's house and Fresno seemed to have changed very much. Not much, he said, but he reminded her that his family had lived in Fresno only a couple of years before he became an aviation cadet. It was Madera that felt more like home to him. He needed to drive over there pretty soon and see how things were.

"Did you know Russ Reiserer came to see me after you'd been shot down?" she asked.

"No," he said. "When was that?"

"After your squadron was rotated back home for R and R before they went out again. I think it was in May."

Dusty thought a minute.

"In May I went from the questioning camp to the stadium camp. That's when I sent the first postcard home."

"We didn't get the postcard until a lot later. We didn't know anything until your radio broadcast at the end of July."

"What did Russ say?"

"He told me what he knew about your squadron, or part of your squadron, getting attacked by Zeros. Chip Reding got back okay and told everybody about it. He was your wing man, wasn't he?"

"Actually I was his wing man. I wondered whether he made it back to the carrier. The last I saw him he had two or three Zeros on his tail."

"Russ said he was okay."

"Good," said Dusty. "I'd sure like to see him. I wonder where he is now." There were others he wanted to know about, too. Especially Jimmy Caldwell and Al Mead.

"Russ was very nice. He made a special trip to see me. Jimmy Flatley had written a letter, but Russ thought he could . . . I don't know . . . comfort me, I suppose. Maybe it helps people to hear firsthand from somebody who was there. I appreciated what he was trying to do. But of course he thought you were dead. He told me I ought to accept the fact that you were really gone. He said I had to get on with my life. That's what they said in the war movies, too. 'You have to get on with your life.' I tried to."

"You were working, I guess."

"Yes . . . that helped. Going about my business and pretending everything was normal. But I didn't think you were ever coming back. I thought Russ knew. I had to believe him. I couldn't believe in a miracle."

Then she told him about a strange experience she'd had back in October of 1942, about the time he was shot down. She and her mother had gone to a movie matinee—she didn't remember what the movie was—but before the movie there was the usual newsreel, about how the war was going in Europe and in the Pacific, as well as on the home front. And then, after the movie, as they were walking up the aisle, she had a feeling that somehow Bud was trying to talk to her. She could hear his voice, but she couldn't make out the words. He was talking very slowly and carefully, as if trying to explain something important.

"What did you think?" he asked.

"I didn't know what to think. I'd never had anything like that happen before. I told Mother about it, and she thought maybe something in the newsreel had made me think about you. I didn't believe in telepathy or anything like that, but I'd read stories, you know, about that kind of thing."

"About people who are in trouble, or maybe dying, and they send a message to someone close to them?"

"Yes."

"Did it scare you?"

"A little. It was weird. I tried to put it out of my mind."

Dusty was intrigued. It could have been just a coincidence. It would probably be impossible now to make a sure match between the time he went down or was sitting in his raft and the time Marian heard his voice. But it could have happened. He was too busy trying to survive to think of anything else at the time, but he'd been aware that at any moment it could be all over. And he'd thought about Marian, and Mom, and God, and how short his life had been, and everything he might do if he lived. And he'd prayed a lot. All in a rush at first, when he was bailing out and scrambling to patch the holes in the raft and hoping the sharks wouldn't arrive until he was out of the water.

Later in the day, and through the harrowing night, he'd done a lot of thinking—about what it meant to be alive and what it would mean if he didn't make it. That kind of concentration was unlike anything he'd ever felt before. If there was such a thing as telepathy, he was probably generating enough energy to send out radio waves, or whatever they were.

Marian had started talking again.

"What made it really spooky is that the next day your mom told me something that happened that same night, just after they'd gone to bed. She'd been reading and put the book down and fallen asleep, she thinks. And then she woke up. She'd heard you knocking at the front door. She knew it was you. She shook your dad and said, 'Welton, Buddy's at the door. Go let him in.'"

"And he said, 'Mae, Buddy's not here. He's in the South Pacific.'

"'But I heard him knock,' she said. 'I'm sure of it. Didn't you hear him?'

"'No, Mae,' he said. But she couldn't let it go. Finally she asked him if he'd please get up and go check, just to satisfy her. So he did, and of course there was nobody there. But it was so real to her. 'I could have sworn it was Buddy,' she said."

Dusty was stunned. "That same night?" he asked.

"Yes, she told me when I talked to her the next day."

"I'll be darned," he said. "She never told me. But we've only seen each other for a few hours. She's probably forgotten about it."

"Ask her," she said.

"I will."

He thought of asking Marian how she'd felt when she heard his radio broadcast from Japan and found out he was alive. But that was too . . . personal, or something.

He asked about Bob Wynne, and Marian said he'd been very helpful to his mom after his dad's death. He was around a lot. Nothing romantic, apparently. He was just a good friend. Dusty told her about Aunt Betty's call and said he was going to try to get to San Francisco for a couple of days. They talked about other relatives and neighbors and friends, and then Marian said that she was sorry if she seemed sort of distant, but she didn't feel like she really knew Bud anymore. So much had changed in three years, and *he'd* changed. She supposed she had, too.

So it was like getting acquainted all over again? he asked. Yes, sort of like that, she said. They'd just have to be patient—she meant she hoped he'd be patient with her—and they'd have to do a lot of talking about all the things that had happened to them while they were apart. That way they'd gradually get to know each other again.

And in the meantime? Should he stay at his mom's house? No, no, not all the time, she said. "We want to see you, too. Mother would think something was wrong if you did that. But your mom has missed you so much. You need to spend some time with her and tell her about all the things that happened to you."

He noticed the "we." "*We* want to see you." *What about your feelings, Marian?* he wondered. *Didn't you miss me, too? And how come you didn't write more often?* But he didn't say those things. Maybe later.

So the readjusting and reacquainting began. Dusty felt that he was having to woo Marian all over again. And she didn't seem to respond as enthusiastically as she had the first time. Things were not going to be easy for them.

But his marriage problems were only a part of his life. There were a lot of other things to think about and to do. And a lot of people who seemed truly glad to see him, or eager to see him if they hadn't yet had the chance.

The second week he was home he got two important phone calls—one from Jimmy Flatley and one from Jean Caldwell, Jimmy Caldwell's wife.

Someone had told Flatley that Dusty's name was on a list of repatriated POWs. He sounded as tickled as Dusty was to be in touch again. Could Dusty join him and a few other Reapers for a reunion at Los Alamitos? That's where he was stationed, temporarily. It would be the first weekend in December.

"Sure, Skipper! Count me in!"

Did Dusty know Al Mead was back, too? He was recuperating at the Naval Hospital in Long Beach. Al would be at the reunion. And eight or ten other guys. And their wives.

"Bring your wife, Dusty."

"I sure will," said Dusty. "Thanks, Skipper. It'll be great to see you."

He was excited. Think of seeing Al again! It would be his second out-of-town social engagement since he got back. The first was with Aunt Betty and Uncle Clifton at the St. Francis Hotel in San Francisco day after tomorrow.

Jean Caldwell had read the article in the *Fresno Bee* saying he was back. She was living in Fresno now. She'd been wanting to call but was afraid to. She was hoping Dusty might have some news about Jimmy. The navy had reported him missing, then killed in action, but she'd kept hoping that he'd been a prisoner like Dusty and maybe Dusty had run into him or heard about him somehow. Then she started to cry. Dusty felt like crying, too. Until her call, he'd thought he might hear any day that Jimmy was okay. He'd half expected he might even show up at the Los Alamitos reunion. No such luck. His best friend—gone for sure.

He told Jean he'd like to see her. It would be better than talking on the phone. So the next afternoon he drove to her house and they spent a couple of hours swapping news and reminiscing. By then Marian had told him she didn't want to go to Los Alamitos, so it seemed like a natural thing to invite Jean. If Jimmy couldn't be there, she could go in his place. She hesitated, then accepted.

Dressed in his navy grays, Dusty drove Marian's car into San Francisco the next afternoon. Thinking ahead to the Los Alamitos reunion, he decided to stop at the Alameda Navy exchange on the way and order another uniform, aviation greens. A tailor took his measurements and Dusty arranged for the uniform to be sent to him in Fresno. He got to

Union Square about five, a couple of hours before his date with Betty and Clifford at the St. Francis, and parked in the hotel garage. Then he walked around Union Square and the nearby streets for a while, taking in the big-city atmosphere.

Dinner in the main dining room of the St. Francis was a special treat. Even if you were living in the Bay Area instead of suffering in a Japanese POW camp, it wasn't the sort of thing you did every day. Betty and Clifford were warm and funny, as always, and though Dusty felt obliged to thank Betty for writing him the news of his dad's death, none of them felt the need to talk much about it. Betty invited him to spend a few days with them whenever he could, and he told them he'd try to work it into his crowded social calendar. Betty said again and again how good he looked, and after a couple of drinks and a great dinner he was willing to believe her.

The next thing on his mental agenda was a visit to Madera, twenty miles north of Fresno on Highway 99. A phone call established a specific reason for the trip. He called the Bondesen home, hoping Everett's mother might tell him that just by chance Jaydolph was home on leave. Unfortunately, he wasn't, but Mrs. Bondesen was pleased to hear from him and insisted he come anyway.

He appreciated the use of Marian's car, but he didn't like depriving her of it. After Dad's death, Mom had turned in his sheriff's car to the county. Sis had heard Dusty talking to Mom about looking for a car of his own, and she'd told him that a friend of Don's had a car he wanted to sell. Dusty went to look at it—a cream-colored two-door 1940 Buick Super with a sloping back. It had had a lot of use, but it was still running. It would be okay until he was ready for a new one, so he bought it.

Midway between Fresno and Madera, he crossed the bridge over the San Joaquin River. The trip brought back memories of his fishing expeditions with his uncles a few miles west on Grandpa Burgess's dairy farm. As the scene changed, he thought of Boy Scout days when he boated and hiked miles along a flume carrying logs downhill from the mountains.

Slowing the car as he entered Madera, Dusty could see the roof of the courthouse ahead just off the highway to the west, on West Yosemite Avenue. His dad's office was there when he was auditor, and Mom had been a secretary in the office. At Yosemite Avenue he turned west off the highway, which had become F Street, toward home. Across from the courthouse was Lincoln Grammar School, which he had attended. Just past the school was the Madera Sanitarium, the lying-in hospital where he'd been born. Delivered and circumcised by Dr. Ransom, practically everybody's family doctor.

Madera (California) Elementary School Band. Buddy Rhodes at far left, with trumpet. Courtesy Raleigh E. Rhodes.

He slowed to a near-stop at 619, the family's home until Dad was appointed U.S. Marshall and he and Mom moved to Fresno. Since Bud had just been elected president of the Student Body at Madera High, they decided he should stay in Madera for the fall term. Everett's family had invited him to live with them, in their two-story house catty-corner across the street. He did a u-turn and stopped in front of the house. He half expected Mrs. Bondesen to be waiting for him on the front porch the way his mother had been, but she came to the door when he rang the bell.

Even though Everett—Jaydolph—was still on active duty, it was good to be back in a house where there were only good memories. Mrs. Bondesen caught him up on Everett's career and his current where-abouts—as far as she could guess.

She showed him some snapshots of Everett in his navy uniform, and said he'd visited a lot of ports and countries in Europe. The ships he'd been on—all destroyers—had mainly escorted convoys back and forth across the Atlantic. After Germany was defeated he'd been moved to the Pacific and given command of an LST, which he called the "USS *Madera*." The Madera Women's Improvement Club decided to sponsor the ship and contributed $250, which Everett used to buy an electric phonograph, an electric mangle, and bats and balls for the use of the crew. The USS *Madera* was in Tokyo Bay at the time of the Japanese surrender.

Everett said he might get out of the navy now, but he hadn't quite made up his mind.

They talked for more than an hour, and then Dusty felt it was time to excuse himself and look around town a little before heading back to Fresno. After parking near the high school, he encountered Ross Kinney, his old history teacher, who asked him to talk to the student body about his war experiences. It felt good to be recognized and appreciated.

When he got home, his mom said she'd been talking on the phone with an old Madera friend who was president of the Soroptimist Club there, and she was excited that Buddy was home and wondered if he'd be willing to talk to the club about some of his experiences.

When he told her about Mr. Kinney's invitation, she said "My, aren't you the celebrity!"

Within a few days the dates were set, but in the meantime he spent more time with Marian and stayed several days with her and her mother. When he asked Mrs. Lowe what he could do to help out around the house, she put him off at first, saying he didn't need to do anything, but when he reminded her he was family, she relented and said it would be a great help if he'd do some grocery shopping for her now and then. He gladly agreed, and made a trip to the market a daily event. It was fun browsing up and down the aisles, drinking in with his eyes the shelves and bins overflowing with foods he'd been dreaming about only three months ago. He improvised with gusto, filling the cart with twice as many things as his mother-in-law had put on the list. Two items they were never in danger of running short of—eggs and milk.

Back at Mom's place there were piles of newpaper clippings and letters and telegrams to look through, and Dusty tried to feel some sense of what it had been like for Sis and Mom and Dad and Marian during those years he'd been in Japan. There was the first postcard he'd written from the stadium camp, after he'd left Ofuna. It was dated May 26, 1943.

"My dear mother and dad and wife," it said. "My prayer is that this finds you well and happy. It seems like many years since I had the pleasure of your company. I hope it won't be much longer till I can again be with you. As POW I am treated well, have good health, and am keeping a bright outlook." He'd lied for two reasons. He didn't want them to worry too much, and he was afraid the Japanese wouldn't let the card go through if he told the truth. It concluded, "Don't worry! I send <u>all</u> my love. Bud." Marian had told him they didn't get that card until well after his recorded message had been broadcast in July.

There was an undated letter he'd written later from the stadium camp—"Tokyo Prisoner of War Camp No. 3."

My dearest Mother, Dad and Marian:
Hi, all! How is everything? Are you getting along okay? Are you all well? I pray with all my heart the answers are in the affirmative. [Obviously, he hadn't received any mail from them yet.] As for me, I am well and getting along okay, just dreaming of the day when we shall all be together again. I hope before too many months have passed that I shall receive mail from you, as some has been arriving from the U. S. Please give Don, Billie, Aden, Bertha, and Ray my love, as well as my best to Jim, Everett, Neil, and any of the gang you might see. . . . Keep your chins up, and don't worry about me, and take care of yourselves. I send you all my love.
I hope I'll be seeing you before long,
Bud.

More reassurances. No real news or facts. Making contact was the main thing. Just letting them know he was alive and thinking about them. It wouldn't do them any good to know what was really going on.

There was a clipping from the *Fresno Bee* dated September 12, 1943. The headline read, "CANNED VOICE FROM TOKIO." The article began

The day Ensign Raleigh E. Rhodes, 25, navy flier, returns from a Japanese prison camp, he will be able to hear the way his voice sounded when it came by radio from Tokio to give his mother and his wife their first definite assurance he did not lose his life in battle near the Santa Cruz Islands. . . .

That must refer to the recording a ham radio operator had made of the broadcast and sent to his Mom weeks later. They'd actually heard it at the end of July or early in August. The article didn't mention Dad. He'd been gone since January.

Then he found a telegram from "Provost Marshal General, Washington, D.C." It began, "The following is from enemy propaganda broadcast from Japan: Hello dearest wife and mother: I hope this finds you in the best of health and lacking in nothing materially." That was a letter he wrote, not a broadcast! He'd only recorded one message. So the Japanese had used a letter he'd written to broadcast on Radio Tokyo. It must have been early in 1944, because he didn't mention Dad, so he'd got Aunt Betty's letter. And later it said, "Give Mr. Martin my best regards and tell him my thanks for the letters." And "Please relay hellos and thanks to all relatives and friends for the letters . . . ." He'd got his first mail from home on Christmas Eve, and that sounded as if he'd had a lot of letters. Maybe late 1944. Still the same cheerful reassurance he was doing fine. Well, he was glad he'd done that. He'd managed to sound pretty chipper, no matter what had really been going on.

Another news clipping may have worried the family, though.

FURY OF 450 B-29S TURNS YOKOHAMA INTO SHAMBLES.
Yokohama, Japan's second port and fifth largest city, was "burning like all hell," after more than 450 Superfortresses poured 3,200 tons of high explosives and incendiary bombs on the city in a daylight fire raid. . . .

The report was dated May 29, 1945. By then he was in Niigata, but Mom and Sis wouldn't have known that. And they would have known that Yokohama was right next door to Tokyo, even if they didn't know that Tokyo Prisoner of War Camp No. 3 was actually in Yokohama. So they probably worried. He knew by now that some POW camps had been hit by bombs. Their locations were often secret, and there were no identifying markings. He didn't know about the stadium camp, but it was because of a fire raid in April that they'd left the brickyard and been taken north to Niigata.

Four hundred and fifty B-29s! They must have kept stepping up the numbers with every raid. From what he'd seen of Tokyo and Yokohama on his way home, there must have been dozens of square miles flattened or burned out. It was amazing the Japanese held out as long as they did. The atom bombs on Hiroshima and Nagasaki must have seemed like a sudden overwhelming escalation of the bombing.

After an hour or so at a time, he didn't want to read any more, so he'd set the piles aside and come back to them in a few days. Marian and Mrs. Lowe had their collections, too, and a lot of it really interested him. Sometimes, though, all the thoughts and feelings that came to him started to confuse him and he had to stop.

The talk for the Soroptimist Club in Madera that he'd promised came the next week. Mom went with him to the Hotel Aragon on the appointed day, and after a light lunch in the meeting room, Dusty explained to a group of very polite and attentive women how he'd become interested in flying through his early reading and the opportunity to enroll in the Civilian Pilot Training program at Fresno State. He briefly summarized his naval cadet training, his commissioning, and his assignment to Fighting Ten. He didn't mention the squadron's nickname, the Grim Reapers. That seemed somehow out of place. Then he told about the day he'd been shot down in the South Pacific and all the perils that followed.

There was generous applause and a murmur of excitement. Just then a door at the side of the room opened and two navy officers walked in. Dusty glanced at them and did a double take. Whitey Feightner and Tommy Harman! Old pals from Fighting Ten! He didn't know what to say, but he waved them to the front of the room. They started with handshakes and fell into warm hugs and back-slapping. After a couple of minutes, as Dusty became aware that the women were both pleased and curious, he began to explain but couldn't find his voice. Whitey stepped into the breach and introduced himself and Tommy. He explained that they had come to surprise Dusty, because they were in Dusty's squadron on the *Enterprise*, and they'd only recently learned he was alive. They'd flown to see him at his mother's home in Fresno, only to learn he'd just left for Madera. So they'd hitched a ride with a friendly neighbor.

"Welcome home, Dusty!" Whitey said.

The applause resumed, and Dusty grabbed them both again for a hug. Then the chairwoman asked if he'd be willing to answer a few questions, and he did, about conditions in the Japanese prison camps and how much weight he'd lost and what the end of the war was like. They all seemed to sense there was more story untold, but he'd talked nearly an hour, and they were polite enough not to press for more, especially with his friends standing by. Dusty invited Whitey and Tommy to ride back to Fresno with him and his mother, and they had an hour or two together before the two had to leave. It was a big day. Their surprise appearance made Dusty feel the Grim Reapers still thought of him as one of them.

His talk at Madera High School came a few days later. Ross Kinney had asked Sheriff Ott Justice to pick up Dusty and bring him to his old high school for an eleven o'clock assembly. Dusty wore his navy blues, and when he took his place at a table in the middle of the school gym with Mr. Kinney and the principal and a couple of other teachers, there was a sudden lessening of chatter among the seated students.

The principal led them in the Pledge of Allegiance, and Dusty saluted, realizing it was the first time he'd said those words in years.

I pledge allegiance to the flag of the United States of America, and to the Republic for which it stands: one nation, indivisible, with liberty and justice for all.

For an instant he was surprised at the tightness in his throat and the tears in his eyes. The flag really did stand for something he felt total loyalty to. He'd never doubted it, but the past three years had made it rock hard. He'd risked his life to defend Mom and Dad and Sis and all these kids. He'd keep on doing it.

When Mr. Kinney introduced Dusty, the welcoming applause was almost embarrassing. But Dusty had a keen sense of exactly the kinds of kids he was talking to. They were pretty much the same kids he'd talked to as student body president. He knew what they wanted and needed to hear. He told it compactly, making it more vivid and dramatic by compressing the story of what happened that October morning over the ocean.

There was too much to tell about the prison camps in Japan, so he selected only the initial beating at Ofuna, working out on the high bar with Sergeant Ito, and fighting the fire after the firebombing at the brickyard. Ending with the image of the surprised guard getting a face full of water from the fire pump left them laughing and finished on a high note. When he thanked them for inviting him and sat down at the table, the whole assembly rose to their feet applauding.

Back home, there was a packet from the Navy Department with a copy of the deposition about his POW experience he'd given in Hawaii on his way home. An accompanying letter asked him to check it for accuracy, sign it, and return it. He had no problem with that, but the letter also said that Sergeant Ito was under suspicion, and might be charged as a war criminal. Dusty immediately grabbed a pen and paper and wrote a letter with several underlined words, expressing as strongly as he could his belief that Ito was innocent of any criminal behavior and had been as fair and considerate a camp commander as could be expected under the circumstances. He hoped the letter, along with what he'd said in favor of Ito-Socho in the deposition, would carry some weight.

Six weeks after he'd been discharged from Oak Knoll Naval Hospital, Dusty got an urgent phone call asking him to report back to the hospital in two days. Puzzled, he appeared as directed and was told there had been an error in his leave orders and they had to be rewritten. He sat for more than an hour waiting to hear what was next. He was surprised when he was given newly cut orders for a ninety-day leave for rest and recuperation. He'd already used up forty-five days of the original ninety! He decided it was no time to argue. He'd think it over. Maybe another ninety would be a good thing.

After a couple more weeks back in Fresno, living at Mom's most of the time and staying periodically with Marian and her mother, he began to wonder if the extended leave was worthwhile. He'd made very little progress in recovering the old closeness and intimacy with Marian, and he was beginning to think it didn't make much difference what he did or said. She seemed to be just going through the motions of a very cool marriage. And then while he was at her house there had been a couple of telephone calls she reacted to uncomfortably, quickly cutting off the caller with some feeble excuse. He didn't ask for explanations and she didn't offer any.

Los Alamitos Naval Air Station was an hour south of Los Angeles, on the eastern edge of Long Beach. It took Dusty and Jean Caldwell a good part of the day to drive there, with a lunch stop en route. They arrived at the gate about 4:30 and were directed to the Officers' Club. Judging from the sound level as they entered, the Grim Reapers' reunion was well under way.

Captain Jimmy Flatley himself was waiting just inside the door, welcoming squadron members with a wide grin and an energetic handshake. Handsome and youthful as ever, he looked sharp in his blues with four gold stripes on the sleeves and a chest full of ribbons. He was clearly delighted to see Dusty, and as warm and chivalrous as possible to Jean when Dusty reminded him who she was. He remembered Jimmy Caldwell fondly, he said, and he knew that he and Dusty had been close friends. He reached out a hand to both of them, and for a minute Dusty felt that their common sense of love and loss was as close a communion as he'd ever known.

The skipper directed them to a room where the group was gathering and suggested they pick up something to drink on the way. Carrying their drinks, they peered tentatively into the room as several heads turned their way and they were waved in with raucous shouts. The men in the room all looked familiar to Dusty, but the names weren't on the tip of his tongue. Al Mead was already making his way toward them, his green uniform and insignia identical to Dusty's. The skipper had said he'd been in the hospital at Long Beach, but he looked really fit.

They hugged each other and started talking at the same time. They stopped and laughed, and Dusty introduced Jean and Al, who remembered each other from Coronado.

"We've got some talking to do," said Al, and Dusty agreed. "First we'd better let these other guys at you," Al said, leading them toward the crowd.

There were a dozen other Reapers there, including Swede Vejtasa, Russ Reiserer, Butch Voris, Wick Wickendoll, Whitey Feightner, Dave Pollock, Jim Billo, Tex Harris, and Tommy Harman, as well as six or seven wives or girl friends. Dusty and Al, it turned out, were the only former POWs in the group. The others had all continued on active duty through the war, most with VF-10, and they'd all ended up flying either Hellcats or Corsairs. Several of them were aces, too, having collected five victories or more—an opportunity Al and Dusty had been so ingloriously deprived of.

But Al had already gotten one up on Dusty, he said, leading him and Jean to a small empty table. He told them how he'd arrived earlier that day at Los Alamitos and wandered out to where some Hellcats were parked on the flight line. On the way he'd run into Tommy Harman, who was now a tech instructor at Los Alamitos. Dusty had just shaken hands with Tommy.

"You want to fly?" Tommy asked Al.

"Sure," said Al.

"Well," said Tommy, "since you're still assigned to the hospital, you can't check out a plane, but you can fly mine."

"No kidding?" Al asked.

"Come on," said Tommy. "I'll check you out in the cockpit, and then I'll check out another plane and fly with you."

So they did. The only thing different about a Hellcat from a Wildcat, Tom told Al, was that you didn't have to crank the wheels up. You just pushed a button. They cleared the tower, took off one after the other, and larked around the area for half an hour or so.

Meanwhile Jimmy Flatley arrived and somehow found out where they were. He was panicked, Al said, laughing. "What's Al doing in that plane he's never seen before, and he hasn't even flown anything for three years?"

"It was the dumbest thing he'd ever heard of, he told me when we landed. But it didn't bother me. An airplane's an airplane."

Later Dusty verified Al's story with Tommy and Jimmy, and he talked with Swede, Russ, Whitey, Butch, and Wick. On the day Dusty was shot down, Swede had splashed *seven* Japanese planes! With the three he'd gotten in the Battle of the Coral Sea, that made him a double ace. The skipper had recommended him for the Medal of Honor, but the navy had awarded him the Navy Cross instead. Russ said the whole squadron had been disappointed with that, since Butch O'Hare had been given the Medal of Honor for shooting down five enemy planes in one day. Why didn't seven in one day and a total of ten count as much?

The *Hornet* had been so heavily damaged that day by Japanese dive bombers and torpedo planes that she had to be abandoned. The next day, after the *Enterprise* and the rest of the task force had left the area, the Japs finished her off and she went to the bottom. The battle was now known as the Battle of the Santa Cruz Islands, or just Santa Cruz.

Russ himself had nailed nine Japanese planes, eight of them in a Hellcat night fighter squadron he joined after the first *Enterprise* cruise. Five of those were in a battle that came to be known as the Marianas Turkey Shoot, where he'd shot down four Val dive bombers and pursued and harassed another until it ran out of fuel and ditched. They'd given him the Navy Cross for that. Russ's night fighter squadron had a phony Latin-sounding motto that translated as "The older we get, the better we used to be."

Whitey Feightner scored five in his Hellcat to add to the four he'd claimed in a Wildcat. Butch Voris had been shot down in a Wildcat and wounded at Guadalcanal, but he'd also joined a Hellcat night fighter squadron and ended the war with eight victories. He'd been in Butch O'Hare's squadron when Butch was accidentally shot down by a marauding Jap. Tommy Harman had six kills in his Hellcat. The Grim Reapers flew Hellcats on their second cruise on the *Enterprise*, and some of them stayed with Fighting Ten for a third cruise, flying F4U Corsairs off USS *Intrepid*.

As they shared their stories, Dusty could visualize the action. He really admired these guys, his buddies. He wished he could have stayed with them instead of taking his Japanese detour. But they all seemed just as impressed by his and Al's special status, and eager to hear everything he could tell them about life in the POW camps.

When Jean was momentarily out of earshot, a couple of the men discreetly asked about Marian, and Dusty said she had a bad cold. He added that he'd brought Jean out of a sense of obligation to his old friend Jimmy. Sitting across the table from Al at dinner, he told him about some of his experiences at the stadium camp, the brickyard, and Niigata. He was surprised to learn that Al had been at Naoetsu, fifty kilometers or so south of Niigata on the west coast of Honshu. Al's experiences after the Japanese surrender were much like Dusty's. He told about the parachuted bale of boots that went through the benjo roof and knocked out a guy, and about Commander Stassen coming to his aid.

Al and his fellow prisoners had also commandeered a train, and en route to Tokyo they'd gorged on Hershey bars, sake, and cigarettes. When he told about the drunken navy pilot who fell off the train and broke his tailbone, Dusty broke in, wide-eyed, to say they must have been on the same train. It was strange how their paths had twice diverged and then converged.

Al got on the same hospital ship that Dusty had scampered over, and in one of the wards he saw the unfortunate navy pilot, lying face down with a large cotton pad on his tailbone. "The nurses would go by and pat him on the ass and call him 'Bunny Rabbit,'" said Al.

He'd flown out of the airstrip at Atsugi instead of Kisarazu as Dusty had, and his homeward course was about the same except that he'd wound up in Long Beach Naval Hospital instead of Oakland. He was about to be released. He'd come through the prison camps in pretty good shape, he said, maybe because working in the kitchen at Ofuna had given him the chance to steal some food, so he hadn't lost weight as fast as most of the prisoners had.

After dinner Captain Flatley made a short speech about what seeing the man again meant to him. As the evening was coming to a close, a navy photographer who'd been popping his flashbulbs from time to time asked Al and Dusty to pose with Jimmy Flatley. Al admired the salad of ribbons on Flatley's chest, and the skipper told them he'd strongly recommended them both for a Silver Star, but the navy had decided on Air Medals instead. He didn't understand why.

On the way back to Fresno, Jean told Dusty that it meant a lot to her to be included. She was glad to be reminded of what a great bunch of guys Jimmy had worked and flown with. Dusty nodded and told her he felt the same way. For the first time since he'd come home from Japan, he felt like he was really a part of the navy again.

Christmas and New Year's came and went peacefully. Christmas dinner was at Aunt Gladys's house on L Street in Madera. The Burgess uncles and aunts were there, and Dusty told them about his Christmases in Japan, especially the one in 1943 at the stadium camp, when he'd got his first mail from home and the guards had brought in musical instruments for the prisoners to play. Marian had warmed up at last, and they'd agreed that she'd go with him to the base at Alameda on San Francisco Bay, where he was scheduled to report in mid-February.

When the time came, he was more than ready. He was eager to get on with his life, which meant his career as a naval aviator, not leave time. He was as recuperated and rehabilitated as he was going to get, back to his normal weight of 155 and fit from daily calisthenics and home cooking. He and Marian moved into married officers' housing on the base, and he was assigned the job of Housing Officer—all pending his orders to Refresher Flight Training, which he could hardly wait to begin.

Grim Reapers reunion at Los Alamitos Naval Air Station, October 1945. Lt. Dusty Rhodes, Capt. Jimmy Flatley, Lt. Al Mead. Official photograph, U.S. Navy.

One day he ran into Vernon Hyde, a lieutenant, who'd been a dentist in Fresno and was now a dentist in the navy. He also met a couple of other old acquaintances, but the best encounter was coming face to face with Phil Souza at the Officers' Club. Phil had gone through naval aviation cadet training at Jacksonville with Dusty and had been flying a Wildcat with VF-72 off *Hornet* the day Dusty was shot down. Phil's mouth opened wide. "Raleigh!" he said. "I thought you were dead!" He insisted on buying Dusty a drink and hearing his story. Then it was Dusty's turn to listen.

Phil was in the first wave of American planes to reach part of the Japanese task force. There were no carriers in sight, just two battleships and some cruisers and destroyers. Gus Widhelm, leading the group's fifteen SBD Dauntless dive bombers, gave orders to climb above their present 12,000 feet before beginning their bombing run.

Just then they were ambushed. Phil was already annoyed at Mike Sanchez, leading Phil's division of four Wildcats, for miscalculating in trying to cover the SBDs from below and behind them. While Sanchez was deciding what to do next, the F4Fs were jumped from above by Zeros. In their loose formation, Phil was tail-end Charlie behind Tom Johnson.

"We were just flying along, and they came from the left, and I looked and I said, 'God, look at those beautiful airplanes!' They were waxed and shiny, and ours were old, dirty, cruddy-looking things. A guy came over the top and I looked back and I said, 'That son of a bitch is trying to kill me!' I started a scissors, a Thach Weave, but that guy just shot the hell out of me. I don't know whether it was the adrenalin in my system that gave me super strength, or whether it was the impact of those bullets, but my plane just did a snap roll. And then he pulled up in front of me, and I nailed him. It was shit luck."

Dusty could see it vividly, remembering his own encounter with Zeros. Phil continued his story.

"I was all alone and I figured they must have got Johnson. I looked around and I saw a Zero working on another F4F down below me. I turned down and poured a big blast into him, and he left smoking. The F4F was piloted by Willie Roberts, the wing man of Sanchez. He was badly shot up. There was blood all over the cockpit. By radio, he said he was in great pain, and I said, 'Give yourself a shot of morphine,' which he did. And he said, 'Maybe you better take me home.' Well, I didn't know where the hell home was. We weren't permitted to put any marks on our navigation charts. The only thing I could figure was just to fly the reciprocal of the outward bound leg."

"Did it work?" asked Dusty.

"Worked fine," said Phil. "I'd already discovered my right aileron was frozen and I had to keep the stick all the way to the left just to fly level. It was working, though. But about fifteen minutes before we got home, five Japanese torpedo planes came out of the clouds, and they were heading right at us. So I opened fire at one of them, and he smoked but he kept going. Right after that, we heard Gus Widhelm on the radio. He'd found a couple of Japanese carriers, but their CAP Zeros were chewing hell out of his SBDs. He let loose with a string of profanity about Sanchez for giving him no fighter cover. It was hilarious!

"Finally we spotted the carrier. She was smoking, though, and listing to starboard. We gave our recognition signal, coming in at a thousand feet, making a 360-degree turn, and dipping our right wings twice before heading in. But the gas was just pouring out of Willie's airplane, and the cruiser San Diego opened fire on us. When they're shooting five-inch shells at you, it kind of scares you and makes you mad."

Dusty nodded and grinned.

"I got on the radio and I said,'You son of a bitch, quit shooting at me! I got enough trouble over here without you screwing things up!'

"They stopped shooting, but about this time Willie ran out of gas and went in the water. Our life rafts were in the fuselage, under the cockpit, and Willie was hurt so bad he couldn't get his out. I saw him in the water and he pulled his dye marker. I circled him for a while, and then he was gone. I don't know if a shark got him, or what happened."

The *Hornet* and the *Enterprise* had split up and were about twenty miles apart by this time. Both of them had been hit by Japanese dive bombers and torpedo planes, and more were on the way. *Enterprise* was trying to land its own planes and take *Hornet*'s planes, too. Phil was almost out of fuel and glad to land anywhere. When he climbed out of the cockpit and took a look at his plane, he could see it was riddled with bullet holes, mostly in the right wing.

The flight deck crew was rushing to make room for the extra aircraft from *Hornet*, and just as they started working on Phil's plane a bunch of Japanese dive bombers came out of the clouds. They ran for cover and the *Enterprise* started twisting and turning. Phil was already in the ready room, but he heard about his plane from the Flight Deck Officer. When a sharp turn of the carrier tilted the deck, it began rolling loose and fell halfway over the side. Too much was going on to fuss with a badly damaged plane, so the Flight Deck Officer ordered it pushed overboard. Too late, Phil remembered that he'd left his favorite tortoise-shell-rimmed sunglasses hanging on the gunsight.

During dinner in the wardroom the captain of *Enterprise* had his lieutenant hand out to *Hornet* pilots laundry bags of clean clothes belonging to *Enterprise* aviators who hadn't returned from the day's actions. By chance, Phil got Dusty's clothes. He was devastated. After losing Johnson and Roberts from his division—Sanchez had survived—he could hardly take Dusty's being gone, too. On the other hand, he admitted, grinning, he was glad to have some clean clothes to wear.

After the battle of the Santa Cruz Islands, Phil went on to say, the VF-72 pilots had been assigned to help out the Marines at Henderson Field on Guadalcanal. The field was being hit by Japanese bombers every day. Every night, too.

"It was interesting," he observed drily. "But we didn't get much sleep."

Then there was Phil's experience landing a damaged Hellcat on the second USS *Lexington* during the battle of Iwo Jima.

"Did you like the Hellcat?" asked Dusty.

"Yeah, it was a great plane. Very forgiving of carelessness and stupidity. And you didn't have to crank the wheels up and down. I don't know about you, but my right forearm is an inch bigger than my left, and that's from cranking the wheels on the F4F. Twenty-eight turns.

"I'd been shot up and I was just happy to get aboard, but the tail hook—I found out about all this later—the tail hook caught on a tie-down plate, which jerked the tail hook off the plane. And then the belly tank fell off and slid forward and the prop hit it and set it on fire. About that time I hit the barrier and nosed up. The seat pulled right out of the floorboard and I smashed my face into the gunsight. I lost half a dozen teeth and had to have about eighteen stitches.

"But the stitches came later. Right then the plane was on fire and I wasn't thinking too clearly. Luckily, a skinny flight surgeon named Benny Bond was there—he was about 135 pounds—and he climbed up on the burning plane and pulled me out of the cockpit! I weighed about 180 pounds. I owe him my life."

Dusty was as impressed by Phil's stories as Phil had been by Dusty's. They both felt good about belonging to a team where everybody seemed to understand that you took care of each other.

When his orders came in March to report to NAS Corpus Christi for Refresher Flight Training, Dusty was already mentally there.

THIRTEEN

REFRESHER

Driving across the southwestern desert was still a long way from being back at the controls of a navy fighter plane, but Dusty wasn't an impatient man. A good thing. Impatient prisoners in Japan always got themselves in trouble. You could count on it. Patience was a survival tactic. It seemed that his patience was in for a long trial in his marriage, too. Marian was with him on the way to Corpus Christi, but just barely. Her hesitations about it had finally provoked him to a reluctant ultimatum. If we're married, he'd told her, come with me. If we're not, stay home. It was that simple.

But it wasn't so simple for Marian. Something was still bothering her, holding her back. Sometimes she seemed relaxed and happy, then the next thing he knew she was having some kind of temperamental spell. For six months now, he'd been handling her with kid gloves, nursing the marriage along the way you'd ease along an airplane or a car when you were low on fuel and a long way from home. He wasn't at all sure they were going to make it, but it was going to be a relief to be an aviator again and not just a husband.

Neither of them had much to say, so the only thing to do was just get there as soon as possible. Drive straight through if necessary, all two thousand miles or whatever it was from Fresno to Corpus Christi. Dusty had never been a sightseer anyway. As it turned out, he was pretty tired by the time they got to Lordsburg, New Mexico, and he thought of stopping ahead in Las Cruces. But then he decided to push on to El Paso so they'd at least be in Texas.

He felt great the next morning, after a good night's sleep in a roadside motel. And he still felt pretty good when they pulled up at the gate to the Corpus Christi Naval Air Station about eleven o'clock that night. A duty officer showed them to a furnished apartment in the Married Officers' Quarters, and when he went to sleep it didn't feel like the end of the road at all. It felt like finishing a rough detour.

For Marian it was very different. Her stomach had been upset most of the trip and she'd eaten very little. The morning after their arrival at Corpus, she woke up with a fever and nausea. She agreed to let Dusty drive her to the base hospital to see a doctor, and she ended up staying there for three days to recover from some kind of intestinal disorder.

Getting back in the air wasn't dramatic or glamorous for Dusty. It was gradual and uneventful. At Alameda he'd put in nearly twenty hours of flight time, but it had all been as co-pilot in a twin-engine Beechcraft SNB or JRB, and he'd taken the controls only occasionally. It was safe, conservative flying—mostly mail runs, in fact—and that was okay for the time being. At Corpus, an Ensign Brown gave him a couple of hour-and-a-half refresher sessions in an SNJ trainer, and that began to feel less routine. With the tandem seating rather than side-by-side and a 600-horsepower Pratt and Whitney that could pull the lightweight plane at over two hundred knots, it was more like a warplane. In fact, he knew that more army and navy fighter pilots had trained in the SNJ than in any other aircraft. He'd flown an SNJ a few times as a cadet, and it was an easy plane to manage. The instrument panel he was most familiar with was the Wildcat's, though, and the SNJ's was different, so he had to pay attention.

The next week the reacquaintance process was interrupted, but agreeably. Jimmy Flatley, who was now directing the Air Advanced Training program at Corpus, invited him on a flying trip to Lima, Ohio, to visit Jack Leppla's mother. Captain Flatley had written her after Lepp disappeared the same day Dusty and Al Mead went down, but now the navy had awarded Lepp a posthumous medal, and Flatley wanted to deliver it in person. Happily, Al was also starting his Refresher at the base, so the three former Reapers could fly the mission together.

They took a JRB-4, with a Lieutenant Potts in the pilot's seat, but Dusty and Al and the skipper traded off with him to get in some extra flying time. Mrs. Leppla was deeply touched by their visit—that not only her son's commanding officer but two of his squadron mates who'd been flying with him that day would make a special trip to visit her. They shared their memories of Lepp with her, and she produced a letter he'd written in the *Enterprise* the night before their mission. She read it aloud:

Somewhere in the Southwest Pacific
October 25, 1942

Dear Mother,
This letter will not be mailed unless I fail to return from an antici-pated mission. Within the next three hours we expect a large scale

battle against an enemy superior in numbers and equipment. There can be no alternative for either side. The battle must be decisive. I hope I can do my part well before I go. I hope there will be no undue sorrow with my passing. Live for the living. We who are gone must be considered the price of freedom. Some must die so that others may live. I am glad to be able to give my life in the hope that someday men will learn to stop fighting and live together peaceably.
Goodbye,
John

When she finished reading, there wasn't a dry eye among them. Lepp's eloquence impressed Dusty. He expressed with absolute truth the feelings of probably every aviator who'd flown that day. "Some must die so that others may live." That obviously included not only his surviving squadron mates, but his mother and millions of others who might not be living if the war had gone differently. Dusty felt proud to have flown in Lepp's division and glad he'd been able to make this visit. Before they left, Mrs. Leppla gave each of them a program from the memorial service for her son at their church. It was a souvenir Dusty would value.

The SNJ practice continued, at a leisurely rate. Captain Flatley had told Dusty and Al, and presumably everybody showing up for Refresher Flight Training, to set their own pace and practice the kinds of things they knew they needed. There was some ground school as well, to familiarize them with systems and procedures put in place since they'd last flown three and a half years ago. It went down easily for Dusty. Everything made sense and he caught on quickly. The only thing he disliked was the mechanical feeling of instrument practice in the Link Trainer, and he spent as little time there as possible.

While Marian was recovering, he started playing a little golf during off-duty hours. Looking for a partner one afternoon, he met another former POW who was in the Refresher program. Lieutenant Wylie Hunt had been co-pilot and navigator on a PBY5-A in the Aleutian Islands, and Zeros from a Japanese task force had shot down his plane on June 3rd, 1942. The wounded pilot had managed to land the amphibian safely in a rough sea, but the nine men aboard knew it would sink soon because of the damage, so they tried to inflate their life rafts and get in. The larger raft, shot full of holes, sank.

Only three survived to be picked up by a Japanese cruiser six or seven hours later. Apparently, the Japanese thought the two enlisted men wouldn't know much of value, so they didn't interrogate them. But they grilled Wylie, and threatened him with bayonets. They wanted to know the location of a new base for American fighter planes that had attacked them. Wylie's PBY had just stopped there for refueling, but he only told them about his home base at Dutch Harbor. Finally they tied a heavy weight around his waist and forced him to stand out on a platform over the water. They said they'd push him off if he didn't answer them. When he still insisted he didn't know any more and asked if he could talk to a priest or minister, they decided to believe him and brought him back on board.

After a week or ten days on the cruiser, he and the others were taken ashore in Japan and sent to Ofuna, the same "questioning camp" where Dusty had been held. But this was early in 1942, and Wylie evidently left there just before Dusty arrived. They knew a few of the same prisoners, like Al Maher, Tommy Payne, and Larry Coulter. Wylie and other prisoners had been beaten often at Ofuna, but never as severely as Dusty had. After that, he was sent briefly to Omori, the island prison camp in Tokyo Bay, and then to Zentsugi farther south on Honshu for the duration of the war. He told Dusty he spent most of his time there playing bridge.

Dusty played several rounds of golf with Wylie at Corpus, but his four weeks there passed quickly. There were a few beach parties for diversion. The main entertainment was provided by a war surplus amphibious commando vehicle that two former POWs had bought together. They were happy to give rides to as many as could pile in, and they roared up and down the beach and out into the surf.

The welcome culmination of the Corpus Christi phase of RFT was a promotion for Dusty to lieutenant commander in June of 1946.

The next stage of his Refresher training was at NAS Pensacola on the panhandle of western Florida. He and Marian drove straight through without an overnight stop. There they settled into a one-story bungalow in the married officers' area on Navy Point, north across the channel from Mainside. He had to drive farther north to Saufley Field, though, on the west side of Pensacola, where all of his flying for the next four weeks was in SNB Twin Beeches, otherwise known as "Double-Breasted Foot Lockers." Navigational experience was the aim here, with a good deal of flying by instruments on IFR—Instrument Flight Rules.

Twin Beeches were sturdy and highly adaptable planes, but no challenge to fly. Even bigger multi-engine planes had no appeal to Dusty now. He remembered the prewar days in Civilian Pilot Training classes when he and Jimmy Caldwell were in love with the huge four-engine China Clippers. They knew they were on the way to becoming naval aviation cadets and naval aviators, but they figured that after their service was over they'd become China Clipper pilots. The war and the chance to fly fighter planes obliterated that dream.

From mid-June to mid-July the flying was routine, with only the challenge of solving navigational problems to lift it above the humdrum. But on the tenth of July, Dusty saw something that reignited his eagerness to fly more than anything else. Instead of going to Saufley that morning, he drove over to Corry Field. Three blue Hellcats were sitting on the parking apron when he joined eighty or a hundred other spectators standing at a chain-link fence along the field. The Hellcats had large gold numerals—1, 2, and 3—on their tail fins, and "U S NAVY" in gold capitals on their fuselages. The pilots had just started the engines, and wheel chocks were being pulled away. Butch Voris and Wick Wickendoll, former Reapers, and who else?

After taxiing into takeoff position and pausing for a minute at the east end of the runway, the Hellcats began their takeoff run. As they passed in front of Dusty, tails lifting, they were in a staggered echelon, no more than a plane length apart. They held the formation as they rose, then at the end of the field climbed steeply in a Chandelle turn[*] to a thousand feet or so. Then here they came, diving in a vee to swoop low over the runway in front of the crowd before roaring into a high loop, upside down at two thousand feet.

Rolling upright, down they came again, with "one hell of a roar," as the Army Air Corps song said, doing over three hundred knots and pulling out less than fifty feet above the ground. Without a pause, they went into a second high loop, repeating the maneuver in the opposite direction—a perfect Cuban Eight.

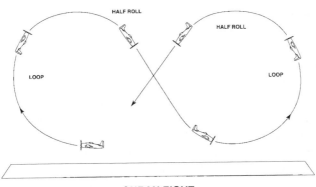

CUBAN EIGHT

Cuban Eight. Drawing by Kent Iwanaga/KBI & Associates.

[*]A high, climbing turn to gain altitude and change direction.

It was a pretty maneuver, especially with the three fighters in a vee, and Dusty was impressed with their precision. An announcer explained the maneuver over a public address system.

At the east end of the field, they pulled up in another Chandelle, coming back over the runway in a vee and then doing a perfectly coordinated horizontal roll, each plane rolling on its axis and their wingtips looking no more than ten feet from each other. Pretty smooth!

After another turn, they returned in a right echelon, corkscrewing into a neat barrel roll as they swept over the field. Reversing direction to repeat the barrel roll, they somehow ended up in a left echelon this time. Was that an accident?

Once more the Hellcats headed back over the runway, well under fifty feet this time—then flipped upside down! They made the inverted pass in a tight vee, flipped upright again, and there was a burst of applause from the crowd, spellbound into silence until then. Dusty clapped hard, aware that he was grinning like a fool.

Just then another plane came buzzing out of the western sky, heading directly at the Hellcats.

"Oh, oh! What's this?" The announcer's voice sounded concerned.

"A Japanese Zero! What's he doing here? Watch out, guys! He's after you!"

But the Hellcat pilots had spotted the intruder and were diving toward him. Dusty could see it was a yellow-painted SNJ trainer, not a Zero, despite the red meatballs on its wings and fuselage. Whose crazy idea was that? The SNJ banked sharply and managed to get on the tail of one Hellcat, but the Hellcat pulled quickly away, and the other two were on the SNJ's tail.

Each time the pilot of the mock Zero tried to line up on one of the Hellcats, another was coming at him, and you could imagine the machine guns firing. The announcer sounded like Don Dunphy describing a prize fight.

Suddenly smoke began pouring from the SNJ and its engine sputtered and missed. It started to lose altitude, its wings rocking as it passed almost directly overhead. The onlookers cheered. Just then a figure tumbled out of the plane, with a partly opened parachute streaming behind it. It hurtled toward the ground, the parachute failing to break its fall, and thudded on the aircraft parking ramp not twenty feet in front of the navy brass sitting inside the fence. Several of them had risen to their feet and started to move out of the way. But they could see then that the figure was a dummy clad in a flight suit, and the impact had burst a sandbag it contained. The spectators behind the fence cheered louder.

The Hellcats followed their smoking victim until it disappeared behind a line of trees at the edge of the field. Then they returned for a Half Cuban Eight in front of the crowd, followed by a right echelon roll and then another in left echelon, all to growing applause. At last they slowed and lost altitude as they approached the runway, staying in a close echelon as they came in for a landing.

Their flaps came down and the three planes touched their wheels to the runway one after the other, separated by only a few seconds and a few feet. Losing speed and settling to the ground, they turned at the end of the runway and taxied back, finally parking close together fifty or sixty feet in front of the spectators. Dusty was excited, and happy for Butch and Wick. He couldn't stop grinning. What a show they'd put on! What a kick it would be to fly like that!

As the three pilots slid back their canopies, the crowd cheered and applauded and whistled. When they pulled off their helmets and waved, standing up in their cockpits, Dusty could recognize Butch and Wick, but not the third pilot. Cassidy or Stouse? Those were the names he thought he remembered hearing. The three jumped off their planes and started toward the crowd. Dusty worked his way to the front and pressed close to the fence behind the chairs where the brass had been sitting. He wanted to shake some hands.

Butch and the other two passed the splattered dummy and said something to each other, shaking their heads. They stopped in front of the admiral and salutes were exchanged. Dusty recognized Vice Admiral Frank Wagner, the chief of Naval Air Training. Butch suddenly dropped to one knee and held his hands together as if he was praying, or maybe begging the admiral for mercy.

"I'm very sorry, sir," Dusty heard him say. "That was a complete accident. The parachute was supposed to open."

Admiral Wagner motioned Butch to his feet.

"Voris," he said. "I've got a suggestion. Move it out a little farther onto the field."

"Yes, sir!" Butch replied.

"But I like it," the admiral continued. "I like it!"

Butch beamed.

A gate opened and the spectators began to push through toward the pilots. Dusty hung back until they had a chance to accept congratulations and talk with other people. They were all wearing standard tan flight coveralls like the ones Dusty wore when he was flying. Butch was a couple of inches taller than the other two. They seemed pleased with the show they'd put on. When he finally got to them, Butch and Wick's faces lit up with surprise. They cranked Dusty's hand while he explained why he was there. Butch suggested they head for the nearby snack bar and get a sandwich and coffee while they talked.

Dusty was happy to see Butch and Wick again. He had seen them both briefly at the Los Alamitos reunion and caught up on their histories. They'd flown Wildcats with him in Fighting Ten in *Enterprise*, and they'd continued flying combat missions in the Pacific for the duration of the war. As experienced combat pilots, they had been serving since the end of the war at the Naval Air Advanced Training Command in Jacksonville, sharing their expertise with new naval aviation instructors. Dusty was introduced to Mel Cassidy, likewise a combat vet who'd known Wick in USS *Langley*, and was also an instructor at NAATC. Gale Stouse, who'd been flying the SNJ, didn't make it to the snack bar.

Dusty had read about the formation of the "flight exhibition team" in the spring and about their first Jacksonville show in mid-June. They'd impressed Fleet Admiral Nimitz at a command performance in Corpus Christi a couple of days later, and they were beginning a tour of various naval air bases around the country. The aim was both to remind the public about the importance of naval aviation and to lure more young men into joining the U.S. Navy.

Butch helped to fill in some of the background of Dusty's impressions. The navy was concerned about the fall-off in enlistments since the end of the war, and about competition from the army, the marines, and especially the army air forces for the available pool of recruits. More than that, the navy brass had been fighting a political battle in Washington to keep the navy's air arm from being swallowed up by a joint air force run by the generals of the AAF, who insisted that long-range "strategic bombardment" by land-based bombers was the key to victory in any future war.

So the U.S. Navy Flight Exhibition Team, Butch understood, was part of a public-relations campaign to remind Americans—especially members of Congress, who held the purse strings—that it was navy air power, launched from carriers, that had turned the tide of the war in the Pacific. The team's early performances in Hellcats, the workhorses of the Pacific air war, demonstrated some of the tactics that had helped navy pilots blast thousands of Zeroes and Bettys out of the sky.

"Gee, I'd sure like to fly with you guys," Dusty said to Butch.

"We'd love to have you," said Butch. "But you're married. The rules say you've gotta be a carefree bachelor."

"I know," Dusty answered. He hesitated, stirring his coffee. "But that could happen. Marian might give me my walking papers if I don't shape up pretty soon."

"Really?" asked Wick. "You been a bad boy? Going back to your wicked ways?"

"Nah. It's just hard to get used to each other again after three and a half years apart. And we'd only been married three months when I shipped out. She's been with me going through RFT at Corpus Christi and here at Pensacola, but I don't think she likes being a navy wife."

"Well, good luck, Dusty," Butch said. "The war's been hard on a lot of marriages."

"Yeah, that's what I've heard," said Dusty.

After Butch and Wick and Mel had left for Jacksonville, he thought of a naval aviator Al Mead had told him about. The flier went back to Iowa and found out his wife had been living with another man. He walked out into a cornfield and blew his brains out. At the Los Alamitos reunion that Jimmy Flatley had organized, he'd heard about a couple of guys in VF-10 who'd already got divorced. There was a saying about being married to the navy. Maybe that was true for him.

At last it was time for the kind of flying Dusty had been waiting for—fighter combat training. For that, he and Marian drove all the way through Florida to NAS Miami on the southeast coast. The fighter training field there was at Opa-locka, a couple of miles inland and just north of the race track at Hialeah. It was where he and Jimmy Caldwell and Phil Souza had their fighter training in Grumman F3Fs when they were naval aviation cadets in 1941. That was when they began to convince themselves they were hot pilots.

Dusty and Marian found a beach bungalow to rent in Hollywood Beach, a few miles north of the field. Except for an initial area checkout with an instructor in an SNJ on August 7, nearly all of Dusty's flying through August and September was in a Chance Vought F4U Corsair.

The process was called "familiarization in type" and typically consisted of two one-hour or hour-and-a-half flights a day every two or three days, plus classes on the Corsair's electrical systems, hydraulics systems, and the like. Satisfying to Dusty as it was to be in a powerful, maneuverable fighter again, the flying was no lark. It was challenging and stressful, and it required his full concentration. Some of it was practicing defensive and offensive maneuvers as tightly and as fast as possible, and a fair part of it was mock dogfighting with another pilot, sometimes an instructor and sometimes a "student," although most of the students were already highly skilled pilots. At least twice, Dusty's skills were checked by wing cameras synchronized with his gun trigger to evaluate his marksmanship.

The Corsair's unusually long nose—twelve feet from cockpit to propeller—gave Dusty the impression that he was sitting behind the biggest, longest engine he'd ever seen. The 2,000-horsepower R-2800 Pratt and Whitney *was* big, but not that big. The Hellcat had essentially the same engine, but without the long nose. The difference was the result of two divergent engineering solutions to the same problem—how to accommodate the big propeller needed for the big engine, so that it cleared the deck. The Hellcat solution was to use long landing gear struts. The Corsair team opted for shorter struts descending from inverted gull wings.

But the Corsair's wing fuel tanks had to be moved when the machine guns were increased from four to six, and the best place turned out to be behind the engine. That meant the cockpit had to be moved back three feet, which severely restricted the pilot's forward view when taxiing. Even raising the seat six inches and adding a bubble canopy didn't solve the problem, and the Corsair's acceptance on carrier flight decks was delayed for months. Navy brass feared the limited forward visibility would be an even worse problem for pilots landing on carriers. In the meantime, marine aviators were handling the plane beautifully from island fields in the South Pacific, and naval aviators soon showed they could manage it on carrier decks well enough.

Whatever its earlier difficulties, for Dusty the Corsair was a pleasure to fly—honest, smooth, relatively quiet—and it produced little vibration. He loved the way it climbed, much faster than a Wildcat, and it was a very stable aircraft, especially noticeable when landing. All the RFT pilots seemed to be in good spirits. Tommy Payne, who like Al Mead had been in the Ofuna questioning camp with Dusty, was the leader of the eight-man group. Individually, in pairs, and in groups of varying sizes, they flew along the coast, over the ocean, and inland over the Florida Everglades, a formidable wilderness. Al Mead recalled his cadet-training fear of crashing in the Everglades—worse, he was sure, than going down in the Jap-infested Pacific. The alligators and poisonous snakes would show him no mercy.

Aerobatics were part of the fighter training, too, and after eight weeks of flying the Corsair every which way but backward, Dusty had only one challenge left—carrier qualification. But that would come back at Pensacola, where he'd finish his last week of Refresher Flight Training.

With the common background the Refresher fliers shared, they were at ease with each other, and often adjourned together after training to their favorite Miami club, Zissen's Bowery. It was a rowdy place, with bowls of peanuts on the tables and peanut shells on the floor, loud music from a jukebox or a live band, and provocative "pin-up" style women painted on the walls, along with funny phrases and directional fingers pointing this way and that. Tables near the door offered views of entering women as they were surprised by a hidden air jet blowing their skirts over their heads.

Dusty remembered coming there with Jimmy Caldwell when they were nearing the end of their naval cadet training in the early months of 1942. There was a period when they were waiting for other groups to finish, so they could all be commissioned together, and Dusty and Jimmy were restless. They had already bought their ensign's uniforms, but they weren't entitled to wear them yet. They did, though, hiding the uniforms under their overcoats until they were off the base, then retrieving their officers' caps from the car trunk and heading for the Bowery.

It was at Opa-locka, while they were waiting for their commissions and their assignment to a fighting squadron, that Dusty and Jimmy had reconsidered their relationships to their girlfriends, Marian and Jean. In that overheated atmosphere of cocksureness in their roles as fighter pilots and conviction that they'd be going overseas to face the enemy in a few months, they quickly concluded that getting married was the only thing to do. The girls were easily persuaded, and after Jimmy and Dusty joined Fighting Ten in San Diego, the four of them shared an apartment off base. The memory of those few months was still sweet.

Now, in their next-to-last week at Opa-locka, Marian told Dusty she needed to go back to Fresno. It was early October and she'd been away from home too long and missed her mother and her friends. She wasn't close to any of the other navy wives, and hadn't made any friends at Hollywood Beach. Navy life so far had been hard for her. This had been obvious to Dusty for a long time, so he didn't object. He had a thirty-day leave coming up, including Thanksgiving, and he could join her then. Two days before his last flight at Opa-locka, he got a letter from a lawyer in Fresno. It said Marian was asking for a divorce.

Glumly considering his options over the next few days, Dusty could see no reason to object to a divorce. They'd tried to work it out, but they were only pretending to be a married couple. The old feelings were gone, and they weren't coming back. It was time to let go. After that, there didn't seem to be much point in going back to Fresno on his leave. He'd go home to see Mom and Sis and the rest of the family at Christmas anyway. Hollywood Beach was a nice enough place to hang around until he decided what to do next.

Al and Tommy and most of the other guys were leaving, but a couple were still on the scene. One night at the Officers' Club, Jack Bauman showed up with an airline stewardess in a Pan American uniform. She was not just pretty, she was cover girl material. When Jack introduced him to her, he felt suddenly awkward, as if all his muscles had gone on strike. Later he wondered if he'd acted like a dunce. He couldn't remember what they'd said, but he remembered her smile, and her beautiful eyes looking at him kindly.

Her name was Pat Collins. She had shoulder-length brown hair curled under in what he thought was called a pageboy style. Her figure wasn't obvious in her airline uniform, but from the way she carried herself she could have been a model or an actress. Dusty wondered if he might have seen her on a poster for Pan Am, her head tilted up slightly, her eyes looking eagerly at the sky where she and her passengers would soon be flying. Marian was pretty, and he'd known other pretty girls before the war, but he couldn't remember anyone who'd seemed so alive as Pat. So *exciting*.

The next day he asked Jack about her, and Jack seemed pretty matter-of-fact. She was just a casual date, nothing serious.

"Would you mind if I asked her for a date?" Dusty inquired.

Patricia Collins, Pan American Airlines stewardess. PAA photo no. 12305.

"No, not at all," said Jack, sharing her phone number. He smiled. "I wouldn't stand in your way, Dusty. She thought you were interesting, she said."

Late that afternoon Dusty called her, and she agreed to meet him at the O Club for dinner. She must have been as ready for him as he was for her. They traded information about themselves, politely and modestly, Dusty feeling more and more that this was an encounter he couldn't afford to bungle. Question, answer. Question, answer. Like a long, graceful exchange in tennis. She was from Chicago. He was from Fresno—no, Madera. She'd been flying South American routes now for a couple of years. Yes, she'd picked up a little Spanish along the way. Well, he didn't know any Spanish, but he could say a few things in Japanese. Oh, how did he happen to learn Japanese? Well, that was a long story. . . .

No, she wasn't seeing anyone seriously at the moment. Was he married? No, he had been, but the war had put an end to that. He'd sure like to take her to dinner again, maybe a little nicer place than this. Was she going to be around for a few days? She was. She'd like to go out again. And so it went.

There was no question where Dusty was going to spend November. If things continued to go the way they'd started out with Pat, it was going to be a good month. She'd be gone for a few days or a week, and then she'd be back with a couple of days off. Repeat. Life was better when the patterns had regular rewards built in. And these rewards could get bigger and better, too.

The week back at Pensacola was a snap. The Corsairs at Whiting Field had been built by Goodyear during the war instead of by Chance Vought. The War Department did that a lot when an original manufacturer's plants didn't have the capacity to fill an order for so many units by a certain deadline. General Motors built Wildcats to Grumman specifications, but the fighters were designated FM-1 instead of F4F. These Corsairs were FG-1s instead of F4Us. But they handled the same, and four days of Field Carrier Landing Practice were so easy they might have seemed just routine if Dusty hadn't been already flying high after beginning his romance with Pat. The FCLP was review and warmup for the actual carrier landings and takeoffs required for carrier qualification.

The icing on the cake was his assignment to the Naval Air Test Center at Patuxent River, Maryland, on completion of Refresher Flight Training, December 10, 1946. The cake itself was served to Dusty that evening by Captain John G. Crommelin, Jr., in the wardroom of the escort carrier USS *Saipan* in recognition of his making the 6,000th landing aboard the

Captain John Crommelin congratulates Lt. Cdr. Rhodes as he presents him the cake made to honor 6,000th landing on USS *Saipan*. Cdr. Hubert Harden in background. Official photograph, U.S. Navy.

ship. Crommelin had been Air Boss in the *Enterprise* in Dusty's time, and Dusty remembered the dynamic pep talk he'd given the aviators of Air Group Ten on the eve of the Battle of Santa Cruz. He was also widely known throughout the navy as a member of the "Three T'gallants'ls," the navy aerobatics team flying Boeing F2B-1s in the early 1930s. He was a big, handsome guy and Dusty had always liked him.

Dusty's six landings that included *Saipan*'s six-thousandth were smooth as silk, and in the culmination of a rich stew of feelings and circumstances, he was ready that night to blow off steam. Jack Bauman and Doc Ferelson, who'd also been going through the fighter combat course, piled into the Pontiac with him for a visit to the navy's favorite watering holes in Pensacola. It was a very satisfactory celebration, and sometime after midnight the three headed back to the Whiting Field BOQ, Dusty at the wheel. He must have been driving cautiously, because when the road took a sudden left and the Pontiac didn't, the minor damage to the bumper, grille, and wheel alignment took only a few days to repair before he could begin his Christmas leave. After picking up a special passenger in Miami, that is.

FOURTEEN

ANGELS AND BEARCATS

It was a warm morning in May 1947. Cradling a mug of coffee in his hands, Dusty leaned back in his desk chair and propped his feet on the desk. He wished he had more work to do and less time to think. He'd lost headway. He was drifting, practically becalmed, and he didn't like the feeling. His job in Operations at the Naval Air Test Center, Patuxent River, was easy, but not very exciting for a fighter pilot who would rather have been testing a new fighter or getting launched from a carrier. Off duty, it wasn't any better. His love life had taken off and flown high for a few months, but then it stalled.

When Marian flew home to Fresno from Opa-locka in October, Dusty wasn't aware she didn't plan to return. But he'd soon learned she was seeing a lawyer about a divorce. Meeting Pat Collins a couple of weeks later was such amazing luck that he'd started thinking "Blue Skies" was written especially for him. "Blue days—all of them gone. Nothing but blue skies from now on!" From the start, he and Pat were simpatico, as she put it. In spite of schedules that rarely harmonized, they got together when they could and wrote letters when they couldn't. November was a lucky month for them, and they saw each other often.

Pat managed to get a furlough from work in mid-December, just as Dusty was beginning a thirty-day leave between Refresher Flight Training and his new assignment at Patuxent River. He planned to deliver Marian's car to Fresno, so on the first leg of the trip he drove Pat to her parents' home in Chicago. Already deeply in love with her and anticipating his divorce from Marian, he began urging Pat to marry him. She was happy and apparently willing, but unexpectedly tearful. There was a serious obstacle. She was Catholic.

Dusty knew her faith was important to her, and he respected that. He was a believer himself, though he seldom attended church. But it hadn't occurred to him to be concerned about the Catholic prohibition against divorce and remarriage, until suddenly it stood in their way. Optimistically, he suggested there must be some way around it. Pat was less hopeful, but she agreed to explore possibilities. Not long after arriving at Patuxent River, Dusty went to talk to the Catholic bishop in Baltimore, hoping he might find some sort of escape clause. The bishop listened sympathetically, then shook his head. There was no way Pat could marry Dusty and stay in the Church. And by then they both knew that marriage was their only chance of staying together, with all the unavoidable separations their careers required. They continued to write and to meet, but their future no longer held a promise.

Neither could Dusty quite see where his navy life was leading him. NAS Patuxent River could have been an exciting place for him, close to the hub of U.S. naval operations. It sat on a peninsula at the mouth of the Patuxent River on Chesapeake Bay, halfway between the Naval Academy at Annapolis to the north and the great naval base at Norfolk to the south, where Chesapeake Bay opens into the Atlantic Ocean. NATC, the Naval Air Test Center, was housed at the Naval Air Station. To be a test pilot at NATC, flying the newest aircraft the navy was evaluating, was a naval aviator's dream. But Operations at NATC was just an ordinary job.

Dusty and the other aviators he worked with were basically utility pilots doing milk runs—carrying cargo and personnel between Pax and other East Coast air stations. In the first week he'd flown one day as copilot with Sponie in a Twin Beech to NAS Floyd Bennett on Long Island, and then back again. Another day Metzner took him on a short run to NAS Anacostia, at the juncture of the Anacostia River and the Potomac, so close to the heart of the capital city that they could see the Washington Monument and the buildings on the Mall. By the next week Dusty was pilot as often as not, visiting stations like Cherry Point and Norfolk and Chincoteague, sometimes in a larger Douglas R4D. Sometimes he ferried navy people from one place to another, or he picked up or delivered cargo. Days when there were no flying assignments were filled with paperwork at his desk. Through the next three months the routine seldom varied.

The other fliers at Pax River were all good guys. Bill Adler and Joe Tucker were the most experienced, so confident of their positions they'd risked a New Year's Eve lark by donning tuxedos and flying a Twin Beech to a party in New York City. For that they'd been put in hack by the CO for a couple of weeks and let out shortly before Dusty arrived at the station. Bill and Joe were fun, whether on duty or off. Commander Jack Blitch, the boss of Operations, had a lengthy combat tour as Air Officer in the *Enterprise* after Dusty was shot down, and he had a wealth of stories to tell. He was a picture-book American war hero, tall, blond, and blue-eyed. Dusty liked him and they got along well.

Still, the "administrative flights" in Twin Beeches and R4Ds were tame stuff. Even ferrying a couple of SNJs to distant fields was hardly enough to get his juices flowing. The Corsairs he'd flown in RFT were more his style. He wondered when he'd get his hands on one again.

Often enough there was neither desk work nor a flying job to do, and he would assume his customary "on break" position, with a mug of coffee in his hands and his feet on the desk. This May morning he was thinking about the medical leave he'd just ended. In late April he had developed a urinary infection and spent a week in the naval hospital in Bethesda. While he was there he got a letter from Marian's lawyer, saying the divorce was final. Later that day, something occurred to him and he got some stationery from an aide and wrote to Butch Voris, the old squadron mate from Fighting Ten in *Enterprise* who was now leading the Blue Angels, the navy "flight exhibition team." Butch might be interested in Dusty's new status.

Just as he was remembering seeing Butch and the exhibition team flat-hatting Hellcats at Pensacola's Corry Field, Butch walked into the office smiling, followed by another tall, good-looking man Dusty didn't know. They were both in flight coveralls.

"Hello, Dusty," said Butch. "Working hard?"

Dusty laughed and stood up to meet them.

"Butch, you son of a gun! What are you doing here?"

"Got your letter from Bethesda. It came at a good time. I'm leaving the Blues at the end of the month and Bob Clarke here is the new leader. He's been with us since December."

Dusty and Clarke shook hands.

"Bob will be running the show at least till the end of the year, but we'll need a good man to lead the team when he leaves. I don't know anybody better qualified for the job than you are. Would you like to do it?"

Dusty was stunned.

"You're kidding," he said, knowing Butch wasn't. "What do I have to do?"

"Not a thing," said Butch. "Just sit tight a few days. You're single, you're a combat veteran, you're a good fighter pilot, and I'm picking you. I'll tell the brass and you'll get orders in a week or less. Your boss here won't object, will he?"

"Blitch? No, he'll be glad to get rid of me. I'm just taking up space."

"I'll talk to him on the way out if he's not busy. Gotta get back to Jax."

Butch offered his hand and Dusty took it.

"You're leaving already?"

"Sorry. We've gotta practice for a show on Saturday. I just thought the quickest way to see if you were available would be to fly up here this morning."

"You flew up here from Jax just to ask me that? You knew what I'd say!"

"Sure, but this is a big decision. I wanted to see your face and shake your hand."

"Butch, you're one in a million."

"That's what they say," said Butch, waving as he left, followed by a grinning Clarke.

"Thank you!" Dusty called.

"Don't mention it," came Butch's voice from the hall.

Dusty walked to the window and saw the two blue Grumman F8F Bearcats parked in the refueling area. He'd read about the Bearcats—the team had started flying them last August. When he'd seen the performance at Corry Field in July, they'd been flying Hellcats, and they were called the U.S. Navy Flight Exhibition Team. Now they were the Blue Angels.

Back at his desk, Dusty shuffled some papers but couldn't concentrate. He kept thinking about the Blue Angels. He imagined flying the close formation vee he'd seen them using at Corry Field. The team's performance then—less than a month since their first performance in June at Jacksonville—was as exciting as any aerobatic flying he'd ever seen. He'd always loved aerobatics, and been good at it. Doing it full time, and leading the navy aerobatics team—that was the top!

Suddenly life looked very different than it had earlier that morning. There was no soothing ointment for his failed marriage with Marian, and the lost promise of his romance with Pat had left him emotionally drained. But Butch's invitation put his naval career in a new light. He was moving again. He was out of the doldrums.

On Friday, June 13, 1947, Dusty Rhodes strapped on a Blue Angels' F8F-1 Bearcat for the first time. When he squeezed into the cockpit and fastened his safety harness, he understood why the other Blues talked about "strapping it on." It was snug like a sports car and felt as if it would handle like one. It was about the same size as a Wildcat, but the pilot sat higher in the cockpit and higher off the ground. And he could fly it about a hundred miles an hour faster.

Dusty ran up the engine and watched the plane captain, Stanzeski, give him okays as he checked out the controls. Monday he'd practice with the team, but today he was on his own, just for fun. They called it "familiarization." Over the weekend he'd refamiliarize himself with Jacksonville, which he hadn't seen since November.

When Stanzeski gave him the go-ahead, he released the brakes and eased the throttle forward, turning past the other parked Bearcats toward the taxiway. He liked the familiar sound of the engine—a Pratt and Whitney R-2800, the same as powered the F4Us he'd flown. In the first F4U he remembered thinking "Gee, what a long engine!" The three-bladed prop was far away, twelve feet or so. The Bearcat's four-bladed prop was closer, and the view from the cockpit was better, not only forward, but all around. It was the first navy fighter to be designed with a bubble canopy. Still, he couldn't see immediately in front of either tail-dragger when they were on the ground, so without a ground crewman he might have to make S-curves when taxiing.

The runway looked clear as he checked with the control tower, and he was okayed for takeoff. As the plane picked up speed and he felt the tail wheel lift off, he remembered reading about the Bearcat's climb record of a minute and a half to 10,000 feet from a standing start. He wouldn't try that on the first takeoff.

She lifted off like a dream, with power to spare. When he was high enough he turned to port and leveled off, then rocked her a little, testing her responsiveness to the stick. Next he stalled her and recovered.

Nice. This kitty could do tricks.

Heading south along the Florida coast, he put the plane through a standard series of basic maneuvers. Then he climbed for altitude to see what she'd do with more challenging stuff. He did a couple of slow rolls, then two or three snap rolls, boring a tunnel in the air. Next a tight loop, tighter than any he'd ever done.

Wow! The folks at the Grumman Iron Works knew how to put a plane together! Upside down at the top of the next loop, he flipped her right side up and went into a full Cuban Eight, tying a bow on a big birthday present for himself. Gravity, but no sweat. You could pull more Gs than in an F4U, but everything felt tighter and surer. She moved with you like a pair of jeans or a gun belt—*that's* what "strapping her on" meant. He wished he could have tried her against a Zero.

He pushed her through every maneuver he knew, always checking the airspace around him, the ocean below him, the instruments on the panel. She did everything he asked her to, with ease and without a complaint. She was a perfect partner for his imagination. After five years, he felt like a fighter pilot again.

Dusty was hungry by the time he touched down. When he looked at his watch, he was surprised that he'd been stressing flesh and metal for over two hours.

He couldn't wait till Monday.

On Monday, Dusty and Jack Thelen, a lieutenant who'd joined the Blues just a month earlier, were in the air twice with the team, observing the routine and getting to know their teammates. They'd begun with a short discussion on the parking apron, the leader Bob Clarke explaining that Chuck Knight would fly the number two position on his right wing, as usual, and Billy May would be number three, on the left. Thelen and Dusty would follow along a couple of hundred feet higher to watch them run through their maneuvers and hear how Clarke signaled them on the intercom. Then they'd come down for a quick debriefing and a cup of coffee and go up again, this time with Dusty and Thelen trading off with Knight and May.

Watching the routine in the air, Dusty was impressed with the coordination of the three-plane vee as they rolled and looped. He was eager to see how well he could do it. When it was his turn after the break to fly on Clarke's right wing, he was keyed up more than the coffee could account for, and every maneuver went like clockwork. Later, taking the number three position on Clarke's left wing was almost as smooth, except for an uneasy moment during a horizontal roll when he lost sight of the other two planes as he rolled to the left and was upside down and still rolling when they came into view again right where they should be. It was the reverse of what happened when he was on the other side, only then the others were out of sight while he was recovering from the inverted position. Skill and trust got you through, but he didn't like his sense of control interrupted.

Bob Clarke had already decided that the in-place roll was too dangerous, and as soon as he became leader he had started working on an alternative. The roll was a staple in the routine, even a highlight, and it couldn't be tossed out overnight. What Clarke wanted was to replace it with a formation barrel roll, moving the whole vee in a corkscrew rather than each plane rolling on its axis. So the team was doing both kinds of roll in practice until the barrel roll was ready.

One of the other IATU instructors, who would be announcing a few of the team's upcoming air shows, watched the practice flights from the ground and gave them a critique afterwards. He mentioned only a couple of minor flubs that everybody already knew about, and he complimented Dusty and Thelen. May and Knight kidded them in a friendly way, and Clarke seemed to be a leader everybody respected. Dusty knew he was going to like this job.

Bob Clarke had been recruited as the second leader of the Blues by Butch Voris, who'd met him at an air show where Clarke was demonstrating the Ryan Fireball. At that time he was working as a test pilot at Pax.

During the war he'd flown a Douglas SBD Dauntless dive bomber and had been awarded a Presidential Citation for bombing a Japanese cruiser at Rabaul in November of 1943. Bob was "tall, dark, and handsome," in the lingo of the day, and projected competence and confidence.

Dusty especially liked Thelen, who was quick-witted and funny. He made "wise-guy" comments about everything. But he was also a hot pilot. He was an ace in the Pacific, with seven kills to his credit, and he'd been recommended by Jimmy Flatley at Corpus Christi for the Blues. He'd flown both Hellcats and Corsairs, as well as Bearcats, but he seemed perfectly happy to fly the SNJ in practice and in air shows. He was good at it.

His name wasn't really Jack, though. It was Bob. In his first wartime squadron, the executive officer's name was Bob, and to avoid confusion Thelen had ended up with "Jack," which he kept for the rest of the war. It was easier that way. After the war he'd reclaimed his real name and was just getting used to it when he joined the Blues and discovered that the leader was named Bob. Since they used nicknames for radio call signs, he inevitably reverted to Jack.

Dusty and Jack often started the evening together at the officers' club, where they met other aviators on the base and often some interesting women. June 26 was Dusty's birthday, and as he and Jack stepped up to the bar he was complaining that he was already over the hump and starting the downhill slide into senility. He was thirty years old.

"Ah, stop cryin' in your beer," said Jack. "Or at least wait till you've got some beer to cry in."

"What'll you have, gentlemen?" asked the bartender.

"A couple of beers and a little sympathy for this old gent. He says he's over the hill."

"That right?"

"Right," said Dusty. "It's my birthday. I'm thirty years old today."

"Lemme see your ID," said the bartender.

Dusty fished out his naval ID card and handed it over. The bartender studied it for a minute, then handed it back.

"You're only twenty-nine. You'll live."

Dusty was startled. He looked at the card and did the mental arithmetic. Eighteen from forty-seven is . . . twenty-nine. He'd lost a year! Or else he was getting sloppy at arithmetic.

"Those years in Japan really screwed up your brain," said Jack.

"I guess so," said Dusty, shaking his head. "So I'm still a kid, huh? Well, I guess we should celebrate. Here's to ya."

As they clinked glasses, they noticed a lieutenant and three good-looking young women approaching them. Jack introduced the lieutenant as Charlie Wall, and Charlie introduced the ladies as his wife Lonnie and her friends Jackee and Frances, all of them stewardesses with National Air Lines. Then he launched into a story about how there were just thirteen airplanes—DC-3s—on National's East Coast routes, with a stewardess for each plane. And since National's boss was named Baker, the thirteen stewardesses were known as Baker's Dozen.

Jack thought that was cute. He also thought Jackee was cute, and he began asking her questions and turning on the charm. Dusty explained that the drinks were on him because it was his birthday, and asked Charlie and the ladies what they'd have. Frances wasn't bad-looking, and it was pretty clear that he had a companion at least for the evening. It might be a happy birthday, after all.

There was an hour-long practice every day for the rest of the week, with Dusty and Jack sometimes observing and sometimes trading positions with Knight and May, now known to them as Chuck and Billy. Next week the team was polishing their act for a weekend air show at Floyd Bennett Naval Air Station in New York, and Dusty was in on only two practice sessions. On Friday, he and Jack flew north with the team, a three-hour trip to Floyd Bennett Field on Long Island, where the Blues performed on Sunday, along with several dozen other aircraft. Dusty and Jack were still "new guys" and not ready yet to fly in the shows, so they sat next to the announcer on the ground and followed the script, preparing for the day when they'd take their turns at announcing.

The show was one of the largest Dusty had seen, with attendance estimated at ten thousand and participants from a variety of naval and marine squadrons. A Navy PB2Y Coronado demonstrated a jet-assisted takeoff from the field, a helicopter simulated an air-sea rescue by picking up a stranded aviator from the top of a hangar, and masses of Hellcats, Corsairs, Avengers, and Helldivers staged mock bombing and strafing runs over the field.

Leaving Floyd Bennett on Monday morning, Dusty thought about Lindbergh taking off from Roosevelt Field, a few miles to the north in Garden City, and heading out across the Atlantic. The Movietone News film of Lindy's takeoff and his landing in Paris had been shown at the Madera Theater less than a week later. The excitement of the crowds—both on the newsreel and in the theater—was electric. Dusty was almost nine years old then, and he'd tried to imagine what it would be like to fly a plane like the *Spirit of St. Louis*. Twenty years later he'd flown a lot of planes, but Lindbergh was still a hero to him.

Floyd Bennett was also a significant name, though much better known around New York than nationally or internationally. Bennett had become briefly famous by flying over the North Pole with Admiral Byrd in 1926. Both men had been awarded the Medal of Honor for the feat. He'd been at Roosevelt Field with Byrd a year later when Byrd was one of a number of potential competitors for the $25,000 prize that Lindbergh would win with his transatlantic flight. Then in 1928, while he was ill with a fever, Bennett had taken off from Detroit on a heroic attempt to rescue a German airship crew that had been forced down in a remote part of Canada. Unsuccessful, he had died of pneumonia and been buried at Arlington National Cemetery.

Dusty had learned all this during his visit to the field named after Bennett, which had been dedicated in 1931 with an air show and great fanfare. A number of famous pilots had begun record-breaking flights from Floyd Bennett Field: Wiley Post, Howard Hughes, Amelia Earhart, Jimmy Doolittle, Jackie Cochran, and even Douglas "Wrong Way" Corrigan. Dusty was always interested in little personal brushes with history, even though they might be remote.

From Floyd Bennett it was a four-hour flight to New Orleans, with refueling stops at airfields in Greenboro, North Carolina, and Montgomery, Alabama. With two nights in New Orleans before an air show there, the team had plenty of time to explore the French Quarter in the steamy evenings, lapping up Dixieland jazz and Kentucky bourbon. Dusty was glad he wasn't scheduled to fly in the show with his headache, and he sat with Thelen while Jack narrated the show, punctuating the prepared script with occasional improvisations. That afternoon they flew on to Pensacola, where the next day Clarke and Knight and May flew while Dusty took over the narrator's duties and Jack kibbitzed.

When the team got back to Jax, there was a message waiting for them from Admiral Wagner at Pensacola. He wanted them to report to his office for a meeting before the air show scheduled for the July Fourth weekend. Could they come early and see him on Thursday? Clarke sent off an affirmative reply, and Dusty joined him and Chuck and Billy on the half-hour flight Wednesday afternoon. Jack would follow later in the SNJ.

Entering the admiral's office Thursday morning, they were surprised to find him flanked by "the two Jimmys"—Captain Jimmy Flatley and Captain Jimmy Thach, legendary among naval aviators for their leadership and tactical innovations in World War II. Something was up.

Salutes and greetings were exchanged, and after a few pleasantries Admiral Wagner got down to business.

"Clarke," he said, "what is the basic fighter formation?"

"Four planes in two two-plane elements, sir," Clarke answered.

Dusty saw Captain Thach and Captain Flatley break into broad smiles. Admiral Wagner glanced at them and absorbed the message.

Addressing Bob Clarke again, he said, "I want you to work out a four-plane routine and come back in a month and show it to me."

"Aye, aye, sir!" said Clarke.

As they left NATC headquarters, they agreed that somebody must have pointed out to Admiral Wagner that it would be more realistic for the Blue Angels to be demonstrating the standard four-plane tactical division than the older three-plane vee. Maybe Jimmy Flatley himself had brought it to the admiral's attention. Early in the war Jimmy Thach had worked out the two- or four-plane defensive maneuver that was soon called the Thach Weave, but it was Flatley who'd done more than anyone else to popularize it among naval aviators.

Clarke had insisted that Dusty attend the meeting, even though he wasn't scheduled to fly in the weekend air show. As the next leader, he ought to be in on important developments. But since he had other business to attend to at Jax on Friday, he flew back Thursday evening, taking with him a copy of the Gosport News, the base newspaper, where he read that the Blue Angels had given over sixty performances in their first year for over a million spectators and traveled "over 35,000 miles to do so." The numbers were impressive, but Dusty wasn't surprised. The combined total flying time of all the team members would be another impressive statistic, if anyone cared to check it out.

With no air shows scheduled for the rest of July, the team continued almost daily practice sessions, trying some new four-plane maneuvers along with the ones already in their repertoire. When the mock-Zero SNJ flown by Jack Thelen made its attack, Clarke and Knight would bracket it in the scissoring Thach Weave tactic, and then Dusty would swoop down to join Billy May as the SNJ was repeatedly caught between the two two-plane elements. After the Zero was dispatched, Dusty would continue as part of a four-plane formation as the team experimented with various loops and echelon rolls. Usually the fourth plane flew off the wing of the number two or three man, in a fingertip formation, roughly in the positions of the fingernails of the extended fingers of either the left or right hand.

Jack sometimes flew a Bearcat instead of the SNJ, and when he and Dusty were in the air while Clarke was practicing with the three-plane vee, one of them would fly into the "slot" directly behind and below

Clarke, where they discovered they had a better vantage point for seeing what was going on. No one else had such a view of the formation.

During breaks between sessions, the pilots in the vee began asking the slot men for critiques. It was a great help to have their own impressions confirmed, or to hear about some little quirk they'd never noticed. Dusty and Jack had the same thing to say about the formation barrel roll. It was certainly safer than the formation roll, but from the slot it looked a little loose. Reports from observers on the ground were positive, and Clarke was hoping they'd be ready to use it in an August show at Jax, before showing it off at Cleveland in September.

Dusty wondered aloud why they shouldn't keep a plane in the slot for the barrel roll. The slot man could help everybody stay tighter and smoother, and besides, they were supposed to be adding four-plane maneuvers, weren't they? Jack seconded Dusty's idea.

"Let's try it," said Clarke, and up they went. Dusty flew the slot, and on the second try the maneuver was as smooth as a Ramos Fizz on a hot day. Everybody knew it before Dusty told them. Jack, watching from above in his Bearcat, confirmed it.

"You guys were as tight as a kite," he said.

The diamond barrel roll was born.

DIAMOND BARREL ROLL

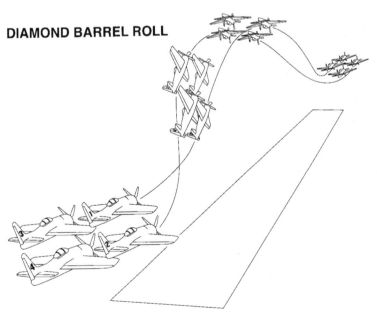

Diamond Barrel Roll. Drawing by Kent Iwanaga/KBI & Associates.

Something about the shape and even the feel of the diamond gave every member of the team a new sensation of unity, as if the four planes were inseparable. They felt the closeness, the tightness, in the way they talked to each other and looked at each other. Within a week they'd added a diamond loop to the routine.

Jack sometimes took a turn at the slot, but for the most part it was Dusty's place now. He'd be in the number one position soon enough. In the meantime, he was on a continuous high. With his eyes fixed on Clarke's Bearcat ahead of him, Knight's and May's planes perfectly framing it, he waited for Clarke's slow and careful call on the intercom.

"Diamond barrel roll."

"Chuck."

"Billy."

"Dusty."

"Get ready . . . ro-o-o-ll."

And over they'd go, in near-perfect synchronization, the distances between wingtips and cockpits as invariable as they could make them, with no more than a few inches' deviation. There was a rhythm to it that you gradually learned with your body as you did it again and again, so that the timing from one repetition to the next scarcely varied. You learned to coordinate it exactly with the others. It was like dancing, only with three partners instead of one.

It seemed funny to Dusty that he was good at formation maneuvers, when he'd been such a lousy dancer in high school and college. He was better at playing on his trumpet than dancing. He'd loved playing in the dance bands he'd been with in high school and college, and even summers at The Falls resort at Bass Lake.

The timing of formation flying was also like the timing of playing in a band. You got so everybody hit the same notes at the same instant, just the way he and Bob and Chuck and Billy moved their sticks and hit their rudder pedals at exactly the same time. The feeling of moving together in the same direction was a beautiful thing. He remembered the rhythm of the Thach Weave, which had probably saved his life when he'd done it with Chip Reding.

Working with the team was sport for Dusty, and the others seemed to feel the same way. They were lucky, even privileged, and nothing was more satisfying than getting better at it day after day. But the mental concentration and the muscular tension made practice days long and tiring, and after hours they shifted quickly into recreational mode. When there was time and when the summer heat and humidity were getting them down, they organized picnics at Jacksonville Beach, ten miles from the Naval Air Station.

Clarke and Knight and May had girl friends, and the girl friends had friends. Several of them were airline stewardesses. They were all pretty, or at least good-looking. Female companionship was never a problem for the Blues. The team, or most of them, would take a couple of cars to the apartment of one of the girls, and the other girls would be there. They'd have sandwiches and watermelon ready, and the gang would stop on the way to the beach for a couple of cases of beer. Frances showed up a couple of times, and occasionally Pat was able to join Dusty when she had time off from her job and could fly up from Miami.

The beach was beautiful, almost as good as southern California beaches, Dusty thought, but he didn't do much swimming, even though he'd been a good swimmer in high school, good enough to be on Madera's swim team a couple of seasons. With his blond hair and good tan and pretty good build—a lot of muscle had come back since Japan—he knew he was attractive to the women, especially since most of them seemed to think fighter pilots were something special. He liked talking to them and asking them about how they spent their days and where they came from and what their hometowns were like.

As a Blue Angel, he didn't think of getting married again, but he enjoyed being with women when they were both pretty and smart, and stewardesses seemed to have a special understanding of the demands of a pilot's life. Besides, the old hormones were still surging, and, in Dusty's life, pretty women gave flying some competition.

Early in August, Dusty flew in his first air show for the local crowd at Jax, but that was just a warmup for the famous Cleveland Air Races, where he flew with the team for two performances. That was the big time, with not only the best air racers in the country barreling around the triangular course marked by tall striped pylons but also famous stunt pilots like Bob Hoover, doing amazing things in his specially modified P-51 Mustang. Cleveland was the perfect place for the Blues to introduce their new diamond formation, and they did it with panache.

The crowds and the newspaper reporters were especially taken with the diamond loop and the diamond barrel roll. A silhouette image of the four Bearcats in one of the papers caught the fancy of the navy public relations people, too, and it began appearing in everything they released about the Blues. Dusty hated it. The planes should have been a lot closer together! Wouldn't you know the photographer would catch them at a bad moment?

Dusty's confidence as a full-fledged Blue Angel was solid enough by this time that it was no comedown for him to spend most of September practicing in the SNJ to play the Zero in the next big show at Harlingen, Texas, in October. Meanwhile, Jack was getting more practice in the diamond.

Dusty flew his Bearcat to Harlingen with the rest of the team, going by way of New Orleans and Corpus Christi. The SNJ had been flown on ahead by Thelen, who checked out local arrangements and then joined the Bearcat formation for the shows. During all three days, it was Dusty who maneuvered the SNJ in a threatening way before the mock Zero was hit by the Bearcats. Then one of the team's mechanics, riding in the rear cockpit, pulled a lanyard to set off a couple of smoke grenades strapped to the fuselage, before throwing out the parachute-equipped dummy that was supposed to be the Japanese pilot. The SNJ's engine sputtered and missed as Dusty pretended to crash it behind a row of buildings at the far side of the field. He knew from his Cleveland experience that the crowd would be applauding loudly.

Local celebrities, especially politicians, often showed up at air shows, and the Blues were usually introduced to them and photographed with them. It was good publicity for both sides. In Harlingen, two colorful state governors made their appearance—Beauford Jester of Texas and Kissin' Jim Folsom of Alabama. There were smiles and handshakes all around, and a great show of jolliness and southern hospitality. Dusty wasn't sure he'd have voted for either of them, but he was happy to be included in the fun.

Team practices in November were intermittent, just enough to keep from getting rusty before the Miami air show coming up in January. The rest of his air time—a dozen hours or so—was spent in SNJs, taking turns "under the hood" with other instructors at IATU getting in their required hours of practice in instrument flying. It was a period of quiet routine before a big end-of-the-year reward: a thirty-day Christmas leave at home in Fresno. That set him up nicely for the big change coming in mid-January, when he would replace Bob Clarke as leader and Officer in Charge of the Blue Angels.

FIFTEEN

TOP CAT

No air traffic in sight. Dusty checked his wing men in the mirror. They were right where they ought to be, nice and tight. In the number two position, Chuck Knight's left wing tip was about twenty feet behind and slightly below Dusty's right wing tip. Mac Mac-Knight was off his left wing as number three. Mac had joined the team in December, when Billy May left. He was a Pacific war veteran with two victories to his credit, and he had a New England accent that tickled Dusty.

Bob Thelen was directly behind and below Dusty in the slot, just far enough back not to catch his turbulence. Thelen liked the slot, and he was really good at it, keeping tabs on everyone's spacing. He and Dusty had helped invent the diamond formation, at least as far as the Blue Angels were concerned. In the early months after they'd joined the team, they'd fooled around flying in and out of the three-plane vee Bob Clarke was leading, and Clarke soon agreed with them that the man in the slot was the key to making the whole formation tighter and smoother.

Dusty spoke slowly and distinctly into his mike: "Loop."

Three voices replied in turn.

"Chuck."

"Mac."

"Bob."

Pause. Then the four-plane diamond rose in perfect synchronization. O-o-ver the top and down.

Accelerating to over 400 knots in the dive before leveling out 100 feet over the beach south of Jacksonville, they could imagine the reactions of sunbathers and beachwalkers below them—frozen in place, necks craned, jaws open, stunned by the sight and sound of four fighter planes hurtling at them. It was a kick for everybody, Dusty thought, smiling as the Bearcats barreled south along the line of white sand and aquamarine ocean.

"Cuban Eight."

"Chuck."

"Mac."

"Bob."

Pause. Once more the 'Cats climbed into a loop, then over the top into a half barrel roll, diving down to repeat the maneuver in the opposite direction. It was a great roller coaster ride, and he knew it looked pretty from the ground, too.

It was their third practice of the day, and they were making progress. They all understood what Dusty wanted, and they wanted it too. They believed they were already the best in the world, but they were getting better. Even though they'd been using the diamond barrel roll in shows since September, Dusty wasn't satisfied with it. It was harder than it looked to do it the way he visualized it. It should never *look* hard. If it didn't look absolutely smooth and trim, there was no reason to do it. They were going to get it right—every time.

Leading the team in a Chandelle turn, Dusty reversed their course. When they'd leveled out at 500 feet, heading north, he checked his mirror again. They were right with him. *Okay, here we go.*

"Diamond roll."

"Chuck."

"Mac."

"Bob."

Pause.

"Ready. . . . Ro-o-ll."

Rolling and rising slowly to the left into a tight corkscrew, Dusty focused on the horizon and the feel of the stick and rudder pedals and the changing pressures on his body. His peripheral vision made him aware of his two wingmen sticking tightly to their positions, Mac cutting back slightly on his power as he rolled under and Chuck pushing his up a little as he rolled over the top.

"That was beautiful," said Thelen's voice as they finished the maneuver.

Dusty was satisfied. "Thanks, guys," he said. "Let's head in."

Dusty felt great. He was doing what he wanted to be doing more than anything else. Flying a hot airplane nearly every day, with buddies who loved flying as much as he did. He liked being the leader, too, the Officer in Charge, for the first time in his career. That is, if you didn't count being senior officer for a hundred POWs at the brickyard in Yokohama.

He remembered flying wing on Chip Reding in the second section of Jack Leppla's division of the attack group off the *Enterprise* that October morning five years ago. He was happy being Tail-end Charlie, as long as he was flying. But just before the Zeros jumped them he'd been thinking that someday it would be his turn to be in Lepp's position. Now here he was. He wished Lepp could be here too. He would have enjoyed this.

Dusty reflected on his new position. Certain people had believed in him, trusted him to be a leader. They must have seen that he never gave his job less than one hundred percent. Any natural ability he had was a gift he couldn't take credit for, but he'd tried to make the most of it. Getting shot down in his first combat and ending up as a POW was just bad luck, but he'd stuck it out and taken care of himself, and eventually he'd had some pretty good luck, too. The score was even now.

Not bad for five years, considering that he was out of action for three of them. His naval career was back on track. From Ensign Rhodes to Lieutenant Commander Rhodes. From Wildcat to Bearcat. He'd skipped a Grumman generation there—the Hellcat—while he was in Japan. From 90 pounds in Yokohama back to 150 within six months of returning. As fit as he'd ever been. From married man to bachelor. *Where do I go from here?*

There was no need to go anywhere or think ahead beyond tomorrow, or the next air show. That would be Pensacola at the end of February. By then he wanted the team's routine to be perfect, as exact as he visualized it. He knew they could do it, even if it took three practice sessions a day. Tomorrow would be another one of those days.

Dusty's six-month apprenticeship to Bob Clarke as Officer in Charge of the Blue Angels had ended in January of 1948. His 149 hours of flying time so far with the Blues, 25 hours a month, had been spent mostly in Bearcats, but it also included a few hours in SNJs, an SB2C, and an R4D, as co-pilot. He'd spent far more hours than that with the other members of the team, on and off duty, getting to know them like brothers. Clarke had groomed him to be the new leader of the Blues, just as he himself had been groomed by Butch Voris. Now it was Dusty's turn.

Clarke's tour with the Blue Angels ended with the annual three-day air show in Miami, where Dusty flew a Bearcat on Friday and Sunday, and the SNJ on Saturday. At the end of January, Clarke left Jacksonville to report to VF-17A, later VF-171, the first jet squadron in the Atlantic Fleet, based at NAS Quonset Point. His jet experience in the YP-59A and the Ryan FR-1 Fireball as a test pilot at Pax, as well as his leadership of the Blues, helped him land this plum assignment.

Back in October, Clarke had been the first Blue Angel to break Butch Voris's taboo against marriage while on the team. He'd married Steele Simmons, a WAVE officer, at her parents' home in Rockingham,

North Carolina, with all the Blues in attendance. The team flew into Pope Army Air Force Base, on the edge of Fort Bragg, thirty miles northeast of Rockingham and just east of Southern Pines, where Steele had arranged for them to stay in a lakeside cottage belonging to one of her cousins.

Before too many drinks, Bob somehow managed to get them to a handsome, rustic restaurant in Southern Pines, where they toasted and roasted him at the traditional bachelor dinner. By the time they returned to the cottage, they had hatched a plan to throw Clarke fully clothed in the lake. But he resisted with surprising energy and ingenuity, escaping their clutches with no more damage than someone's elbow in his eye. Steele was not amused when he appeared for the ceremony the next day with a shiner, but the Blues looked smart in their uniforms and behaved like gentlemen.

In the aftermath, it appeared that a couple of other members of the team were already thinking about marriage themselves. Bob Thelen was the first to raise the subject with Dusty at the end of January. He'd reverted to "Bob" from "Jack" now that Bob Clarke had left the team. He and Jackee had hit it off from the start eight months ago, and lately they'd been talking seriously about tying the knot. There wasn't another air show scheduled until late February. Besides, he'd be leaving the team before long, and . . .

Dusty had stepped up the intensity of practices and needed to keep the team's attention focused, but a short break in the schedule wouldn't hurt. He okayed Bob and Jackee's request for Sunday, February 8, with a three-day honeymoon. The wedding took place in the base chapel, with the team in their dress blues holding swords in a ceremonial arch for the newly married couple to walk under.

On February 19, Dusty counted the hours in his log. In sixteen days of practice since the 16th of January, when they'd stepped up the tempo, they'd had thirty-one hour-long practice sessions. To ease the pressure and keep from getting too wound up, they seldom flew more than two days in a row, and in mid-February they were all so tense that Dusty gave the team five days off. Chuck had been holding the stick so tight that he was coming down from practice flights with a lump on the muscle of his right forearm. But they were shaping up.

And despite the tension of holding four four-ton aircraft within a few feet of each other for twenty-five minutes at a time while rolling and looping and turning at nearly four hundred miles an hour, every one of them loved it. They threw all their energy into it. They came back for more.

Pulling out of a grueling maneuver, or a series of maneuvers, more than once they heard Thelen's voice in their ears: "Let's do it again, Skipper!"

Between sessions on days when they went up two or three times, they'd have coffee together and talk about what they'd done well or hadn't done well enough, and almost always somebody would have a suggestion to make it better the next time. And up they'd go again.

With five days until they left for Pensacola, Dusty was satisfied. They were as good as they were going to get, at least for this month. He was proud of how much they'd improved since Miami, and they were good even then. Taking the team to an air show at Pensacola was a kind of homecoming. Like almost every navy flier, he saw Pensacola as the hub of naval aviation. Besides, it was only a year and a half ago that he'd seen Butch and his team put on their show at Pensacola, and now he was going back in Butch's place.

It would be his first show as the team's leader, the first with a big gold number "1" on his Bearcat's tail fin and "Lt. Cdr. R. E. Rhodes" lettered in gold under the cockpit. The glory was there, but the responsibility concerned him more. The number one responsibility was the safety of the team—to do everything he could to ensure their safest possible passage through some admittedly risky flying. But there was also his responsibility to the navy—to lead the team in a way that would bring honor to the navy and naval aviation.

All the people that meant the most to him now were navy. He owed them something, every one of them—Jimmy Caldwell, Chip Reding, Al Mead, Jack Leppla, Jimmy Flatley, Russ Reiserer, Phil Souza, Swede Vejtasa, Whitey Feightner, Al Maher, Larry Coulter, Dave Hurt, Al Blinn, Everett Bondesen, Butch Voris, Wick Wickendoll . . . There were a lot of them. They were a family he couldn't let down.

Those were the responsibilities he thought about. The other things most people would call responsibilities were just duties, things you did because they had to be done and you were the guy to do them. Mostly, that meant making arrangements for air shows. He didn't schedule the shows. OPNAV, the Office of Naval Operations, did that, after they approved requests for the Blue Angels from various civilian and military groups that wanted them. These sponsors had to pay all the expenses, for insurance and aviation fuel as well as food, lodging, and sometimes entertainment for the team. And they had to convince OPNAV that there was some charitable or public service purpose behind the air show.

After OPNAV scheduled the year's shows, or started to schedule them, Dusty got a list of dates and places, and it was up to him then to make the local contacts and be sure the arrangements were safe and adequate.

Lt. Cdr. Raleigh E. "Dusty" Rhodes, Officer in Charge of the U.S. Navy Flight Demonstration Team, January 1948. Official photograph, U.S. Navy.

Most shows were at military airfields, even when they were sponsored, or co-sponsored, by civic organizations like the Junior Chamber of Commerce, so working with each site's Public Information Officer was usually pretty easy. They were used to handling that sort of thing. Whoever was acting as the team's announcer and advance man took care of some of the arrangements, and when a permanent announcer arrived in the middle of the year, Dusty hoped to shift even more of those responsibilities his way.

As Officer in Charge, he accepted the administrative duties—the paperwork and personnel side of it—as part of his job, even though the main job, the biggest satisfaction, was in flying. But he was finding that delegating tasks was easier than he'd expected. The members of the team and other people he dealt with always seemed willing to do the things he asked them to. It was when he had to make requests in writing, usually up the ladder, that he sometimes met resistance. When he made contact face to face, or even voice to voice on the telephone, he usually got what he wanted.

The team was hot for the Pensacola show. Everybody was as eager as Dusty was to make it good, and they did. The base newspaper published articles full of praise for their performance, and so did the local civilian paper.

The Blue Angels, January 1948. Lt. JG H. R. "Hal" Heagerty, Lt. R. H. "Bob" Thelen, Lt. Cdr. Raleigh E. "Dusty" Rhodes, Lt. Charles "Chuck" Knight, Lt. JG H. C. "Mac" MacKnight. Official photograph, U.S. Navy.

There was another Pensacola show exactly a month later, at the end of March, with a third replay scheduled for late April. Before that third one there were three other shows, or four, counting two "exhibitions" in a row at Jacksonville's Craig Field, just before leaving for Pensacola. The big show, in mid-April, was at Dannelly Field in Montgomery, Alabama, the 1948 Southern States Air Carnival, an annual event sponsored by the Junior Chamber of Commerce.

Betty Skelton, a young stunt flyer Dusty had seen performing at Cleveland, showed up again in Montgomery in the tough little red-and-white Pitts S-1C biplane she'd christened "L'il Stinker." She'd recently won the 1948 National Aerobatics Championship at the age of twenty-one, and when some forward-looking public-relations type at OPNAV noticed that the Montgomery show would take place during National Sweethearts Week, he suggested that Betty should be chosen as "the Sweetheart of the Blue Angels." Dusty and the team had no objection to that, so she was duly elected and then photographed standing on the wing of Thelen's Bearcat, which happened to be handy, smiling at Dusty in the cockpit, while Knight, Mac, Thelen, and Hal Heagerty looked on approvingly. Hal, who had joined the team early in March, flew the SNJ for the show.

Betty had recently appeared on the back covers of several popular magazines—*Life*, *Look*, *Colliers*, and the like—in an ad for Camel cigarettes. "Watch that wing!" the reader was advised in bold red letters. Then in black letters on a yellow background: "Daring Betty Skelton calls it precision flying, but few men would try it." Several cartoon-style panel drawings showed spectators marveling at her stunts, such as flying ten feet above the ground at 130 miles an hour to snatch colored ribbons tied between poles with her wingtip. The last panel was a color photograph of Betty holding a Camel and smiling. "Experience is the best teacher," she was saying, "in precision flying, and in choosing a cigarette, too."

Betty Skelton with Blue Angels Chuck Knight, Mac Mac-Knight, Bob Thelen, Hal Heagerty, and Dusty Rhodes (in cockpit) at Southern States Air Carnival, Montgomery, Alabama, April 1948. Photo by Collier, Pierce & Kraus.

Betty was irresistible: a pretty, charming young woman as well as a fearless and gifted aviator, and the whole team fell for her. She was flattered and amused at the attention of so many handsome young fighter pilots, as they tried to outmaneuver each other. Although she parried their invitations graciously, it was clear that she favored Chuck Knight. When the session with the photographers and local reporters was over and the team was heading back to their planes, Chuck was the only one with a firm promise of a date. Betty would be at the two Craig Field exhibitions the next week. Dusty was happy for Chuck, but disappointed for himself. Still, nothing was settled. It was only a preliminary skirmish.

The day before the first Craig Field show, Dusty announced a practice session at an outlying field. He told the team he had to be at the field an hour early to work out some scheduling details with a few other performers. He'd meet the team there. Sure enough, Betty Skelton was there on time and seemed pleased to see Dusty. She was also agreeable to his invitation to dinner that night. Dusty had guessed correctly that she hadn't planned to see Chuck until the following night. Betty looked especially pert and pretty at dinner, and even though Dusty understood from their conversation that romance wasn't on the agenda, he enjoyed the evening.

The third Pensacola show, at the end of April, came off as smoothly as the others. The Blue Angels were on a roll, and Dusty was in his element.

The May air shows at Memphis, Raleigh-Durham, and Charlotte all drew crowds of close to twenty-five thousand. At Charlotte, Dusty ran into Haskell Deaton, whom he'd talked with at a couple of earlier air shows. Haskell had organized a loose coalition of aerobatic performers he advertised as a "Flying Circus," and he was full of wild stories and the latest gossip on the air show circuit. He was also an accomplished ventriloquist, which led to a prank on Jim "Killer" Kane.

There had been another Killer Kane in VF-10, the Grim Reapers, Dusty's squadron in *Enterprise*. But this was "Woman Killer" Kane—Commander James B. Kane—who'd been a schoolmate of Haskell's in Charlotte. He was now CO of a Corsair training squadron at Jacksonville and loved to go to air shows. Dusty knew he was flying "Rusty," his specially painted F4U with whitewall tires, into Charlotte late Friday afternoon, so he and Haskell met him at the airport in Haskell's car. As they drove down one of the main streets toward the center of town, Haskell at the wheel, they began to hear voices that seemed to come from people along the way.

"Hey, look! It's Jim Kane!"

"Wow! Jim Kane's in town!"

"Hurray for Jim Kane!"

Kane looked surprised but waved out the window.

"Hey, Jim!" said Dusty. "They really remember you here!"

Haskell had been staring soberly ahead, but he turned his head to say, "I wouldn't think so many people would recognize you!"

Kane seemed mystified and a little disoriented by the experience. It was only later, over dinner, that they let him in on the joke.

On June 2nd and 3rd, the Blue Angels roared low over the graduation ceremonies at the United States Naval Academy at Annapolis, Maryland. They took off from NAS Patuxent River, fifty miles south along Chesapeake Bay, where they'd stayed overnight in the BOQ. Approaching Annapolis over the Bay, Dusty could see a forest of sailboat masts in the marina along the shore. Then they flashed over the white-uniformed graduates, and Dusty could imagine their feelings. He'd never attended Annapolis, but the day he got his commission at Miami in 1942 was unforgettable.

Announcing the Annapolis performance was Lieutenant (Junior Grade) George Hoskins, and flying the SNJ was Lieutenant (JG) Fritz Roth. Both had recently reported to the team. In their first assignment after completing training, they had flown Corsairs in VF-74 on the first cruise of the brand-new carrier, USS *Midway*, for exercises in the North Atlantic. Then they'd served in USS *Franklin D. Roosevelt* for a Mediterranean cruise, logging more carrier experience. They'd come with strong recommendations from Commander Emmett Riera, their air group commander at NAS Oceana in 1947. After taking them up for a skill check in Bearcats, Dusty had verified their abilities. They were the first new Blues he'd checked out as leader, and he hoped later candidates for the team would be as good.

Back at Jax, the team took a week-long break before swinging into an intensive summer schedule, with an air show—sometimes two or three—every week. First there was Raleigh, North Carolina, and then a long flight to NAS Minneapolis for an overnight stay before going on to Bemidji, Minnesota, for a two-day show. The fame of the Blue Angels was growing, and so were the crowds. Bemidji was a small town, but the *Bemidji Daily Pioneer* on Sunday morning estimated "up to 50,000 to see Air Days finale."

Practicing over the field early Saturday morning, Dusty was just starting his call for a right echelon roll when a spot suddenly appeared in the sky dead ahead, swelling in size.

"Scatter!" yelled Dusty into the intercom, and the four Bearcats split in four directions. Glancing over his shoulder, he saw a Navy F2H-1 Banshee streak through the airspace where he'd just been. Too close. He should have known better than to take the team up at the same time as that jet jockey, whom they'd seen on the ground swilling oxygen to clear his head after overindulgence at Friday night's reception for air show performers.

There was a welcome rest for the team after the weekend shows. The local sponsors had thoughtfully booked them into Rutgers' Lodge, a luxury resort on Lake Bemidji, one of the "10,000 lakes" that Minnesota claimed. They had two comfortable cabins set among the tall pines overlooking a sandy beach, and on Monday and Tuesday they all had a shot at rowing out on the lake and trolling or bait-casting for walleyed pike. There was a golf course, too, where Dusty played a couple of rounds with Thelen. Meals at the main lodge—walleyed pike, naturally—were generous and delicious. The owners, Don and Louise Rutger, were especially interested in Dusty and pumped him for stories about his experiences as an aviator and a prisoner of war. The photographer for the *Daily Pioneer* knew the Rutgers, and on Saturday he'd persuaded Louise to pose standing on the wing of Dusty's Bearcat while Dusty stood below.

Fritz Roth, one of the new Blues, had unexpectedly been tapped to make the trip with the team and fly the SNJ when Hal Heagerty got sick. This had nearly upset his wedding plans, but he made the adjustment. Missing the vacation at Rutgers' Lodge, he left Monday morning for Jacksonville by commercial airlines, then drove all night to Norfolk, Virginia, to get married on Tuesday. Dusty was sympathetic. Since coming close to marrying Pat, he could understand the urgency.

Besides, there was a new girl on his horizon, a twenty-year-old charmer from Jacksonville named Betty Jean Williams. One evening in May he'd noticed her waiting in the BOQ lounge for a lieutenant Dusty knew slightly. When he saw the lieutenant the next morning at breakfast, he asked him about his date. The lieutenant was in a foul mood; he'd asked her to marry him and she'd turned him down. He was through with her. In that case, said Dusty, would the lieutenant mind sharing her name and phone number?

Betty's mother answered the phone and was impressed when Dusty introduced himself. A lieutenant commander! Leader of the Blue Angels! She excitedly conveyed her approval to Betty and urged her to accept Dusty's request for a date. They'd dated several times since then, and Dusty found her as interesting as she was pretty. She'd attended Stetson University in DeLand for two and a half years, where she'd majored in

Louise Rutger, Bemidji, Minnesota, on wing of Dusty's Bearcat, June 1948.
Reprinted with permission of *Bemidji Pioneer*.

journalism and been recruited by a sorority. She'd loved the social whirl,
but quit the university to take a bookkeeping job when she felt she was
becoming a financial burden on her mother, who was divorced and working. Betty had a combination of conscientiousness and playfulness that
intrigued Dusty.

The month of June ended with Dusty's thirtieth birthday and a show
for the second anniversary of the Naval Reserve Air Station in Atlanta.

On the program with the Blue Angels was a group of five twin-jet McDonnell FH-1 Phantoms led by Lieutenant Colonel Marion Carl of the Marine Corps, who held the official world speed record for jet planes. Carl was a World War II ace in the Pacific, with eighteen downed enemy planes, two Navy Crosses, and four Distinguished Flying Crosses to his credit. He was currently leading a marine jet demonstration group of varying size, and Dusty had met him briefly at a couple of previous air shows. In Atlanta, the Phantoms handled the speed, streaking across the field at over five hundred miles an hour, and the Blue Angels handled the intricate maneuvers. According to the *Atlanta Constitution*, it was a thrilling show. But the next month brought the Blues two of the biggest and best-publicized shows they'd ever done.

"Two Million Review US Air Arm at Air Show" said the headline in the *New York Daily Mirror*. Two million! The Coney Island show on Friday, July 2, featured air groups from the navy, air force, and marines, showing off some of their newest aircraft for the huge crowd spread out for miles along the beaches. There were specialty civilian acts as well, and Corky Meyer, Grumman's chief test pilot, did some impressive "trick flying" in a Bearcat. The *Daily Mirror* reporter's adrenalin was still pumping when he described the finale:

> A few minutes later the fabulous Blue Angels, the Navy's answer to any and all hot pilot groups, took over with a simulated air battle that made everyone's heart leap. While Lt Cdr Dusty Rhodes and Lts Jack Thelen, Charles Knight, and Mac MacKnight hovered high in the skies like a wolf pack, Lt Harold Heagerty flew by in a disguised Jap Zero. The pack leaped on him, and as the air was rent with gunfire, smoke suddenly shot up from the Zero and it began a dizzy dive earthward. Screams rose from the watchers all along the beach front, but Army and Navy loudspeakers quickly assured the crowd that it was all simulated, and sure enough Heagerty leveled off as he neared the water and flew away with his buddies to the accompaniment of tremendous cheers.

Two days earlier, when the Blues had landed at NAS Floyd Bennett, a few miles east of Coney Island, they had been welcomed by Grover Whelan, New York City's famous greeter, who informed them that they would be the guests of the city at the amusement park the next day. Whelan had welcomed hundreds of celebrities to the city, including the most famous of all twenty-one years earlier—Charles Lindbergh. Though it was Thursday, the summer crowds were out in force at Coney Island, and the team reveled in the festive atmosphere. Dusty rode three successive tours on the merry-go-round, insisting with a straight face that the other rides were too wild for him.

After Coney Island, July had the air of a run-up to the end-of-the-month climax at the grand opening of Idlewild International Airport, a week-long celebration in which the Blues were scheduled for six performances. Two days after Coney Island, there were holiday shows on July 4 and 5 at Columbus, Ohio; then mid-month sorties to Chattanooga and Knoxville for one-day shows before flying on to Worcester, Massachusetts, for a centennial celebration. To warm up for the Worcester show, the team took a short hop east to Weymouth, Mac MacKnight's hometown, and treated his family and neighbors to a few minutes of fancy flying.

That was good for Mac's morale, which had been anemic ever since an accident in practice at Port Columbus Municipal Airport the day before the Columbus show. Dusty had been thinking about going directly into a Half Cuban Eight on takeoff, which would be a spectacular beginning. The Bearcats could easily handle it, and the team, on a high the day after the Coney Island show, were ready to try it.

For some reason, Mac lost his concentration as the Bearcats began their in-line run down the runway, and before he'd built up enough airspeed to become airborne, he inadvertently retracted the landing gear. Dusty, glancing down from the top of the loop, was astonished to see Mac's plane skidding along the runway, where it came to rest with a badly bent prop. Mac was deeply embarrassed but unhurt, and he was able to fly their spare fifth plane in the Columbus show.

Meanwhile Lieutenant Commander Charlie Brostrom, the maintenance officer for the Naval Reserve squadron at Port Columbus, saved Dusty the trouble and embarrassment of filing an accident report. He assured Dusty that he'd take care of everything, and ten days later the plane was like new and ready for Dusty and Mac to pick up. The navy never knew.

Time magazine called the 1948 Idlewild dedication "the greatest peacetime display of aerial might in US history." The air show ran from July 31 to August 8 and amazed spectators with the numbers of its aircraft as well as the quality of its airmanship. "One thousand planes came from bases in 15 states, and from Navy carriers at sea," said *Time*. "Winging in over Jamaica Bay, 200 B-29s thundered by in massive formation, Fairchild flying boxcars lumbered past and three six-engined B-36s, the world's largest bombers, cruised slowly across the far edge of the field."

Dusty Rhodes on carousel at Euclid Beach Park, Cleveland. Photo by Horton. Courtesy of Raleigh E. Rhodes.

Lieutenant Colonel Marion Carl from marine squadron VMF-122 led four FH-1 Phantoms over the field, and the Gray Angels, "three flying admirals," buzzed the field in their own Phantoms. A lone Grumman F9F Panther jet, probably piloted by Corky Meyer from Grumman, flew past the grandstand very low at over six hundred miles per hour. According to a newspaper account, "shock waves visible like vapor trails formed around the pointed fuselage just forward of the cockpit."

A British Navy team showed their skills in four Hawker Hurricanes, and on the last day, designated Navy and Marine Day, with 265,000 spectators present, they were joined in a sweep over the field by the Blue Angels, who had already performed on five previous days. During a break at Floyd Bennett Field, where the Brits and the Blues were staging, Dusty watched one Hurricane pilot fly so low over the runway that he bent the tips of his five-bladed propeller.

Not to worry. The Hurricane landed and the ground crew got to work. After sawing off the tip of the most damaged blade, they jury-rigged a marker on the ground—a wooden crate that the sawed-off blade just cleared—then rotated the prop and sawed off the other four blades to match. Dusty was impressed by the casualness of their solution.

There were other minor mishaps. One of the Gray Angels, Rear Admiral Edgar "Bat" Cruise, age forty-nine, had a flame-out in his Phantom jet at five thousand feet and nursed the plane safely in to a dead-stick landing. And when somehow the Blue Angels in a low pass over the field found themselves confronted head-on by the Gray Angels, whose two other members were Rear Admirals Apollo Soucek, fifty-one, and Dan Gallery, forty-seven, Dusty's quick "Scatter!" saved the day.

Air Force General Hoyt Vandenberg, on hand to appreciate and take credit for his service's participation, was more than mildly upset when a flight of B-29s from Hawaii, scheduled to appear precisely on the announcer's cue, never materialized. The printable part of his reaction was rendered as "Somebody's going to hear about this."

President Harry Truman was welcomed by New York's governor, Thomas E. Dewey, his opponent in the presidential election campaign then under way. The two were photographed smiling and shaking hands. But President Truman may have suspected sabotage when a flight of Lockheed F-80 Shooting Stars whooshed over the field during his short address to the crowd and drowned out most of his words.

The Idlewild opening was nevertheless a great success, and in the opinion of *Time*, "the Navy stole the show. Its 200 fighters and dive bombers flew in tight, ground-hugging formations, swept over and simulated mass attacks. The famed Blue Angels, led by Lt Cdr Raleigh 'Dusty' Rhodes, stunted with the precision of a chorus line. Grumman Bearcats crumpled the walls of a painted target, revealing the word 'Navy' in glowing block letters, as the President, an old Artillery captain, chuckled appreciatively."

After their final triumphant sweep of the field in the company of the British Hurricanes, the Blues relaxed contentedly on their nonstop three-

and-a-half-hour flight home to Jacksonville. They had done themselves—and the U.S. Navy—proud.

After a four-day break, the Blues were back in the air again for a Friday air show at Jax, then off the same day for Columbus, Ohio, the staging field for a Sunday airshow at Lima. After the show the whole team was invited by Jack Leppla's mother to have dinner at her home. Dusty had visited her during his Refresher Flight Training in 1946, when Jimmy Flatley at Corpus Christi suggested they should fly up to pay their respects. She was visibly moved on both occasions, and it was an emotional reminder for Dusty too.

Meanwhile, Dusty's friendship with Betty had become a romance, warmly smiled on by her mother and stepfather. Dusty was surprised to learn that her father was the manager and sometimes bartender at the George Washington Hotel in Jacksonville, a favorite off-duty hangout for navy airmen.

With the Blues' busy travel schedule, it was hard for Dusty to spend much time with Betty, but they kept in touch by telephone. He was coming to believe she was too good to let get away, and he wooed her with flowers and candy and funny greeting cards. He knew there were other men waiting to step in if he failed to keep her full attention.

The Cleveland Air Races the first week of September kicked off the fall season, and in the following months the Blues were all over the map—Watertown, South Dakota; Anacostia in Washington, D.C.; Burlington, Iowa; Miami again; a Navy Day show in Minneapolis; Jacksonville again.

The Philadelphia show scheduled for November 2 had to be canceled at the last minute—not just the Blue Angels' portion, but the whole show. Flying up from Jacksonville, the team refueled at Pope Army Air Force Base, but when Dusty radioed Philadelphia for landing clearance, he was told the field had been shut down because a thick cloud of smog had rolled in, suffocating the city. The Blues turned west as Dusty began checking other possible landing sites, but fields that were open when he first contacted them closed before they could be reached. Steel mills in Pittsburgh and all across the state were churning out fumes that the prevailing winds carried east, and the sun in its westward course converted them into a blinding, toxic cloud.

As a precaution, Dusty ordered rpm's cut back to save fuel. Akron, a major field, was open and would probably remain so, but that was all the way across Pennsylvania and into Ohio. Watching the fuel gauge as the miles and minutes ticked by, Dusty could see it was going to be close, but he thought they could make it. The others agreed.

Over Akron the sky was clear but there were a lot of planes needing to land, and the control tower was trying to get the most desperate ones down first. The Bearcats had to circle twice before entering the landing pattern, and Chuck and Mac were reporting empty tanks. When the planes hit the runway one after the other, Dusty could imagine every pilot breathing easier. On the taxiway, though, first Mac's plane and then Chuck's sputtered and stopped. Their tanks were dry.

The team ate while the planes were refueled, and then they headed home, looking forward to a little rest before the next show, four days later, at Orlando. It was a long day, including more than six and a half hours in the air. Dusty read in the paper the next morning that a number of people had died from the effects of the smog in Donora, Pennsylvania.

There were four more shows before the Christmas holidays, but only one memorable one. At Toledo on December 6, a snowstorm with considerable wind required some serious evaluation, but the visibility was acceptable and the Blues went up. There were hundreds of cars at the airport and people were staying in them. Doing loops and the Cuban Eight, Dusty knew they were out of sight in the clouds and snow part of the time, but the carloads of spectators stayed and the show went on. Fritz Roth, a new team member, was flying the SNJ, newly christened "Beetle Bomb," and over the runway in front of the half-empty grandstand and acres of cars he throttled back and put his flaps down while heading into the wind. Beetle Bomb flew slowly backwards. Fritz said later he thought those poor people who came out in the cold deserved something special.

In the midst of a tight schedule of shows, the Blue Angels found their home base relocated when the whole Naval Air Advanced Training Command was ordered to move from Jacksonville to Corpus Christi on the Texas coast. On Monday, November 8, they put on a farewell performance over the water south of the St. John's River bridge. On Saturday, after a hectic week of packing and shipping their support materiel, they flew to Corpus Christi, with refueling stops at Pensacola and Lake Charles, Louisiana. Two days later, on Monday, they celebrated their arrival at their new home with an air show performance at the Kingsville field, a few miles to the southwest. The rest of November was spent getting settled into their new station and overseeing the reinstallation of equipment by the maintenance crew, which by now had grown to about thirty men.

After a week of making sure everything was in order, Dusty flew back to Jacksonville by transport to keep a previous engagement. Just before leaving there, he'd proposed marriage to Betty. He'd pointed out that con-

Betty Jean (Williams) Rhodes, November 1948. Courtesy of Raleigh E. Rhodes.

tinuing their romance when he was based in Corpus Christi would be hard. She agreed, and because Georgia, unlike Florida, had no waiting period, they decided to drive across the state line the Saturday after Thanksgiving and get married by a justice of the peace.

The wedding, though rushed, came off as planned. Mr. and Mrs. Griffin, Betty's mother and stepfather, accompanied them in a separate car to act as witnesses. Folkston, Georgia, was only forty miles from Jacksonville, and Betty's blue and gray gabardine suit was hardly rumpled. Her mother was her sole attendant, and her stepfather gave her away. After the ceremony and farewells, the newlyweds left for a brief honeymoon in New Orleans.

SIXTEEN

JOINING THE JET SET

In their '42 Plymouth coupe, bought cheaply from a buddy, Dusty and his bride arrived at NAS Corpus Christi at 3 A.M. Wednesday, December 1, 1948, his first duty day at the new base. They'd stretched their honeymoon to the limit, and there was still time for a few hours' sleep before Dusty suited up and joined the team on the field at noon.

The Blues had one day—time for a couple of practice flights—before they left for shows at Grosse Ile, Michigan, and Toledo, Ohio, a tour that kept them flying for six days. After a few more duty days on base, they were ready for Christmas leave. Instead of returning to Fresno as he'd done the year before, Dusty celebrated Christmas with Betty in their new, if temporary, home in the married officers' quarters at Rodd Field.

When he reported for duty on January 3, 1949, he'd worked out a solution to the first problem of the new year: the team hadn't flown since December 6 and were coming off the usual stresses and indulgences of the Christmas holidays. In only four days they'd begin three days of performances at the Miami Air Maneuvers. How was he going to get them to Miami safe and rested and still have time for the necessary practice sessions?

The solution was simple. Instead of practicing in Corpus with the usual distractions, including new marital ones, and then flying for four and a half hours plus fuel and lunch stops, they'd leave the next day and take it in stages, practicing formation maneuvers en route. Corpus to Lake Charles on Tuesday, a short hop to New Orleans on Wednesday, then on to Miami on Thursday, with a fuel stop at Tyndall Field in Panama City, Florida. Then they'd go up early on Friday morning for a little fine-tuning before the first show.

The team liked the plan, and it worked neatly. In the cockpit about an hour each time, they were rested and in good spirits when they arrived in Miami. The practice maneuvers along the route were sharp. The team hadn't lost its edge. The new man, Lieutenant Jake Robcke, replacing Mac MacKnight, fit in like an old hand.

The Miami Air Maneuvers had glitz and glamor. Zack Mosley, the creator of the aviation-oriented comic strip *Smilin' Jack*, was there to do crayon caricatures of the performers and to present a trophy to the winner of a local beauty contest. Eighteen-year-old Ann Williamson of Hialeah was named "Miss De-Icer of 1949," after a running joke in *Smilin' Jack*. Betty Skelton was there with "Li'l Stinker," along with Billy Light, a young Hollywood stunt man who did a wing-walking routine, and Johnny Vasey of Austin, Minnesota, whom they'd seen at Bemidji. Don and Louise Rutger had also flown in from Bemidji, and Dusty took them to dinner at The Bowery, the colorful nightclub Dusty had come to love during Refresher Flight Training two years ago. Louise was prettily embarrassed when a jet of air at the doorway blew her skirt over her head.

With three days of performances, there was time for other entertainment as well. Roger Kahn, the Grumman liaison, who often flew his custom red Bearcat to shows, this time arrived in a luxurious two-engine Grumman Mallard amphibian and brought along his friend Arthur Godfrey, famous across the country for his breakfast-time radio show. On Sunday morning, Kahn took them all up for a flight over Miami Beach and invited them to take turns at the controls of the Mallard, including making water landings. That turned out to be easier and more fun than they expected. When it was Godfrey's turn, he insisted instead on circling low around a large ocean-front hotel, the Kennilworth. His motive was mysterious until he pointed out to all of them a shapely woman sunbathing naked on one of the private balconies. She turned out to be his wife.

Godfrey loved flying and was just getting his pilot's license. He'd heard about the Blue Angels and had seen them perform on Saturday. Obviously impressed, he bombarded them with questions and ended up inviting them to appear on one of his new television shows as soon as possible. Dusty was flattered and tentatively accepted; he thought it wouldn't be too hard to convince OPNAV of the publicity value of such an appearance.[*]

Back at Corpus, the Blues had a month to settle into their new quarters and into a comparatively relaxed practice schedule before returning to the East Coast for a late February show at Columbia, South Carolina. A feature story appeared in the *Corpus Christi Caller* on the home life of the Blue Angels, showing them in various off-duty activities. Here were

---

[*]Dusty recalls flying to New York with his team to appear on one of Godfrey's shows. Responding to a question from Godfrey, he described the team's dinner with Governor Strom Thurmond. But that is all he remembers about the Godfrey show, and he has no clippings in his scrapbook.

the famous aviators with their helmets and goggles off, being ordinary guys for a few hours. But readers were reminded that the hot planes that took them "almost straight up" into their opening Half Cuban Eight could also reach ten thousand feet in just one minute and forty seconds from a standing start.

Thumbnail sketches of the team told Dusty's POW story and summarized the wartime exploits of Heagerty and MacKnight. Since the paper's reporter and photographer had been on the base in December, Mac was included but not Jake. Though combat experience had been one of the original qualifications for a Blue Angel, nearly four years after the end of the war it had gone the way of the bachelorhood requirement. George Hoskins had been too young for action in the war, but he'd served on several cruises in USS *Midway*. Fritz Roth, "one of the latest additions" to the team, had also served with George in *Midway*. In three years, this elite team with its evolving membership had "performed before more than ten million spectators in air shows and civic events throughout the country."

The Blue Angels were a new source of pride for both the base and the community, and they were prevailed upon to give two public performances at Corpus Christi before the end of the month.

The show at the Capitol Airport in Columbia, South Carolina, sponsored by the American Legion, gave Dusty the opportunity to add another colorful governor to his list of celebrity acquaintances, after Kissin' Jim Folsom and Beauford Jester. The Blues were invited to dinner at the governor's mansion, where they met J. Strom Thurmond and his wife. Governor Thurmond was a popular southern politician, who'd been a Dixiecrat "States' Rights" presidential candidate in 1948.

Roger Kahn had told Dusty in Miami that Grumman wanted to provide the team with colorful flight coveralls for their shows, but Dusty had turned down the offer. He was aware that among other naval aviators there was sometimes a feeling, seldom expressed openly, that the Blue Angels thought too well of themselves and were pampered by the navy. Anything that might encourage that suspicion was not a good idea, so the Blues continued to wear their standard-issue coveralls.

On the other hand, the Blue Angels were a distinct unit, elite or not, and they were entitled to some distinctive insignia, like a shoulder patch. After sharing this opinion with Betty one evening, Dusty got a pencil and paper and drew a rough sketch, showing four Bearcats completing the diamond barrel roll, which had become the Blues' trademark maneuver. When he got as far as he could with his design, he sent it off with a letter outlining his intentions to Margaret Jacobson, the wife of his cousin Jake in Madera.

Margaret was a commercial artist and quickly sent back several handsome versions of Dusty's idea. He took her sketches to Rear Admiral Ernest "Ernie" Litch, who agreed that the Blue Angels needed an insignia and turned Margaret's sketches over to a civilian staff artist, Virginia Porter, for polishing. In a few days Dusty was called in to approve the finished design and patches were ordered. On a traditional armorial shield a diagonal line ran from the upper left corner to the lower right. Above the line the four Bearcats roared out of a diamond roll against a white cloud. Below, a circle above a set of navy wings enclosed a plane lifting off a carrier deck. Under the shield, a banner carried the words "Blue Angels." It was a small thing, but something the team members would wear with pride.

It was also becoming clear to Dusty and to other members of the team that in order to represent the navy's best, they ought to be flying jet-propelled fighters. Happy as they were with the zippy, nimble Bearcats, the times were changing, and Marion Carl's marine squadron of Phantom jets had already been appearing at air shows for six months or more. The navy couldn't afford to be left behind much longer.

In early April, Dusty and Commander Bill Dean from Admiral Litch's staff flew to Washington, D.C. on a navy transport to see Admiral Putnam Storrs at the Pentagon. They expected a sympathetic hearing for their request, and they weren't disappointed. Put Storrs had belonged to one of the navy's earliest flying teams, the Three Sea Hawks, which had gained fame with a series of sensational demonstrations in 1928. He'd been following the exploits of the Blue Angels with great interest.

Armed with information from numerous sources, Dusty and Bill explained to the admiral why they believed the new Grumman F9F Panther jet was the ideal plane to ratchet the Blue Angels to a higher level of performance. Its performance in tests was impressive, and the navy had already ordered fifty-two Panthers for two trial squadrons. Grumman sturdiness and reliability were proven factors, and the factory at Bethpage could supply six planes in a matter of weeks once the order was received.

Dusty had one special request. The F9F-3 now in production for the navy had an Allison J-33 centrifugal-flow engine that compared unfavorably with the British axial-flow J-42 Nene engine in the F9F-2. Dusty had been assured that Grumman could supply enough F9F-2s for the Blues. Admiral Storrs agreed to every detail of the request for the new jets and said it would be forwarded with his approval immediately. Dusty was elated. The Blue Angels were about to get new wings.

April brought another reason for anticipation. Betty announced she was pregnant. When she and Dusty did the arithmetic, they discovered the baby was due in December. It was going to be another special Christmas.

In the meantime there was a high priority air show at the Oakland NAS in Alameda. Alameda was one of the two major naval air bases on the West Coast, along with San Diego. The San Francisco Bay area also held a lot of memories for Dusty. He'd started his navy career there when he was processed at the Oakland E-base before shipping out to Jacksonville for naval aviation cadet training. He'd sailed from the San Francisco Port of Embarkation with the Grim Reapers early in 1942 for training on Maui before deployment in *Enterprise*. And as a returning prisoner of war, he'd been processed at Alameda after a checkup at Oak Knoll Naval Hospital, receiving his back pay of over $6,000, a promotion from ensign to lieutenant, and a ninety-day leave.

So it was special to return to Alameda leading the Blue Angels. And Fresno, his hometown, wasn't far away. In fact, there was time for the team—Dusty, MacKnight, Robcke, Heagerty, and Roth—to stop over at Fresno for a couple of days and enjoy some hometown hospitality. Dusty knew the *Fresno Bee* would alert people that he would be leading the Blues in Oakland, and some of them would surely want to make the trip.

As it turned out, Fresno got its own performance. Dusty's old friend Bob Wynne, a member of the local Navy Club, appeared at the airport with the president of the club, James Dermer, in tow. They asked him what it would take for them to get a show. Dusty suggested a wire to Washington, and he got an okay from OPNAV before the Blues left for Oakland. Three days later, an article in the Sunday *Fresno Bee* headlined "Famed Navy Fliers Will Appear Today" turned out a lively crowd later estimated at twenty-five thousand at the Fresno air terminal. Though it didn't set a record for sheer numbers, it probably did for the number of spectators who knew Dusty personally.

The Oakland NAS performance was the usual twenty-minute "aerial ballet" by the Blues alone, not as part of a larger air show. It was the first time the Blues had been there since Butch's team in 1946.

The Blue Angels did an air show nearly every weekend in April and May—Atlanta; Raymondville, Texas, near Harlingen; Corpus Christi; Pensacola; Denver; Pueblo, Colorado; and Pensacola again. Then after two shows in Maryland the first week of June, they flew to NAS Sand Point in Olathe, Kansas, outside Kansas City, where they left the Bearcats and boarded a transport for NAS North Island in San Diego.

The Blues were about to become jet jockeys. Before they took the controls of their own Grumman Panthers, they'd have ten hours of familiarization in Lockheed F-80 Shooting Stars, the first wartime fighter jets, famous for their blazing speed and incredibly smooth ride. Five Blues went through the training: Dusty, Fritz Roth, Jake Robcke, and two new members, Lieutenants Ray Hawkins and Bob Longworth. To everyone's surprise and disappointment, Hal Heagerty failed the eye examination in their initial physical and left the team soon after.

The Blues were temporarily attached to VF-52, the navy's only jet training squadron, whose executive officer had recently been Lieutenant Commander "Dangerous Dave" Pollack, a former VF-10 aviator who was now skipper of VF-51, a squadron of North American FJ-1 Fury jets. But VF-51 and VF-52 and three other squadrons of Air Group Five shared a hangar across the street from the BOQ where Victor's Bar was located, and Victor's was the regular after-duty watering hole for many of the pilots. So it was there that Dusty caught up with Dave Pollack and a lot of scuttlebutt about recent activities and personalities of Air Group Five.

Preceding Pollack as CO of VF-51 had been Lieutenant Commander Bob Elder and, before him, Commander Pete Aurand. Aurand and Elder had been CO and Exec of VF-5A, the predecessor of squadrons 51 and 52, and it was then, in the early months of 1948, that they'd been the first pilots to land jets—FJ-1 Furies—on a fleet carrier, USS *Boxer*. Shortly after that, they'd won the national coast-to-coast Bendix Trophy race in the same Furies. They'd moved on to other assignments before the Blues arrived in June, but both VF-51 and VF-52 still had a number of exceptionally skilled and experienced pilots. At Victor's and on the field, Dusty met Don Engen and Johnny Magda, both of whom he'd later get to know better.

The jet transition training was a crash course. After a few hours of classroom introduction to the mechanics of jet engines and the aerodynamic qualities of jet fighters, the fledgling jet pilots were introduced to the TO-1, as the F-80 was known to the navy. Some aviators who had previously been through the training had been given forty-five hours of ground classes and twenty hours of solo flying. The Blues had ten hours each in the Shooting Star.

On his first day up in the TO-1, Dusty was struck by two big differences from the Bearcat and other prop-driven planes: the engine was much quieter and there was practically no vibration. The feel of the plane was astonishing. He wasn't so much flying it as it was flying him. It started slowly, but then accelerated with a great surge, pressing him back in the seat with a force of several Gs. He knew he'd pull quite a few Gs on some maneuvers, and he wondered if the Blues would have to wear G-suits. The climb was amazing, almost straight up with no loss of airspeed. Great aerodynamics—very thin wings and lean fuselage meant little air resistance. Besides, it was a beautiful plane to look at, sleek and shapely.

All the Blues were asked to record data on airspeed, fuel, and the like on cards attached to the kneepads of their flight coveralls. Fuel consumption was fierce in a jet, and they were supposed to be back over the field with 450 pounds of fuel left in case of any delays in landing. After a few minutes in the air, though, Dusty could see that note-taking was a distraction. It was easier to keep track of the time and come in just under an hour. *Whoops! The lead on the pencil broke! Too bad.*

The airspeed indicator was calibrated in Mach units rather than knots. The math was no problem once you'd done a few conversions to miles per hour. Instead of multiplying the indicated knots by 1.2—or 1.15 if you were fussy—to get miles per hour, you started with Mach 1, the speed of sound, 760 miles per hour at sea level. You ordinarily cruised at .7 or .8 Mach, between 530 and 600 miles per hour. But that was all relative and approximate because the speed of sound varied with altitude or air pressure, and you didn't need to think in miles per hour anyway. In any case, the cruising speed of the TO-1 was easily half again that of a Bearcat and twice what the old Wildcat could do. It was a hell of an airplane.

Dusty was already thinking of ways their air show performance would have to be adjusted. With the jets' speed, it would be harder to keep the planes in front of the audience. They wouldn't turn around so fast. And no Half Cuban Eight on takeoff. The jets just didn't have the gravel-scratching start the Bearcats did. A Bearcat could get off the ground faster than a TO-1 or an F9F and beat it to a thousand feet, even to ten thousand. Still, the jets would create new excitement.

The team finished their week-long familiarization course with no mishaps and in good spirits. They were looking forward to getting their hands on the Panthers. Returning by transport to Olathe, they picked up their Bearcats and headed for their next air show, to help dedicate a new airport in Winona, Minnesota, on the Mississippi River.

In Corpus Christi, meanwhile, Betty was starting to prepare a landing field for the stork, whose ETA was still six months away.

Between Winona on June 19 and Pensacola on July 7, the Blue Angels gave six other performances. The highlight of that period was a three-day Fourth of July weekend show at Elmira, New York, for the sixteenth annual National Soaring Contest, hosted by the Schweitzer Aircraft and Glider Company. The owner of the company, Pete Schweitzer, took Dusty up in a two-place sailplane and let him take over the controls. It was a far cry from a Bearcat or F-80 jet, but it put an aviator back in touch with the simplest elements of flying, especially the way the airflow over the craft's surfaces supported it and easily lifted it in an updraft. And it was so quiet! Dusty loved it.

He learned that Elmira had been one of the premier soaring centers in the United States since a group of German sailplane pilots migrated there in 1930. He also learned that Pete's wife, Ginny, was the only American woman, among eighty-nine men, including Pete, to hold the Silver C award from the Soaring Society of America. To qualify, she had to make a flight of at least five hours, thirty-one miles, and 3200 feet above the altitude at which she released from the towplane. Dusty was impressed.

Elmira is in western New York, just north of the Pennsylvania border and south of the beautiful Finger Lakes region. The topography provides plenty of updrafts for soaring, as well as natural beauty. It was Mark Twain's favorite summer vacation spot for twenty years. It was unfamiliar country to Dusty and the other Blues, and they enjoyed driving excursions into the countryside with their hosts.

The setting for the Blue Angels' three performances was also a treat, for them as well as the crowd of five thousand spectators. The glider field they flew over was on a plateau between two river valleys. The Blues would fly up one valley and go into a diamond barrel roll over the field, rolling out over the other valley. That put them low and upside down almost over the crowd. Local newspaper writers were ecstatic.

Dusty, Fritz Roth, Jake Robcke, and George Hoskins flew the four-plane diamond, while Bob Longworth and Ray Hawkins took turns in Beetle Bomb for the mock air battles.

An extra thrill for the team was the discovery that there were a lot of air force men in the crowd, and they were wildly appreciative, hooting and hollering and waving their caps as the Blues taxied in after their performance and deplaned in front of the grandstand. The U.S. Air Force and the U.S. Navy were lively competitors, and that ovation was a rare compliment.

Between air shows Dusty squeezed in two visits to the Grumman plant at Bethpage on Long Island, where he checked out final preparations of the six new Panthers and watched Corky Meyer demonstrate the plane's maneuverability. On one flight Corky had the teardrop-shaped auxiliary fuel tanks on the wingtips filled with colored water, which he jettisoned in a long, curving, yellow vapor trail. Dusty began thinking what the Blues could do with that.

In mid-July, Dusty, Fritz, George, Jake, Ray, and Bob flew by transport to Bethpage to take possession of their six new F9F-2 Panthers, which sat in a row on the airport apron, their blue paint gleaming. On the ground a Panther looked fatter through the midsection than the TO-1, like a seal or a tuna, but that could well mean smoother airflow and less drag.

Corky Meyer and a couple of other Grumman people introduced the Panthers to their pilots. They assured Dusty that these were the Panthers with the Nene engines, which developed an amazing five thousand pounds thrust. The Nene, it turned out, was named after a little-known Canadian gray goose.

"That must be a hell of a goose," said Fritz.

Corky reviewed a few other technical and aerodynamic characteristics of the Panther. To no one's surprise after their TO-1 experience, the F9F was also slow to reach takeoff speed, and fully loaded on a hot day, it might eat up 3,000 feet of runway before it could lift off. Even then it climbed at only 6,000 feet per minute, compared to the Bearcat's 8,000. The 120-gallon wingtip fuel tanks, surprisingly, actually improved the plane's aerodynamics, reducing drag and aiding aileron response.

In starting, the jet turbine had to be turned over by an external Auxiliary Power Unit, or APU. When the turbine was whirling, the pilot touched a button to ignite the jet fuel, and he was in business. The Blues would have their own Monster, as the APU was called, to take with them on their support transport.

The cockpits were comfortable and beautifully designed, with instruments placed for quick and accurate reading. There was even air conditioning, which was pretty luxurious. The bubble canopy gave them a good view, much like the TO-1's, and it opened easily, sliding back on twin rails.

When the Blues took to the air, one at a time, they were happy with the feel of the planes. They certainly lacked the nimbleness of the Bearcats, which could turn on a dime. With no prop torque and that smooth, powerful engine under you, though, you could get awfully close to another plane without getting anxious. And if the other guy pulled up close, you didn't have to worry that his prop was going to chew your elevators or ailerons off. The diamond formations were going to get tighter.

Landing the F9F should have been pretty much like landing the TO-1, but there was a hitch. Fritz Roth had asked Corky Meyer what the landing speed was, and Corky had said, "Oh, about ninety-five knots." That sounded a little slow to Fritz, but he thought, "If he can do it, I can do it." He was the first to land. On the approach, he cut his power and watched the airspeed indicator drop. At about one hundred knots, and not over the runway yet, the plane threatened to stall.

Fritz added power and pulled the stick back slightly as he felt his speed pick up. Just over the end of the runway at less than twenty feet, he eased the throttle back a quarter of an inch and the plane dropped like lead. As it bounced, he struggled for control and prepared to crash, but managed to wrestle it to a safe landing.

"Watch it, George, watch it!" he radioed to Hoskins, who was next in line. "Keep your airspeed up!"

Hoskins and the others landed smoothly, helped by Fritz's scare. Fritz wondered whether he and Corky had misunderstood each other. That evening, when he called his wife Sage, she asked how the day had gone.

"What did they do? Did they give you a lesson?"

"No," said Fritz, "they just gave us a plane to fly."

After two short flights of a little over half an hour each, the Blues said goodbye to Grumman and headed south along the coast, planning to refuel at Patuxent River. They moved naturally into the diamond formation, with Fritz and George on Dusty's wings and Jake in the slot. Ray Hawkins and Bob Longworth paired up a short distance away. Dusty noticed that Fritz and George were having trouble staying in position. On the radio they both told him the Panthers' aileron response was so sensitive that the smallest stick movement made the planes jerk. Dusty and the other three were noticing the same thing. No matter how slowly or how little they moved their sticks, the sudden jerks still happened. Close formations would be risky as well as sloppy. That wouldn't do.

At Pax, Dusty described the problem to the chief engineer and then called the Grumman liaison, Goldie Glenn. There were guesses about the cause of the problem, but no reassuring answer. That could take a few days. Flying the planes on to Corpus Christi probably wouldn't be dangerous, but if they had to go back to the factory to have the problem fixed, it would be a shorter return from Pax.

The Blues couldn't wait for a diagnosis; they had performances scheduled. After an overnight in the BOQ, they flew home to Corpus by transport for another overnight, and then strapped on the Bearcats the next day to head for Chattanooga. The Seventh Annual All-Dixie Air Show came off at Lovell Field with the help of the Blue Angels, Zack Mosley of *Smilin' Jack* fame, glamorous stunt flier Rae Parry, and other celebrities of the skies.

When the team returned to Corpus Christi, there was word from Grumman: the critical aileron response was caused by the fluid in the hydraulic control system being at a stand-still until the stick was moved, then jerking into action. The problem could be fixed by modifying the system so the fluid was moving continuously. The Blues' own maintenance team could install the necessary parts, which were being shipped from the factory to Corpus.

After a day's rest, the team boarded a transport to return to Patuxent River and pick up the Panthers. On July 21, Dusty took off from Pax in his personal F9F-2, name stenciled in gold under the cockpit, and returned to home base with George Hoskins, Fritz Roth, and Bob Longworth. The planes of Ray Hawkins and Jake Robcke needed some minor adjustments, so their return was delayed a day.

The *Corpus Christi Caller* for Friday morning, July 22, heralded the arrival of the glamorous new jets. Headlined "Navy Jets Land After 1800-Mile Flight to NAS," the article described the "half-million dollar" aircraft—costing approximately $450,000 each—in words of awe, including the British-made emergency ejection seat, which would use a gunpowder charge to blow the pilot and his parachute eighty feet from the plane at six hundred miles per hour. Clearly, the Panthers would only increase the public's appetite for the Blue Angels' performances.

After a three-day break to modify the Panthers' hydraulic systems, the Blues went up three successive days for hour-long familiarization flights, finding out what their jets could do. The program would need a few changes, most of them probably improvements. Everything would take more air space, not only because the performance speed was higher—maybe 500 knots instead of 450—but because the turning radius was longer. They could still do a Cuban Eight, but not from takeoff. Echelon rolls and the diamond barrel roll were better because without prop torque and turbulence, they could tighten up the formations to half the distances they maintained in the Bearcats. Jake Robcke, in the slot, had to stay below Dusty's jet blast, but he had already learned to avoid the Bearcat's propwash. A new wrinkle was that if Jake got too close, Dusty could feel his plane being pushed by the shock waves from the nose of Jake's jet.

Until the modified Panthers were thoroughly tested and new routines were worked out, they continued to fly the Bearcats in shows. On practice days they usually flew once in Bearcats and once in Panthers. Virginia Porter's aid was enlisted again to change the image on their insignia from Bearcats to Panthers. The big Cleveland Air Show was coming up Labor Day weekend, and they planned to fly the Panthers there. In three smaller shows at the end of August, they could try out the jets and iron out any wrinkles. Meanwhile, they flew the Bearcats at NAS Sand Point in Olathe, Kansas, the last weekend of July. In early August there was another West Coast tour—Salem, Oregon; Seattle; Portland—with a one-day rest stop in Fresno on the way home.

August was a blur. From the Sand Point show the last two days of July through the Cincinnati show on August 28, they did six performances in Bearcats and three in Panthers. Air mileage between shows was more than anyone could keep track of, but their logs showed forty-eight hours traveling time. Add the hours they were in the air for shows and for practice, and the sum was sixty-five hours. An average of two hours a day in the air for a month might not sound like much to a groundling, but that was only a fraction of their total hours on duty, which included time spent refueling and checking out various mechanical problems with the ground crew, as well as the paperwork of flight plans and communications with OPNAV and the station admiral's staff at Corpus Christi, not to mention the sponsors and organizers of the various air shows. It surprised everyone how much time they spent on the ground before and after practices and shows just talking about what hadn't quite clicked and how one thing or another could be made better.

There were also hours of public relations activities related to the air shows—interviews, photo sessions, receptions, dinners and banquets, visits to children's hospitals. Another photo session with the *Corpus Christi Caller* had to be squeezed in. Dusty's early weeks with the team two years ago seemed leisurely by comparison.

Most of the acceleration of the Blue Angels' schedule was the result of an increasing number of requests for appearances streaming into OPNAV. Recently, Operations had told Dusty they were averaging seven requests a week! Not all the potential sponsors could meet the navy's minimum requirements for facilities and financing, but even so, at one air show a week and sometimes two, the Blues couldn't keep up with the demand. Somebody in Washington had to be making a lot of hard decisions. Dusty was glad he didn't have to do it.

The jets could go faster and farther without refueling than the Bearcats, so that was starting to save them some time. In the Bearcats it had taken more than three hours between Corpus Christi and Pensacola, with a stopover at New Orleans or Lake Charles. In the Panthers it took little more than an hour, nonstop.

Before they said good-bye to their Bearcats, they decided to keep one of them for the new Beetle Bomb. The old SNJ would look silly pitted against the Panthers, but a yellow Bearcat might give them a challenge.

The Cleveland National Air Show, better known as the Cleveland Air Races, kicked off the equally busy fall season. There were thirteen shows scheduled through the end of November, before things wound down after Thanksgiving. In the middle of all that there was another cross-country relocation, this time to Whiting Field at Pensacola. The navy had decided to keep all its jets together at the same place, because parts and tools and mechanics trained to work on jets were still in short supply. The move would be sandwiched between the Cleveland show and the dedication of the new O'Hare International Airport at Chicago.

There was another West Coast visit in October, with shows at Oakland and Los Alamitos and a chance for another stopover in Fresno. Right after that, a big show was scheduled at South Bend, Indiana, with an invitation for the Blues to be guests of honor at a Notre Dame football game. To top off the year, *Life* magazine was sending a team to Whiting Field to take pictures and do interviews for a feature article on the team. From the standpoint of publicity and getting navy aviation in the public eye, that was about the best you could do. Everybody read *Life*. It had more readers than any American magazine except *Reader's Digest*—and the *Digest* didn't have pictures.

The Blue Angels had two surprises in store for the crowd at Cleveland, on top of the sheer speed and flashiness of the blue and gold Panther jets. They took off in the diamond formation, Dusty's plane and the planes of his two wing men tied together with bungee cords. The slot plane wasn't tied, but that hardly mattered. The cords showed dramatically how tight the formation was and how tight it stayed through the takeoff, into a sharp climbing turn and then the patented diamond barrel roll above the field, followed by a high-speed loop. The cords were attached to the Panthers' speed brakes on the belly, just forward of the cockpit, and when the team popped the speed brakes coming out of the loop, the cords flew off. As one newspaper reporter noted, the plane-tying trick had been done years before with slow-moving prop planes, but with shorter cords and jet speeds the unvarying tightness of the formation through maneuvers was astonishing.

The other surprise was turning on streams of colored water vapor from the Panthers' wingtip fuel tanks as they started the diamond barrel roll and continued through the loop. Other performers used clear water for white trails, and Dusty had seen Corky Meyer use yellow with a Panther. Any trails were eye-catching, but Frank Graham, announcing the show, agreed with Dusty that more color would be even better. So with the help of generous doses of red and blue dye, at Cleveland the formation left behind a patriotic bunting of red, white, and blue.

The new generation Beetle Bomb act was a hit, too, with Ray Hawkins putting up a good fight in his yellow Bearcat before the Panthers nailed him and sent him smoking out of sight behind the hangars on the near side of the field. There were the usual aerobatic acts and military fly-overs, including the Gray Angels, as well as the noisy air races around the triangular course. The only blot on the whole exciting weekend was the fatal crash of an Air Force F-80 pilot terrifyingly near a crowd of specta-tors. The accident refueled existing controversy over dangers to the pub-lic from high-speed, low-flying, aircraft, and there was talk in the papers of moving the site of the air races to a more spacious location.

The Blue Angels returned in glory from the spectacular national debut of their Panthers in Cleveland. The first Panther performance had been two weeks earlier in Beaumont, Texas, followed by appearances at Pensacola and Cincinnatti, but the huge Cleveland show on Labor Day weekend was the test. If they looked good there, in the company of the best aircraft and aviators in the country, they would look good anywhere.

Short as their tenure at Corpus Christi had been—just ten months—there were emotional good-byes as they prepared to move back east to Pensacola. People in town as well as on the base were proud and fond of them. The Blues responded with a farewell performance and then streaked to Whiting Field in just over an hour. Betty Rhodes and Sage Roth followed more slowly with the light personal and household baggage they'd learned to live with. Now six months pregnant, Betty carried an additional bundle.

With information supplied by Betty's mother, by now one of the biggest fans of the Blue Angels and her son-in-law, the Jacksonville paper announced the return of the Blues to Florida. "According to information compiled by Mrs. John H. Griffin Jr.," the article explained, the Blue Angels had been "featured in every air meet of national importance" since their founding in Jacksonville in 1946. Mrs. Griffin also earnestly told the paper that Dusty was a graduate of the University of California and enlarged upon his combat encounter with the enemy: "Early in the war, with three other planes, he participated in an attack on 20 Jap Zeros. Before their ships were riddled with bullets, Rhodes and his companion pilots accounted for 19 of the enemy planes." Dusty courteously neglected to correct his mother-in-law.

Flying his Panther to Chicago a week later for the dedication of O'Hare Field was another sentimental journey for Dusty. He had the great-est respect for the late Butch O'Hare's remarkable combat achievements and sympathy for Butch's mother. As an ensign training on Maui for his first combat deployment, he'd had little contact with Lieutenant Commander O'Hare, skipper of a fighter squadron and already an ace and holder of the Medal of Honor. Six months earlier near Rabaul in the South Pacific, Butch had helped save his carrier, *Lexington*, from an attack by a swarm of Japanese Betty bombers by shooting down five of them in a matter of minutes. It was only after the war ended that Dusty learned Butch was killed on a night-fighter mission early in 1943.

Though far from rivaling the Idlewild celebration, the one-day O'Hare Field dedication drew a crowd of 200,000 and involved nearly two hundred planes. Only George and Jake made the flight with Dusty for an abbreviated performance, but the audience enjoyed it. A reporter for the *Chicago Tribune* described the Panthers as "flying as tho their wings were strapped together," doing "slow rolls, Immelman turns, and loops over the crowd," and making "speed runs for the spectators at less than 30 feet."

Enthusiasm got the better of accuracy when the same writer claimed that "the jets showed their ability to get off the ground in a few hundred feet, and demonstrated a rate of climb of nearly 14,000 feet per minute." Dusty had learned to shrug off journalistic exaggerations, so reading the article the next day he was only pleased for the positive notice. Mrs. Selma O'Hare, Butch's mother, was brought from St. Louis for the occasion, and Dusty was able to speak with her after the show and accept her thanks.

After a week's breather at Corpus Christi, the Blues took off for a West Coast trip, with a performance en route at Joplin, Missouri, and then at Oakland and Los Alamitos, with a stopover in Fresno between. While the rest of the team flew on to Los Alamitos, Dusty stayed behind to speak about the Blue Angels to a Navy League meeting at the Fresno Hotel. Also on the program was Captain John Crommelin, who'd been skipper of the USS *Saipan* when Dusty was treated to a cake and coffee party in the wardroom for making the 6,000th landing on the carrier's deck. That was off Pensacola during Dusty's Refresher Flight Training.

In the meantime, while landing at Los Alamitos, George Hoskins's landing gear collapsed and his Panther dug up the field as it skidded to a stop, but George was unhurt. The traveling crew of Blues mechanics assured the team they'd have the gear repaired and the plane ready to go by Sunday's air show. Dusty learned the details when he arrived in Los Alamitos on Friday.

With no plans on Saturday morning, Dusty decided to call his old Grim Reaper and POW buddy Al Mead, who was married and living in

San Gabriel, near Pasadena. He told Al he was doing a Sunday air show at Los Alamitos and apologized for not getting in touch with him earlier. Al was happy to hear from Dusty and told him to sit tight—he and his wife would drive down as soon as they could arrange for a babysitter. At the officers' club, Dusty met Barbara Mead, a lovely Los Angeles girl who'd married Al in February of 1947, when Dusty was at Patuxent River.

After a couple of hours trading news and reminiscences over drinks, they discovered that the officers' club was closing. Dusty suggested they go off base for another drink, which they did. Then, as it began to get late, Barbara invited Dusty back to San Gabriel with them, where she fixed them supper while they continued their conversation. During and after supper, the conversation got livelier as they polished off several half-empty bottles from Al's pantry.

They even got back to remembering the Grumman F3F biplanes they'd flown in gunnery training out of Opa-locka as aviation cadets. They had to take along rags to keep the windshields wiped off because the engines threw back so much oil.

The next morning Barbara rousted them out of a deep sleep with "Wake up, you guys! Dusty's got a show to do!" After breakfast and black coffee, Al and Barbara drove Dusty back to Los Alamitos. In fact, Barbara drove, since Al was seeing rainbows around everything. He wondered how Dusty was feeling and whether he'd be able to fly. Dusty assured him he was used to such a regimen and could handle it. As visiting celebrities, the Blue Angels were usually treated by their hosts to a big party with plenty of food and drink on the evening before a performance, and they were experienced at limiting their fuel intake to manageable levels.

Entering the long entrance drive at Los Alamitos, Al remembered their postwar reunion there with a dozen or so Fighting Ten members, which Jimmy Flatley had organized. Al had told Dusty then about his unauthorized first flight in a Hellcat when he was barely out of the hospital, scaring Jimmy Flatley to death.

There was time before the show for Dusty to show Al his Panther, and Al climbed into the cockpit while Dusty explained the gauges and controls.

"Are you gonna let me fly it?" Al asked.

Dusty shook his head, recalling Al's old fear of bailing out over the Everglades. "Too many alligators in the swamps."

Mid-October brought a visit to South Bend, Indiana, to help dedicate the new five thousand-foot runway at St. Joseph County Airport. It also brought an invitation from the chairman of the board of Chrysler Corporation, a

Notre Dame alumnus, for the whole team to join him at Saturday's Notre Dame football game. Though he'd joined the team too recently to fly, Lieutenant Commander Johnny Magda, slated to replace Dusty as leader in January, made the trip with them. Chrysler limousines carried the Blues to and from the game, as well as to a Saturday evening dinner and dance and to the field for Sunday's air show. Sunday's *South Bend Tribune* devoted a full page to introducing the Blue Angels, and Monday's paper reported "one of the worst auto traffic jams on record" as some sixty thousand motorists, avid to see "four jet-propelled Angels . . . , fought for car-length space to get near the airport. Some never got within miles."

In early November, J. R. Eyerman, a photographer for *Life* magazine, spent several days shooting pictures of team members and their Panthers in flight, for an article that appeared in the December 5, 1949, issue. The color photos of the Panthers in the diamond, trailing colored streams of water vapor, were stunning, but the text was minimal—*Life* being chiefly a picture magazine. The whole team was shown in a small black-and-white shot, with Dusty, Fritz, George, and Jake in hard jet helmets demonstrating a maneuver with their hands while Bob Longworth, Ray Hawkins, and Johnny Magda, without helmets, looked on. The helmets were standard jet pilot equipment, but the Blues actually wore the same soft headgear they'd worn in the Bearcats. They'd found the hard hats fit poorly and they couldn't hear each other through the earphones as well as they needed to.

Only three of the team were named, however, as they were shown in close-up cockpit portraits: Dusty, with mention of his service in Fighting Ten aboard *Enterprise*, as well as his POW experience; Johnny Magda, "the next leader," with note of his carrier experience aboard *Hornet*, *Saratoga*, and *Boxer* and his Distinguished Flying Cross for "shooting down five Japs"; and the most decorated, Ray Hawkins, "who shot down 14 planes, sank a 5,000-ton Jap tanker and helped sink a carrier in Kure Harbor. He won three Navy Crosses and a D.F.C. with two gold stars." That may have been enough to give the reader an idea of the team's qualifications to represent the best of the navy's aviators.

On a routine errand from Pensacola to Bethpage in mid-November, Dusty and Johnny Magda, flying their Panthers, unintentionally set a new speed record for the route—one hour and fifty-seven minutes. In the new jet age, speed records were being set and broken with dizzying frequency, and this was nothing exceptional. Several other jets currently flying were faster. Still, any little bit of good publicity for the Blues and for the navy was welcome. This was especially true under the current secretary of

Life photographer J. R. Eyerman with Dusty Rhodes, center, and Lt. Cdr. John J. "Johnny" Magda, Pensacola, November 1949. Official photograph, U.S. Navy.

defense, Louis Johnson, whose unfriendliness to the navy, especially naval aviation, was notorious. His presence at the Blues' air show at Whiting Field that month seemed to some as likely to result in a budget slash as in an increase.

Returning to Whiting from Bethpage the next day, Dusty's Panther developed engine trouble, and he made an emergency landing at Lawson Field near Columbus, Georgia. The F9F's fuel pumps had burned out, and it had to be left at the field for repair. An SNB dispatched from Whiting

November 1949

Date	Type of Machine	Number of Machine	Duration of Flight	Chase seat of Flight	Time	Passengers	REMARKS
1	F9F-2	125746	.8	Z	Self		Show at Whiting field
2	"	"	1.5	Z	"	2.3		Life Mag. Photography
3	"	"	2.3	M	"	4.6		Whiting to Glenview
4	"	"	.6	M	"	5.2		Glenview to Grosse Ile.
5	"	"	.8	Z	"	6.0		Air Show at Grosse Ile.
6	"	"	1.9	M	"	7.9		Grosse Ile to Whiting field
7	"	"	1.3	Z	"	9.2		Photography for Life Mag.
7	"	"	1.0	Z	"	10.2		Air Show for Sec. Johnson
8	"	"	1.2	Z	"	11.4		Pictures for Life Magazine
8	"	"	.6	Z	"	11.9		
11	"	"	1.8	M	"	13.7		Whiting field to Corpus Christi
12	"	"	.4	M	"	14.1		Corpus Christi to Kingsville
12	"	"	.8	Z	"	14.9		Air Show at Kingsville
13	"	"	.9	Z	"	15.8		
14	"	"	.3	M	"	16.1		Kingsville to Corpus Christi
14	"	"	1.5	M	"	17.6		Corpus Christi to Whiting field
17	"	"	2.0	M	"	19.6		Whiting field to Bethlehem
18	"	"	2.5	M	"	22.1		Bethel Page to Lawson field Ga
19	SNB4	51836	1.4	M	co-Pilot	23.5		Lawson field to Whiting field
19	F9F-2	125589	.4	M	Pilot	23.9		Whiting field to Mobile, Ala
	Total time to date						

Page of Dusty's flight log for November 1949 showing Blue Angels' air shows, cross-country flights, and photo sessions. Courtesy of Raleigh E. Rhodes.

picked up Dusty the next day and brought him home in time to make a practice run with the team to Bates Field in Mobile, Alabama, in preparation for the air show there the following day. The repaired Panther was ferried back to Whiting just in time for Dusty to fly it in the show—gratifying because it was his last performance as leader of the Blue Angels.

Betty, eight months pregnant, wanted very much to attend, and Mobile was only about sixty miles away. Sage Roth was ready to drive her in the Roths' new black 1948 Buick convertible with red leather upholstery—top down, of course. But Fritz chivalrously insisted that he should drive. Bob or Ray would ferry his Panther to Mobile for him. It was a good plan except for the impenetrable traffic jam created by the thousands of cars heading for Bates Field. Fritz fretted and finally pulled off the road to phone Dusty at the field. Resourcefully, Dusty called the Alabama Highway Patrol, who alerted the Florida Highway patrol, and NAS Mobile sent out a search helicopter equipped with a description of the car. The pilot quickly found the stranded trio and landed in a field by the highway. Fritz turned over the car to Sage and rode the 'copter to Bates Field. Sage and Betty were a little late but in time for most of the performance.

Thanksgiving 1949 was a reminder to Dusty of how much he had to be thankful for. Never had life seemed so full and the future so promising. Leading the Blues had been the high point of his life, and he doubted that anything else would ever match it. He felt too lucky to give in to any regrets, and new lives lay just ahead—first as a father, then as executive officer of a Panther squadron, VF-112, in USS *Philippine Sea*, based at North Island in San Diego.

Raleigh Ernest Rhodes, Jr., was born in Florida on December 18, and Dusty's last flight as a Blue Angel, after testing the new engine installed in his Panther, was an early January solo performance dedicated to his three-week-old son, snuggled in his mother's arms and blinking into the morning light over Whiting Field.

SEVENTEEN

PANTHERS OVER KOREA

On the morning of July 5, 1950, ten days after North Korean troops had burst across the thirty-eighth parallel into South Korea, Dusty stood with hundreds of other men on the flight deck of USS *Philippine Sea* as the 27,000-ton carrier, assisted by tugs, eased away from the dock at North Island in San Diego Bay. At first light outside their rented house on Point Loma, he'd loaded his gear and Betty and six-month-old Raleigh into their new 1949 Pontiac "fastback" coupe and driven to the dock. Betty was on the verge of tears, and there was nothing left to say when they hugged good-bye. Now the wives and children and parents of the ship's crew and Air Group Eleven stood sad-faced and silent on the dock, some waving intermittently. The inevitability of the moment was emphasized by the slow, steady progress of the great ship toward the channel leading to the open sea. The early morning coastal clouds obscured the sun.

Five years ago some of the officers and men now aboard had come home from the war on the other side of the Pacific; now they were going back to a new war. Maybe they were a little less eager to test their courage and skills than the men too young to have fought against the Japanese. And maybe everyone's mood was less resolute and less aggressive than it would have been if American military forces rather than South Korean ones had been attacked.

In fact, no war had been declared. President Truman had committed U.S. forces to a "police action," along with air, sea, and ground forces from other members of the United Nations. What that might mean—how hot it might get, what the enemy was like, how soon they could expect to come home—was imponderable.

Most of them knew their mission was necessary. They had been well informed of the Communist threat to the free world, and, like their government leaders, they believed that if the Communists were successful in

South Korea, they would continue to gobble up weaker countries around the world until they were powerful enough to come knocking at American shores. Protecting South Korea was protecting the United States.

Dusty had shared in the fruits of victory in World War II. His navy career was solidly back on track, he'd had some glory as a Blue Angel, he had a new wife and a son, some savings and enough credit to buy a car or a house. It wasn't pleasant to have all this put in jeopardy, but it was his job to defend it. He had no doubts about that. He had the skills and the equipment and the commitment to make a contribution to whatever the navy and his country called on him to do.

During the past four months, he'd been training for a possibility like this. He'd been the only one in his squadron with experience flying Panthers, and he'd felt satisfaction teaching younger aviators what he knew about handling them in tactical situations. His four-man division was shaping up well, developing the kind of teamwork he'd known in the Blues. They were dependable guys; he could count on them.

He'd liked coming back to North Island and Coronado again. There were a lot of changes. Everything had expanded and developed, and much of it was brand-new. But the good things were still there—the sea air, the sunrises and sunsets over the harbor, the handsome old Hotel del Coronado where in 1942, thanks to a navy billeting shuffle to accommodate crowds of servicemen in transit, he'd stayed rent-free for a few weeks before shipping out for the South Pacific with Fighting Ten. Even Victor's Bar in the BOQ was pretty much the same, and to his surprise Victor had remembered him!

As executive officer of VF-112, second in command, he was on the way to eventual command of his own squadron. That was as far as he cared to think ahead. He had some models to look up to: Jimmy Flatley, of course, and Swede Vejtasa and Butch Voris had already had their own squadrons. He didn't expect he'd ever be the leader that Jimmy Flatley had been with VF-10. Men who'd served under Flatley then still spoke of him with respect and affection. He'd earned that by getting to know them all individually and expecting great things from them. They couldn't let him down.

Dusty hadn't gotten to know VF-112's original skipper, Commander Frank Lawler, very well. For some reason, Lawler hadn't deployed with the squadron. Commander Ralph Weymouth had replaced him, and there hadn't been time yet to take his measure. Dusty was closer to the former exec, Lieutenant Commander John Butts, who radiated friendliness and confidence. He had an unflappable "can do" air about him. But John had joined the admiral's staff and wasn't around as much. The air group com-mander was R. W. "Sully" Vogel, Jr., a well-liked old hand Dusty hoped to get to know better.

Dusty led one of five divisions in the squadron. His wing man was Lieutenant Dick Adams, and Lieutenant JG Earl Godfrey led the second section. Earl had been chosen by *Life* magazine as the subject of an article about how a naval aviator and his family prepare for his shipping out. The *Life* reporter and photographer had spent a couple of days with them at North Island, but the article hadn't come out yet. Earl's wing man was Lieutenant Bill Gillen. They were a tight, tough team, and Dusty was proud of them, even though he hadn't become close friends with any of them. They were younger, by ten years or so.

Their Panthers were Grumman F9F-2s, such as Dusty had been fly-ing with the Blues, except that their engines weren't the original British Nenes but American copies called J42s, made by Pratt and Whitney. Dusty couldn't tell the difference, but he was glad the planes were -2s and not -3s, which had Allison engines and less power. There were eighteen Panthers in the squadron, and twenty-seven pilots, which would let them keep the maximum number of planes in the air and give the pilots some breaks on rotation. The other Panther squadron aboard, VF-111 under Lieutenant Commander Tom Amen, had about the same number of planes and men, dictated by the capacity of the carrier.

The jets were a darker shade of blue than the Blues' Panthers, and they were marked differently—no gold trim, but a white three-digit numeral on the nose cowling, just behind a white blaze around the four 20-millimeter cannon, a U.S. star-and-bar insignia under the cockpit for-ward of the wing, and "NAVY" in white block letters at the rear of the fuselage, above a smaller "VF-112." The tail fin bore the letter V, the tail code for Carrier Air Group Eleven, which was repeated on the right wing next to the three-digit aircraft number, inboard from one of the 120-gallon wingtip fuel tanks.

The rest of the eighty-five planes on *Phil Sea* were made up of two F4U Corsair squadrons (VF-113, the "Stingers," and VF-114, the "Execu-tioners"), a squadron of Douglas AD Skyraider dive bombers, and three small composite squadrons made up chiefly of other ADs equipped for spe-cial purposes—night attack, antisubmarine warfare, and airborne early warning. Finally, there were a couple of new lightweight helicopters that would be used mainly to pick up downed aviators, either near the ship or at a distance. Dusty's squadron had no name to compare with the Stingers or the Executioners. What it had was a fancy Latin motto, *Custode Armis*

Dusty's VF-112 division of F9F Panthers, with Dusty in flight gear, inset. Official photograph, U.S. Navy.

Pacis, whose meaning Dusty had trouble remembering. "Guard peace with arms," or something like that.

Being aboard *Phil Sea* was something new. They'd loaded the aircraft and almost everything else overnight, and nobody from CAG-11 had been aboard before that. So they had carrier landing qualification to do yet, after they got to Hawaii. It had been the same way with *Enterprise.* Fighting Ten had trained on Maui for four months, and then once *Enterprise* had patched up the damage she'd sustained in the Eastern Solomons and put to sea, the squadron flew their Wildcats aboard. That seemed to be SOP, hitching up the carriers and their aircraft at the last minute, like a shotgun wedding. No time to get nervous about it. You just did it.

Until Hawaii, then, there wasn't a lot to do except get acquainted with the ship and play some poker and see some movies. There were routine duties, of course. The carrier wasn't exactly a cruise ship or luxury liner, though Air Group Eleven was definitely on a cruise. She was bigger and better equipped than *Enterprise,* having been completed in 1946, after the war was over. *Enterprise* was a prewar carrier like *Hornet* and *Yorktown,* both of which had been sunk in the war. She had a displacement of about twenty thousand tons and an overall length of 809 feet, compared to *Phil Sea*'s twenty-seven thousand tons and 888 feet. But she carried about the same number of planes. Both were dwarfed by the three *Midway*-class carriers, also completed near the end of the war. *Midway, Coral Sea,* and *Franklin Delano Roosevelt* were 968 feet long and displaced 45,000 tons. They could carry nearly 140 aircraft. But *Phil Sea* felt familiar to Dusty, even though he hadn't spent any time on a carrier for nearly eight years. The cramped quarters and noisy air conditioner blowers and banging hatches annoyed some air group members, but to him they were just inevitable parts of shipboard life. The things that mattered most were how much room he had to land on the deck and how good the catapults were at getting him launched.

Landing a Wildcat on *Enterprise* had been tricky, but with a landing speed of 85 knots minus the 30 knots or so the ship was making, the little F4F wasn't exactly an incoming missile. An arrested landing felt something like stopping a car on a country road when a tractor pulled out a block ahead of you. In a Panther, though, you landed at 115 knots, and the harder jerk was really welcome. If a pilot got a wave-off from the LSO (landing signal officer) at the last second, he had to goose the throttle and hope the jet turbine spooled up fast enough to carry him over the planes parked on the deck ahead of him. Wildcats and the much heavier Dauntlesses and Avengers had their share of crashes, but the jets with their higher landing speed and slower acceleration were more vulnerable on that score.

On *Enterprise* you didn't use a catapult. You just shoved the throttle ahead till you felt maximum power, then released the brakes and let 'er rip. Getting airborne was seldom a problem unless the pitching ship dropped out from under your aircraft before it had enough airspeed. In a Panther on the *Phil Sea*, a pilot was at the mercy of the catapults—eighty-foot-long hydraulic jobs that had to move the plane from zero to 115 knots, including the carrier's speed, in less than two seconds. It was a real kick in the pants. If the cat failed for some reason and the pilot had a cold shot, he would have a couple of seconds to feel his plane falling out from under him and see the water coming up to meet him. Then WHAM! and he'd hope the ship's bow wave didn't swamp him before he got out.

Dusty didn't know what the percentage of cold shots was, and he didn't want to know. On any given shot the odds of getting airborne were pretty good, and that's what he needed to think about. In a week or so he and the rest of the squadron—all the squadrons on the ship—would have half a dozen chances to try it out. It was absolutely essential practice for everybody aboard, from the man at the ship's helm to the air boss and the deck crew and the pilots themselves. Qualifying everybody in carrier landings would either precede or be part of the Operational Readiness Inspection, which could take several days before the admiral of the fleet said you were ready to deploy. That would come after a week or ten days of taking on supplies and practicing combat tactics, along with some welcome shore leave on Waikiki.

Meanwhile, there was just the steady progress at thirty knots toward Hawaii. The pilots and crewmen of Air Group Eleven had time on their hands. Their inactivity was notorious among the ship's officers and crew, whose time-honored complaint was that "all they do is eat, squawk, and shit." Some of the younger men spent hours writing letters, leading others to speculate about how many romances they were trying to keep alive back home. Just talking with old friends or new acquaintances aboard seemed to satisfy many airmen and air crew members—or "airdales," as the ship's crew called them. But aside from the regular evening movies, which drew big crowds, the most popular time-killing activity was playing cards, usually poker or pinochle. Liquor was forbidden, but not gambling. There wasn't much else to spend their pay on, and hopes of making a killing were fanned by stories about the big pot somebody won last night.

Dusty was a sociable man, and with little else to lubricate the tedious passing of off-duty hours, he distracted himself with poker, which could get pretty lively with the right players. Since he was well known in his squadron and looked up to by most of the younger pilots, he could hardly walk through the ready room without being invited to join a game in progress. After a few evenings, certain regular groups coalesced, and Dusty often ended up spending time with three younger men from other divisions: Ensign Allen "Boot" Hill, Ensign Auz Aslund, and Ensign Dayl Crow. Dayl, known as "Smoe" to his friends, was an especially congenial sort who usually organized the games, and Dusty liked his cheerfulness and entertaining patter as they played.

But the week went quickly, maybe because so much was new and there was a lot to think about as they headed for action. As they neared Oahu, the aircraft had to be flown to NAS Barber's Point, a few miles west of Pearl Harbor. After both Panther squadrons were launched, there was deck room for the Corsairs and ADs to take off.

For those still aboard, the carrier's first entrance into Pearl Harbor was a solemn and ceremonial occasion, with most hands standing silently in formation on deck as it steamed slowly past Battleship Row, where USS *Arizona* and a number of other great ships had been bombed and sunk on

December 7, 1941. Returning to Pearl, by sea or air, was still an emotional occasion for Dusty and probably always would be. But he doubted that any return would ever match the thrill of that day in September 1945 when he'd seen the harbor from the air on his way home from three years in Japanese prison camps.

Once *Phil Sea's* stores were replenished, she put to sea again and CAG-11 took off from Barber's Point to rejoin her for carrier landing qualifications. Two full days were spent in carrier quals, with each pilot of each squadron making six successful arrested landings on the deck, each one for a jet preceded by a catapult launch. Tension ran high throughout the ship, with emergency crews standing by and men with a few free minutes mounting to "Vultures' Row" near the air officer's deck, where they carried on good-natured critiques of each landing. Their banter helped to cover up both hopes and fears of witnessing an accident. There was a welcome break in the tension when the squawk box announced that Ensign Lowell Brewer of VF-111 had just made the 25,000th landing aboard *Philippine Sea*. Late that afternoon a huge decorated cake—described by the cooks as weighing eight hundred pounds but in reality closer to eighty—was served with coffee to all comers. The carrier quals ended without a single mishap.

After they entered Pearl Harbor that evening and were released for shore leave, the considerable remains of the cake were carried ashore by Brewer and several of his squadron mates and convoyed proudly to a room in the Moana Hotel at Waikiki Beach, where they remained as the centerpiece of a celebration that continued sporadically for several days.

Once everyone was carrier qualified, the squadrons geared up for combat readiness. For VF-112 this included calibrating the HVAR rockets newly installed on outboard wing racks and practicing strafing runs with their 20-millimeter cannons. Their targets were on a small island near Maui. Twice they flew air cover while the ADs practiced dive bombing. With each flight they moved mentally closer to the real thing. Every step of every procedure, every item of equipment, was reviewed. Remembering his own sadly neglected emergency kit when he was splashed by the Zeros, Dusty encouraged every pilot in the squadron to double-check the shark repellent, dye markers, flares, signal mirror, flashlight, first-aid kit, compass, Halazone tablets and vitamin pills, antibacterial drugs, fishing gear, knives, and sidearm ammunition. Dusty carried a Colt .45 automatic, as he had in Fighting Ten; most others carried a standard-issue Smith and Wesson .38 revolver.

Whenever there was off-duty time, all the pilots headed for the Moana Hotel at Waikiki. The nearby Royal Hawaiian was too expensive.

Besides, the Moana had a huge banyan tree in the courtyard where drinks were served, and its low, spreading branches were inviting. One Saturday night it looked as if the whole air group had managed to climb into the tree. Unfortunately, nobody had brought a camera. There was one minor but widely noted accident, later referred to as "our first cruise casualty," when John Butts fell down a short flight of steps while leaving the courtyard. Air group members received the news with amusement but no surprise.

On the day VF-112 finished its third straight day of strafing practice, Air Group Eleven and *Philippine Sea* successfully completed the Operational Readiness Inspection and received orders from Admiral Radford, commander in chief of the Pacific Fleet, to deploy. Stocked with fresh stores and ammunition, the *Phil Sea's* first port of call was Buckner Bay, Okinawa, almost 4,500 miles due west of Pearl Harbor and about 400 miles south of the Japanese mainland. Navy tankers would refuel the carrier en route. Another week at sea with no flying, no action. Night skies were alight with stars, sunsets and sunrises were often gorgeous, the sea was endlessly changing—but these were not pleasures with enduring appeal for young aviators. They distracted themselves with more card playing, skeet shooting off the rear hangar deck to keep trigger fingers limber, and reminiscences of the two weeks in Hawaii. They anticipated the attractions of Buckner Bay and Sasebo, the naval base on Kyushu, from which *Phil Sea* and other carriers would sail into Korean waters.

Buckner Bay was notable, Dusty and the others were told, for its cheap whiskey. On arrival all available hands swarmed ashore for a day of liberty, and the rumor was verified—bourbon and scotch were cheaper than beer! All the best brands were available. Doubles were the order of the day.

On the first of August, *Philippine Sea* approached the harbor at Sasebo on the west coast of Kyushu, facing the Korea Strait, about one hundred miles wide. As the carrier moved slowly up the channel toward her anchorage, she passed through submarine nets and between green, terraced hillsides. Here and there were abandoned, crumbling Japanese gun emplacements that had not guarded the harbor for five years now. Numerous small wood-frame houses looked like shacks to American eyes accustomed to more impressive dwellings.

Already in the harbor were the British carrier HMS *Triumph* and USS *Valley Forge*, both of which had arrived off the coast of Korea nearly a month before, in early July. There was time for a brief shore leave and for visits with the personnel of the other carriers. The Panther, Corsair, and Skyraider squadrons of *Valley Forge* had already flown many bombing

USS *Philippine Sea* at anchor, Sasebo, Japan, January 1951. Official photograph, U.S. Navy.

and strafing missions over Korea, from off both coasts. *Triumph's* Seafires (converted Spitfires) had likewise been busy. Most of North Korea's Yak and MiG fighters had been destroyed in the first few weeks of the war, some on the ground and some in the air. U.S. Air Force P-51s and P-80s, operating at first from South Korean airfields and then from Japan, had joined the carrier-based aircraft in decimating the enemy's air force, and the few survivors had retreated north to airfields beyond the Yalu River in Chinese Manchuria, forbidden territory for U.S. and UN planes.

On August 3, *Phil Sea* and *Valley Forge* both left Sasebo as part of Task Force Seventy-seven under the command of Rear Admiral Edward C. Ewen. *Valley Forge* headed into the Yellow Sea off the west coast of Korea, and *Philippine Sea* moved into the Sea of Japan off Korea's east coast. On August 5th the first strikes were launched from *Phil Sea* against ground targets, with the ADs and Corsairs bombing and strafing and the Panthers providing cover for them until they had used up their ordnance and headed back to the carrier. Then it was the Panthers' turn to come down and unleash their five-inch HVAR rockets and twenty-millimeter cannon against anything that looked like a worthwhile target.

From this first strike through the entire Korean tour of duty, the squadrons of *Philippine Sea*, like those of other U.S. and British carriers, flew "missions of interdiction" against railroad trains, truck convoys, anti-aircraft installations, industrial sites, and the like—everything that could support the North Korean war effort. The jet squadrons as well as the ADs and Corsairs took their shots. There were no MiGs or Yaks, though—no air resistance of any kind. That was a disappointment to the fighter pilots, who wanted more than anything to test their skills against the latest model MiGs flown by North Korean or Chinese pilots. Interestingly, the early MiGs had the same engines as the Panthers, based on the British Nene. They were also faster and carried heavier armament. But the fighter squadrons of *Valley Forge* and *Triumph*, along with Air Force fighters, had long since cleared the skies of opposition.

When assigned ground targets had been blasted or couldn't be found, pilots looked for "targets of opportunity"—locomotives hidden in the mouths of tunnels, trucks concealed under trees or bridges, anything that might be carrying military supplies or personnel. Lieutenant Don Engen, flying an F9F-3 off *Valley Forge*, finished a sortie with his wingman against the airfield at Pyongyang and still had ammunition left. Flying low over the nearby countryside, they spotted a long plume of dust kicked up by a yellow 1941 Chevy convertible barreling down a dirt road. When they could see clearly that the driver was wearing a uniform, said Don, they "rolled in on the Chevrolet from 5,000 feet."

The problem sometimes seemed to be the scarcity of significant targets. Firing on civilians was strictly forbidden, but bored pilots teased each other about how many ox carts or Good Humor wagons they'd nailed. Dusty led his division on six "boring" missions in August, all of them requiring between an hour and a half and two hours in the air. Faster than the ADs and Corsairs, the Panthers left the carrier later and caught up with them over the target. The skies were clear, and returning, they could see *Phil Sea* from a great distance. For weeks the weather continued hot and clear, and on the carrier life between missions was often surprisingly peaceful.

But wars bring tremendous disparities in the experiences of combatants, even in the experiences of one combatant from day to day and week to week. While Dusty's division was having a comparatively easy time of it in mid-August, another *Phil Sea* attack group raiding enemy installations at Seoul, the South Korean capital then in possession of the North Koreans, encountered heavy anti-aircraft fire. Sully Vogel, the commander of Air Group Eleven, was hit by flak in his AD while destroying a whole span of a vital bridge. He and his crewman bailed out, but Vogel's parachute failed to open. His death jolted the whole fleet. Dusty regretted not having time to know him better.

ADs were slower and bigger targets for ground fire than Panthers or even Corsairs, and other AD pilots besides Sully Vogel were victims. Some escaped alive, though. Lieutenant Commander Jerry Lake of VF-115 was shot down and managed a Mayday call before he crash-landed on a sandbar in a river behind enemy lines. He piled out of the wrecked plane and spotted an enemy platoon on the river bank starting to come after him. With his .38, he held them off long enough for a Sikorsky HO3S helicopter to arrive and hoist him to safety while a couple of Corsair pilots strafed the enemy troops.

Low-level flying was risky for all the planes, but especially for the Corsairs of VF-113 and VF-114. A single rifle bullet in the engine could drain the oil cooler, and the engine would seize, forcing the pilot to crash land wherever he could—too often behind enemy lines. Most pilots wore a large white patch with flags of the United States, the United Nations, the United Kingdom, and South Korea sewn to the back of their flight coveralls. An accompanying message written in Korean, Chinese, Japanese, and English said: "I am an American (United Nations) flier. My plane has been shot down and I am helpless; but I want to get back and fight again for the peace of the world and your country. If you will help me and yourselves by getting me to the nearest American unit, my government will reward you well. Help us and we will help you."

Dusty never heard whether this patch saved anyone's life. Later, in December, a Corsair pilot's engine for some reason caught fire and he made a safe landing in a snow-covered field. Luckily, there was a marine platoon nearby who saw him land and took him in. An AD pilot named Denny Crist had to ditch behind enemy lines, and he and his crewman reached cover in a hole on a rocky ridge. A couple of Corsair pilots who saw them go down strafed approaching enemy troops until a marine helicopter arrived to rescue them. But there were others who were either killed or captured. From what they'd heard of North Korean treatment of captives, some of the pilots thought they'd rather be Killed in Action than Missing in Action.

After a month at sea, *Philippine Sea* returned on September 5 to the base at Sasebo to renew stores and ammunition and to offer her sailors and fliers a welcome shore leave. "Sasebo" in naval usage had a double meaning. There was the huge American naval base established after the war, and there was the city itself, the anticipated playground of liberty-bound navy men. Taken ashore in relays of motor launches, they explored the narrow streets and alleys with wide eyes and wrinkled noses. It was the most exotic place most of them had ever seen. The dirty gutters and peculiar stinks were surprising to those who'd heard of the legendary cleanliness of the Japanese. Maybe the overcrowding and postwar poverty explained it.

But the sailors were there for recreation and entertainment, and they searched it out quickly, guided by instinct, memorized Japanese phrases, or directions from more experienced shipmates. Cheap souvenirs and trinkets were easy enough to find, but they were after better things. The value of Dusty's wartime experience was later acknowledged by the author of VF-112's chapter in the air group's cruise book: "We found that we were fortunate indeed to have a man that could converse with the Japanese in their own tongue. So we all followed Dusty, eagerly planning to drive many a shrewd bargain with some local shopkeeper, only to hear the words, 'Boy-San, one bourbon and water!'"

In fact, Dusty and several companions lost no time in making their way by hired rickshaw to a rendezvous point prearranged for all air group officers: a large, impressive-looking entertainment palace that specialized not only in ample servings of tasty sukiyaki and other Japanese delicacies but also in fine whiskey, beer, and sake, and best of all, dancing girls with sparkling eyes and flirtatious smiles.

Astonishingly, they were bare-breasted and wore only grass skirts as they stepped and twirled across the raised stage at one end of the large room. There were a dozen or so dancers, every one inviting and desirable. Near the stage a small band accompanied them on American-style instruments. Someone had managed to save Dusty a seat at a table near the stage, and he appreciated the thoughtfulness. Sipping the tumbler of bourbon he'd brought to the table with him, he heard a voice say, "My God, they don't have any pants on!"

It was Chooch—Ensign Ted McGinnis from Dusty's squadron. When the dancers finally finished their performance and quickly disappeared, it was Chooch who pulled out a roll of bills and negotiated with the band for the rental of their instruments. He grabbed a guitar and motioned for Dusty and the others to join him. While they were deciding who would play what, several of the dancers re-entered the room, dressed in kimonos. They were delighted with the re-forming band, and a couple of them wanted to play. One seized the violin, and the other picked up the trombone. Ensign Vince Moore had taken over the small drum set and Dusty found a trumpet.

It fell to Dusty to suggest the tunes and set the tempo, and after a couple of false starts ending in giggles and guffaws, he finally got them all going on "Don't Be That Way." It was a good dance tempo, and some quick-thinking officers grabbed the remaining girls as partners while others pushed back the tables to clear a dance floor. A good time was had by all.

The next morning they learned that returning enlisted men had been met at the heads of ramps by the ship's medics, passing out what they called "after-diddley mints."

As *Philippine Sea* headed into the Korea Strait toward Point Oboe, the designated latitude and longitude for rendezvous with other task force vessels and departure for either the Yellow Sea or the Sea of Japan, reports spread through the ship of an ominous incident on September 4, as they had been approaching Sasebo. A Corsair division from *Valley Forge*, then operating in the Yellow Sea, had intercepted a bogey heading directly toward the carrier. Rear Admiral Hoskins had ordered them to make an identification pass over the intruder and to fire if fired upon. It turned out to be a twin-engine Tupolev bomber, red stars clearly visible on wings and fuselage. When the Corsair division leader made his pass, he was fired on by the tail gunner. His wingman let go with his twenty-millimeter cannon, sending the Tupolev into a smoking dive into the water.

An American destroyer on the scene found just one survivor, who died soon after being rescued. Papers in his flight suit identified him as a Soviet pilot. Since the United States and Soviet Union were not at war, it was a serious incident, and there was a flurry of communications between Washington and Moscow. The Russian bear and the Chinese dragon were dormant at the moment, but the danger of rousing them was on everybody's mind. Task Force Seventy-seven, working right in "Uncle Joe's back yard," would be among the first victims of a sudden onslaught by either of these potential enemies.

The corpse of the Russian pilot was delivered by the destroyer to *Valley Forge*, where it was temporarily stored in a freezer before being transferred to another on *Philippine Sea*. Dusty heard that those curious and ingenious enough to finagle a peek reported that the corpse appeared to have chrome-plated teeth.

Phil Sea and the rest of Task Force Seventy-seven joined a growing fleet in the Yellow Sea the second week of September. At first the weather and calm seas seemed completely out of keeping with the combat preparations aboard. Lieutenant Commander Angus Ross, the editor of Air Group Eleven's cruise book and author of its "official history," drafted descriptions that echoed idyllic passages in Melville's *Moby-Dick*: "The heat and humidity of the Okinawa and Korean area was forgotten at times when the ship sailed through the mirror-like waters of the Yellow Sea, through myriads of large, translucent jellyfish, countless flocks of sea birds; through waters where porpoises played and huge blue marlin spiked the water in their lunges for small prey."

But something was brewing. In a little over two months, the invading North Koreans had pushed Allied forces almost off the Korean peninsula, except for a small area with a radius of about fifty miles from Pusan on the southeast coast—the "Pusan Perimeter." But General Douglas MacArthur, the supreme commander of UN forces, had devised a daring counterattack—an invasion on the west coast at Inchon. Marine and U.S. Eighth Army troops driving inland from Inchon would quickly retake Seoul and cut off supply routes to North Korean troops south of that point. The strategy succeeded brilliantly.

Dusty's Panther division was aloft on three days in a row, from September 13 through the 15th, for just under two hours each time. On the 13th and 14th, CAP gave Dusty and other carrier pilots a ringside seat for the initial artillery barrage against shore defenses from heavy cruisers and battleships. On the 15th, when the invasion began, with landing craft swarming like water bugs to the beaches, they flew an additional sortie to strafe enemy airfields in the vicinity with rockets and cannon shells. Corsair and AD squadrons from *Philippine Sea* as well as *Valley Forge* and *Boxer* carried out bombing attacks and flew cover over the invading troops. As the Eighth Army under General Matthew Ridgway pushed inland, Dusty's division joined two more sweeps of North Korean airfields on September 17 and 21. Virtually no enemy planes made it into the air to harass the Allied forces. After the airfield strafing, *Phil Sea* Panthers continued to fly cover for the next couple of weeks over reinforcements going ashore and over Corsairs and ADs bombing and strafing enemy emplacements. From all reports, U.S. forces were advancing steadily, turning north toward Pyongyang, the North Korean capital, after recapturing Seoul.

Late on October 3, after nearly a month in the Yellow Sea, *Philippine Sea* headed back toward Japan to replenish supplies and ammunition, and *Valley Forge* followed two days later. With overlapping six-day liberties, the men of both carriers welcomed the break. As Panther pilot Don Engen aboard *Valley Forge* wrote later, "After you have been at sea for a month, land can have a definite and different identifiable smell. Once ashore, trees and flowers have individual smells, and you detect the slightest whiff of perfume almost immediately."

The editor of *Phil Sea*'s cruise book wrote simply, "We retook Sasebo."

From the wharf there was the simple pleasure of rickshaw races to various destinations, including "Black Market Alley," where bargains abounded and nearly anything could be had for a price. There were attractive souvenirs and gifts for girl friends, wives, and other family members. One of the most appealing bargains for the knowledgeable was a ninety-two-piece set of Noritake china, well packed for shipping.

But with six days to spend, Sasebo's interests were soon exhausted. Many signed up for tours by bus to the Koransha porcelain factory in Arita and the Mikimoto pearl farm on a small peninsula not far away. Some took an overnight tour to Nagasaki, fifty miles to the south, where pleasant rooms and first-rate food at the Kanko Hotel afforded comfort after the shock of the indescribable devastation of the ruined city. Dusty's duties as Exec kept him from the tours, but his friends filled him in. They found the human scenery along the road unfamiliar and fascinating. In school yards there were boys with shaved heads and girls in black bloomers. Sometimes in sheds near the road people were weaving mats from bamboo strips or other fibers. In the rice and barley fields bare-breasted older women worked alongside a few older men.

On October 10 the carrier sailed north again, this time into the Sea of Japan off Korea's eastern coast. From the 11th through the 19th, Dusty's division flew several CAPs, lasting about an hour and a half each. Sometimes these were routine sector patrols, with the hard parachute seat pack getting very uncomfortable. Sometimes while aloft they received orders for attacks on sites along the coast. The weather was changing, cooling from the heat of August and September, but still with more clear skies than cloudy ones. ADs and Corsairs went off on several missions that kept them in the air at least twice as long as the Panther squadrons, but they returned without casualties or serious damage. Shipboard life grew increasingly boring, and the card games and movies and letter writing offered little relief. The best thing was the weekly mail call, when a destroyer would pull alongside to deliver ten or a dozen large canvas bags and a few hours later shipboard morale would rise.

By mid-October 1950 United Nations forces were pushing rapidly north from Seoul, and on the 19th they retook Pyongyang, halfway to the Chinese border on the Yalu River. Toward the end of October the Tenth Corps, including the First Marine Division, landed on the east coast and pushed northwards, in the wake of South Korean troops already advancing there. As the enemy territory diminished, so did obvious targets, and the number of air missions dropped off sharply. There were reports that General MacArthur considered the war almost over.

Philippine Sea operations in the Sea of Japan broke off in late October, and another shore leave appeared to be in the offing. To everyone's satisfaction, they learned they were bound for Tokyo on the eastern coast of Honshu, the largest island in the Japanese archipelago. They'd have five days to explore the city, take a train to Yokosuka with its well-known cabarets and army PXs, or even visit resort hotels in the mountains.

Philippine Sea entered the harbor on a sunny morning the first day of November. In the hazy distance the cone of Fujiyama was unmistakable. Those with liberty dispersed quickly, and Dusty decided to see if he could locate the site of the questioning camp at Ofuna, near Yokosuka, where he'd been imprisoned for five months. But he delayed his liberty to finish up some business, and the next morning there was bad news. A huge number of Chinese troops were already in the mountains of northwest Korea and doing serious damage to UN forces. A message was sent out from *Phil Sea*, ordering the men to return to quarters immediately.

The carrier was under way early on November 4, heading for Wonsan on the east coast of North Korea. *Valley Forge* had already been recalled from Sasebo into the Yellow Sea, and its ADs, F4Us, and F9Fs began hitting targets in North Korea on November 7. But they reported nasty changes in the weather, with snow and ice on the deck slowing the morning launches of aircraft. From the Sea of Japan on the 10th, *Phil Sea* launched air strikes against bridges on the Yalu near Sinuiju and Hyesanjin, but apparently tens of thousands of Chinese troops were already in North Korea and headed south at high speed. Aware of a degree of futility in their mission, pilots bombing and strafing the Yalu bridges ran into frustrations and dangers as well. Anti-aircraft batteries on the Chinese side of the river hurled flak at them, and they were forbidden to fly into Chinese air space either to attack the AA artillery or to pursue enemy MiGs and Yaks that dashed out to harass them. Besides that, the best way to hit a long, narrow target like a bridge was to fly the length of it, but that would take them into China.

The first pilots on these missions to have a shot at a MiG were doubly frustrated to discover that the cold front pushing south from Manchuria had caused their guns to freeze. But on the 12th, when Dusty's gang was among several Panther divisions flying high cover over attacking ADs and F4Us at Sinuiju, VF-111's skipper, Tom Amen, shot down a MiG-15, the first MiG downed by a navy fighter in the war. That produced a wild celebration back on the carrier. Two Panther pilots from *Valley Forge* shared credit for another MiG kill. Still, air-to-air action was limited, and suspicions that Chinese or Russian pilots were flying the MiGs remained unconfirmed.

Winter flying called for some adjustments. For one thing, there were the poofy suits—rubberized exposure suits that were supposed to form a snug seal at your ankles, wrists, and neck and puff up like a balloon if you had to hit the water so that you could stay afloat and dry until you were rescued. The trouble was, they were more likely to fill with water because of a tear or gap of some kind and drag you down. Besides, they weren't even insulated, so they were no protection in icy water. Everybody called them "poopy suits" in disgust. Most of Dusty's friends didn't wear them, nor did he. The cockpit was heated, once he got there.

But first he had to make his way across the deck to his plane, sometimes in a 20-knot wind. He wore longhandles under his coveralls and a wool sweater and leather flight jacket over them, plus extra socks in his boots and two or three pair of gloves. Plus his high-impact plastic helmet, snugged tight. His already frozen plane handler helped him into the cockpit where, as one pilot described it, "you shrugged and wiggled into your chute, plugged in your G suit, attached your bail out oxygen bottle, made sure your life raft lanyard was hooked up, connected your radio transmitter and receiver cords, fastened your shoulder straps to the safety belt and pulled them up tight." But even when it was cold, pilots left the canopy open until they were safely air-borne, just in case they had a cold catapult shot and had to get out of the cockpit fast—after unplugging and unfastening all those things.

One frigid morning the mission took Dusty and his division north along the coast toward Vladivostok, there in the invisible distance. There were heavy clouds from a thousand feet on up to five thousand, and once above the clouds and cruising at Mach .6, about 450 mph, Dusty plotted their course by map and instruments and settled in for the thirty-minute trip. When his watch told him they were there, he signaled to his gang to follow him down, and just under a thousand they came through the clouds over the water and spotted the port and their target, a large factory complex, dead ahead. It was a kick when it worked that well. Even better, there was no flak, and they fired all their HVARs, assessed the damage, and were on their way home in less than two minutes.

They breathed easier after unloading their ordnance, even though they still had a couple of problems to solve. They'd been watching their fuel gauges all the time and had a comfortable margin for the return trip. Finding the ship usually wasn't hard, because you flew the reciprocal of your outbound course, you picked up a homing signal from the ship on your "Bird Dog" ARN-6 radio, and since you were flying at all, it was unlikely that the clouds or fog were socked in right down to the deck. Sometimes somebody went astray for one reason or another. Horton of the "Friendly Squadron" took a hit and couldn't make it back to *Phil Sea*, but he managed to get aboard *Leyte*. Noonan ditched within sight of *Phil Sea*, but he couldn't get clear of his plane and went down with it.

Once they were over the carrier at 20,000 feet, Dusty and his division stayed high to conserve fuel in the thinner atmosphere. You liked to have 2,500 pounds or so left. They checked in with the Air Operations Officer, cut air speed, and orbited while they waited for their Signal Charlie. When they got it, they came down to starboard of the island at 300 feet, paralleling the course of the ship, and made an easy racetrack-shaped turn around the ship until they lined up on her stern, all the while adjusting their airspeed, lowering their flaps, and shoving back their canopies. When Dusty had the right attitude, altitude, speed, and course, and the LSO was holding both paddles straight out, he was in the groove, and if he'd remembered to drop his tail hook, everything should be okay. Of course it wasn't always okay. A dozen things could go wrong.

The most common was missing all of the five cables stretched across the deck. Maybe you bounced, or the ship bounced, or your tailhook was just having a bad day, but Dusty had already seen a couple of planes plow into the tractors parked across the deck to protect the parked planes forward. It wasn't pretty, and if some fuel caught fire it was touch and go to get the pilot out. So far there hadn't been any casualties on deck. And on this mission all of Dusty's division landed safely.

Flight assignments somehow limited Dusty's gang to CAP for most of November, even though reports of enemy advances on the ground continued to worsen with the weather. Strangely, it was reported that *Valley Forge* had left the action and gone to Yokosuka. *Boxer* was temporarily out of action with a damaged propeller shaft, but Dusty assumed there were other carriers still operating—the second *Hornet* and *Leyte* had seen considerable action, and there was talk of others on the way.

On Thanksgiving Day, November 23, *Philippine Sea* was wallowing in a choppy gray sea under a gray sky off the east coast of North Korea. A cold wind whipped across the flight deck, where two Panthers poised on catapults seemed unlikely to be launched. Their canopies were closed, and both pilots, on Condition Ten, were reading books. In the wardroom mess there was an impressive Thanksgiving dinner. There was even a printed menu: Cream of Tomato Soup, Cheese and Ham Canapes; Mixed Olives and Pickles, Crisp Saltines, Roasted Young Tom Turkey, Oyster Dressing/Stuffing, Baked Virginia Ham with Candied Pineapple, Buttered Green Peas, Pumpkin Pie with Whipped Cream, Parker House Rolls, Cranberry Sauce, Giblet Gravy, After-Dinner Coffee.

Ashore, in snowy valleys and on frozen flatlands, there was a lull in the fighting. Around small fires marines and army infantrymen in parkas and ponchos stood or squatted, clutching aluminum mess kits filled with slices of lukewarm turkey breast and scoops of mashed potatoes smothered in cooling brown gravy. There were square chunks of pumpkin pie shoveled from large baking sheets for those who'd finished their turkey. And plenty of hot coffee for their canteen cups.

Was the Chinese invasion faltering? MacArthur announced that U.S. troops were going to be home by Christmas, and United Nations forces began a counterattack on the 24th of November. But two days later, a massive Chinese army estimated at 300,000 men stormed south from the border—evidently unhampered by damage to the Yalu bridges—and threatened to overwhelm UN forces. Aboard *Philippine Sea*, everyone read the daily newspaper and listened to the nightly news reports read by the chaplain over the P. A. system.

News of the ground war grew more depressing. The sheer numbers of Chinese troops were often irresistible. They seemed completely unfazed by murderous machine gun and mortar fire. Dozens or hundreds would fall and others just kept coming. They advanced in waves, running, shouting, and blowing bugles. Troops in the third and fourth waves sometimes had no weapons—they picked up weapons from those who had been killed in earlier waves.

On the night of November 28, the First Marine Division at Chosin Reservoir—"Frozen Chosin"—was hit by something like seventy thousand Chinese troops. They retreated toward the south end of the reservoir, taking with them as many of their fifteen hundred casualties as they could. An attached infantry task force on the east side of the reservoir was decimated. There were over two thousand casualties. Converging at Hakawoo-ri, where there was an airstrip, they managed together to hold off the advancing Chinese long enough to evacuate more than four thousand casualties by air.

Retreating down the winding mountain road toward Hungnam, they found that the bridge over a 1,500-foot gorge had been blown. Miraculously, they managed to call in an air drop from a C-130 transport of six or eight two-ton steel bridge sections, with which they were able to reconstruct a makeshift bridge. The painful retreat continued, hardly mitigated by the bitter humor of Major General Oliver Smith, who told some war correspondents, "Gentlemen, we are not retreating. We are merely attacking in another direction."

Overhead, relays of aircraft from *Phil Sea* did what they could with cannon and rocket fire to delay and discourage the pursuing Chinese. But with troops of both sides spread over a large area, it was hard to spot targets through breaks in the weather, especially since the Chinese were skillful at making themselves invisible. Nearly every day the carriers were at sea, missions were launched continuously. ADs and Corsairs would go first, and the Panthers would catch up with them over the targets. For every five missions flown, each aviator was awarded an air medal.

Air medals were so plentiful they were devalued among the owners, but they impressed families and newspaper reporters back home. Dusty's second air medal received notice in the *Fresno Bee*, and a paper in Jacksonville, Florida, gave him an impromptu promotion on the basis of a phone call from his mother-in-law, who'd enlarged on the news in a letter from Betty.

> Lieut. Comdr. R.E. (Dusty) Rhodes, commanding officer of Fighter Squadron 112 and former leader of the Navy's crack "Blue Angels" aerobatic team, led his jet squadron into Korea Monday night for an effective raid, it was learned yesterday.

To add to their woes, American and other United Nations troops were inadequately equipped for the freezing winter weather. Why hadn't they been issued enough warm clothing, and why couldn't they be supplied when the weather suddenly turned bad? Aboard the carriers offshore, navy men were puzzled by the reports and at the same time grateful for their own comparative security and comfort. They congratulated each other on their good sense or luck in choosing the navy.

It seemed to be difficult sometimes for the brass to figure out where air strikes could be most effective. The front lines were changing rapidly, and reports only hours old were unreliable. The targets—advancing enemy troops—were spread out over hilly and mountainous terrain, and the weather made it almost impossible to locate them anyway. Cloud ceilings were low, and you couldn't risk going down for a look-see when you might fly into a mountain. The high-speed Panthers were of little use in such circumstances.

Every pilot now wore the extra insulation of long underwear, and was grateful for a heated cockpit. There was sometimes ice or snow on the planes and flight deck in the morning, and the deck crews would clear it away with brooms or even small tractor snowplows. When it continued to snow during the day, there were no flights at all. Often pilots sat a long time in their planes on Condition Ten—just waiting for the weather to clear. On the few days he was aloft and it was clear enough to see the ocean below, Dusty spotted small icebergs here and there. Less than two hundred miles north was Vladivostok, in Soviet Siberia.

The first week of December there were other defensive and protective missions—flying cover for Corsairs and ADs hitting enemy forces surrounding the coastal city of Wonsan, where what was left of the U.S.

Tenth Corps was being evacuated by landing craft in a Dunkirk-style operation. A week later Dusty's team was back north, off the coast of Hungnam, covering the evacuation of the survivors of the First Marine Division who had fought their way back from the Chosin Reservoir.

After fifty-one days of continuous operations, their longest time at sea so far, all hands aboard *Philippine Sea* were ready for shore and a Christmas holiday leave. A dispatch from fleet headquarters ordered all officers and men of Air Group Eleven to Yokosuka for "ten days' leave, recreation, and upkeep." On Christmas Eve they were still at sea, and a Twin Beech landed with a welcome COD (Carrier On-board Delivery) load of small Christmas trees, along with a dozen mailbags. "Home by Christmas" had become a sour joke. But the trees and Christmas cards and presents from home helped boost everybody's morale, and all over the ship there were small Christmas parties and carol singing that evening and into Christmas Day.

Dusty got Christmas cards from Betty and Raleigh, as well as tightly wrapped packages of socks and underwear and clippings from the *Fresno Bee* and the *Madera Citizen*. An editorial from the Madera newspaper, dated October 19, was headed "He's Our Madera Boy." The writer pointed out that Dusty was not really from Fresno, as most naval news releases said, but from Madera. "This kid, who is one of the crack pilots in the Navy, is just as much a Madera home product as the cotton and grapes that grow in our own county." A week later, a well-written feature article about Dusty, headed "The Citizen Salutes," carried a photo of him in dress uniform, with medals and ribbons.

From Yokosuka a large contingent from CAG-11 left by train for a couple of resort hotels in the nearby mountains. Enlisted men detrained at the Gohra Hotel and officers went to the Fujiya. The rooms were small by American standards, but furnished with "real beds," two to a room. Dusty and his wingman, Dick Adams, shared a room.

Besides walks around the grounds of the hotel and in the nearby woods, the airmen found other simple but satisfying ways to relax—over meals, in a huge hotsi bath where twenty men at a time could soak comfortably, and with a pitcher full of brandy Alexanders, a bargain at the local equivalent of a quarter. It was easy not to think of how the ground troops must be observing the holidays back in Korea.

There had been rumors since arriving at Yokosuka that Air Group Eleven might be going home in January, but at the end of the first week they were headed instead back to the cold gray Sea of Japan. There were more Condition Ten days, days with snow on the deck or snow flurries so thick there was no thought of launching planes. When the sky cleared enough for a mission or Combat Air Patrol, there was more anxiety about cold shots on the catapults. For various reasons they didn't work as well during winter weather, and when a cat failed to reach full acceleration, the aircraft usually ended up in the water. There had been a cold shot early in the cruise when the port catapult dumped Ensign Max Killingsworth of VF-111 and his Panther into the Pacific. The weather was clear and the water was warm, and he cleared the plane quickly and was picked up by a following destroyer. He later insisted he should be credited with two jellyfish and wanted them painted on the fuselage of his new plane.

Reports from the ground war indicated that the powerful enemy offensive was faltering, even though by early January their troops were estimated to number as many as 500,000—400,000 of them Chinese and 100,000 North Korean. As their supply lines were stretched, they were unable to keep their front-line troops supported, evidently for several reasons: the nasty weather, their shortage of trucks and trains, and the success of navy and air force planes in picking off whatever vehicles appeared on roads or rails. Once, while Dusty and his gang were following a line of railroad tracks near the Yalu River, hedge-hopping because of low clouds, they surprised two or three "locos" on the tracks—locomotives pulling several freight cars—and made a run over the trains in single file, smoking them with their 20-millimeter cannons. When they had to pull up suddenly to avoid a mountain where the tracks went into a tunnel, their fuel gauges said it was time to head home. By the end of January, the Communist offensive seemed to be stalled. There were reports of a possible cease-fire or armistice, but the two sides kept disagreeing on acceptable terms.

All through January and February, *Philippine Sea* moved up and down the east coast of Korea. Dusty's flight log showed four missions in January and six in February. He learned that *Valley Forge* had in fact left the area in late November to return to San Diego but had no sooner arrived there than she was ordered back to Korea with a new air group and was now operating off Korea's west coast. Don Engen, who'd been flying a Panther with Air Group Five on *Valley Forge*, later wrote in his book *Wings and Warriors* about the mood aboard ship when it had been nearly two months since they'd seen port.

"Everyone was grumpy from the daily flying routine, and the wardroom crackers had weevils. We would break the crackers in half to knock out the weevils before we ate them." And at the same time, "green vegetables, fruit and tempers began to run short!"

Worse than that, fellow pilots had been killed, missions grew increasingly tedious and frustrating, and the war looked as if it might drag on indefinitely.

"The days droned on," Engen continued. "War fighting is not much fun. The thrill of coasting in over a hostile coastline and attacking a large target complex, or looking for an enemy fighter airplane with which to test your skills, can break the monotony, but the thrill soon disappears as the daily dirty drudgery of strafing trucks and looking for soldiers on the ground to kill, as they try to kill you, begins to dull your mind. One day melds into another, and administrative duties on board become chores to take your mind off tomorrow. At night you dream of improbable war fighting situations and wake to begin another day of the same slugging dirty war."

That mood had settled on Dusty and most of the other aviators of Air Group Eleven. Then in late February there came two pieces of good news. First, the carrier USS *Princeton* was arriving in the area, bearing Air Group Nineteen, which included VF-191, the Panther squadron led by Lieutenant Commander Johnny Magda, who'd followed Dusty as leader of the Blue Angels. Also in the squadron were four other former Blues that Dusty had flown with—Fritz Roth, George Hoskins, Jake Robcke, and Ray Hawkins—and two later additions to the team he hadn't met, Pat Murphy and Bob Belt. Because of the war, the Blue Angels had been deactivated in July, when *Phil Sea* was en route to Korea, and they'd become the nucleus of VF-191, with the nickname "Satan's Kittens." After training at North Island, they'd arrived in Korea in late December.

The second piece of good news was that Air Group Eleven would soon be heading back to the States—it was official. They'd learn the details soon.

Dusty was eager to see his old pals from the Blues, and when *Princeton* and *Phil Sea* rendezvoused with a refueling vessel on the same day, he shuttled over by helicopter. It was a cold day on deck but a warm reunion in the wardroom, with Dusty eager to hear how the team had done after he'd left, and the others, still new to the cold waters of Korea, happy to have any tips Dusty could give them. Dusty gave them the low-down on poopy suits, leaving them wondering whether they'd rather risk dying from hypothermia if they went in the water, or chance being pulled under by a water-filled exposure suit.

Johnny Magda never got a chance to decide about the suit. A few weeks later he got fatally hung up on the horns of another dilemma. Dusty heard the news on his way home in early March. Johnny's F9F had been hit by flak over Wonsan and had caught fire. His wingman urged him on the radio to eject, but Johnny said he was going to try to make it back to

Princeton. The fire spread quickly, and he was nowhere close to the carrier when he splashed. Everyone who knew him was sure it wasn't fear of the icy water that kept him from bailing out. It was fear of the ejection seat, which he'd told Dusty and others he would never use.

The Panther's Martin-Baker ejection seat, made in England, was infamous among Panther pilots because its sudden explosive propulsion had seriously damaged the spines of many who'd used it. That threat was scarier to Magda than the consequence of staying with his plane too long. Whether he could have saved himself was pointless to debate.

Dusty's last launch from *Phil Sea* was on March 4, and the next day the carrier headed back to Sasebo. There, to everyone's surprise, Air Group Eleven was ordered to say good-bye to the "Showboat" and transfer to the "Happy Valley"—*Valley Forge*—for the voyage home.

Ignoring Madera's claims, Fresno claimed Dusty as its own in a March 30th article in the *Fresno Bee* headlined "Fresno Flier Is Coming Home from Korea with New Honors." The honors were a gold star in lieu of a third air medal, and the article listed some of the targets his squadron had hit, also mentioning their cover for the Inchon and Wonsan landings and the retreat from the Chosin Reservoir.

An air group statistician had time on the homeward cruise to total several sets of figures: In 215 days at sea, the aircraft of Carrier Air Group Eleven, collectively, had been in the air for 23,107 hours, which included 10,114 sorties, 8,673 of which were in combat. They had dropped 4,848 tons of bombs and fired nearly a million and a half rounds of 20-millimeter ammunition. Put like that, it sounded like a very busy time. Taken plane by plane and pilot by pilot, the experience had been an assortment of extremes—from wilting heat to shivering cold, from hair-raising action to yawning boredom, from sensuous comfort to breath-catching pain, from whooping hilarity to aching tears.

For Dusty, his return from the Pacific was less emotional than it had been five and a half years earlier. He'd been away nine months, not three years, and despite the dangers, he'd felt pretty comfortable and secure. He'd missed Betty and Raleigh, but separations went with the job. A few pilots had seen more exciting action than he had, but like most, he'd flown a lot of useful routine missions in a way he was satisfied with, even proud of. Now it was on to General Line School in Monterey. He'd already received the orders. It was the next step in his navy career. First, though, he'd use his post-cruise leave to collect Betty and Raleigh from Jacksonville. To do that, he'd need to get the car out of storage in San Diego. From a Panther to a Pontiac. Slower, maybe, but the flying was a lot closer to the ground.

NO MORE BLUES

Following his Korean tour and nine months in General Line School, Dusty joined his old Fighting Ten mate Swede Vejtasa at China Lake Naval Air Facility, where he was operations officer for a year. With his promotion to commander, he became skipper of a Cougar jet fighter squadron at Miramar Naval Air Station in San Diego, and took the squadron on a Western Pacific cruise aboard USS *Hancock*. Briefly, he served as air operations officer in USS *Shangri-La*.

In presiding over their transition from propeller-driven to jet-powered fighters, Dusty helped bring the Blue Angels into the modern age. A

September 30, 2005. Cdr. Raleigh E. "Dusty" Rhodes, USN (Ret.), inducted into American Combat Airman Hall of Fame, Midland, Texas. Photo by Brad Helliwell.

decade later, he served for four years (1957–1961) as the navy's representative on the Airways Modernization Board and Federal Aviation Administration, which helped bring this country's modern air traffic control system into existence. Coincidentally, Dusty's primary concern in both these roles was making flying as safe as possible.

Dusty left the navy in late 1961 when he was forced to choose between accepting a new overseas assignment or staying stateside to ensure that his fourth child received the best possible medical treatment for a congenital hip displacement. For the next thirty years he was a project planner at Lockheed Missiles and Space Company. Most of his projects there were Classified (secret) because they were related to national defense. In the second half of his naval career and in his civilian career, Dusty's life and work enhanced the safety and freedom of all Americans. For fifty years, from 1942 to 1992, he served his country.

GLOSSARY

AIRCRAFT

Beechcraft JRB: twin-engine utility transport; also called "Twin Beech"; same airframe as SNB

Beechcraft SNB: twin-engine navigation trainer; also called "Double-Breasted Foot Locker"; same airframe as JRB

Bell YP59-A Airacomet: twin-engine jet fighter, trial model

Betty: Mitsubishi G4M2 two-engine Japanese bomber

Boeing B-17 Flying Fortress: four-engine bomber

Chance Vought F4U Corsair: single-engine fighter with inverted gull wing

Consolidated Vultee PBY (PBY5-A) Catalina: two-engine patrol-bomber flying boat

Consolidated Vultee PB2Y Coronado: four-engine patrol-bomber flying boat

Consolidated Vultee PB4Y Liberator: four-engine bomber (Air Force B-24)

Curtiss SB2C Helldiver: single-engine dive bomber

Douglas R4D: two-engine transport (civilian DC-3)

Douglas R5D: four-engine transport (civilian DC-4)

Douglas SBD Dauntless: single-engine dive bomber also used for scouting missions

General Motors FM-1 Corsair: single-engine fighter built by General Motors to same specifications as Chance Vought F4U Corsair

Goodyear FG-1 Corsair: single-engine fighter built by Goodyear to same specifications as Chance Vought F4U Corsair

Grumman F3F: biplane fighter, predecessor of the F4F

Grumman F4F-4 Wildcat: single-engine fighter

Grumman F6F Hellcat: single-engine fighter

Grumman F8F-1 Bearcat: single-engine fighter

Grumman F9F-2 Panther: single-engine jet fighter

Grumman TBF Avenger: single-engine torpedo bomber ("Torpecker")

Hawker Hurricane: single-engine British fighter

Lockheed F-80 Shooting Star: single-engine jet fighter; first operational U.S. jet fighter in World War II (Navy TO-1)

McDonnell F2H-1 Banshee: single-engine jet fighter

GLOSSARY

MiG: Russian-made single-engine jet fighter

North American B-25: twin-engine bomber (Navy PBJ)

North American FJ-3 Fury: single-engine jet fighter

North American P-51 Mustang: single-engine fighter

North American SNJ Texan: single-engine fighter trainer

Ryan FR-1 Fireball: fighter aircraft powered by both a radial engine and a turbo-jet

Stearman N2N: biplane trainer, usually painted yellow ("Yellow Peril")

Supermarine Seafire: single-engine British fighter (naval adaptation of Spitfire)

Yak: Russian-made single-engine fighter

Zero (Mitsubishi A62M): single-engine Japanese fighter (also "Zeke")

OTHER TERMS

BOQ: Bachelor Officers' Quarters

CAP: Combat Air Patrol

Chandelle turn: climbing turn to gain altitude while reversing direction

charge guns: pull spring-loading lanyard to make guns ready to fire

Colt .45: seven-shot .45 caliber semiautomatic pistol (not the older Colt .45 revolver)

cowl, cowling: removable engine cover

Cuban Eight: complete double loop resembling a horizontal figure eight

ditch: make an emergency landing on water

division: group of four to nine aircraft (in VF-10 and VF-112, four)

echelon (right or left): three or more aircraft in diagonal formation (rather than abreast or in line)

FCLP: Field Carrier Landing Practice; simulated carrier landing on dry land

fingertip formation: four aircraft in formation resembling relative positions of extended fingertips

firewall: insulated protective barrier between cockpit and engine compartment

IATU: Instructors Advanced Training Unit

knot: one nautical mile (1.15 statute miles) per hour; thus 25 knots = about 29 miles per hour

Link Trainer: motor-driven simulated cockpit with instruments and controls to teach instrument flying by approximating movements of aircraft

LSO: Landing Signal Officer, who directs landings aboard an aircraft carrier

LST: Landing Ship, Tank; large sea-going vessel used in an amphibious assault to carry tanks, trucks, etc., to the beach

Mogami-class cruiser: modern, heavily-armed Japanese cruiser with distinctive single funnel

NAS: Naval Air Station

operational altitude: optimum altitude for aircraft to perform essential functions

plane captain: chief mechanic who oversees maintenance and readiness of a particular aircraft

port: to the left; the left side

PT boat: small (80-foot), fast (40-knot) motorboat designed to launch torpedos against enemy ships

quadrant: an area between two main compass points, such as "the northwest quadrant"

RFT: Refresher Flight Training

rpm's: revolutions per minute (of an engine)

section: group of two to four aircraft (in VF-10, two)

skipper: the commander of any naval unit, such as a ship or a squadron of aircraft

squadron: group of six to thirty-six aircraft

starboard: to the right; the right side

tatami: mat of woven straw

Thach Weave: defensive maneuver in which two aircraft or two pairs of aircraft sharply diverge and then turn towards each other so that one unit can fire at enemy aircraft on the other's tail; also "beam defense maneuver." Devised early in World War II by Lt. Cdr. John S. "Jimmy" Thach

tracers: bullets tipped with a chemical that ignites and shows the bullets' path

vector: a course or compass direction, especially for aircraft

SOURCES

INTERVIEWS

Commander Raleigh E. "Dusty" Rhodes, USN (Ret.)
Captain Stanley W. "Swede" Vejtasa, USN (Ret.)
Captain Russell L. Reiserer, USN (Ret.)
Captain Roy M. "Butch" Voris, USN (Ret.) (d. 8/9/05)
Captain Robert A. Clarke, USN (Ret.)
Commander Robert H. "Jack" Thelen, USN (Ret.)(d. 9/14/03)
Commander Philip E. Souza, USN (Ret.)
Commander Wylie Hunt, USNR (Ret.)
Commander Dayl E. Crow, USN (Ret.)
Lieutenant Commander Al Mead, USNR (Ret.) (d. 11/19/98)
Lieutenant Commander Edward F. "Fritz" Roth, USNR (Ret.)
Captain Everett Bondesen, USN (Ret.)

PRINT

Angell, Roger. "Dry Martini," *The New Yorker* (August 19 and 26, 2002): 68.
"Battle of Santa Cruz Islands," in *Solomon Islands Campaign*. Washington, D.C.:
U.S. Navy, 1943.
Billo, James D. "First Combat," in *American Fighter Aces and Friends Bulletin* 14,
no. 4 (Winter 1997): 11–12.
Boyington, Col. Gregory. *Baa Baa Black Sheep*. New York: Putnam, 1958.
Brickhill, Paul. *Reach for the Sky: The Story of Douglas Bader, Legless Ace of the Bat-
tle of Britain*. Annapolis: Naval Institute Press, 2001.
Cambon, Kenneth, M.D. *Guest of Hirohito*. Vancouver, BC: PW Press, 1990.
Daws, Gavan. *Prisoners of the Japanese*. Scanton, Pa.: Morrow, 1994.
Engen, Donald D. *Wings and Warriors: My Life as a Naval Aviator*. Washington,
D.C.: Smithsonian, 1997.
Ewing, Steve. *Reaper Leader: The Life of Jimmy Flatley*. Annapolis: Naval Institute
Press, 2002.
———. *Thach Weave: The Life of Jimmy Thach*. Annapolis: Naval Institute Press,
2004.

Ewing, Steve, and John B. Lundstrom. *Fateful Rendezvous: The Life of Butch O'Hare*. Annapolis: Naval Institute Press, 1997.

Fahey, James C. *The Ships and Aircraft of the United States Fleet*. New York: Ships and Aircraft, 1945.

Frank, Richard B. *Downfall: The End of the Imperial Japanese Empire*. New York: Random House, 1999.

Gamble, Lt. Bruce D. "First Mission Blues: The Story of Rear Admiral James W. Condit, USNR (Ret.)," Parts One and Two. *Foundation* 23, nos. 1–2 (Spring and Fall 2002): 8–19.

Giles, Donald T. *Captive of the Rising Sun: the POW Memoirs of Rear Admiral Donald T. Giles, USN*. Annapolis: Naval Institute Press, 1994.

Grady, Frank J., and Rebecca Dickson. *Surviving the Day: An American POW in Japan*. Annapolis: Naval Institute Press, 1997.

Guyton, Boone T. "The Blue Angels," *United States Naval Institute Proceedings* (April 1950).

Halloran, Ray "Hap" and Chester Marshall. *Hap's War: The Incredible Survival Story of a P.O.W. Slated for Execution*. Menlo Park, Calif.: Hallmark Press, 1997.

Hata, Ikuhiko, and Yasuho Izawa. *Japanese Naval Aces and Fighter Units in World War II*. Translated by Don Cyril Gorham. Annapolis: Naval Institute Press, 1989.

Holland, Lawrence. *Battlehawks 1942*. (Text accompanying computer simulation.) San Rafael, Calif.: Lucasfilm Games, 1989.

Hoover, R. A. (Bob). *Forever Flying*. New York: Pocket Books, 1996.

Horikoshi, Jiro. *Eagles of Mitsubishi: The Story of the Zero Fighter*. With Shojiro Shindo and Harold N. Wantiez. Seattle: University of Washington Press, 1981.

Hynes, Samuel. *Flights of Passage: Reflections of a World War II Aviator*. Annapolis: Naval Institute Press, 1988.

———. *The Soldiers' Tale*. New York: Viking Penguin, 1997.

Johnston, Stanley. *The Grim Reapers*. New York: Dutton, 1943.

Lundstrom, John B. *The First Team and the Guadalcanal Campaign*. Annapolis: Naval Institute Press, 1994.

Maloney, Edward T. *Grumman F8F Bearcat*. Fallbrook, Calif.: Aero, 1969.

Marshall, Chester. *B-29 Superfortress*. Osceola, Wis.: Motorbooks, 1993.

Mersky, Peter. *The Grim Reapers: Fighting Squadron Ten in WW II*. Mesa, Ariz: Champlin Museum Press, 1986.

Miller, Thomas G., Jr. *The Cactus Air Force*. New York: Harper, 1969.

Morison, Samuel Eliot. *The Struggle for Guadalcanal*. Boston: Little, Brown, 1954.

Morrison, Wilbur H. *Birds from Hell: History of the B-29*. Central Point, Ore.: Hellgate Press, 2001.

Nesmith, Jeff. *No Higher Honor: The USS Yorktown at the Battle of Midway.* Atlanta: Longstreet, 1999.

Porter, Col. R. Bruce. *Ace! A Marine Night-Fighter Pilot in World War II.* Pacifica, Calif.: Pacifica Press, 1985.

Rausa, Rosario. *The Blue Angels: An Illustrated History.* Baton Rouge, La.: Moran, 1979.

Rhodes, R. E. (Dusty). "We're Taming the Panthers," *Air Navy* (October 1949): 4–6.

Sakai, Saburo. *Samurai!* With Martin Caidin and Fred Saito. New York: Dutton, 1957.

Salter, James. *Burning the Days.* New York: Random House, 1997.

Scheuer, Dave. "The Birth of the Blues." *Foundation* 17, no. 1 (Spring 1996): 8–20.

Spector, Ronald H. *Eagle against the Sun: The American War with Japan.* Old Tappan, N.J.: Free Press, 1985.

Stafford, Edward P. *The Big E.* Annapolis: Naval Institute Press, 1988.

———. "Action Off Santa Cruz," in *The United States Navy in World War II.* Edited by S. E. Smith. New York: Morrow, 1966.

Stewart, William H. *Ghost Fleet of the Truk Lagoon.* Missoula, Mont.: Pictorial Histories Publishing Co., 1985.

Tillman, Barrett. *U.S. Navy Fighter Squadrons in World War II.* North Branch, Minn.: Specialty, 1997.

Treadwell, Terry. *Ironworks: A History of Grumman's Fighting Aeroplanes.* Osceola, Wis.: Motorbooks, 1990.

Wilcox, Robert K. *First Blue: The Story of World War Ace Butch Voris and the Creation of the Blue Angels.* New York: St. Martin's Press, 2004.

Wolff, Alexander. "Tonelli's Run," *Sports Illustrated* (January 27, 2003): 76–83.

Zamperini, Louis. *Devil at My Heels.* New York: Dutton, 1956.

ACKNOWLEDGMENTS

Dusty read, corrected, and approved the entire text. Portions of the text were read, corrected, and approved by Butch Voris, Swede Vejtasa, Al Mead, Phil Souza, Bob Clarke, Bob Thelen, Fritz Roth, Everett Bondesen, Russ Reiserer, Wylie Hunt, and Dayl Crow. Betty Rhodes, Barbara Mead, Thea Voris, and Sage Roth contributed precious tidbits. Early encouragement in the writing came from Lynette Armstrong, Herb Guthmann, Viki Anderson, Al Bell, and Bob Armstrong. Later advisers included Joe Collignon, Bill Smith, Bob Wicks, and Bill Patrick. I am indebted to them all.

Charles E. Rankin, Editor-in-Chief of the University of Oklahoma Press, has shepherded my manuscript through months of improvement, and to him more than to anyone else I owe the publication of this book. Thank you, Chuck. And special thanks to Steven B. Baker, manuscript editor; Jay Fultz, copy editor; and Tony Roberts, book jacket designer. Thanks, too, to the rest of the staff at the University of Oklahoma Press, and to the two anonymous readers who evaluated the manuscript for the Press and recommended its publication.

For special information and advice I am grateful to Steve Ewing, retired as Senior Curator at Patriots Point Naval and Maritime Museum; Joel Shepherd of cv6.org (the web site dedicated to USS *Enterprise*); Virginia Porter; Lou Emmert of the Madera County Historical Society; Raymond "Hap" Halloran; Pauline Seabaugh; Bob Kanze; Len Mozey of the Blue Angels Alumni Association; Penne Franklin; Rick Padilla of the Bataan Memorial Military Museum and Library in Santa Fe; and Mario and Peggy De Luca of the Blue Angel Archives at the National Museum of Naval Aviation.

For indispensable assistance, I wish to thank the U.S. Postal Service, especially Gonzalo Trevino of the Placentia Post Office and Sherry, Carolyn, Jere, and Maria of the Yorba Linda Post Office.

Finally, I am inexpressibly grateful to Nell and Tess for their constant companionship at my desk.

Made in the USA
Monee, IL
01 March 2021